OTHER VOICE

To Phyllis,
With thanks for your
support & friendship
over the years,
Timmy
12 July 2006.

OTHER VOICES,
OTHER WORLDS

The Global Church Speaks Out on Homosexuality

Edited by
Terry Brown

CHURCH PUBLISHING
an imprint of
Church Publishing Incorporated, New York

First published in 2006 by
Darton, Longman and Todd Ltd
1 Spencer Court
140–142 Wandsworth High Street
London SW18 4JJ

ISBN 0–89869–519–8
ISBN13: 978–0–89869–519–9

A catalogue record for this book is available from Library of Congress

Designed by Sandie Boccacci

Church Publishing, Incorporated.
445 Fifth Avenue
New York, New York 10016

Printed in Great Britain

Always when I read the Gospels I wonder what was really said, how far the evangelists had got it right, and how much they left out, writing it down long after, and some of the things they forgot and left out might have been very important, and some of the things they put in they perhaps got wrong, for some sound unlikely for him to have said. And that is a vexation about the Gospels, you cannot be sure what was said, unless you are a fundamentalist and must believe every word, or have an infallible Church. Anglicans have less certainty but more scope, and can use their imaginations more. My father, however, used to say that we must not pick and choose and invent, for where would that end? We had to take it or leave it, my father would say, and Father Chantry-Pigg said the same, but that is where the clergy make a mistake, for there is no need to be so drastic, and few things are ever put down quite right, even at the time.

Rose Macaulay, *The Towers of Trebizond*

The one who finds his or her homeland sweet is still a tender beginner; the one to whom every soil is as his or her native one is already strong; but the one is perfect to whom the entire world is as a foreign land.

Hugh of St Victor

CONTENTS

PREFACE AND ACKNOWLEDGEMENTS

This book, a collection of global Christian reflections on homosexuality – largely Anglican but also ecumenical – came out of the shock of the 1998 Lambeth Conference plenary debate and resolution unambiguously declaring any homosexual practice incompatible with Scripture and, therefore, a sin.

From experience and reading, the media's simplification of the controversy as one of 'North' versus 'South' Anglicanism seemed to me quite untrue. From my experience of Oceania and Asia, which I know best, it was certainly untrue.

At first I thought to write something on Oceania and homosexuality alone. But thanks to Brendan Walsh at Darton, Longman and Todd, I broadened the topic to global Christian reflections on homosexuality – though still largely Anglican, as I am an Anglican and it is in this church that the conflict is being played out most dramatically today. My apologies to readers who find any of the essays that follow too Anglican – but it is wise to follow carefully what is happening on this issue in the Anglican Communion, as all churches, despite attempts to stifle debate by pronouncements and decrees, will continue to have to face this ethical issue.

Therefore, I express my thanks to the publishers of this volume, especially Brendan Walsh at Darton, Longman and Todd and Cynthia Shattuck at Church Publishing Inc. for their constant encouragement, advice and freedom given during the development of this book. Darton, Longman and Todd's initial early commitment to this book made its writing possible. I am also grateful for Kathy Dyke's copy-editing at DLT and to all of the staff there.

Secondly, I am indebted to all the contributors – for their willingness to write and to trust that their inclusion in this volume is a good thing. I am quite aware that the contributors are not all in complete agreement with one another. However, I do not believe that this is a problem, as this is an area where the church is still finding its way and a variety of approaches is useful. I am not aware of an unkind word exchanged in any of the editing. I only wish we could be all together at some point, rather than linked only by the Internet.

I am grateful to all those who assisted in finding contributors to this volume, particularly to Yong Ting Jin, Richard Kirker and Andrea Mann. I am grateful to Melba O'Reardon and Cyril Powles for their

translations from the Spanish and Japanese respectively. My thanks to
Karen Evans, Librarian of General Synod of the Anglican Church of
Canada, for her help in providing bibliographical information, advice
and encouragement.

Many friends have provided material assistance by way of computers,
computer equipment and computer assistance. I particularly want to
mention David Akin, Ben Burt, Mariana Bell, Gary Fagg, Michael
Ingham, Jennifer Matthews, Lorna Reevely and Matthew Smith. In a
place as isolated and technologically problematic as the Solomon
Islands, this assistance has been invaluable.

I am thankful for hospitality extended to me by: the Community of
the Sisters of the Church at Tetete ni Koluvuti (Solomon Islands) and
Ham Common (England); the Society of St Francis in Brisbane; and
many friends around the world as I often wrote and edited in transit.

Many have offered encouragement in the development of this volume, not least countless friends and family with whom I have discussed
this issue over the years. My parents have been particularly supportive,
although my mother did not live to see the book's publication. I am
especially grateful to Marjorie and Cyril Powles, Mary Brown Parlee,
Sister Anita CSC, Richard Carter and John Blyth. Among those who have
gone before and are at rest, I would especially mention Pauline
Bradbrook, Celia Hannant and John Rye. I am also grateful for the
encouragement of the Archbishops of Canterbury and Melanesia.
Beyond these family and friends are countless others too numerous to
list. My thanks go to all of you.

This may prove to be a controversial book. But it is written and edited
with prayer and respect for Scripture and the tradition, with the hope that
the church can move constructively forward on this difficult but
challenging issue.

BISHOP TERRY BROWN
Auki, Malaita Province, Solomon Islands
Epiphany 2006

INTRODUCTION

Terry Brown

The controversy on homosexuality continues to rage in the Anglican Communion and to a lesser extent in other churches. It is difficult to say what new enlightenment another book will bring; but there are some major and hitherto unexplored areas, which it aims to address.

The 1998 Lambeth Conference commended the Communion to listen to the experiences and voices of homosexual people. These voices have been largely coming from the global North. There are other voices to be heard from the global South – from lesbian and gay Christians (including Anglicans) there and their friends. This book allows some of these voices to be heard.

Unfortunately, the media, and to some extent the protagonists themselves, have bought into the view that homosexuality is a reality and concern largely in the global North, indeed, some would maintain, an obsession amongst 'liberal' Christians there.

However, as the following essays show, homosexuality is a global phenomenon and always has been, present in all cultures and religions, even where it is anathematised by the culture or religion. One has only to browse the internet to discover Jewish, Muslim, Buddhist, Hindu – and even Mormon, Seventh Day Adventist and Jehovah's Witness – websites for their homosexual members. Many of the following chapters make it clear that homosexual orientation and practice is not foreign to Islam, Hinduism and other religious traditions.

Some of the authors in this book write from within cultures that from before Christianity had some positive assessment of homosexual orientation and practice (for example, Oceanic and Native North American cultures and, of course, Asia). The authors here encourage the church to build upon these cultural gifts rather than destroy them.

Nor is what is developing among lesbian and gay Christians in the global South a weak clone of the North American and European 'gay liberation' movement, yet another product of western imperialism. (This analysis of gay and lesbian Christians in the global North is also, of course, highly problematic.) Rather, emerging lesbian and gay theologies (indeed, practice) are highly contextual, while not without reference to what is happening in the global North and the broader biblical and theological traditions of the churches concerned. The rise of new churches, for example, in Hong Kong and Singapore, discussed in this book, focused on the hopes, experiences and needs of their lesbian

and gay members, is an entirely local phenomenon, echoing Roland
Allen's description of the 'spontaneous growth' of Christianity in the
early church.

Nor has the church in the global South been entirely non-pastoral in
its approach to homosexuality. Various contributors to this volume in
their stories and experience make this pastoral openness clear.

As many have noted, at the heart of much of the controversy are
different ways of reading the Bible. Many contributors to this volume
point out how unsustainable is an overly literal and de-contextualised way
of reading the Bible, dependent on only a few key texts. They also reject
a hermeneutics (in this case, the theory and practice of biblical interpretation across great gaps of time and culture) that *a priori* excludes only one
subject, homosexuality, from further hermeneutical scrutiny.

Unfortunately, this has largely been the position of the Anglican
Primates, the Lambeth Commission on Communion that produced the
Windsor Report in 2004, and the Anglican Consultative Council since
the 1998 Lambeth Conference, which first promulgated this limitation.
While hermeneutics cannot be just a way of getting what one wants,
neither can it be simply a way of excluding what one does not want.
Several of the authors in this volume address the hermeneutical question, pressing for a fuller reading of Scripture beyond the standard
'proof' texts.

The theme of liberty and freedom has strong biblical roots in both the
Old and New Testaments. Global theology in the last thirty years has
seen the rise of a variety of liberation movements. Not surprisingly,
several of the chapters in this book reflect this theme. However, the
authors are also aware of the careful work needed in relating (and,
indeed, critiquing) biblical, ideological and experiential understandings
of freedom and its limitations.

Finally, this is a book largely by Anglican theologians and pastors.
The shadow of the perhaps defining Anglican theologian, Richard
Hooker (*c*.1553–1600), however interpreted and expanded (Hooker too
is subject to hermeneutical debate), hovers over this book. The interaction of 'what Scripture doth plainly deliver', what one can 'necessarily
conclude from the force of reason' and 'the voice of the Church',[1] often
abbreviated as 'Scripture', 'Reason' and 'Tradition', in their local
contexts is a concern of many of the authors in this book.

It is perhaps this interaction that is key to moving forward on this
issue. As authors in this volume point out, recent international Anglican
consultations and bodies from the 1998 Lambeth Conference onwards
(though not before) have concentrated on Scripture (its 'authority'
poorly understood at Lambeth 1998 but much better understood in the
2004 Windsor Report) and 'the voice of the Church' (indeed, uncriti-

cally regarding the 1998 Lambeth Conference resolution declaring all homosexual practice without exception contrary to Scripture as that voice). This has been to the exclusion of human reason, the physical and social sciences and, indeed, simple human experience, including that of lesbian and gay Christians from around the world in their particular contexts. Scripture, reason and the voice of the church have not been allowed their full freedom to range across history, cultures and the broad range of human experience and have instead been narrowed into one proposition – all homosexual practice is evil — which is then imposed upon the church as doctrine. Contributors to this volume challenge this ultimately oppressive model. It is a model that does not bode well for the future of the Anglican Communion.

I have edited this volume as a bishop, mindful of my vocation to uphold, strengthen and enhance the unity of the church, but also to challenge the church. My own personal experience has been largely as one whose sexual orientation is homosexual. Most of my life has been spent in celibacy. However, there have been some experiences of same-sex intimacy in my life that I have experienced as grace. I realise that even this admission puts me beyond the pale in the minds of many, including many of my fellow bishops. However, I believe it is important that even bishops say 'we' rather than 'they' when talking of homosexual persons.

I am a North American bishop who has worked for many years in a global South diocese, in a culture where same-sex friendships (usually without but occasionally with sexual intimacy) are developed beyond anything imaginable in contemporary western culture. I have had my own narrow boundaries, fear of touch, suspicion of intimacy, love of privacy, indeed, my deep individualism challenged.[2] It is a culture in which 'homosexual marriage' seems utterly absurd but in which multiple, deep and affectionate same-sex relationships and friendships abound (for personhood *is* relationality), including across (what in the global North would often be boundaries of) age, educational level, family, marital status, position of power or weakness, language group and, indeed, sexual orientation. I add the latter because even here, with or without the hostility of family and friends, some people are beginning to declare themselves as 'gay' or 'lesbian' or, if unable to use such words (they are not local words – naming is an issue that contributors to this volume address), proclaim it by their appearance, mannerisms and actions. In the Oceanic tradition, discussed elsewhere in this volume, there is also much ambiguity, hence one is not surprised that the plenitude of relationships includes a certain amount of bisexuality. Down the road, even 'homosexual marriage' may make sense here for some (as heterosexual marriage does for others) as an alternative to what risks becoming promiscuity. But in relatively well-ordered cultures of deep, complex and meaningful relationships (strengthened by the church), 'faithful friendship', however expressed, is another alternative.[3] Of course, one must always guard against the potential for abuse. Contributors to this volume explore the various models of same-sex marriage and friendship that might be open to Christians.

If there is one lesson to be learned from this volume, it is that there is no single solution or simple answer – but that all solutions and answers must be rooted in deep and prayerful faith in Jesus Christ, manifested in Scripture, human reason, the tradition of the church and human experience, including the great complexity of human history and cultures. Inevitably there will be disagreements. Alas, one size does not fit all; even human reason tells us that. Therefore, virtues of charitable listening and mutual understanding need to be developed.

Indeed, as Sarah Coakley's Afterword reminds us, even this volume is still but an incomplete contribution to the ongoing conversation. There are always more biblical, theological, historical and experiential insights to be discovered and considered; and always the need to see our flawed but redeemed lives and views more critically and in need of further Christian transformation – whatever our position on this issue. For theologians of the global north, this ongoing transformation may mean setting aside western ideology and simply listening to and relating with those very different from ourselves. For those in positions of power, especially church leaders, whether 'north or south', this ongoing transformation requires a self-emptying of certainty to enable listening. Nor are gay and lesbian Christians exempt from listening to those who find our lives and views greatly problematic.

Fortunately, I am writing from within a culture that still listens – relational personhood requires listening for mutual support to flourish. I believe this openness to listening is also a part of most other global south communities, even if some of their leaders, overly active on the international stage, have ceased to listen. Contributors to this volume have listened to their people. The Archbishop of Canterbury has exhausted himself urging all parties to continue to listen to one another. As the editor of this volume, I can only urge the same: Listen to the voice of 'the other'.

NOTES

1. Richard Hooker, *Laws of Ecclesiastical* Polity, Book V, 8:2.
2. See my article, 'Personhood as a Tool to Reflect upon *Koinonia*', *Anglican Theological Review* 88:2 (Spring 2006) pp.163–79, based on lectures given to the theological *hui* (gathering) of the Anglican Church of Aotearoa, New Zealand and Polynesia at St John's Theological College, Auckland, in August 2005. The full lectures are available on the ACANZP theological *hui* and AnthroGlobe websites under the title 'Communion and Personhood'.
3. A very significant recent survey of such friendships in the history of the church is Alan Bray, *The Friend* (Chicago: University of Chicago Press, 2003).

Chapter 1

LAKOTA HCA

Martin Brokenleg

Introduction

Imagine a reservation in the United States fifty years ago. In a small
Sioux community a feast is being held with a social dance following.
Three hundred Sioux, who call themselves Lakota, gather beneath shade
trees in a large, grassy area. The group is seated in a circle stretching
fifty metres across. Most of the people are speaking in quiet voices with
one another. The men are dressed in jeans, western boots, western shirts
and western hats. The women are all in dresses, many covering their
shoulders with colourful shawls. All the women over fifty years of age
wear headscarves or hairnets covered with large sequins. The Lakota
men speak the men's form of the language. The women speak the form
appropriate to their gender.

There is one man not sitting with the other men. He sits instead with
the women and speaks Lakota using the grammar and sentence structure
appropriate for women. He covers his mouth with the back of his left
hand when he laughs, and his intonation is that of a woman. As the food
is served to the men, children and women who are guests, this man helps
with the serving – performing all the tasks of a woman. As the feast ends
and the seated people put their dishes away, the singers take their respective places around the large central drum and the music, typical rhythmic
Lakota music, begins. A few dancers adorn themselves with outfits
reminiscent of the formal dress of the Lakota at the end of the nineteenth
century. Some of the women dancers do not appear in the traditional
beaded buckskin dresses of their ancestors but instead wear a colourful,
fringed-cloth shawl.

The man, the one who speaks like a woman, stands when some of the
women begin to dance. Although dressed in slacks, a patterned long-
sleeved shirt and beaded moccasins, he also wears the ankle-length bone
breastplate typical of Lakota women's wear. A sequinned hairnet covers
his short, businessperson's style haircut, and his shoulders are draped
with a long-fringed shawl Lakota women wear. Dressed in eagle feather
outfits, the other Lakota men dance in the centre of the circle, but this
man shuffles to the circle's perimeter and stands side-by-side with the
women dancing in the bended-knee style of Lakota women.

This man who speaks 'Women's Lakota' does so with no embarrassment, and he dances as an honoured member of the Lakota community. He is *wi'i'nkte* – a man who speaks with women's language. In traditional Lakota culture he holds a distinctive place of importance, and traditional Lakota people regard him as a sacred person who is understood to be powerful. Those who do not speak Lakota well will eventually change the term by which he is known, and it will become 'winkte' – kills-woman – a nonsensical term; and later, as well, Christian missionaries will condemn any man such as this one and the role he plays in Lakota culture. Nevertheless, the *wi'i'nkte* manifests a long cultural tradition of alternative gender roles in Lakota culture. Appropriately then, the title of this chapter is *Lakota Hca* and translates as 'intensely Lakota' or 'truly Lakota', which this man-who-speaks-like-a-woman truly and intensely is.

Gender roles, the spirit world, and Lakota society

In the field of human sexuality, a clear distinction between sex and gender is necessary. 'Sex' is the term used to refer to fundamental biological or physical characteristics of being male or female – 'the plumbing'. 'Gender' is understood to refer to the cultural way one lives out a social role – the lifestyle. While many societies have two gender roles, Lakota culture has three and other Native American cultures have even more. Historically, indigenous cultures across the Pacific and North America have been and continue to be accepting of and open to differences in gender role and in sexual orientation as well.

Native North American cultures are normally female-led cultures. Some cultures such as the Navajo are matrilineal and matriarchal. In Navajo society one's self-introduction begins by announcing that the speaker is of the mother's clan, 'born for' the father's clan. In Navajo society, all property including the children, the home, the sheep, even all the man's clothing and most of his possessions, belongs to the woman. Technically the woman owns these, but the man may use the appropriate items. He will have ownership only of his weapons and religious items. The woman owns all other property.[1]

In First Nations North American warrior cultures, one might expect males to be dominant, as would be the case in other parts of the world. But even in these cultures, women are very powerful, possessing voice and vote, and may still run the foundational aspects of that culture. This is certainly true of Lakota culture. Men own their own property, but Lakota women are responsible for what is considered the most important aspects of life – the home, children and the first teachings.

The role for Lakota men involves survival skills such as food acquisition and protection from enemies. Men are, in a sense, 'disposable' in Lakota culture but the place for women is vital. If a culturally traditional Lakota couple were walking somewhere on my reservation, the man would precede the woman. This would not be an indication of male dominance, however. This order allows the woman time to get away should danger surprise the couple. The man receives the danger and handles it on behalf of the woman so she can escape.

The spirit world

Differences between religious systems native to North America and Christianity are apparent in gender patterns. In world religions originating in the Middle East such as Islam, Judaism and Christianity, the major heroes are male. This would include Muhammad, Moses and Jesus. In these religious systems, female heroes are few in number and hold much less prominent roles. It should not be surprising, then, to note that cultures influenced by these religions are male dominated.

In contrast to Middle Eastern patterns, the religions with origins in North America usually have major heroes who are female. Spider Grandmother, in the Hopi belief system, wove the physical world into being. According to the Navajos this world was made safe through the efforts of Turquoise Woman and her son Monster Slayer with the help of White Shell Woman. The Lakota declare Pte San Win, White Buffalo Calf Woman, to be 'messiah'. She revealed all of the traditional ceremonies and the teachings that make up the Lakota way of life.

Careful observation reveals that Native women are always strong, if not the dominant gender in Native North American cultures.[2] A Lakota woman follows a man while travelling in order to be protected, not to show that she is subservient. A Blackfoot woman may sit on the ground as a sign of her connection to Mother Earth, not because she must show her humility. To see an Iroquois man speaking in public or even presiding over his clan and then to assume that he is in charge would be a mistake because it is the clan grandmother who actually directs him.

Western anthropologists who come from male-dominated cultures do not always note the importance of Native women. James Walker collected ethnographic interviews in his thirty-year tenure as a physician among the Oglala division of the Lakota.[3] He became fluent in our language and took dictation in Lakota. In all of the published material of his interviews, there is not one interview with a Lakota woman. One result of this omission is a distorted understanding of gender in Lakota culture, not to mention ignoring the true status of Lakota women.

Lakota society

Gender roles are rigid in Lakota society. The role of a Lakota man is essentially that of provider and protector. He owns his own clothes, weapons and religious items. To provide for his extended family and relatives is his life's work. He must, therefore, be a good hunter and a brave warrior. If he has high status he might belong to a warrior society that assigns him duties of protecting the community at certain times and hunting for those unable to provide for themselves.[4] A Lakota man is expected to participate in ceremonies and religious activities. Religion is permissible for a woman for the reasons cited below.

The role for a Lakota woman is broader than that of a Lakota man. A Lakota woman has responsibilities in the most foundational aspects of Lakota culture – home, children and teaching the Lakota way. A Lakota woman owns the home and she is its strength. Lakota elders teach that while the man is like the tent cover, sheltering those inside, the woman is like the poles, providing the strength and shaping the entire structure. The *tipi*, literally 'the living place', belongs to the woman. At the time a woman is eligible for marriage, her kinswomen help her construct her *tipi*. After marriage, when the woman occupies her home, it belongs completely to her. Her husband will be permitted to paint his designs on the outside cover, but the *tipi* always is the property of the woman.

In Lakota thinking, any activity required to maintain the *tipi* is also the woman's responsibility. This is why Lakota women chop wood and carry water. They both pertain to running the home, which is the foundation of the Lakota community, and it therefore belongs in the realm of the woman, the foundational gender.

Also in the woman's domain are pregnancy, childbirth and childcare. The foundational teachings and instructions, the *Lakol Wicoh'an*, the Lakota way to live, are the responsibility and possession of the woman. The mother's role of mentor is lifelong for a daughter, but for a son only until he begins to grow up, about ten years of age in the Lakota understanding. The boy will then be turned over to his father and his uncles who will teach him the ideals of Lakota manhood.

A specific ceremony, *Isnati Awicalowan*, marks the coming to adulthood for the young woman. This ceremony is held during the first few days of her 'moon time', her menstruation. She sits alone in the community women's *tipi* while the other women sing over her. For the Lakota this time is the mark of the woman's carrying of life, and it is defined as very sacred. A woman has a lifelong experience of this 28-day rhythm in her life and so is considered unlikely to lose spiritual balance. Having no similar rhythm in his life, a man must make use of religious ceremonies to keep balanced.

Alternative gender

First Nations such as the Blackfoot have four genders with alternative gender roles for both men and women. Blackfoot women warriors are well known. The Lakota have only the three genders. Lakota culture has long recognised that the male role may not be appropriate for all males. In its reluctance to force someone to live in an inappropriate way, Lakota society allows for a gender role differing from the traditional male role. In Lakota society it is assumed that someone in the family will know if a boy is unsuited for the life of hunter and warrior. If there is uncertainty within the family, then a ceremony is held to help the family discern the path for the young boy. This ceremony is conducted when the child is four or five years old.

As the family gathers together, objects typical of the male role, such as a spear, an arrow or a bow, and objects typical of the female role, such as sewing items, women's arts tools and cooking items, are placed on the ground. The child's role will be defined by whichever items he picks, and whichever gender role the child chooses results in no shame or embarrassment. If he chooses the men's items he will be taught the life of a hunter and warrior. If he chooses the women's items, he will be taught the women's life and arts. In that case, he will also speak the women's form of the Lakota language. Whatever form of Lakota language this child speaks will define him from this time on. Women's Lakota, 'slow Lakota', is characterised by full and poetic imagery in sentence construction while Men's Lakota, 'fast Lakota', has a terse and idiomatic communication style. Both Women's and Men's Lakota have terms, vocabulary and grammar rules defined by Lakota culture. Of course, Lakota men and women can understand one another, but it is an obvious grammatical mistake when a woman constructs a sentence the way a man should and *vice versa*. The dominant characteristic of a man who lives in the woman's gender role is that he speaks as a woman speaks, a *wi'i'nkte*.[5]

The *wi'i'nkte* role

The gender role for 'men-who-speak-with-women's-grammar' is broadly defined as that of a Lakota woman. There are additional functions as well. A *wi'i'nkte* is defined as different and, as such, sacred. To some degree, sacred power, the *wakan*, exists in all things, but there are particular places where the *wakan* is especially strong. Some people are also *wakan* and possess a distinct closeness to the sacred.

Among those thought of as *wakan* would be *wi'i'nkte*. *Wi'i'nkte* are considered to mediate the *wakan* and so are consulted for a name for most children. Selecting a name for a child is done carefully since it will define the child and may determine the child's life. Any object created by a *wi'i'nkte* is considered sacred and Lakota try to possess those items. The *wi'i'nkte* are also responsible for remembering how to conduct ceremonies and to remember sacred songs.

Even today certain sacred songs use women's grammar since they were taught by *wi'i'nkte*. Knowledge of the arts is a responsibility of this gender since the arts are a mediation of sacred power. Because they are a gender 'between' men and women the *wi'i'nkte* are also frequently consulted in matters of romance and act as go-betweens to facilitate relationships. *Wi'i'nkte* address one another by female kinship terms such as sister and are not known to live with another *wi'i'nkte*. The usual pattern for a *wi'i'nkte* would be to live with a defined man or in a household composed of relatives from the *wi'i'nkte's* family of origin.

As a gender, the *wi'i'nkte* may or may not be same-sex oriented. Gender is a cultural role and so is not biologically defined. Sexual orientation is more in the biological realm.[6] Most *wi'i'nkte* were probably same-sex oriented, but the man cited at the beginning of this chapter had a wife and children. Contemporary authorities report that the Lakota refusal to discuss sexual behaviour makes drawing conclusions in contemporary times tenuous.[7] In traditional times, a man might have been sexually active with other men, yet define himself as a man, a warrior and a hunter. His relatives and community would then understand him as a traditional man as well. A *wi'i'nkte* might be other-sex oriented but be known by his gender role and not his sexual behaviour. The gender role of *wi'i'nkte* is not as broad as the contemporary understanding of same-sex orientation. Several contemporary writers mistakenly assume the alternative gender role is identical to being gay in the contemporary understanding.[8]

Westernisation and missionaries

Some comparable aspects of western culture appeared among Lakota people long before white people were physically near the Lakota. Tools and materials would be pre-contact aspects of physical culture. The philosophical and social changes, which had an intense impact on Lakota culture, came with the physical presence of white people, including missionaries. Three western institutions – the church, the federal government and education – created profound cultural change for the Lakota society.

Christian missionaries of that time were generally unwelcoming of any aspect of Lakota culture, with the exception of the Lakota language. But later efforts would even be made to reduce the use of Lakota language. Deep inner wounds were created when Lakota children were removed from home and culture and placed in boarding schools. The US government used both treaties and the military to defeat Lakota people and take their land. Even contrary to the US Constitution, the Lakota sun dance was declared illegal for nearly 100 years.

The missionaries particularly rejected Lakota sexual ethics. The Lakota solution to having more women than men was to allow men to take more than one wife. Although not all Lakota men did so, if such was the case, he would usually marry the sister or cousin of the first wife. The women would usually welcome the division of labour in maintaining the home and family life. Missionaries required Lakota couples to have a church marriage even if they had been together for many years. If a man had more than one wife he was to separate from all but one and never see the other wives again. However, he did have to provide for the now-rejected wives. My grandfather kept his favourite first wife and continued to raise the children, all of whom had been born of his second wife.

Missionaries were deeply offended that Lakotas allowed for the alternative male gender. The *wi'i'nkte* were an embarrassment to them, and they always assumed the *wi'i'nkte* were same-sex oriented. Nor did they seem to understand that a Lakota man might define himself as a man and yet have a sexual relationship with another man.

From 1874 to 1890 the US government followed a policy called 'The Quaker Plan'. This plan assigned official Christian missions to each Native nation to the exclusion of all others. The Sioux Nation was assigned to the Episcopalians, the branch of Anglicanism in the US. At a later time Roman Catholic missions were also permitted. These two denominations are the main churches with Lakota membership today.

My life

I grew up in the Episcopal Church, to which my parents and grandparents had also belonged, and the small reservation churches were filled mostly with my relatives. My father was an Episcopal priest with several chapels as his cure and I spent many happy times in church. I loved the liturgy, the social dynamics and the feasting. Church was always home.

I had a sense of being different as a child, but I did not have language or insight to understand how or why I was different. I had the usual childhood experience of 'playing doctor' but didn't find it very interesting. Now, I wonder if this was because my childhood neighbours were girls. When I was in high school I thought I should become a monk since I enjoyed church so much. I was not conscious of monastic communities being male. I attended a military high school for the last two years of high school. It was there that I observed and took part in same-sex experimentation. I had read that it was a phase for some youth and thought I was in that phase. It was not until years later that I realised I was too old for that phase. University years were also a time of same-sex activity for me but I had planned to marry and eventually did.

During the last year of university I became engaged to a wonderful woman and we married immediately after my graduation. By this time I

had decided to go to seminary and become a parish priest. After ordination and full-time parish work for three years, I became a university
professor and a non-stipendiary canon at the local cathedral. During the
following years we had three children. After nearly twenty years of
marriage my wife and I admitted our relationship could not endure.
Although I did not want the divorce I did not contest it. The factors of
personality were the main issue pushing us apart. Had she not wanted
the divorce, I believe I might still be married today.

For several years I worked hard at examining my life, mostly in
efforts to improve it. I was able to let surface experiences of sexual abuse
that had occurred when I was a toddler and in early adolescence. Both
of these abusers were male. I entered therapy for the turmoil and pain
that remained from those experiences. I also became conscious of the
two-year-long sexual relationship I had had with my parish priest when
I was a teenager. This experience was an abuse of power, and it was the
most difficult experience to resolve. It still surfaces at times. Eventually
I felt whole enough that I believed I could live the rest of my life well.
What is clear to me now is that my childhood and teen sexual abuse
experiences had caused me to find males repugnant. When I had
sufficiently resolved those abuse memories, I could find males attractive
and understand myself as a gay man. I found that I even had a level of
passion I had never experienced before.

After several years of not being in a relationship, I had the opportunity to become reacquainted with a former friend, openly gay, who now
lived in a far away city. Bill (not his real name) and I had dinner one
evening when I was visiting in his city for a conference. We ended up
spending not just the evening but also the entire weekend together. It was
the beginning of a two-year, long-distance relationship. Then, when the
time was right, Bill said he felt his role in our (and my first) gay relationship had been to bring me out. He also said we would always be
friends but that I would probably find someone I wanted to be with and
that would be all right. I was a bit taken aback by what he said but would
come to realise before long that Bill was quite correct.

For a number of years I had been associated with a monastery in
northeast South Dakota and was there on retreat when I met Gene, a man
I had previously known only through a brief e-mail dialogue. Our original contact was made when I was working at the university counselling
offices and the director asked if I would mind corresponding with a
friend of hers, a married man who was gay. We exchanged a few e-mail
notes about his coming out and I shared my story. Eventually he said he
was moving to another part of the country and thanked me for the
correspondence. Gene was also at the monastery visiting one of the
monks he knew before moving away. We met, had a good conversation,

and said goodbye. I assumed I would never see him again but did mention that I had an extra bedroom if he was ever in town. A few days later Gene called to ask if that offer to use the spare room was still open, as his plans had changed. I welcomed him and he moved in for what we both thought would be only a few days. After more than nine months, as we were having dinner one evening, we realised we had a relationship and that a move to greater intimacy was right for us.

Throughout all the changes in my life, church has continued to be a major part of my life, and I was open with fellow clergy at the cathedral and with my bishop about the relationship Gene and I shared. All were accepting of both Gene and me and welcomed us into their hearts and homes. We had also established a connection with openly gay friends at the Metropolitan Community Church (MCC) in town. They were all immensely welcoming. Eventually some controversies in that congregation caused the pastor and most of the congregation to leave MCC. They came to the Episcopal cathedral and found a place to worship – perhaps because I was there. Most of the former MCC people, including the pastor, became Episcopalians, but the transition was not easy. The cathedral congregation generally welcomes gay people, as they had Gene and me, as does the bishop and the clergy, but this is generally not the case around the diocese of South Dakota, however.

Gene and I have now been together for more than ten years. In November 2003, we came to Canada and were legally married. This made our later move to British Columbia much easier. Part of the reason we moved to Canada from the US, where we had lived all of our lives, was due to the open welcome and legal status we have as married gay men. Everywhere we have been in British Columbia, from our church, to the mortgage broker, to our neighbours, we have been warmly received. The Anglican bishop of this area of British Columbia welcomed me into his diocese and always asks after Gene. This is, after all, a diocese in which a same-sex couple can be officially blessed in the Anglican Church.

The only significant negative encounter has been that the school of theology where I teach has experienced bitter hostility from one Anglican bishop, who severed his relationship with the seminary. This was entirely due to the seminary's hiring me – an openly gay man in a legal marriage. Before signing the offered contract I asked the seminary principal to check again with the board to make sure they were willing to hire me, and the board was again unanimous in my hiring.

The Vancouver School of Theology is a loving and welcoming community of affirmation and caring for both Gene and me. Here we can live our lives as gay men dedicated to Jesus Christ. Here First Nations' culture is an accepted and nurtured foundation for the Christian faith. In

the culture of British Columbia and Canada we have a welcoming of
diversity in all its forms. In the diocese of New Westminster I have
experienced a foretaste of the kingdom of God, a life full of real love and
acceptance. People here are understanding and not defensive about their
lives. I can live an openly gay and openly Anglican Christian life as a
First Nations' man. I will never return to a life among the 'innocent'.

Perhaps my newly experienced contentment is what *wi'i'nkte* have
always known in traditional Lakota culture. Perhaps now, for the first
time, I too can be *Lakota hca*.

NOTES
1. Bishop Steven Plummer, personal conversation, 1992.
2. Peggy Beck, Anna Walters and Nina San Francisco, *The Sacred: Ways of Knowledge, Sources of Life* (Tsalee: Arizona, Dine College Press, 1992).
3. James Walker, *Lakota Belief and Ritual* (Lincoln: The University of Nebraska Press, 1980).
4. Thomas Mails, *The Mystic Warriors of the Plains* (Garden City, New York: Doubleday and Company, 1972), p.37.
5. Arthur Eagle Elk, Sioux Falls, South Dakota, public lecture, 'The Lakota Way', March 2003.
6. Robert Crook and Karla Bauer, *Our Sexuality* (Pacific Grove, California: Wadsworth Group, 2002).
7. Albert White Hat, personal conversation, Mission, South Dakota, 2003.
8. Will Roscoe, *Changing Ones: Third and Fourth Genders in Native North America* (New York: St Martin's Press, 1998), p.5. Roscoe discusses and accounts for all this variety.

Chapter 2

THEOLOGY AND THE POLITICS OF EXCLUSION: AN INDIGENOUS WOMAN'S PERSPECTIVE

Jenny Plane Te Paa

Racism and sexism and the Anglican Church in Aotearoa New Zealand and Polynesia

Fifteen years ago it was quite difficult to find good books on *race* politics. At that time I was desperately trying to theorise why and how it was that Pakeha[1] Anglican theological educators had, for the past 150 odd years, managed to prevent indigenous Anglicans from 'succeeding'. This lack of 'success' (acquiring institutionally recognised and/or awarded academic theological educational qualifications) was in spite of their long experience of 'participation' in the formal study of theology and in ministry formation and practice. I was at the time writing my master's thesis on the historical experience of Maori students who had attended St John's Theological College between 1843 and 1990.

The College of St John the Evangelist is the oldest institution of higher learning in Aotearoa New Zealand. Its beginnings and its legacy are part of the enduring historical record of colonial imposition upon indigenous interests. The history of the college from the perspective of Maori Anglicans is both compelling in its apparent promise of possibility for effective mission and ministry and yet profoundly sad in the extant reality of systemic theological educational injustice. The end result of this injustice is seen in the tragic record of academic under-achievement by Maori Anglicans admitted to the College right from its earliest beginnings in the mid-1800s through to the early 1990s, a period of almost 150 years. It is also seen in any critical historical examination of the wider realm of church activity into which theology graduates might naturally aspire: church and academic leadership, and decision-making roles.

Until the early 1990s and the change of the Constitution of the Anglican Church in Aotearoa New Zealand and Polynesia,[2] Maori participation in church leadership was minimal, often token and always vulnerable to dominant Pakeha interests. For example, although the 1928 General Synod passed a statute entitled 'Of Episcopal Supervision of the Maori Race', which provided for the position of an assistant bishop (who would be Maori) to work under the supervision and guidance of a non-Maori diocesan bishop, this suffragan arrangement soon became untenable as successive diocesan bishops used their power to restrict the movement of both Maori Anglicans and/or their bishop in very unhelpful and often offensive ways. Because of the restrictions implicit in diocesan boundaries, it also meant Maori Anglicans living outside the diocesan area in question felt denied access to the bishop of their first choosing.

When I graduated in 1992 from the University of Auckland with an undergraduate academic degree in theology, the local daily newspaper, the *New Zealand Herald*, made much of the fact that I was the first *Maori* ever to do so. Since it was a secular publication, that I was a lay person, divorced and a woman, seemed not to make too much difference! It was around this time that I began to feel somewhat uneasy at the thought that, whereas I was interpreting the academic plight of Maori in theological education to be a simple issue of *race politics*, there was in fact something far more complex and multi-layered at work. I began to get a sense of how single-identity politics were being used and could be used to institutionally reposition those previously excluded. The problem lay and still lies in the challenge of controlling for professional integrity and accountability.

My simplistic emergent theory was limited to populist race-based rhetoric: *Maori are and have been intentionally systemically marginalised and subsequently disenfranchised by dominant and inherently racist Pakeha.* This, I concluded, was not an intentionally *physically brutal* politics of outright exclusion, rather it was one of subtle, intentional, potent structural disadvantage – it was the more *emotionally and spiritually brutal* politics of exclusion. It was the devastatingly harmful reality of institutional racism. At the time I had already been heavily involved in the feminist movement for many years so I figured I could bring to bear some of my laboriously acquired feminist understandings of *gender* politics, especially given their apparently 'obvious' relevance and comparability to the situation concerning Maori in theological education. I saw a clear parallel in terms of the fundamental politics of *exclusion*. After all, there were the same socio-political power plays present in the church realm as I had witnessed and experienced in the secular civil society realm. Here were the very same uneven or unjust politics, which enabled those with power (acquired through unjust institutionalised advantage) to act intentionally and usually with impunity (protected by institutionalised advantage) to control, oppress, define or exclude 'the other'.

And so in my naivety I assumed that the same counter strategies as those employed by feminist activists would also serve to confront and begin to dismantle the evil of racism. We had to begin by naming the 'evil', developing critical strategies of determined resistance, engaging in sustained and intense struggle and above all else we had to remain ever hope-filled and confident that our attempts to transform the situation from one of oppression to one of mutual liberation would, on some glorious future day, be realised.

The early 1990s were my 'heady' days as an emergent theologian. Then (and still now) I remain profoundly grateful for the incredibly precious gift of a combined university and seminary-based ecumenical theological education at the feet of a wide range of outstanding teachers. My earliest theological 'informants', and those by whom I proudly concede to have been most deeply influenced, would be those broadly described as the authors of liberating Catholic social teachings. These teachings fit so closely with my own lived politics and with my own fledgling theology of recognising God's promise of unconditional inclusion *of all whom God created* as inherently good and beautiful. Mission and ministry, it seemed to me, were the purpose of our lives. That purpose was in turn to ensure the realisation of God's promise that none should ever be excluded, that none should ever seek or be enabled to unjustly dominate others, that all in God's creation deserve to be treasured, nurtured and enabled to flourish in freedom and in peace.

In 2006 I still hold strongly to the basic theological tenets expressed here. I believe my mission responsibility is to challenge and attempt to transform any and all unjust structures, whether social, political or ecclesial, which militate against the *inclusion* of any of God's people. Because I am blessed to work within the privileged realm of higher theological education, this has become the prime site within which I am determined to work. Here I seek to ensure that all who yearn for access to the academy are enabled to do so. And I also seek that those previously excluded are enabled to benefit from the experience, in ways that enhance not only their life chances but those of the people whom they, in turn, seek to nurture, protect and serve.

Heterosexism and the Anglican Church in Aotearoa New Zealand and Polynesia

Gay politics have always been on the 'radar' of my political and subsequent theological activism, as much as gender and race, but perhaps without the same intense singular focus. During the heady days of feminist struggle in Aotearoa New Zealand, it was so often incredibly gifted lesbian women who provided a clear and courageous leadership example. I tended to defer respectfully to their skill and experience and to concentrate instead on confronting what was still *for me* the 'higher' priority of race politics. I still had not made the connection between all of these 'competing' single-identity oppressions and neither had I come to a conscious awareness of the double bind of human and sexual 'invisibility' which gay people alone are far more readily spiritually debilitated by. It had not occurred to me to consider how either *being* Maori, *being* either male or female and *being* heterosexual, is an emotional, physical and spiritual *state of being*, which is usually fairly obviously codified either by physical appearance or by socially explicit indicators. Regrettably, it took me a lot longer to understand and to deeply appreciate the excruciatingly cruel personal dilemma which inevitably confronts those who are gay. Race is usually visibly obvious and *is now* OK to publicly proclaim. Gender is usually visibly obvious and *is* OK to publicly proclaim. Heterosexuality is rendered visibly obvious by the dominant social codes, which utterly privilege heterosexual relationships whether in civil marriage or in all manner of legislation, public data collection and declarations. But for those who are gay, the same taken-for-granted social 'norms' are subtly but surely denied. My lengthy preoccupation with race and gender politics regrettably subsumed my activism in gay politics until perhaps the last decade or so. Like so many of my peers, my own underdeveloped critical consciousness of the evil effects of heterosexism rendered me complicit, albeit unwittingly, in the politics of excluding those whom God created and whose sexuality is determined by same-sex preference.

Having 'confessed' to recognition of my own lack of awareness and thus a distinctive lack of conscious advocacy and/or direct activism in the cause of gay interests, I was not, however, entirely passive. In my work for the church in Aotearoa New Zealand and Polynesia, I was certainly not unaware of the inherently homophobic attitudes and practices of many who held positions of power. It was, as I now realise, simply a case of being far more radically and instinctively attuned to sexism and racism (which affected me personally) than to heterosexism (which did not affect me personally). It did not, however, mean I was totally unaware of, nor indifferent to, the plight of gay students who sought admission to the theological college.

During the 1990s the College Board of Governors from time to time debated the issue of whether or not 'openly' gay students ought to be admitted to the residential community at St John's College. I do recall being outraged by the mere fact that one's sexuality, normally a matter of private and sacred individual preference, could ever become such a matter of public concern. After 1995, when I was appointed Head of College, I had more direct influence over the recruitment and selection of students for admission. From that point, I consciously opted to use the power I held to enable the entry of all whom I believed deserved access to the riches of the theological academy. While my priority advocacy was for women and for Maori, it was during the mid-1990s that I also

officially enrolled the first *openly* gay Maori student as a full-time residential student of the college I am still responsible for leading. I was
criticised by individual board members for having done so and was
reminded of the current position taken by dominant Pakeha members of
the board on behalf of their college society.[3] Their decision had been
consistently to disallow the enrolment of any *openly* gay student to the
residential community because of its inherently disruptive effect. It was
from around this time that I began to better appreciate and publicly act
and speak against the subtlety and the insidiously cruel nature of
heterosexism. I began to use the many public speaking and preaching
invitations I receive in my role as academic leader to continue, as I had
always done, to name the theological indefensibility of *excluding* anyone
from full participation in the 'Body of Christ'. But now I did so with
particular condemnation of those who used their power and privilege to
exclude those of God's people who are born to be gay.

In retrospect, I consider my emergent political consciousness and
then my subsequent advocacy for gay interests to be akin to those I have
always asserted for women, lay people and young people, indeed, for
those 'on the margins' for any reason. Only now I was also deeply
committed to understanding the very specific politics and practice of
heterosexism. I needed to know far more than I currently did about how
this brutally discriminatory practice had developed, how it was
structurally maintained, what was its point of convergence with other
exclusionary practices and what were the points of divergence.

Unlike sexism and racism (which I knew very well from extensive
and always incredibly hurtful personal and professional experiences) I
needed to understand why heterosexism so clearly provoked even more
intensely and utterly unacceptable ugly human behaviour. In all my years
of encountering sexism and racism I had never witnessed nor been on
the receiving end of such intense and irrational personal rejection,
profound bigotry, or potential and actual violence. Neither had I witnessed such extraordinarily and embarrassingly heightened sexual
insecurity. All of these responses seemed, in varying degrees, to charac-
terise the attitudes of those determined to exclude gay people from
belonging, from being able to be and to flourish as God's people in any
sphere of social, political or ecclesial involvement of their choosing.

From my vantage point as a 'straight' Maori woman, as I reflect more
specifically and more critically on the last thirty years or so, and as I
have spoken with many gay Anglican priests and lay people of their
experiences of being 'in' the church, I realise I had perhaps unwisely
(certainly uncritically) assumed that the Anglican Church in Aotearoa
New Zealand and Polynesia had not been especially *actively* antagonis-
tic to gay interests. Rather it was more a case of the church being

unhelpful and indifferent, even disinterested. This attitude it seemed to me has prevailed in both Pakeha and Hui Amorangi (Maori) dioceses. But then, of course, I also realise that, because of the prevailing social attitudes and legislative position, neither have gay Anglicans felt or necessarily been able to actively agitate for anything in particular over this same time period.

I can see now how the situation was really one of powerless passivity for gay Anglicans – one could belong fully and mostly *invisibly* as a lay person without any difficulty at all. Ordination was best and more likely achieved without public declaration or at least with a minimum of fuss and was more likely to happen in some regions than others. In spite of the situation at college, it was also the case that openly Pakeha gay men and women were being and had been ordained, rather than Maori. And yet there remains a poignant irony in this statistical reality borne out of the facts of history.

Gay Maori Anglicans: a true story of acceptance

One of the more contemporary congregational sites within which gay, transgendered and bisexual Maori Anglicans have always traditionally worshipped is not in Aotearoa New Zealand but in Sydney, Australia. For it was to Sydney that thousands of Maori shifted during the 1960s onwards. All went in search of better social and economic opportunities; and gay Maori went especially to find respite from the subtle, relentless and always cruel expressions of homophobia to which many were subjected, either by their own *whanau* (family), *iwi* (tribe) or by society generally. In the Sydney diaspora a very famous coterie of gay Maori leaders soon emerged. Led by legendary icons such as Carmen, many in the gay Maori community soon became famous for their personal flamboyance, their daring creativity, their outrageous glamour and their enviable propensity for stunningly beautiful fashion choices.[4] Not only was Sydney a city mature and cosmopolitan enough to accept and ulti-mately to celebrate the presence of gay Maori but it has since become world renowned, alongside San Francisco, as a gay haven.

Tragically for most Maori their enforced choice of a 'sympathetic' homeland meant a consequential 'disconnection' from the land of their birth, the land of the ancestors. Such loss of relationship to the land and by implication the culture that sustains it is for any indigenous peoples always especially painful and 'costly' in emotional and spiritual terms. However, in spite of living in virtual exile, gay Maori living in Sydney kept alive many aspects of Maori culture, language and customs and many maintained in various ways their adherence to the Anglican faith into which probably the majority had been baptised. In the early 1980s a proposal to establish a Maori Mission in Sydney was negotiated and accepted. When the work began on its emerging mission and ministry, it was the gay Maori community who were particularly generous in making financial and personal contributions. The Sydney Maori Mission parish, based in the suburb of Redfern and known as Te Wairua Tapu or the Church of the Holy Spirit, went on to become one of the most vibrant and successful Maori Anglican church sites. It was a church where gay and straight Maori Anglicans got on with the priority work of *being* church and of strengthening the cultural survival project of being Maori. There was no overt discrimination, no attempts to exclude – it was difficult enough just being Maori and having to cope with the diaspora experience without adding any unnecessarily divisive elements.[5]

What would Jesus say and do?

In terms of theologising my position on the politics of exclusion I hold to the very simple Gospel-based instructions offered by Jesus and recorded in John 13:34–35:

> I give you a new commandment, that you love one another. Just as I have loved you, you also should love one another. By this everyone will know you are my disciples, if you have love for one another.

This very simple, unambiguous, unequivocal, and tenderly phrased teaching of the One in whose name we pray provides me with a sort of inbuilt moral compass for my day-to-day thinking, behaving, teaching and praying.

And so it was that when speculation first began to emerge throughout the Anglican Communion about the implications of ordaining a gay man as bishop, I tended to be naively dismissive of what I assumed to be merely typically unhelpful media hype. I would never have imagined that the reaction of some to the decision of one autonomous ecclesiastical province to act in accordance with its own canons and constitution would turn our beloved Communion into the site of such brutal human encounter that it has since become. For example, I am appalled at the ways in which Scripture has become a tool of weaponry, whereas in the context of my own Anglican upbringing I am accustomed to its use as the church's primary teaching and learning resource, intended to enable gracious, compassionate and reflective enlightenment among the people of God.

Now I know the vexed question of hermeneutics easily arises as one turns to Scripture for an authoritative bolstering of a strongly held position. Those opposed to any consideration of the issue of homosexual love are the first to uncritically employ any number of Scriptures as 'evidence' for their case against what is popularly described as 'the gay agenda'. But so too it could be said that I am equally culpable in my 'selective' rendering of John 13.

I do not, however, concede to this simplistic refutation of my hermeneutical claim.

Rather, I believe the difference is in the universal acceptability of the scriptural injunction contained in the gospel message – it is not one I have ever heard refuted, qualified, challenged, or deeply interrogated for possible double meaning or even irrelevance. On the other hand, most if not all of the commonly asserted counter-claims or those biblical texts used to 'prove' the unacceptability or outright rejection of homosexual love are all in some ways contestable, and many are certainly somewhat ambiguous.

None of this is to suggest that it simply comes down to a matter of 'competing' to see who has the 'best' scriptural arguments – those arguments are usually circular at best and increasingly vitriolic at worst.

The solution to the problem of how best to *reconcile* those who hold seemingly irresolvable differences of attitude, opinion, understanding and acceptance of homosexual love appears at times to be one proving too hard to identify. Within the global Anglican Communion some key factional interests, especially those holding extremely conservative views, appear to be hardening their positions rather than demonstrating fundamental Christian willingness to even engage in respectful mutually informing conversations. Their priority focus upon *positionality* as opposed to *relationality* is deeply troubling and is, in my view, theo-logically unacceptable. It would appear that what may well be needed at this current moment is for an increased emphasis to be placed upon the overarching teachings and example of Jesus, for all Christians to *be as sisters and brothers* with and for one another. The gospel imperative is always for us to be in right relationship with one another, not as and when we choose, or even *if* we choose. Therefore I support the urgings of those church leaders who are desperately seeking for ways of modelling willingness and ability to place *relationality in Christ* as the priority and only starting point of conversation and engagement. This means a willingness to be at all times and in all ways working sacramen-tally and, therefore, unconditionally toward reconciliation between and among all of God's people. To continue to allow *positionality* to be the primary determinant of whether or not God's people will even consider engaging relationally with one another is to doom the Communion to inevitable schism. Single-identity issues and their resultant competing oppressions, whether to do with race, gender or sexuality, must not be allowed to distract us from our primary mission and ministry.

As an academic I cannot help but yearn for the opportunity to develop an appropriate theological educational response to the current crisis. It is my belief that we could for example use critical theological thinking and understandings, informed by contemporary scientific research insights, to reveal how our sexual, racial and gender identities are constructed without our conscious notice. I would also insist upon teaching about the methods those with power use to oppress others, particularly those declared by the powerful, to be 'different'. Are we educating for liberation or we are educating for domination? There is, therefore, a need for all people to have a deep understanding of the inextricable link between the pursuit of God's justice for all people and the need to expose and rid the world of all competing oppressions.

The question is also how the church can and should contribute to the achievement of a stable, inclusive and loving society where there is an instinctive morally grounded yearning among all citizens for the good life for all – something of the vision of Martin Luther King's 'Beloved Community'.[6]

The church as a major ecclesial institution is inescapably morally obligated to exemplify at all times the qualities of compassion for those who suffer. It is also morally obligated to pursue justice for those who are oppressed, assume a position of fearless advocacy for those unable to enjoy basic human rights, and always demonstrate a willingness 'to do justice and to love kindness and to walk humbly with God' (Micah 6:8).

I hold a profound hope for the liberation potential of theological education to provide the language of hope, justice and freedom. I look to theological insight for the tools of critique essential for exposing all manner of structural injustices, and I look to theological wisdom for the caution to humility, compassion and tolerance.

My theological education project does not presuppose an easy transition. The task of establishing and honouring pluralism and inclusivity of any sort in any society is especially demanding moral work. That theology is, however, a crucial central undergirding to the project is immensely reassuring, for here is the discourse of justice, inclusivity, peace and liberation. Pluralism (the capacity and the will to build bridges of loyalty across ethnic, gender, sexual and other differences) must be mobilised in theological education. It is the only way of making sure we care enough about people who are different from ourselves to stop us from using those differences to destroy one another. The task is not to replace one ethnocentrism with another, neither is it to assimilate all peoples into one hybrid 'normal' being. The risk of that hybrid being straight white Anglo-Saxon male is too great a risk to take! The only alternative that does not threaten us all with potential schism is the hard work of forging, maintaining and renewing engaged partnership relationships. These are partnerships that accept the diversity inherent in

our homelands, our churches and our communities and those that rejoice
in the opportunities to learn endlessly of the ways of God, and of the
God-given worth of others.

What is needed in order for the project to succeed is neither a pristine
theoretical model, nor an impressive institutional site. What is needed is
what Stephen Carter describes as a commitment to reconstructing
ecclesial civility, 'for us all to learn anew the virtue of acting with love
toward our neighbours ... a revival of all that is the best in religion as a
force in our public life. Only religion possesses the majesty, the power,
and the sacred language to teach all of us ... the genuine appreciation
for each other on which a successful [ecclesial] civility must rest.'[7]

What is needed is transcendent theological imagination – one
inspired by the instinctive human yearning for community, and one
sustained by the instinctive human 'knowing' that to do God's good
works is indeed to serve the common good.[8]

John's gospel is indeed irrefutable in its clear, concise and transpar-
ent yearning for authentic Christlike discipleship today and always, to
exemplify human love one for another, unconditionally, non-selectively,
non-judgementally – just as Jesus did, so also should we do similarly ...
please Lord, from this day forward, let it be so. Amen.

NOTES

1. Although now a justifiably contested word among many New Zealand aca-
   demics and writers, for the purposes of this paper I am using the term Pakeha to
   describe those people who are descended from English and other early-
   nineteenth-century settlers and colonials and who choose to identify strongly
   with the customs and traditions of those early immigrants.
2. In May 1992 the Anglican Church in Aotearoa New Zealand and Polynesia
   officially adopted a revised constitution. The revised document contains within
   it clauses and provisions which represent a radical departure from the original
   constitution which merely embedded Pakeha ecclesial imperialism. In the 1992
   version, Maori Anglican interests are for the first time ever expressed in
   appropriate detail as a form of bicultural partnership and they are protected
   legislatively. See also Provincial Secretary of the Church of the Province of New
   Zealand, *Te Kaupapa Tikanga Rua Bicultural Development*, 1986.
3. By legal implication the Constitutional Revisions of 1992 required amendments
   to the canon relating to the previously monolingual, monocultural provincial
   theological college known as St John's. The new canon reads, 'the College shall
   comprise a President and two societies, one consisting of a dean, fellows, the
   teaching faculty and scholars, together with other students whose names are or
   may hereafter be entered onto the College Register; the other known as Te Rau
   Kahikatea, consisting of Te Ahorangi, fellows, the teaching faculty and scholars
   together with other students whose names are or may hereafter be entered on the
   register of Te Rau Kahikatea.' A fully autonomous Anglican theological
   educational institution was thus created.
4. Trevor Rupe, more commonly known as Carmen, was born in Taumarunui, New
   Zealand just 69 years ago. Carmen launched his career as one of Australasia's

most famous drag queens in the early 1970s at the Balcony Nightclub in Wellington. See also Paul Martin, *Carmen: My Life, as told to Paul Martin* (New Zealand: Benton Press, 1988).

5. Tom Ihaka, son of the first Maori Anglican Missioner to Sydney, Archdeacon Sir Kingi Ihaka, confirms this account.

6. Martin Luther King has always been a profoundly influential figure in the development of my own scholarship, particularly in the area of race politics and theological understanding. King's concept of the 'Beloved Community' has always been evocative of shared commitments and responsibilities in terms of 'race relations'. The notion of 'Beloved Community' or the idea of 'the mutually cooperative and voluntary venture of all moral and rational persons' was at the core of King's political theology. For an extensive and sensitive treatment of King's insight into the essential democratic ideals of the beloved community, see Lewis V. Baldwin, *Toward the Beloved Community: Martin Luther King Jr. and South Africa* (Cleveland, Ohio: Pilgrim Press, 1996).

7. Stephen L. Carter, *Civility: Manners, Morals and the Etiquette of Democracy* (New York: Basic Books, 1998), p.18.

8. Jennifer L. Plane Te Paa, 'Contestations: Bicultural Theological Education in Aotearoa New Zealand', unpublished PhD dissertation, Graduate Theological Union, Berkeley, California, 2001, p.295.

Chapter 3

MOANA WAVES: OCEANIA AND HOMOSEXUALITY

Winston Halapua

Introduction

The failure of the wider church in Oceania to listen to people of different sexual orientations perpetuates violence within the church and in society. This chapter argues the importance of listening and talking openly in the midst of this crisis. Hope will emerge as we listen, talk and learn from one another. Hope becomes evident in Oceania through the stories of the *leiti* and *fa'afafine* who are gifts of Oceania to the ongoing discourse on this important issue of sexuality. *Leiti* in the words of the president of the Tongan *Leiti* Association are 'men who identify themselves as women'.[1] *Fa'afafine* is the word for their counterparts in Samoa. Johanna Schmidt argues that, '*Fa'afafine* are biological males who express feminine gender identities in a range of ways.'[2]

The approach of this chapter takes into consideration legal positions, broad scientific research and theological understanding as I seek to allow voices from Oceania to speak. It is my intention to encourage robust debate and action. Attention to the voices of the *leiti* and *fa'afafine* within the worldview of Oceania helps towards gaining a holistic understanding of homosexuality.

Moana in the title of this chapter is the Polynesian word for ocean and is used to express an Oceanic worldview. The vast space of the ocean powerfully shapes the environment and lives of people and *moana*, as a metaphor, is used for the wide network of relationship. Homosexuality viewed from within the worldview of Oceania is only one of the waves of a wider network of relationships. *Moana* waves, as a title, offers an invitation in this discourse to launch out into the deep.

The use of our own indigenous language *moana* is deliberate. Language expresses our interconnectedness or spirituality. The intentional choice of *moana*, rather than Oceania, in the title signifies a theological statement. The use of *moana* signals that this chapter seeks to embody the distinct voice of Oceania in relation to the whole world.

Life stories in Tonga and Samoa: *leiti* and *fa'afanine*

Early in 2004 I made arrangements to travel from New Zealand to Tonga to interview the President of the *leiti* community, which I did in July. In Apia, Samoa at the end of the year, I made an appointment to interview the president of the *fa'afafine* community.[3] The ethos and aspirations of the two associations have much in common. The two communities have different locations in different Polynesian island states, yet there I found that the leaders spoke similarly with passion and integrity about their own pain and their own celebrations and hopes.

My interest in the very human situation of the *leiti* and the *fa'afafine* with their issues over sexual orientation and their rightful place in the Polynesian communities did not arise out of the blue. Before I undertook this exploration, I had had many encounters with individual *leiti* and *fa'afafine* and some of their counterparts in these and other island states in Oceania over the years. When I was appointed as the Diocese of Polynesia Vicar General based in Fiji, some of my responsibilities included visits to Samoa, American Samoa, Tonga and Nauru. In the 1980s I worked very closely with the Episcopal Church in Hawaii. In the 1990s, I was the General Secretary of the South Pacific Association of Theological Schools and this position enabled me to travel widely in Oceania. This work not only allowed me to observe widely the current views on issues of sexuality from within but also to witness how people with different sexual orientation are accepted.

When I was a young person, my father was a vicar and then a bishop in Tonga. During special celebrations of the parish, my father often turned to a particular person and encouraged his leadership to organise and take care of key occasions. This person was also known as a *leiti* and the church community celebrated his gifts and interpersonal skills. Having won the respect of others his sexual orientation was accepted.

I have become aware of similar situations in village life in Samoa. *Fa'afafine* are regarded as loyal parishioners. They belong to the village and their parish community where they have their own rights, privileges and obligations. I have marvelled at their participation in both village community and parish events. In my 2004 interview with the Reverend Paulo Koria, the General Secretary of the Christian Congregational Church, which has the largest number of adherents of all the churches in Samoa, he bore witness to the unique services and contribution of the *fa'afafine* in the village context.

I worked in Fiji for over thirty years. The active participation in village and urban activities of the *vakasalewalewa* (the Fijian counterpart of *fa'afafine*) is similar to the *fa'afafine* in other parts of Oceania. In French Polynesia, the name is *mahu*. I was in French Polynesia at the time of the celebration of the two-hundredth anniversary of the arrival of the missionaries in Tahiti. *Mahu*, in their capacity as citizens and parishioners, participated and contributed to the celebration like anybody else. From my observation the communities did not think of them as any lesser human beings than others.

So, in Oceania, *leiti*, *fa'afafine*, *vakasalewalewa* and *mahu* are many and different names for men who have a different sexual orientation. Members of this distinct community are not deprived of their roles in village communal life or of their rights or privileges to contribute their gifts as baptised Christians. Members of this group have very often evoked a kindly and loving understanding within communities. An appreciation of their presence and service within the communities is heightened by the kindly regard in which they are often held.

In the light of the interviews with the leader of the Tongan *Leiti* Association and the leader of the Samoan *Fa'afafine* Organisation, and my observance of general attitudes to a different sexual orientation, identical fundamental Oceanic values emerged. The two interviews were arranged independently of each other.

Identified Oceanic values

Belonging

Members of the *Leiti* and *Fa'afafine* Associations fully belong to the communities and the countries of their birth. They have full privileges and rights along with other people in their own location. They belong to the wider community and no one can take that privilege and obligation from them.

To belong is a fundamental human need and this concept of belonging is strong in Oceania. It arises in our spirituality and understanding of the whole interconnectedness of the land and the ocean. It arises in our deep affinity with the environment, the importance of our kinship systems and the honouring of our ancestors. The future generations belong to us and it is our duty to provide for them.

In this holistic understanding of the place or land of birth, the various words for 'land' in Oceania express relationship. From before memory people have been bound together by a multiple range of relationships to the *fonua*. The word for land in Tonga and Samoa is *fonua*, the same word for the womb. The word for land in Fiji is *vanua*. The Maori word for land is *whenua*. *Fonua*, *vanua* and *whenua* signify an ecological worldview. They express connection and relationship. The use of the word *fonua* implies ancestors, people, culture, leadership, land, sea, environment, past, present and the future.

Within an Oceanic worldview, the right of belonging embraces people irrespective of sexual orientation, whether they are in their villages or in urban situations. This powerful wholesome sense of belonging embraces people in their families, extended families, villages and urban areas.

Belonging, obligation and privileges are intertwined. This strong sense of belonging is not restricted to those who live today but extends to those who have gone before us and to the generations to come.[4]

Most people in Oceania are baptised Christians and, as mentioned earlier, *leiti* and *fa'afafine* communities are mostly baptised people. Their participation in parish and community activities puts into action their own commitment as members of the whole Body of Christ. In my interviews with some leading women and men theologians in Oceania, the active participation and commitment of people with different sexual orientations was undisputed.[5]

Participation and obligation

My previous experience of people with different sexual orientation was confirmed by my more recent interviews with the leader of the Tongan *Leiti* Association and the Samoan *Fa'afafine* Organisation. In the villages and at national level members of *leiti* and *fa'afafine* communities are at the forefront of activities and their individual skills and gifts contribute to community life at all levels. Some take strong leadership roles, some hold national leadership positions in specialised professions while others prefer to participate faithfully in less prominent ways.

The President of the *Leiti* in Tonga enthusiastically shared with me his appreciation of the abundant community services contributed by the members of the *Leiti* Association. The Association offers scholarships to underprivileged people and provides voluntary hospital services and community care. Members of the Association whose formal education is limited are encouraged and enabled to set up small businesses to use such skills as sewing, baking and catering.

The Association holds an annual national pageant which hosts a *leiti* beauty contest alongside the *Heilala* Festival 'Miss Heilala' beauty contest. The pageant is hugely popular. It follows the more formal Miss Heilala contest and people enter into the informality and the humour of the event, encouraging the *leiti* to celebrate their own beauty, distinctness and sexual orientation. This beauty contest gives an opportunity for the nation to offer affirmation and popular support for the *leiti*. The public's support for the pageant has been overwhelming, with the business community giving phenomenal financial backing. The pageant is popular in Tonga because the *Leiti* Association offers an event of festivity that is original, inclusive, creative and affirms realities. People are enabled to laugh at themselves and there is a healthy exposure of the way Tongan patriarchal males behave at times. While the proceeds from the pageant festivity fund most of the community services of the Association, the wider community gain from the energy of the Association. Members of the Tongan *Leiti* Association joyfully and passionately take pride in what they give and what they receive.

The leader of the Samoan *Fa'afafine* Organisation enthusiastically told me of the services and other activities of the organisation in which they participate and provide for the wider society. In the early stages of his leadership, the President sought advice from the government and worked in consultation with the Prime Minister on important issues. As we talked, I became aware that the members of the organisation function mostly in the urban capital. Individual *fa'afafine* in village and rural areas contribute as members of their respective communities.

It is the view of the President of the Samoan *Fa'afafine* Organisation that sexual relationships between male Samoans are among the many relationships within the cultural context and that these relationships existed before contact with the West. Historical and anthropological evidence confirms both these views.[6]

Within the *aiga* (Samoan concept of community life), activities are generally divided between the women and men.[7] The division of labour often separates young men and women. This cultural trait for communal obligations and activities encourages group participation according to gender especially among the young people in the village. Within this lifestyle, according to the President, a young *fa'afafine* may find himself in a sexual relationship with another young man. This was one of the many forms of relationships such as mentor, friend and co-worker. The *fa'afafine* participated in working in different professions, sport, arts, plantation work, carving, tattooing, fishing, caring for children and meeting obligations for the *aiga* and the wider village community.

According to the President, when the partner of a *fa'afafine* eventually finds a female partner to live with permanently, the sexual relationship between the male partners ceases but friendship remains. This relationship becomes a treasured friendship known only to the two males and they often regard one another as confidantes.

Identity

The President of the Tongan *Leiti* Organisation recalled: 'On many occasions people affirmed my unique potentiality and integrity. But there is also an expression that I am unfulfilled and wasted because I am not married with a family.' The President went on to express his own sense of identity: 'The most precious gift that God has given me is who I am and what I have achieved.' I reflected on this powerful statement and understand it to mean that he is affirming his identity as a *leiti*. That is the identity he passionately claims as his own and given by God. His personality, creativity and unique potentiality are God's gifts and he is different from the prevailing dominant heterosexual majority.

In conversation, the President of the Samoan *Fa'afafine* Organisation traced the vision, formation and the history of the movement in Samoa. The organisation was formed to protect, maintain and develop the identity of the members. Their identity as *fa'afafine* who are distinct human beings and people of Samoa motivates their service to the community. *Fa'afafine*, according to the President, is the Samoan word which means 'to be like a woman'.[8] He argued that the *fa'afafine* is part of an ancient culture in Samoa. This identity was and is an integral part of the ancient civilisation of the *aiga* and *fonua*.

Identity features strongly in the dynamics of formation, aspirations and the belief system of the two national networks and speaks powerfully of solidarity. The *leiti* and the *fa'afafine* are predominantly men with different sexual orientations, but simplistic assumptions about their identity are to be avoided. The stories that are shared by the *leiti* and *fa'afafine* networks reveal human faces that are integral members of the community.

A sociological and theological approach

Research recently published on the *leiti* and *fa'afafine* has thrown new light on our understanding of people with different sexual orientation in Oceania. Paul Miles provides a comprehensive bird's-eye view of the *fa'afafine*, *fakaleiti* [*leiti*] and *mahu*.[9] Miles locates the three counterparts in their historical context. This trend was integral to the Oceanic community before contact with the West. Johanna Schmidt has helped me to locate how this community functions not only in Tonga and Samoa but also in relation to the Pacific Islanders born in New Zealand.[10] Sue Farran, a senior lecturer in the School of Law at the University of the South Pacific, Emalus Campus, Vanuatu, takes the plight of the Tongan *fakafa'fine* [*leiti*] and Samoan *fa'afafine* and locates their difficulties in the current legislations of the island states in Oceania. She provides legal, biological and scientific interpretation and underlines the complexity which surrounds human sexuality and sexual orientation.[11]

Some of the public homophobic outcry after the release of *Lambeth Commission on Communion: The Windsor Report 2004* potentially blocks the opportunity for further dialogue on the issue of homosexuality. The findings of the Commission appear to be taken out of context. Archbishop Barry Morgan of Wales stated the brief of the Commission: 'It was not asked and has not tried to tackle the issue of human sexuality. Its brief was, given the fact that different provinces have different attitudes and understanding of various contentious matters, how do they acknowledge the fact and consult the wider Communion before making decisions that inevitably impact on the life of that wider Communion.'[12]

The recommendations of *The Windsor Report 2004* on an Anglican 'covenant' and the Archbishop of Canterbury are suspect. I contend that before consideration of relevant structures within the Communion, *talanoa* offers a mechanism for ongoing dialogue in order to let go of homophobia, to build up relationships and foster mutual inter-dependence and interconnectedness. Within such a safe environment or *moana*, the integrity of different voices, including those of people whose sexual orientations are different, will be honoured and the welfare of all will be secured.

Talanoa is a Tongan word for all levels of conversations and inter-actions. The Fijians and Samoans have the same word, which is common to many parts of Oceania. *Talanoa* is comprised of two words:

> ... tala meaning talking or telling stories and noa meaning zero or without concealment. Our construction of the meaning of talanoa tells us that it can mean talking with or telling stories to each other, without concealment (i.e. zero concealment) of our inner feelings and experiences that resonate in our hearts and minds. Talanoa embraces our worldviews of how we can and ought to live and work together collectively, and relate to one another in a good, relational way as different cultural members of society.[13]

Within this concept and process of *talanoa*, the identity of *leiti* and *fa'afafine* and other forms of homosexuality may be located and analysed holistically.

I believe that we should applaud certain public responses to current controversies for clarifying for us how to communicate issues of homo-sexuality in language relevant for the twenty-first century. Stephen Bates, a British journalist specialising in church affairs, provides a deep insight into the history and key players in the Church of England and their networking within the Anglican Communion.[14] Among the issues that arise in his book is that of power and control. From my perspective, it is fundamental to re-examine the ideological underpinnings that protect the power base of the few who are in control. Some of my questions are: Whose theology do we maintain in relation to human sexuality and sexual orientation? Whose ideological context drives this theology? To what extent is theology informed by working in partnership with science and other disciplines? Is theology contextual, allowing for different voices including those of indigenous peoples?

A major component of the status quo in theology stems from the kind of theology brought by the pioneering missionaries in Oceania. Missionaries have contributed remarkably to many facets of transforma-tion in Oceania.[15] As more people are more informed now about their own contexts and the importance of using the indigenous language in research methods, more insight about local people, identity and feelings becomes evident. There has previously been an absence of indigenous voices writing the history of missionaries from the perspective of Oceania.[16] The vast number of the storytellers of mission in Oceania were from the West. The critique mainly identified and re-examined by indigenous historians is the failure of western historians to detect the western ideology and theology that contributed to subjugating some of the ancient Oceanic worldviews to a subservient status.[17]

Since World War II, the ideological concept of assimilation, which has dominated western views of Oceania, has been debated. The legacy of dualism and the Age of Enlightenment in Europe is now suspect. When these two ideological concepts are identified as among the key driving forces in colonialism and imperialism, how could the pioneering missionaries and their worldviews be independent from the context of their upbringing?

The concept of assimilation had a great influence among the early missionaries. What is assimilation? The *Collins Dictionary of Sociology* defines it as '(especially in race relations) the process in which a minority group adopts the values and patterns of behaviour of a majority group or host culture, ultimately becoming absorbed by the majority group ...'[18] In my definition, assimilation is an ideological tool which enshrines the unjust mindset of the dominant section, imposing it on the powerless vast majority of people in the society. The approach of assimilation conceals the exploitation and violence of the few who are in power positions exploiting the system for their own advantage. A similar argument is articulated from North America:

> This paradigm conceived of society as a largely homogeneous social system integrated around core values and norms, in which stable equilibrium between structure and functions of component systems sustained social order. Such conception of society is built into old assimilation formulation of the core Anglo-American middle-class culture and society the putative mainstream which was the end point of assimilation.[19]

A dualistic view of life is another worldview of the missionaries. Natives were subsumed as pagan and subhuman. Founding philosophers who contributed to the laying down of a dualistic worldview, including Aristotle, Socrates, Kant and Plato, perceived the world and context as a different realm from the world of the mind and spirit.[20] The Romans consolidated this trend of the Greek dualistic approach by weaving it into their legal system. The Enlightenment period in Europe incorporated the dualistic worldview into its thought, which later spread far and wide to other parts of the globe through colonialism and the early missionary movement.

The assimilating and dualistic worldview of the pioneering missionaries contributed to and framed the core theological underpinnings of
human sexuality including homosexuality. The current scientific and
psychological knowledge of the whole issue of sexuality was not
available. Furthermore, the dominant ideological worldview that shaped
the attitude of the missionaries and their interpretation of the Bible was
from the top down. The peoples and the worldview of Oceania were subjugated. Oceanic peoples were regarded as less human and incapable of
imagination and rationality. To be fully human was to be civilised. That
was taken to mean learning and behaving as people of the West. To
acquire understanding of God and the Bible was to adopt the way
missionaries perceived Oceania. In the context of human sexuality, the
Oceanic ancient values were uprooted indiscriminately. In the terms of
dualism, the theology of the missionaries superseded indigenous values.
This is the very essence of the assimilating paradigm.

In my reflection on most of the contemporary discussions on human
sexuality, a major contributing factor to the misunderstanding and crossing and passing each other is a theological problem. Some people from
the global 'South' refer to their values opposing homosexuality as
though their cultural values were in place before contact with the West.
A major part of our cultural values we hold sacred about the Bible and
its teaching on homosexuality is deeply rooted in the theology brought
by pioneering missionaries. Some of the theological assertions of the
pioneering missionaries need re-examining and even, perhaps, uproot-
ing. When theology perpetuates injustice and subjugating fellow human
beings, such theology is part to the doctrine of dehumanisation in the
name of God.

This chapter, as the title 'Moana Waves' suggests, supports an intentional departure from the monopoly of the western ideological
constraints. Holding on to western worldviews of assimilation and
dualism perpetuates and maintains the injustice and dehumanising of
people with different sexual orientations. It is important for the welfare
of all people in Oceania to depart from the tyrannical aspects of theological status quo. Why has *moana* interconnectedness embraced the
leiti and *fa'afafine* but not the official theology, teaching and attitudes of
the churches?

Moana waves

The *moana* worldview, as I suggest, is bigger than the worldviews of
assimilation and dualism. It is transformative, creative, inclusive and
integrating. *Moana* is closer to postmodernism. O'Donnell asserts:
'Postmodernism shuns grand theories and the attempts to ground ethics
in fixed "truths", but it has a real contribution to make. Postmodern

philosophers stress how reality is societal and relational; we are not alone.'[21] The interconnected view of the *moana* concept embraces the context, spirit, mind and all, including the ancestors, the present and the future. The very core of the *concept* contributes to a view of the whole interconnectedness of life. Every voice is not in isolation. Differences are integral and are not to be undermined or subjugated.

The reclaiming of the *moana* values and spirituality is imperative. It is our responsibility as indigenous theologians to participate constructively, imaginatively and vigorously in mission which is relevant to our present fast-changing context. We are an integral part of a global village and technology will continue to shape our world. The reclaiming of the *moana* values such as in the acceptance of the *fa'afafine* and *leiti* within the Oceanic communities will be powerfully instrumental in the transformation of the patriarchal and heterosexual dominance in official theological attitudes of the mainline and newly established Pentecostal churches towards human sexuality. Such a courageous move would honour by putting into practice one of the mission statements of the Anglican Consultative Council – that is, to transform the unjust structures. To transform unjust structures gives integrity and relevance to our mission today. It is to be in line with the spirit of Christ.

Moana values and spirituality have been integral to the very core of our ancient identity and challenge the uncritical maintenance of theological positions within the churches in Oceania with regard to homosexuality. Conservative theological positions on human sexuality derive from the theological legacy of the pioneering missionaries of eighteenth-century Europe. They do not emerge from deep within the Oceanic experience.

The refusal of the mainline and Pentecostal churches to ordain homosexual people contradicts the wide acceptance of the same people within the Oceanic communities. The *moana* or the ancient concept of Oceanic interconnectedness celebrates the *fa'afafine, leiti, vakasalewalewa* and *mahu*. While church people celebrate their faithful participation in mission, the official line supports the denial of their humanity. There is a great contradiction here.

Does the theology of ordination give a just space for voices from the margins? In my interviews with the *fa'afafine* and *leiti*, in my wide contact with people from the marginalised sections of our community, many give their all to God. Why are they deprived of participation in mission in the ordained ministry? Have we heard from our gay people their understanding of ordination? The churches in Oceania will be impoverished in mission without their participation.

The 2004 Conference of the Methodist Church in New Zealand, with its large Oceanic membership, endorsed the ordination of gay and

lesbian people. The importance of this decision was made clear not only
in English but in the Fijian, Samoan and Tongan language versions of
the motion. This decision was supported by a Memorandum of
Understanding to protect individuals and groups who hold different
stances. The theological acknowledgement of the justice of the ordination of those with different sexual orientation will have a huge impact on
people of Oceania.

The realisation of the theological and paradigm shift on the issue of
human sexuality has already taken place. In the Oceanic context, ongoing interaction and *talanoa* on the issues surrounding the ordination
of gay and lesbian human beings are no longer being seen as alien and
something from the West. The decision of the Conference includes
voices of people from Oceania who are Methodists. The impact of the
Oceania values of interconnectedness such as *moana*, *aiga*, *fonua* and
talanoa will not only enhance wider and open dialogue but provide
robust ongoing debate on human sexuality in Pacific cultures and
languages. Theological considerations from another part of the world in
English will no longer unilaterally dominate the dialogue on human
sexuality. It is imperative that Oceanic values provide the context in
which the new ecological theology, human rights and recent scientific
findings continue in *talanoa*.

This chapter celebrates homosexuality as integral to wider issues of
sexuality. When an understanding of homosexuality is located within
Oceanic values and interconnectedness in the stories of the *leiti* and
fa'afafine, homosexuality is accepted and celebrated as one of the many
waves of the *moana*. Waves dance to the currents of the ocean depths
and waves faithfully touch the island shores to embrace all, small or big,
mountainous or flat, volcanic or golden sand, to remind us all that the
moana is very much alive. The paradigm shift in a new theology of the
moana places emphasis on the inclusive embracing of all the richness of
human sexuality. A *moana* perspective is about transformative relationship – about seeing ourselves and others in the context of God's
embracing love which is as deep and wide as the ocean.

My realisation that I am not alone strengthens my stance on homosexuality. As I tell the story of my journey with others in this process of
discourse, it is obvious to me as a person from Oceania that the whole
worldview of the *moana* has not yet been given the grace to manifest
itself to its full potential. The theology of the *moana* is about the whole
interconnectedness of the environment and humanity. The theology of
the *moana* helps towards a heightened understanding of our triune God
who is the Creator, Redeemer and Life-Giver. The Three Persons of the
Trinity are the expression of God's love and are interconnected. The
image of the *moana* for the Oceanic people contributes to an under-

standing of the uniqueness of the divine love expressed in the triune
God. Recent writings give new interpretations of the Bible through the
insights of an eco-justice hermeneutic, emphasising the interconnectedness of all things within God's love.[22]

Our worldview of Oceanic interconnectedness is empowered by a
ground-swelling of grace and warmth from inside a people, arising from
encounters that deeply move those involved. Reciprocity as an English
word for giving something in return does not fully embrace this Oceanic
worldview. The *moana* worldview of reciprocity is closer to a form of
giving which does not entail conditions. It is a giving of grace for grace.
Before contact with the West, in Tonga reciprocity was contained in
people's greeting of one another. The meeting point is not isolated from
the whole way of life. The actual greeting is *si'oto 'ofa* which means my
whole (*si'oto*) life (including the environment, the past and the future)
or love (*'ofa*) is yours too. The response is returned in the same spirit.
The Fijian word for greetings is *bula*, which means life in its fullness. In
Samoa, the greeting *talofa* is about fullness of life. This implies the
interconnectedness of individual life to the ancestors, environment and
the future. Reciprocity means voluntarily extending life with all its
interconnectedness and mutuality to the person encountered.

Central to the way of life evolving from reciprocity is the importance
of relationships. I have arrived at a point in my life and ministry where
I can passionately say that journeying with God is not so much about
believing in God but rather a living relationship with those on the
margins. I cannot support the displacement of those with different sexual
orientations, which treats people as less than God's love intends.

Hidden in the whole discourse on homosexuality is the issue of patri-
archy. Patriarchal and heterosexual arguments dominate in the debate on
issues of human sexuality. The *moana* worldview of family is about
relationship within the extended family unit that comprises many
components. It challenges western heterosexual emphasis on the nuclear
family and locates homosexuality within wider, more inclusive families.
As all people are made in God's image, the whole interconnectedness of
God's love is the bigger picture that needs to be seen.

In Christ I find the full expression of the reciprocity of the triune
God. My choice of the title of this chapter – *Moana* Waves – reflects my
theological position on issues concerning the sacred area of human
sexuality. The writing of this chapter is my commitment to the empowering of the *leiti* and *fa'afafine* who are for the most part accepted
culturally. Their strong sense of identity and belonging are gifts from
God, which wait to be fully celebrated by the church. In this way we are
releasing reciprocity for the benefit of the whole humanity and the
world. When we seek to do justice to *leiti*, *fa'afafine* and others with

different sexual orientations we shall also do justice to all people because our wellbeing is always interconnected with that of others.

NOTES
1. Interview with Joey Mataele, 23 July 2004.
2. Joanna Schmidt, 'Redefining fa'afafine: Western discourses and the construction of transgenderism in Samoa', *Intersections* 6, 2001, p.1. http://wwwsshe.murdoch.edu.au/intersections/issue6/schmidt.html
3. Interviewed 26 November 2004.
4. See I. S. Tuwere, *Vanua: Towards a Fijian theology of place* (Suva, Institute of Pacific Studies: Suva, 2002); A. Tofaeono, *World Mission Scripts. Eco-Theology: AIGA – The Household of Life* (Erlangen: World Mission Script 7, 2000); W. Halapua, *Tradition, Lotu & Militarism in Fiji* (Fiji Institute of Applied Studies: Lautoka, 2003); Sitiveni Halapua, in *Peace, Conflict, and Development: Walking the knife-edged pathways in multiculturalism*, a public lecture in 2003.
5. Interviews with Sister Dr Keiti Kanongataa (Tonga), 1 August 2004; Lorini Tevi (Fiji), 2 August 2004, Alice Akao (Solomon Islands), 3 August 2004 and Rev. Dr Paulo Koria (Samoa), 26 November 2004.
6. See, for example, Douglas L. Oliver, *Oceania: The Native cultures of Australia and the Pacific Islands* (Honolulu: University of Hawaii Press, 1989), pp.635–6.
7. Schmidt, op. cit., p.5.
8. Interview with Ken Moale, 27 November 2004.
9. Paul Miles, ' "*Fa'afafine, fakaleiti* and *mahu*" transgender in the Pacific', 2003. http://europa.eu.int/comm/development/body/publications/courier/courier183/en/en_045.ni.pdf.
10. Schmidt, op. cit.
11. Sue Farran, 'Transexuals, Fa'afafine, Fakaleiti and Marriage Law in the Pacific: Considerations for the future', *Journal of the Polynesian Society*, 113:2 (June 2004).
12. 'Statement from the Archbishop of Wales, member of the Lambeth Commission, on the Windsor Report 2004', *Anglican Communion News Service*, 3901 (19 October 2004).
13. Sitiveni Halapua, op. cit., p.6.
14. Stephen Bates, *A Church at War: Anglicans and Homosexuality* (London: I. B. Tauris and Co. Ltd, 2004).
15. See N. Gunson, *Messengers of Grace: Evangelical Missionaries in the South Seas, 1797–1860* (Melbourne: Oxford University Press, 1978); John Garrett, *To Live Among the Stars: Christian Origins in Oceania* (Geneva and Suva: World Council of Churches, in association with the Institute of Pacific Studies, University of South Pacific, 1982); M. T. Crocombe (ed.), *Cannibals and Convents: Radical change in the Cook Islands by Maretu* (Suva: University of the South Pacific, 1983); Allan K. Davidson, 'Culture and Ecclesiology: The Church Missionary Society and New Zealand', in Kevin Ward and Brian Stanley (eds), *The Church Mission Society and World Christianity, 1799–1999*,(Grand Rapids: Eerdmans, and Richmond: Curzons, 2000), pp.198–9; and B. V. Lal and K. Fortune (eds), *Coup Reflections on the Political Crisis in Fiji* (Canberra: Pandanus Books, 2001).
16. See E. Waddell, V. Naidu, and E. Hau'ofa (eds), *A New Oceania: Rediscovering Our Sea of Islands* (Suva: University of the South Pacific, 1993); N. Maclellan and J. Chesneaux, *After Mururoa: France and the South Pacific* (Melbourne: Ocean Press, 1998); I. S. Tuwere, *Vanua: Towards a Fijian Theology of Place*

(Suva: Institute of Pacific Studies, and Auckland: College of St John the Evangelist, 2002); and Sitiveni Halapua, op. cit., 2003.

17. See A. Sharp, *Ancient Voyages in Polynesia* (Auckland and Hamilton: Paul's Book Arcade, 1963); Patrick Vinton Kirch, *The Lapita Peoples: Ancestors of the Oceanic World* (Malden, Massachusetts: Blackwell Publishers, 1997).

18. *Collins Dictionary of Sociology* (New York: HarperCollins, 1991), pp.31–2.

19. Richard Alba and Victor Nee, *Remaking the American Mainstream: Assimilation and Contemporary Immigration* (Cambridge: Harvard University Press, 2003), p.10.

20. Kevin O'Donnell, *Postmodernism* (Oxford: Lion Publishing, 2003), p.98.

21. ibid., p.99.

22. See Norman C. Habel, *Readings from the Perspective of the Earth* (Sheffield: Sheffield Academic Press Ltd, 2000); Norman C. Habel and Shirley Wurst (eds), *The Earth Story in Wisdom Traditions* (Sheffield: Sheffield Academic Press, 2001) and Norman C. Habel and Vicky Balabanski (eds), *The Earth Story in the New Testament* (Sheffield: Sheffield Academic Press, 2002).

Chapter 4

A STORY OF ITS OWN NAME: HONG KONG'S TONGZHI CULTURE AND MOVEMENT

Rose Wu

Introduction: The identity politics of Hong Kong

Hong Kong has been known as the 'Pearl of the Orient' by the West since its colonisation by Britain in 1842. According to Edward W. Said, 'The word "Orient" is not an inert fact of nature. It is not merely there, just as the Occident itself is not just there either ... It is an idea that has a history and a tradition of thought, imagery, and vocabulary that have given it reality and presence in and for the West.'[1] If we look closely at the history of European colonisation, we will see that the relationship between Occident and Orient is a relationship of power, domination and varying degrees of a complex hegemony between the coloniser and the colonised.

A consequence of this process of colonisation has been the construction of an East–West binary in which the West has defined itself in relation to the people of Asia and, by authoring the East as 'others', has sought to justify western imperial domination. Today, although most of the colonies have gained their political independence, we know as we reflect on the present global situation that western colonialism is still very much alive except that it is now much more subtle, much more legitimate in the guise of 'globalisation'. For me, the East–West binary discourse of colonialism is linked directly to the western construction of gender, race, class and sexual differences in our contemporary societies. Thus, one major question that concerns me in this chapter is how the Orientalist relationship between East and West constructs the stereotypical representations of Hong Kong's culture of sexuality – its confrontation between heterosexual and homosexual relationships.

With the end of British colonialism in Hong Kong on 1 July 1997, the community became a Special Administrative Region (SAR) of the People's Republic of China. In contrast to the Chinese government's propaganda, the majority of Hong Kong people do not share its triumphal and optimistic view about the hand-over and their future. Hong Kong's postcolonial period is marked by double oppression: by the previous British colonial government and by the new Beijing government.

Based on the same polarised logic of 'West vs East' or 'coloniser Britain vs native China', there is no alternative available for the people than to acquire another, more positive identity. What we need is to create a third space between the coloniser and the dominant native culture in which we reclaim our own identity. To seek liberation, we must move beyond the simplistic dichotomy of West vs East and explore alternative ways of thinking about cross-cultural and cross-boundary perspectives that exceed the dualistic framework of the East–West binary context. If we do not do so, any theory will only reinforce the presumption of stable identities and continue the problems of binary categories, instead of transforming unjust power structures of colonialism, nationalism, racism, patriarchalism, heterosexism and many other 'isms'.

With this in mind, the task of this chapter is first to examine the influence of both Chinese heritage and western colonialism on the social-political aspects of Hong Kong sexuality, which has been structured by an unconscious process of domination. I shall then try to capture how Hong Kong's *tongzhi* culture and the Christian movement have acted as a path of negotiation and re-creation between the two aggressors, Britain and China.

Sexuality in the Chinese tradition

In Hong Kong, as a Chinese society, the culture was strongly influenced by Confucian and Taoist teachings. In Chinese culture, we do not have an equivalent for the English word 'sex'.[2] We have *jiao-he*, which means sexual intercourse, *fang-shin*, which means things one does in his or her private room, and *se*, which has multiple meanings of erotic, sexual sensation and pleasure. According to Confucius, 'Eating and *se* are human nature.' Therefore, *se* is not something separated from our daily life activities. Research on early Chinese sexuality by the Dutch author Robert Van Gulik, a former ambassador to China, found that traditional Taoist teachings of sexual norms understood sexual relationships to be healthy and neither 'repressed' nor 'perverted'.

Sex, however, was not viewed as a private matter until the beginning of the Han Dynasty (206 BCE to 220 CE).[3] The earliest study and teaching of *fang chong shu* – the skill we use in our private room – was found in the Han Dynasty and seen as one of the four major skills in practical subjects in ancient Chinese education. In fact, one meaning of Lao-tze's *Tao* is the womb of the earth; it was seen as a gate to enter all mysteries of life. Both Confucianism and Taoism affirm that human sexual intercourse has two functions, namely, for reproduction and for health.[4] The restriction of sex was not imposed as a social control until the emergence of New-Confucianism in the Song Dynasty (960–1275 CE).

However, Charlotte Furth describes Van Gulik's attempt to idealise Chinese attitudes, particularly the notion of the Taoist sexual arts as being the antithesis of Victorian repression, as a part of the general phenomenon of Orientalism critiqued by Said. Using a feminist critique, Furth makes the following observation:

> From the very beginning in medieval times, bedchamber arts had been embedded in medical and religious discourses which were not 'about' pleasure or women simply as objects of desire, but about what medieval Chinese understood as serious goals of life and death, linking health, spirituality, and social purposes. They were linked to modes of male empowerment which we may define very loosely here as Confucianist or Taoist. The erotic could be seen as a vehicle for social reproduction and the conception of descendants or for individual self-transformation and sagehood. Both of these alternatives require women to serve male goals.[5]

Furth suggests that both Confucian and Taoist constructions of *eros* are better thought of as constituting a historically contingent experience than as either fulfilling or repressing natural instincts. Following Furth's critique, I conclude that the problem of Van Gulik's perspective is that he overlooks the contradiction in the open view that ancient Chinese took on sex, namely their attitude towards women as harsh and humiliating. Therefore, sexual pleasure was a privilege only for men, particularly the emperors and males of the landed aristocracy. Foot-binding and polygamy were the usual practice all over China until the revolution of Sun Yat-sen and the formation of the Chinese Communist Party (CCP) in the twentieth century. In the Chinese feudalistic family system, both women and serfs were treated as property of men.

In terms of homosexual and transsexual culture, many people think that Chinese society is more repressive than western society. Some Chinese people even claim that homosexuality was imported from the West. They believe it was never an issue in Chinese culture previously.

However, ancient Chinese literature points to a different reality. According to the most representational study, *The History of Homosexuality in China* by Xiaomingxiong, homo-, bi- and transsexual practices were very common phenomena.[6] Many Chinese emperors were fond of male companionship and openly practised pederasty. Women in the palace also formed couples known as *dui shi*, literally meaning 'paired eating'.[7] Other popular examples in Chinese history include male homosexuals in Fujian Province and *tzu shu nü* and *chin-lan hui* in Shunde in Guangdong Province.[8] Many classical Chinese novels, operas, songs and poems were full of male–male and/or female–female romances, like the stories about Pao Yu, Chin Zhong, Zheng Yuxian and Xe Bao in *Hong Liu Meng* (*The Dream of the Red Chamber*).[9]

According to Chau Wah-san, the English noun 'homosexual' does not have the same meaning in the Chinese language because in Chinese culture 'sex' can only be used to identify an act, a relationship or a sex role. It is not used to denote certain categories of people as the western meanings of 'homosexual' and 'heterosexual' often do.[10] While traditional Chinese culture was tolerant toward sexual minorities, this open attitude toward homosexuality and transsexual culture was based on the hierarchy of gender and class. Only male elites in society had the privilege to exercise their sexual freedom. Many women and people of lower classes lived under the triple oppression of patriarchalism, heterosexism and feudalism.

According to Xiaomingxiong, homosexuality was tolerated and accepted only when it was not threatening to the basic heterosexual family structure. Men were allowed to have sex with other men; but they were also expected to fulfil the duty of husband and fathers. Thus, in Chinese tradition, oppression of sexual minorities was not based on their sexual behaviour as non-heterosexuals. Homosexuals, bisexuals and transsexuals were not treated as abnormal or sinful. Rather, discrimination was based on the gender and class hierarchy of society. Compared to the explicit homophobic culture of the West, Xiaomingxiong describes the Chinese homophobic culture as an implicit homophobia.[11]

Legislation to eliminate discrimination

Shifts in Chinese attitudes toward sexuality began in the late nineteenth and early twentieth centuries when China was threatened by European power. At this time, some intellectuals began the May Fourth Movement (1919) to push for the modernisation of China, a movement that favoured many western ideologies, systems and values. Science and democracy were the two major themes of the movement which believed that by adopting aspects of western civilisation China would be transformed from a backward society to a modern and scientific country. Consequently, the western Christian view of sex and homosexuality gradually influenced Chinese societies, particularly Hong Kong after British colonisation.

As history shows, the import of Christianity into China accompanied European imperialism, creating a golden opportunity for Christian missionaries to set up churches, schools and hospitals in many parts of China. As a result, western Christian culture was introduced and slowly influenced the local Christian community. However, this cross-cultural process was under the colonial construction of the East–West binary relationship, through which the West defined itself as the norm against the East – the 'other' – a justification for western imperial domination.

One major criticism that Christian missionaries made about Chinese traditions involved issues of marriage and sexuality. Judging Chinese practices of polygamy and homo-, bi- and transsexual behaviour as deviant, missionaries tried to impose Christian norms of sex and marriage, setting a moral standard in which sex is only permitted in a heterosexual marriage relationship. Thus, polygamous, homo-, bi- and transsexual behaviours were all condemned as sinful and immoral acts.

How did the colonial discourse on sexuality manifest itself in Hong Kong's legislation? Since the beginning of British colonisation, Hong Kong inherited the British common law system deeply influenced by the nineteenth-century Victorian prejudice against male homosexuality. As a result, Hong Kong criminalised homosexual acts between two male adults (over the age of 21) in any public and private place. The highest penalty was a life sentence. The criminalisation of male homosexuality in Hong Kong was not abolished until 1991 after almost ten years of struggle and resistance.

As the issue of decriminalising male homosexual acts became debated publicly, the majority of Hong Kong people took a conservative position against homosexuality and assumed that this was a bad cultural practice introduced from the West. The church was one of the major voices fighting against decriminalisation because of its desire to protect the Christian value of marriage and the Chinese family structure. There were a few Christian groups, including the Hong Kong Women Christian Council (HKWCC) and the Student Christian Movement (SCM), that took a prophetic stance with other feminist and human rights groups to support the decriminalisation of male homosexual acts in Hong Kong. The debate continued until 1991 when Hong Kong's Legislative Council finally abolished the law that made male homosexual acts a criminal offence. In late 1993, Legislative Councillor Anna Wu urged the Hong Kong government to introduce an Equal Opportunities Bill that would cover many types of discrimination such as that based on gender, age, sexual orientation, disability, race, political and religious beliefs, union membership and previous criminal record. The government delayed the process for a year until the end of 1994 when, under tremendous public pressure, it finally introduced two bills. One was the Sex Discrimination Ordinance enacted on 28 June 1995, which prohibits discrimination based on gender, marital status and pregnancy, as well as sexual harassment. One month later the Disability Discrimination Ordinance was passed, prohibiting discrimination, harassment and slander on the grounds of disability. In addition, the legislation created an Equal Opportunities Commission (EOC) in 1996 to oversee enforcement of these new anti-discrimination laws. However, the church was exempted from these ordinances on the principle of religious freedom.

Unfortunately, the government was successful in lobbying the legislature in 1995 to defeat additional legislative proposals that would have prohibited discrimination on other grounds – e.g. sexual orientation, age and race. The major forces opposed to protecting people with different sexual orientations were business, religious and pro-Chinese government groups. Their argument was that society has different opinions and levels of acceptance towards homosexual persons and that most people have very limited knowledge about homosexuality; therefore, public education must be strengthened before introducing any legislation. Instead of introducing equal opportunity legislation, the government established a special fund to promote equal opportunities for people with different sexual orientations.

Hong Kong's *tongzhi* culture and movement

There have been two major struggles since Hong Kong's sexual minorities began their movement in the early 1970s. The first has been its identity of representation; the second, its strategies for resistance and survival. Because Hong Kong identity has been a contested site for imperial coloniser Britain and the national regime of China, there is a need to seek Hong Kong's own voice and write its own history. How do these two dominant powers affect Hong Kong's *tongzhi* culture and movement in the shaping of its local identity of representation?

In a study done by Chau Wah-san, there was no particular term to identify sexual minorities in Hong Kong before the 1970s. News media generally associated homosexuality with certain sexual behaviours between male homosexual persons, relating them to criminal offences. Female homosexuals were not visible because only male homosexuals were bound by the law and its penalties. Therefore, many people wrongly believed that homosexuality only occurred among males. Indeed, one characteristic of sexual minority communities from the 1960s to the 1970s was that they were dominated by either white or Chinese male elites who were once educated in the West. The public and mass media did not at all recognise the existence of lesbians and bi- and transsexual people.[12]

Since the mid-1980s, the social and political atmosphere has been much more open in Hong Kong. More feminist and human rights groups have been formed, which has affected the public debate on the issue of homosexuality. Moreover, after the decriminalisation of male homosexual acts in 1991, many local gay and lesbian groups were registered as non-governmental organisations (NGOs), such as the 10 Percent Club and Horizons.

Although these changes have opened up more public space for homosexual persons in Hong Kong, lesbians have still been treated as second-class members of the homosexual movement. This phenomenon is illustrated by the use of language. For instance, the Chinese word *kei*, the same pronunciation as gay, became popular to identify all homosexuals. However, according to Anson Mak and Mary Ann King, the

founding members of Zimeri-Tongzhi (Queer Sisters),[13] very few
female homosexual persons would call themselves *kei* because the word
delegates women to a subordinate role, as it is usually associated with
male homosexuals. Female homosexual persons would usually call
themselves *tzu kei yar*, meaning 'buddies from the same community', or
ngau hai, meaning 'I am', because they refuse to use any label that
restricts them to a specific social identity.

The word *tongzhi* first appeared to identify gays and lesbians in the
bulletin of a local Lesbian and Gay Film Festival in 1988. After that, the
word was well received by all sexual minorities in Hong Kong and was
commonly used by many gay and lesbian organisations as well as the
media. The word *tongzhi* has spread beyond the borders of Hong Kong
to China, Taiwan and other overseas Chinese gay and lesbian
communities. Why was the word *tongzhi* so attractive to the Chinese?
According to Mak and King, *tongzhi* is a word of multiple meanings and
possible interpretations.[14] The literal meaning of *tongzhi* is 'common
goals and aspirations' in Chinese. Although it is also a word of respect
meaning 'comrade', as used by the Chinese Communists, it gradually
and ironically has become a word used pejoratively in Hong Kong to
describe Chinese officials coming from mainland China who represent
the authority of Beijing – a use of language indicating the fear and help-
lessness of Hong Kong people about the transfer of their destiny to
China in 1997.

Chau explains that there are many good reasons for using *tongzhi* as
a word to name the translesbigay identity. First, *tongzhi* is not limited to
any fixed identity, like homosexual, heterosexual or bisexual. Thus, it
has the potential to be an inclusive word, which embraces all the sexual
identities of people. Second, *tongzhi* has meaning beyond simply
sexual identity; it points to a respectful ideal of people who share the
same goals and aspirations. Third, it breaks the dualistic dichotomies of
'homosexual' vs 'heterosexual', 'East' vs 'West', 'body' vs 'spirit', etc.,
and allows flexibility, fluidity and freedom for movement and change.
The last reason is that, politically, it is a wise choice for Hong Kong's
translesbigay movement because it shares the same cultural and
ideological heritage with the Chinese Communists.[15]

To me, the construction of the *tongzhi* identity marks a significant
point in Hong Kong's unique postcolonial discourse. According to
queer[16] and postcolonial politics, it fulfils at least two functions. The
first is described by Cindy Patton as rhetorical reversal and counter-
reversal,[17] for sexual minorities in Hong Kong have reclaimed for
themselves the term *tongzhi*, a word that is considered part of the
hegemonic vocabulary imposed by China's political regime on Hong
Kong, and yet, it is also a word of respect used to represent Chinese

Communists. Thus, it functions as a paradoxical political term with both positive and negative meanings in Hong Kong and China's contexts. Reversing the negative sense of such terms as homo-, bi- and trans-sexuality, it produces a positive and inclusive identity. The second function is the deconstruction of Hong Kong's colonial identity. It breaks the western imperialist cultural tradition and transforms it into a Chinese-owned terminology.

This historical review shows how Hong Kong's *tongzhi* movement seeks its own representation by shifting both inside and outside of its relationship to the hegemony of the dominant powers of Britain and China. The construction of this complex identity that crosses gender, cultural, class and political forces includes the strategies of subordination, resistance, negotiation and integration.

As for the strategies of resistance and survival, there are some observations that I think are closely related to Hong Kong's postcolonial context. First of all, the choice of Zimei-Tongzhi (Queer Sisters), which uses both *tongzhi* and *queer* for their Chinese and English names, is a way to signify their determination to cross borders and boundaries. Instead of importing the western concept of 'queer', they have succeeded in contextualising queer ideology in the Chinese concept of *tongzhi* based on Hong Kong's own socio-political culture. As a strategy, they have decided not to put sexually subaltern women in the category of female homosexuality. Instead, they have emphasised that women have the right to explore, rethink and choose how they pursue interconnected-ness, heterogeneity and multiplicity of sexualities. Furthermore, while challenging the existing male homocentric *tongzhi* communities that often overshadow women and people of different sexualities, Queer Sisters has taken the lead to move beyond sexual rights concerns and has played an active role in different kinds of social and political movements in Hong Kong. They have criticised the apolitical stance of many *tongzhi* groups. By avoiding involvement in any political issues, some groups in the *tongzhi* movement have become merely engaged in social activities within *tongzhi* circles.[18]

The second strategy of resistance and survival that Hong Kong's *tongzhi* movement has often emphasised is a conscious move to avoid adopting the 'coming-out' politics of the western translesbigay movement and to disclaim its use as a universal norm with which to judge other cultural situations.[19] To me, this is part of Hong Kong's decolonisation process. As Kwok Pui-lan puts it:

> The assumption that the human experience of Western people is the norm for everybody is not just an intellectual blind spot, but is heavily influenced by the colonial experience. The appeal to

universal human experience and the inability to respect diverse
cultures are expressions of a colonizing motive: the incorporation
of the other into one's own culture or perspective.[20]

Instead of choosing to come out as individuals, Queer Sisters has chosen
to stand in solidarity with all other marginal people in Hong Kong and
to come out as political activists to seek liberation for all people as its
strategy of resistance and survival. We should not take 'coming out' as a
rigid norm for all sexual minorities universally. 'Coming out' has a deep
spiritual meaning. It is a lifelong challenge for all to pass from one well-
defined state of being to another. It is also important to be reminded that
'coming out' is not an individual act; rather, it involves communal
participation because we need the support and love of others to help us
through the process of moving from the old into the new, just like the rite
of baptism.

The third strategy of the *tongzhi* movement is to return to the Chinese
heritage and traditions. Since the hand-over of Hong Kong, the local
tongzhi movement has chosen to emphasise the prevalence of homosexuality in Chinese history and the pluralistic sexual culture in ancient
China. One example is the decision by local gay activists in June 1999
to hold the first Tongzhi Day in Hong Kong during the traditional
Chinese Dragon Boat Festival. The festival commemorates Qu Yuan,
who has been honoured and remembered in Chinese history as a patriot
and poet and who was allegedly a lover of his emperor in the Chu
Dynasty.[21] This strategy was quite successful in drawing the attention of
the media and public to the existence of homosexuality in Chinese
history as well as in contemporary society. However, many lesbians and
bisexual people criticised the ideological assumption behind the Tongzhi
Day because it unwittingly represented only male homosexuals and
excluded other sexual minorities.

Another development is the creation by Chinese translesbigay communities all over the world of a network organised through the Global
Chinese Tongzhi Annual Conference that has been held every year since
1997. This shift of focus towards strengthening the Chinese identity and
the promotion of a worldwide Chinese *tongzhi* network indicates that
there is an attempt to dismiss homo-, bi- and transsexual movements as
products of westernisation and colonisation and to rediscover the cultural
roots of homo-, bi- and transsexuality within Chinese history and
traditions. While I agree on the necessity of the Chinese *tongzhi*
movement to reclaim its cultural tradition and to deconstruct the
colonialist representation of Chinese *tongzhi* history and culture, I also
want to emphasise that it is just as problematic to preserve and glorify
the Chinese traditions of the past without a critical examination of the

particular cultural practices and institutions that were discussed earlier.

The fourth strategy of Hong Kong's *tongzhi* movement is its willingness to embrace more diversified and marginalised groups informing coalitions to fight against oppression. One of the incidents that sparked this broad-based coalition was the criticism of the Red Cross guidelines for blood donors which mentioned that all people are welcome to donate their blood except gays, lesbians, sex workers and AIDS patients. Because of this prohibition, the coalition was successful in bringing together many translesbigay communities, concern groups for sex workers and AIDS patients to fight against the social stigmatisation and discrimination of sexual minorities, sex workers and AIDS patients.

The challenge of homosexuality to Hong Kong's Christian community

During the public debate on decriminalising male homosexual acts in the 1980s, the Christian response to homosexual issues was varied. The strongest objections were from a few evangelical church leaders, including ministers from the Baptist Church, Hong Kong Alliance Church and the director of Breakthrough, Dr Chow Yuen-wan.[22] They succeeded in lobbying the Hong Kong Chinese Christian Churches Union (HKCC-CU), which represents the majority of Chinese congregations across denominational lines, to issue a public statement to object to the government's decriminalising of male homosexual acts.

The Hong Kong Catholic Youth Council (HKCYC) also organised an anti-decriminalisation campaign. The Hong Kong Christian Council (HKCC),[23] which represented more liberal views within Hong Kong's Christian community at that time, chose to issue a study report on homosexuality instead of making a statement on their position in order to avoid direct conflicts with other members of the local Christian community.

Since the passing of the legislation that decriminalises male homosexual acts in 1991, institutional churches in Hong Kong have not been actively involved in any public debate related to homosexual issues. However, one new phenomenon that I have observed recently is the beginning of an anti-sex and anti-homosexual Christian movement in Hong Kong through the formation of the Society for Truth and Light in 1996. Part of their agenda is to monitor the government and the media on issues of sexuality, including homosexuality, based on their perception of Christian moral values of family and fidelity. They opposed the government's legislation prohibiting discrimination on the grounds of sexual orientation as well as the government's special fund for public education to promote equal opportunities for sexual minorities.

On 17 August 2003, two groups of activists, Rainbow Action and Youth Commune, stormed into the Roman Catholic Cathedral of the

Immaculate Conception. On the television news that evening, two activists were seen being pushed onto the ground outside the cathedral, activists were chanting slogans against Bishop Joseph Zen and the Catholic Church, and two lesbians were kissing each other while walking down the aisle. Same-sex marriage was the cause for which the two groups of activists took this radical, at least in the eyes of the general public, path of action. They demonstrated against the Catholic Diocese of Hong Kong's republication of two Vatican articles against same-sex marriage in their official newsletter, *Kung Kao Po*, which reiterated the Vatican's position against homosexuality: that it is a sin and same-sex marriage erodes the institution of marriage and results in violence towards children.

It is true that the incident did disrupt the service for about ten minutes and shocked both the congregation and some viewers of the nightly news. However, the activists did not see the ten-minute disruption as of any significance compared to the ongoing, lifelong influence exerted by the Catholic Church on the daily lives of homosexuals. As Roddy Shaw of the Civil Rights for Sexual Diversity pointed out,

> [T]he matter has to be analysed in view of the huge power differential between the Catholic Church and the Tongzhi community. Despite the fact that both communities are minorities in Hong Kong, the Catholic Church definitely has more power in terms of resources, public recognition and social status. Its historical development has lent great power to its social influence. Although its population may be small, the institution constructed by its religious values and doctrines is by no means insignificant, for the extensive network of local educational and social service institutions founded by the Catholic Church and its social influence is quite extensive.
>
> By contrast, the Tongzhi community is just slowly overcoming the barrier in visibility. Despite the 20-odd organisations representing roughly 2,000 members in the Tongzhi community, those who can be 'out' publicly are still in the dozens. Because of the lack of anti-discrimination legislation, the Tongzhi community is still largely in the closet for fear of being discriminated against once they come 'out'. Any Tongzhi who is 'out' or 'outed' stands the risk of losing their job, family and friends. The fear of being visible creates a grave hurdle for organising Tongzhis, not to mention activism. Oftentimes, this is the reason why a few activists may take the radical way, so as to maximise the impact and public debate with the least resources.[24]

At the beginning of 2005, the Home Affairs Bureau informed the

Hong Kong community that as it had been ten years since the government conducted its last survey on sexual orientation, the government believed it was appropriate to conduct a telephone survey of about 2,000 people to gauge their attitudes towards homosexual people and to examine possible legislation against discrimination based on sexual orientation. While sexual minorities see the legislation as a necessary step towards equal opportunities, Christian and family concern groups believe it will unleash a dangerous tide of tolerance and upset society's fundamental family values.

As we look at the reality of our world and our church, we must admit that there are brothers and sisters who have different sexual orientations than heterosexuals. Because of the mainstream position of the Christian churches that condemn homosexual acts as sin, many sexual minorities continue to hide themselves in the closet, try to change their sexual orientations, leave the church and join other Christian communities-in-exile or even give up their faith. However, I want to point out that, no matter what positions we take, we are still one family in Christ. As Paul told the Corinthians, 'All of you are Christ's body, and each one is a part of it. We cannot do without the parts of the body that seem to be weaker, and those parts that we think are not worth very much are the ones which we treat with greater care … God has put the body together in such a way as to give greater honour to those parts that need it. And so there is no division in the body, but all its different parts have the same concern for one another' (1 Corinthians 12). The purpose of God's creation is not to mould everyone into being the same; rather, God's purpose is to teach us to love and care for one another and to appreciate our differences.

If we embrace our homosexual brothers and sisters as one family and relate to them with genuine care at this initial stage of Hong Kong's development, we must then ask how we can transform our church as a safe place for all of them even though we may take a different position on homosexuality. Thus, I suggest that our church open its space and its heart to allow our brothers and sisters who have other sexual orientations to become a part of our community and to have the same equal rights to participate in all of our religious rituals and activities, including attending worship services and Sunday school, receiving Holy Communion and accepting lay leadership roles. Moreover, we also have to support sexual minorities to fight for their equal rights in society, such as their rights to employment, education, housing, etc.

Secondly, before we condemn homosexuality as sin, we must acknowledge that this stance is not the only or the final and absolute truth. In the past few decades, there have been other alternative interpretations of the Bible that use a hermeneutical approach together with theological reflection about human sexuality that is more inclusive and liberating. We need to change the present top-down approach of moral teaching and transform it into a more inclusive and open dialogical approach of theological reflection. More importantly, we must respect and include minority voices and experiences as our primary source of theological input in our process of theologising. The purpose is not to seek absolute authority; rather, it is to explore an inclusive and empowering approach for enhancing our mutual understanding and solidarity among all parties of the Christian community.

Regarding same-sex marriages, based on the principles of human rights and justice, I personally support same-sex marriages as having the same rights as heterosexual marriages. However, I also understand and accept that there are churches which take the opposite view, based on their inter-pretation of the biblical condemnation of homosexuality, treating homo-sexuality as a violation of God's procreation. To me though, the challenge that God puts to us is not whether homosexuality is a sin but rather how we treat each other even though we bear a different image of God.

An Exodus community and its path of healing and liberation

Owing to the conservative view of homosexuality held by many people in Hong Kong and the oppressive and heterosexist culture of the Chinese church, many gay and lesbian Christians find no other alternative but to turn away from the church or to keep silent and figuratively hide themselves in closets. There are incidents in which some gay and lesbian Christians, including seminarians, were immediately forced to leave their church or seminary or advised to go for counselling and medical help when their sexual identities were exposed, so that their homosexual behaviour could be purportedly 'corrected'.

However, we witnessed a glimpse of hope when three gay Christians decided in July 1992 to move from being in exile to forming an Exodus community[25] – a Christian fellowship under the umbrella of the 10 Percent Club. During the first stage of its development, the fellowship maintained itself as a private gathering at members' homes. A year later, as the membership grew from three to more than thirty, the fellowship began to meet in St John's Cathedral of Hong Kong Sheng Kung Hui (Anglican Diocese of Hong Kong) once a month. Their activities in-cluded prayers, hymn singing, and Bible studies. During this period, the fellowship also began a joint project with HKWCC to organise theology courses for their members as well as for other Christians. These courses, which are ongoing, aim to provide an alternative interpretation of Christian theology and biblical reflection on homosexuality.

Five years later the fellowship registered with the Hong Kong govern-ment as an independent organisation named the Hong Kong Blessed Minority Christian Fellowship (HKBMCF). As its name indicates, the group's aim is to witness to the love and blessing of God among sexual minorities. In October 1997, the fellowship was able to rent an apartment for their office and functions. In the past two years, membership has grown to more than 100. Like a regular church, they meet every Sunday afternoon for worship. They have Sunday school, Bible study and a choir. Like other churches in Hong Kong, they elect their board members once a year. The only difference is that they are not attached to any denomination and have no ordained minister. Each Sunday they invite a minister to preach, and once a month they ask an ordained minister to conduct the Eucharist. What I see as a major success of HKBMCF is their ability to raise a new breed of young leaders from among their members.

Since they became an independent organisation, HKBMCF has come out as a visible Christian witness in Hong Kong. Their constitution lists three objectives: (1) to promote the Christian community's understanding and respect for sexual minorities; (2) to offer support and mutual care for gay and lesbian Christians to worship, pray for and empower each other; and (3) to seek equal rights and dignity in the church and society for all, regardless of one's gender and sexual orientation.

Since its inception in July 1992, HKBMCF has gone through thirteen summers with its congregation growing to more than 100 people now. About thirty people have received baptism since this sacrament was introduced in 2001. With the guidance of the Holy Spirit and the devotion of the HKBMCF, Selina Sun was ordained as their pastor on 5 October 2004.

The following is the testimony of Pastor Selina Sun to explain why she chose to be ordained by HKBMCF:

> My bond with HKBMCF has developed since 2002. At the beginning, I was merely invited to deliver some training courses in the church. However, to better understand the needs of HKBMCF, I attended their meetings as well. Having got along with them for some time, I began to identify with all sides of their struggle and became involved in their lives.
>
> It is really God's grace that my encounter with HKBMCF has grown into a loving relationship. My involvement in HKBMCF is also the answer that I have awaited from God over the past five years. When seeking ordination five years ago, I prudently pondered on my vocation to the pastorate, the meaning of becoming a pastor and its role in society as well as in the church. As such, I came to a definition like this: The mission and role of a pastor should be living among people; a pastor is not someone who lives a life secured by stable incomes or someone who occupies herself

with a variety of church chores and yet fails to respond to God's ultimate calling. Hence, I asked God to send me to the flock that is uncared for and to those who linger at the door of his temple and yet feel too ashamed to enter the house of worship.

Through my interaction with HKBMCF and through each and every single story that I heard there, I realised that the sheep in HKBMCF were exactly the answer to my question posed five years ago. Without much hesitation, I accepted their invitation to become their pastor. One and a half years have passed since I accepted the offer in February 2003. As I have not been ordained yet under the institution of the church, I am only a minister, not a reverend, albeit the duties of both sacred positions are more or less the same. Nevertheless, upon meditating on the existence of HKBMCF, I believe that HKBMCF should, by all means, be a living testimony to sexual minority groups, society and even the church of Christ. She should take on a prophetic role and mission, standing as a bridge of reconciliation in a world of prejudice and discord. Thus, HKBMCF deserves other people's acknowledgement. Although the administration of HKBMCF is on the right track, what she needs at this stage is a prominent spiritual leader who can lead the congregation to reach out to society, other bodies of Christ and even the sexual minority community so that the Reign of God shall be magnified.

Personally speaking, it is not my concern whether outsiders recognise my ordination or not. What is important to me is the meaning behind this vocation, which I believe is God's special kindness to me, the most precious moment in my life and a personal experience of walking with God. My Sovereign Lord has shown me how to live humbly and how to view this world and the people living in it with his love and mercy. Just as our Lord says, 'Remain in me, and I will remain in you' (John 15:4–10), the meaning behind a vocation is the covenant of his love.[26]

Towards a liberation theology of 'right relation'

In order to bring liberation to sexual minorities, we must first liberate the church from homophobia and heterosexism and construct a liberation theology which truly reflects the justice and love of God among all of God's people, especially those who are marginalised and excluded because of their different sexual preferences. To do this, I propose two alternative interpretations of theology of the triune God and human sexuality which touch upon both the doctrine of God and Christian anthropology.

To me, the triune God enables us to rediscover the profoundly relational character of the mystery which reaffirms our unity in diversity, our connectedness as a community, and/or erotic power that is sexual, spiritual and just. Brazilian liberation theologian Leonardo Boff points out that because the Trinity is a mystery of relationships existing among divine co-equals, a society that is to be a sign and sacrament of the Trinity will be a society that is based on relationships of equality, participation, inclusion and communion.[27]

Feminist theologian Carter Heyward criticises the notion of God as controlling power, which has become the cancerous seed for the growth of sexism and heterosexism in the church and society. To transform this misogynist (woman-hating) and erotophobic (sex-fearing) religion, Heyward chooses *Christa* – a bronze crucifix of a naked female Christ – as a transitional Christian symbol of sacred power. She argues that the power of *Christa* is in the connection she makes between our erotic power and the sacred power in our most profoundly human, most deeply embodied belief of who we are – a relational body of incarnate love.[28] Heyward says that God is justice, and justice is right relation, and right relation is mutual relation. She criticises the church's efforts to keep God and sex separate and to imagine God as a male master of the world, a deity who rules nations, families and women as well as their sexual behaviour. These are the root causes of sexism, hierarchicalism, colonialism, neo-colonialism, heterosexism and patriarchalism. The mystery of the Trinity reveals to us that God is not a solitary divine being but a God of communion and solidarity.

Another proposal, in view of the pervasive fear of sex and homosexuality within the church, is for the church to construct a sexual theology which connects sexual relations with justice-making. To do this, we must transform our ethic of control to an ethic of solidarity. We must transform the binary logic of either/or to a trinitarian logic of relationship based on freedom, love and justice. In her newest book, *Saving Jesus from Those Who Are Right: Rethinking What It Means to Be Christian*, Heyward distinguishes between self-righteousness and right relation. Self-righteous Christians are those who claim that they have all of the right answers and the right to rule and control others. Their ethical theology is based on fear and control. Creating right relation, by contrast, means to seek justice through a dynamic relational commitment with others and God. The ethics of theology is based on Christians' conviction of love, faith and solidarity in mutuality.[29]

What is a spirituality of solidarity? Put in practical terms, it is a construction of a new kind of 'coalitional politics'. As Henry Louis Gates writes, 'The challenge is to move from a politics of identity to a politics of identification ... A politics of identification doesn't enjoin us to ignore or devalue our collective identities. For it's only by exploring the multiplicity of human life in culture that we can come to terms with the commonalities that cement communities.'[30] As a Christian community, we are constantly called to participate in the ministry of loving our neighbours as ourselves. This is a ministry that moves us towards the healing of divisions, overcoming brokenness, and ultimately towards achieving wholeness. We as individuals cannot become whole without helping others to become whole. To embrace sexual minorities as equal members of our Christian family is a hospitable act in which our ethics of morality is measured by the whole, the community, the Body of Christ, instead of by individuals. For the church in Hong Kong to become an inclusive Christian community requires us to have faith in 'the other who is larger than the self'. Only through our sense of connecting with 'the other' – the larger community, nature and God – can we grasp a glimpse of hope for life.

NOTES

1. Edward W. Said, *Orientalism* (New York: Pantheon Books, 1978), pp.4–5.
2. In Chinese, the word 'sex' is different from the western meaning of sexual instincts or sexual intercourse. In Chinese, it means 'human nature'.
3. Robert Van Gulik, *Sexual Life in Ancient China: A Preliminary Survey of Chinese Sex and Society from ca. 1500 BC till 1644 AD*, trans. Lee Ling and others (Shanghai: Shanghai People's Press, 1990), pp.1–18.
4. ibid., p.8.
5. Charlotte Furth, 'Rethinking Van Gulik: Sexuality and Reproduction in traditional Chinese Medicine', in Christiana K. Gilmartin and others (eds), *Engendering China: Women, Culture, and the State* (Cambridge: Harvard University Press, 1994), pp.130–1.
6. Xianomingxiong, *The History of Homosexuality in China* (Hong Kong: Siuming and Rosa Winkel Press, 1997), pp.4–21.
7. Bret Hinsch, 'Lesbianism in Imperial China', in his *Passions of the Cut Sleeve: The Male Homosexual Tradition in China* (Cambridge: Harvard University Press, 1990), p.174.
8. Xianomingxiong, op. cit., p.302. The *tzu-shu nü* in Shunde was a well-known tradition in Qing and contemporary times. Those women who decided to join the community house were called 'old maids' because they had to leave their own family and vowed not to marry as a lifelong covenant. Some women would find another woman with whom they wanted to live, and they would form a couple called *chin-lan hui*. After making their vows to each other in the official ceremony, the women were supposed to live together as a married couple and not live apart.
9. *Hong Liu Meng* is one of the world's most well-known Chinese novels written by Tso Jin in the eighteenth century. The story presents a very clear picture of the corruption of Chinese feudal families and society in the Qing period.
10. Chau, Wah-san, *Post-colonial Tongzhi* (Hong Kong: Hong Kong Tongzhi Research Institute, 1997), pp.348–59.
11. Xianomingxiong, op. cit., pp.4–21.
12. Chau, op. cit., pp.348–59.
13. Zimei-Tongzhi (Queer Sisters) was founded in early 1995 as one of the first

feminist queer organisations in Hong Kong as well as in Asia.

14. Anson Mak and Mary Ann King, 'Hong Kong's Tongzhi Movement: Through the Eyes of Queer Sisters', in *Hong Kong's Social Movements; Forces from the Margins* (Hong Kong, July 1 Link and Hong Kong Women Christian Council, 1997), p.100.

15. Chau, op. cit., pp.360–9.

16. Eve Kosofsky Sedgwick, *Epistemology of the Closet* (Berkeley: University of California Press, 1990), p.xii.

17. Cindy Patton, 'Tremble, Hetero Swine!', in Michael Warner (ed.), *Fear of a Queer Planet: Queer Politics and Social Theory* (Minneapolis: University of Minneapolis, 1993), p.146.

18. Mak and King, op. cit., pp.104–8.

19. ibid., p.104.

20. Kwok Pui-lan, 'The Sources and Resources of Feminist Theologies: A Post-colonial Perspective', in *Yearbook of the European Society of Women in Theological Research* (1997), p.9.

21. On 18 June 1999, twenty-two Tongzhi organisations and other support groups organised the first Tongzhi Day in Hong Kong. The objective was to educate the public that homosexuality and bisexuality are not only found in the western world but are also evident in ancient Chinese traditions.

22. Breakthrough is a Christian organisation formed in the early 1970s to serve as a centre for youth counselling and youth education. One of their objectives is to reach out to young people in the community.

23. HKCC was founded in 1954; its membership is denominational and ecumenical.

24. Roddy Shaw, 'Same-Sex Marriage and Religious Tolerance', *Hong Kong Christian Institute Newsletter*, No. 182 (October 2003), 3–4.

25. This poetic image was used by Rosemary R. Ruether in her book *Women-Church: Theology and Practice of Feminist Liturgical Communities* (San Francisco: Harper and Row, 1985) to describe how Women-Church as an ex-cluded community within the patriarchal Church is still determined to seek liberation and thus become an Exodus community. I find that this theological image reflects the journey of the Hong Kong Blessed Minority Christian Fellowship (HKBMCF).

26. Selina Sun, 'Why I Chose to Be Ordained by BMCF', *Hong Kong Christian Institute Newsletter*, No. 194 (November 2004), 3–4.

27. Leonardo Boff, *Trinity and Society* (New York: Orbis Books, 1988), p.3.

28. Carter Heyward, *Touching Our Strength: The Erotic as Power and the Love of God* (New York: University Press of America, 1982), pp.114–18. *Christa* is a bronze crucifix of a female Christ made by British sculptor Edwina Sandys. It was displayed in New York's Cathedral of St John the Divine during the Lenten season of 1984. According to Heyward, this display generated a stir among the Christian community.

29. Carter Heyward, *Saving Jesus from Those Who Are Right: Rethinking What It Means to Be Christian* (Minneapolis: Fortress Press, 1999), pp.1–30.

30. Henry Louis Gates, 'A Liberalism of Heart and Spine', *New York Times*, 27 March 1994.

Chapter 5

THE MYTHIC-LITERALISTS IN THE PROVINCE OF SOUTHEAST ASIA

Leng Lim with Kim-Hao Yap and Tuck-Leong Lee

Introduction

The purpose of this essay is to shed light on the Anglican Province of Southeast Asia to understand how, under the leadership of Archbishop Moses Tay, former Bishop of Singapore and the first Primate, it has come to exert such a prominent role in the ongoing controversy over homosexuality in the Anglican Communion. The writers of this essay are all Singaporeans. While Southeast Asia comprises eleven countries and 500 million people of diverse ethnicities, the actual reach of the province is largely confined to the former British colonies of Singapore and Malaysia, with parishioners drawn mainly from the minority Chinese immigrant population of the region.

The presenting issues are homosexuality, the question of biblical authority and church unity. Mindful that one may apply theological, historical or political modes of analyses to the situation, this essay instead uses moral and faith developmental frameworks and makes the case that what is at stake is wholesome spirituality.

Human development

Development as a *universal* process is evident all around us. A child becomes a teenager and then matures into an adult. Some of this development unfolds naturally (as in the onset of puberty), and some of it must be consciously chosen (as in the development of one's adult character). Regardless, the child, the teenager and the adult are equal *to the extent that they are all human beings*, but they are also unequal and vastly different in the way they are able to actualise and manifest human capacities and potential. Only the adult is capable of manifesting the potential of all three stages.

Developmental processes have been observed beyond the biological. Their description and characterisation may not be completely tidy and may even contain flaws but developmental hierarchies exist. In the moral sphere, Lawrence Kohlberg has observed six stages in moral development.[1] In the area of education, Robert Kegan has studied five levels of the developing adult mind.[2] In the cultural, Ken Wilber and Clare Graves in 'Spiral Dynamics' recognise eight levels in the development of societies and cultures.[3] In leadership, Bill Torbert has studied seven transformations[4] and in spiritual life, James Fowler has identified six stages of faith development.[5] Even Confucius in ancient China observed six stages of the evolving self.[6]

A development narrative is universal across human cultures and a human being, by passing through these stages, experiences more and more of what it is to be fully human. There is greater complexity and greater order as one develops. We might even say that these more 'evolved' humans show us more fully what God looks like.

What is common in these developmental frameworks is that at the higher levels the mind is able to work with more complexity and ambiguity; the heart of faith is inclusive of difference; and the sense of self, and who one is, becomes paradoxically more individuated and autonomous, and at the same time more connected to other beings. Society and culture at the upper levels integrate the material, the cultural, the rational and the spiritual, the seen with the unseen worlds. The higher stages make sense of and integrate a larger amount of data – whether physical, metaphysical, emotional, cultural, psychological or spiritual.

A developmental narrative will displease both conservatives and liberals in the church. While conservatives do not dispute the existence of hierarchies and indeed think of themselves at the top of the pyramid of moral development, they will be disappointed to know that all of the developmental frameworks would place them in the middle, or even at lower rungs of development. On the other hand, liberals and progressives are much developed, yet they will be chagrined because they take umbrage at the whole idea of development itself. For them, a narrative of development implies hierarchy and judgement and that sounds too much like what conservatives do!

This essay will argue that the Anglican Diocese of Singapore has been at a lower level of faith and consciousness development, and that it has in recent years regressed. However, this regression is not necessarily pathological, and there are in fact instances in which its expression of faith is both normal and life-giving. However, there are enough instances of the expressions of pathology within the regression to the lower levels of faith and consciousness development that the situation is worthy of attention and concern.

The Anglican Diocese of Singapore

James Fowler, in his groundbreaking book, *Stages of Faith Development*, describes six stages of faith development, with people moving up the stages, but not always reaching the higher ones. Stage 1,

'Intuitive-Projective', occurs in early childhood. Stage 2, 'Mythic-Literal', takes place in late childhood and adolescence. By adulthood, many would have reached Stage 3, the 'Synthetic-Conventional'. Progress beyond that might occur with age but is not assured.

Stage 3, the 'Synthetic-Conventional Faith', describes the Singapore Anglican Diocese under British colonial rule. The Anglican Church, as an integral part of the colonial structure, was 'liberal', in that it was committed to public education in the English language and to the promotion of education of women. These 'liberal norms' were of course the *conventional* values of late-nineteenth-century colonialism. In contrast to other countries, where Christians were engaged in the fight for national independence, Anglicans in Malaysia and Singapore did not become involved in such struggles because their countries gained independence peacefully from the British. A consequence is that they adopted a private and personal faith, for the most part remaining uninvolved with the issues of society. 'Synthetic-Conventional', therefore, refers to that stage of faith development in which religious values are *tacit*, and the more demanding aspects of religious faith are all but ignored.

The leadership of the Diocese of Singapore changed into local hands with the consecration in 1966 of Bishop Joshua Chiu Ban It. He was an ethnic Chinese, but in the racial nomenclature of Singapore, was 'English educated'. In the beginning, Chiu continued on the liberal/conventional path, giving leadership to the ecumenical movement and even becoming President of the Christian Conference of Asia (a liberal ecumenical group) from 1970 to 1972. However, these credentials made it difficult for him to relate to his Chinese and more conservative base. The turning point came in 1972, while Chiu was attending the Salvation Today conference organised by the World Council of Churches in Bangkok. Manik Corea, in an unpublished report, describes Chiu's new conversion:

> The Anglican Bishop, Chiu Ban It, had come into his own experience of the Holy Spirit in Bangkok in December 1972. While attending a Christian conference, a Fijian colleague handed him a book, *Nine O'clock in the Morning* by Rev. Dennis Bennet, which described the exciting and powerful work and move of the Holy Spirit in an Episcopal (Anglican) Church in America. Bishop Chiu contrasted that with his rather dry and insipid experience of Christianity thus far. Quite frankly bored with the proceedings at the conference, Bishop Chiu had returned to the hotel one afternoon and though not naturally attracted to the supernatural work of God, he prayed for a similar experience as that which had transformed Rev. Bennet's ministry. He then dozed off only to awaken

with a quickening of the presence of God. His heart was filled with joy and he burst forth in praise to God. When he ran out of words, he found himself praying in tongues.[7]

Chiu then influenced the English-speaking Anglican congregations to adopt charismatic worship. Believing that it was no longer necessary for Anglican ordinands to pursue the normal course of theological studies at Trinity Theological College – an ecumenical institution founded by Anglicans, Methodists and Presbyterians – he directed ordinands to enrol in a small Bible college that focused on the experience of the Holy Spirit. His successor, Dr Moses Tay, even made speaking in tongues a requirement for ordination. Charismatic congregations led to church growth, and the numerical (and financial) success of this was appealing and therefore propagated. While Chiu was genuinely renewed by his religious experience and the church did grow in numbers, the church had renewed itself by *regressing* to Stage 2, the 'Mythic-Literal'.

According to James Fowler's typology, the 'Mythic-Literal' is

> the stage where the person takes on for him- or herself the stories, beliefs and observances that symbolize belonging to his or her community. Beliefs are appropriated with literal interpretations, as are moral rules and attitudes. Symbols are taken as one-dimensional and literal in meaning ... This is the faith stage of the school child (though we sometimes find the structures dominant in adolescents and in adults) ... The actors in their cosmic stories are anthropomorphic. [Those at this stage] can be affected deeply and powerfully by symbolic and dramatic materials and can describe in endlessly detailed narrative what has occurred. They do not, however, *step back from the flow* [italics mine] of stories to formulate reflective, conceptual meanings. For this stage, the meaning is both carried and 'trapped' in the narrative.[8]

In the Mythic-Literal stage, the sacred texts are understood literally. Hermeneutics is tacit and thus never explicitly examined as a *process in itself*.

For some Mythic-Literalists, the events of daily life can reflect a cosmic showdown between Good and Evil. Elevating this conflict into a Manichean heresy, the larger charismatic movement in Singapore has had a preoccupation with evil spirits and the end times. American Christian science-fiction authors like Hal Lindsay (*The Late Great Planet Earth*) and the *Left Behind* series of books have been a common staple of a large section of Singaporean Christians, Anglicans and otherwise. Mythic-Literal Christians look at current political events, assign to them apocalyptic meanings and so herd their believers into various zealous positions of one sort or another. Archbishop Moses Tay in his retirement has joined a millennium messianic Jewish Christian community looking for the return of the Messiah.[9] This preoccupation with the end times interprets secular events as divine clues of the Second Coming, whether these clues have to do with the formation of the modern State of Israel in 1948 (the *sine qua non* for these sign-watchers) or the acceptance of homosexuality (equated with the apostasy and degeneracy that herald the apocalypse). In this heightened urgency for purity and zeal (in order for the chosen few to make it into the Rapture), theological diversity becomes a sign of an impure church; ecumenism and interfaith dialogues become signs of a whoring church that has rejected the *exclusivity* of Christ; and international co-operation becomes a sign of the Anti-Christ's one-world government (hence Lindsay's hysterical interpretation of the European Economic Community as the resurrected Beast portrayed in The Revelation to John).

The Mythical-Literal, with its devotionalism, superstition, magic and fundamentalism, is also descriptive of other religious expressions in the region. Southeast Asian Taoism is not of the high metaphysical kind that has attracted so many in the West but is subsumed in the world of magical spirits and spells and duelling deities. Because the Mythic-Literal is an essential part of the fabric of Southeast Asian life, Bishop Tay's well-publicised destruction and exorcism of an antique chest with Chinese dragons on it (symbols of the devil) was a manifestation of this generic level of faith development.

There is, strictly speaking, nothing wrong with Stage 2 Mythic-Literal. It is one valid way by which human beings express their spirituality. Indeed, the passion, commitments, zeal, energy, faithfulness and orderliness that are part of Stage 2 are admirable qualities. However, because of its self-imposed barrier against questioning of authority, it is prone to the pathological abuse of power. So, while no harm comes out of believing that Jonah was literally swallowed by a whale, it also succumbs to the temptation to use other biblical motifs (hellfire, damnation, apocalypse) to induce guilt and shame, particularly around the areas of sexuality (gay or straight), in order to exert control over the lives of others. And since control is synonymous with order and order is something God ordains, human power and cosmic power are collapsed, and the conditions for abuse are set.

We see this descent into pathology for Mythic-Literal Anglicans in Singapore in their understanding of human depravity. Adhering to a narrow and heavy Augustinian understanding of the Fall and of Original Sin, they view the entire human capacity for knowing to have been impaired by Adam's disobedience. Humans therefore cannot trust in any kind of human capacity for knowing. This position leads to two consequences: first, objective data, gathered through scientific inquiry, is suspect when it does not conform to *a priori* Mythic-Literal positions. Hence, no amount of scientific data about the normalcy of homosexuality (or evolution) is acceptable, except for reparative therapy (and creation science). Secondly, subjective data, from personal or communal experience, is even more suspect. When gay and lesbian Christians speak from experience of having known God's grace in their same-sex relationships, their testimony is not just suspect, but considered a hideous lie. For Mythic-Literalists, noone can rely on their faculties for discerning truth because of the Fall. But if the Fall's impact is so far-reaching, then how might human beings, regardless of sexual orientation, ever discern any kinds of truths, including biblical ones?

The conservative Christian at the Mythic-Literal stage views God in strict Origenist terms (*Cur Deus Homo*, How God became man), where a feudal God, offended by the misdemeanours of his subjects, cannot make himself just to accept the contrition of his lowly subjects. Instead, someone of his same stature must pay the price to restore his honour; thus, the death of his Son as substitution. But such a strict and singular view of salvation has two unfortunate effects. The first is the necessity of violence as a yardstick of being loved – a belief portrayed in Mel Gibson's *Passion*, which swept Christian circles in Singapore like a cult movie. Second, by contrasting the efficacy of the crucifixion with the futility of Old Testament temple sacrifices, conservatives negate other orthodox biblical ways in which God has saved: for example, the Noahic Covenant, where the flood stops after forty days (an allusion to the completion of time) because God simply had enough of destruction, and chooses to save life instead; or the Exodus, in which God delivers the Hebrew people from slavery because the cries of the oppressed and suffering are enough to move God; or in the gospels, where Jesus forgives sins simply by proclaiming them forgiven.

What then is the nature of the God of Mythic-Literalists? There is a Hollywood film called *Stargate*, where a group of humans stumble upon a round Egyptian stone gate, which enables them to travel to another planet. There, they find other humans living in fear and terror of a god who returns to judge and punish them. There is opposition, but they are rounded up as heretics and rebels and punished. No questioning or thinking is allowed. In the film, this god does in fact return – in a spaceship the shape of an Egyptian pyramid. And the god looks like the Egyptian Sun-god Ra. As it turns out, Ra is an advanced and powerful alien creature, who is the last survivor of his species. But it doesn't matter that he is not actually God – the God of Love, Truth or Goodness – because to his weaker subjects, Ra is *like a god*.

To unpack this theology, which has its cognates in various parts of the 'right' wing of the Christian church throughout the world, the Mythic-Literal Christ is *Stargate*'s Ra. In the worldview promulgated by Bishop Tay and other Mythic-Literal leaders, all other religions are false and their adherents destroyed in Christ's Second Coming. (The *Left Behind* series has a gory scene of a returning Christ sending non-Christians to a hideous destruction.) To the question of why a loving God would create a world where other religions falsely claim to have the truth but whose adherents are somehow unfortunate enough to believe in them, the answer is that God chose to have counterfeits to test the wisdom and devotion of human beings.

But what an unfair test! Human beings, already blind and incapable because of Original Sin, are now also to be tested? It is like asking a blind paraplegic to jump rope through a maze. There is only one consequence here: to keep believers in hyper-vigilance, ostensibly against external threats like false leaders (presumably from the Episcopal Church and the rest of the apostate West) and evil spirits, but really, to control them through fear, guilt and shame. This is spiritual pathology, because it creates an endless and unnecessary vigilant war against the self – against human beings' God-given gifts of human reason, human feelings, human intuition and human experience.

For years now, one excess of the charismatic movement under Bishop Tay is that common physical illnesses like arthritis have been interpreted as evil spirits possessing the knee joints, or miscarriages as generational curses. A well-educated banker once responded to my suggestion that she take up yoga as an exercise by saying that yoga was satanic. But the glaring question is: if Christians can be possessed by the devil, what on earth is the value of Christ's death and resurrection? Indeed, if Christians can be assured of so little protection from the devil, why indeed might the Bible itself not be susceptible to the devil? Might there not be some parts of the Bible that are actually inspired by the devil to lead even the elect astray?

Ridiculous? Then, consider a Singaporean Anglican teaching that masturbation is equal to fornication and will lead to demon possession, all based on a literal proof-texting of the Song of Songs – in which 'the little foxes that are ruining the vineyards' (2:12) symbolise masturbation.[10] To turn an innocent bodily action into an occasion for cosmic destruction would be laughable were it not abusive. Abuse – emotional, sexual or spiritual – is simply an opportunistic ploy by those with more power, to take something innocent, vulnerable and perhaps as yet unformed or insecure in a less powerful person, and turn it back onto that person to victimise, terrorise and punish him or her. In sexual abuse, for example, a more powerful adult comes upon a less powerful child, who has a natural but as yet unformed set of needs. The adult then promises something that is not objectively possible. The act itself is traumatic. But the deeper damage lies in the child growing up and perpetually negating their own judgements, abilities and sense of self-trust. They think they are to be blamed for what happened, when it is in fact the abusing adult. Likewise, spiritual abuse is where church leaders use religion to engage the individuals under their care in a perpetual make-believe war against themselves.

But beyond the spiritual abuse is another abuse. Who is this god who is being invoked? He is clearly powerful, and seems to be all-knowing – he knows why some are born gay and thus will have to cope with a predilection their entire lives that constantly jeopardises their salvation; he has a reason why the devil can even successfully tempt the elect in ways that outwit their ability to resist; he has a reason why he has created a world, purportedly in love, but in which some are elected to salvation while others – and for Southeast Asians, this means 250 million Muslim souls – are damned to hell. This god has reasons, but *we never know what they are!* The cruelty of the pathological Mythic-Literal god of transcendence is that it mocks God's actual goodness and love. This is no God, but *Stargate*'s Ra.

The western liberal church

One might erroneously surmise that the Episcopal Church has always been liberal. But, until recently, it was dubbed the Republican Party at prayer, and perceived to be a bastion of the status quo. Perhaps nothing better symbolised its establishment stature than a letter from George Murray, Bishop of Alabama, to Martin Luther King in 1963, telling him to desist from the civil rights struggle. Racial segregation was the norm of society at that time, and thus religious faith at Stage 3 in the Episcopal Church misconstrued human prejudice to reflect God's will. King responded with the famous 'Letter from Birmingham Jail', writing that, 'injustice anywhere is a threat to justice everywhere'.

Thankfully, a turning point occurred shortly afterwards, with Bishop John Hines' term as Presiding Bishop (1965–74). He took a radical stance for racial integration, earning the charge by his critics that he had 'communistic aims'. He said at the General Convention of 1970:

> Against even the worst of possibilities, must be set the inescapable obligations of Christians, that the Body of Christ must be prepared to offer itself up for the sake of the healing and the solidarity of the whole human family, whatever its religious or racial identities. Especially must the Body of Christ risk its own life in bearing and sharing the burdens of those who are being exploited, humiliated, and disinherited![11]

And so with great pain, anguish and loss of membership, the centre of gravity in the Episcopal Church moved to Stage 4, the Individuative Faith where the individual reflects upon and critiques his or her own received faith to reinvigorate it with new meaning. Fowler writes:

> Stage 4 most appropriately takes form in young adulthood (but ... many adults do not construct it, and ... for a significant group it emerges only in the mid-thirties and forties). This stage is marked by a double development. The self, previously sustained in its identity and faith compositions by an interpersonal circle of significant others, now claims an identity no longer defined by the composite of one's roles or meanings to others ... This is the demythologizing stage, and its ascendant strength is its capacity for critical reflection on identify (self) and outlook (ideology).[12]

The Episcopal Church progressed rather than regressed because US society in the 1960s was itself undergoing several revolutions. But perhaps no other person inspired faith development in the US as much as Dr Martin Luther King Jr. He showed the way towards a more mature faith development for diverse sectors of people, religious and otherwise. Resisting the accepted norms of decades of Bible-sponsored racism (that arose out of Stage 3 faith), he advocated a Bible-inspired civil disobedience (Stage 4 faith) for the sake of truer community. By the strength inherent in the vulnerability it takes to be open to one's enemies, King was an exemplar of Stage 5 Conjunctive Faith. And finally, by crossing religious boundaries through his embrace of the universal (his alliance with the Vietnamese monk Thich Nhat Hanh over the evil of the Vietnam War), King showed us Stage 6, the Christlike universalising love that transgresses human boundaries and prejudices, and which in many instances leads to martyrdom.

Fowler writes:

> 'Stage 6 is exceedingly rare. The persons best described by it have generated faith compositions in which their felt sense of an ultimate environment is inclusive of all being. They have become incarnators and actualizers of the spirit of an inclusive and fulfilled human community. They are 'contagious' in the sense that they create zones of liberation from the social, political, economic and ideological shackles we place and endure.[12]

It would therefore follow that in the Episcopal Church a collective church conscience awakened by the Gospel to seek justice for African Americans (by a very white church) would result in similar quests for justice for women's ordination and the inclusion of gay and lesbian people in the church. Likewise, a Canadian church that has woken up to the evil of church-sponsored abuse of Native-Canadian children in the nineteenth century, would move quickly from Stage 3 to 4 and 5 and find itself wholeheartedly embracing inclusion. Inclusion and universalism mark upward development.

It must be noted that higher faith development exists in non-western provinces. Consider the Nippon Seikōkai (the Anglican Church of Japan) or Desmond Tutu and the church in South Africa. They are supportive of gay people because their faith development (Stage 5 or 6) can accept complexity and paradox in a spirit of openness.

This is not to say that there are no pathologies peculiar to Stages 4 and 5. The failure of western liberals at Stage 5 is self-satisfaction masquerading as inclusion. With regards to the pathology of Mythical-Literalists in the Anglican Communion, liberals in the western church have too long acquiesced with their pathology – in the name of inclusion and anti-racism. Too afraid to own up to their tradition of colonialism, they are unable to say anything critical to non-whites in the church, because they are not brave enough to face up to the accusation of being racists (which they may or may not be). But without a stomach for a committed critique of pathology found in non-white groups, the only safe critique is to engage pre-emptively in self-criticism of their colonialist past. Attached to the rationalist mode of biblical higher criticisms, they have considered Mythic-Literalists in both the West and the East as stupid and unsophisticated. This, of course, is never publicly said but it justifies their disengagement. Naively believing in inclusion as the be-all and end-all value of Christian living, and allergic to value judgements of any kind, the liberal pathology is that it is cowardly and lazy. What then passes for vigour in postmodern liberalism is endless engagement in the 'hermeneutics of suspicion'. But the pathology is that language itself and meaning-making are mocked. By rejecting hierarchy and the developmental spiral, they miss the validity and actuality of direct spiritual experience of transcendence and immanence – the heart of the religious enterprise – that are above rationalism and political correctness.[14]

In the 1980s and 1990s several Singaporean Anglicans, the authors included, made representations to Archbishop George Carey about the disappearance of Anglican practices, liturgies and traditions under then Bishop Moses Tay. Specifically, we were dismayed at the replacement of the use of the Prayer Book (local version or otherwise), in almost all of the churches, with total free-form worship resembling that of Pentecostalists during the principal Sunday services. Altars were removed and replaced with stages for rock bands; regular lectionary readings were replaced with scriptural verses chosen at the discretion of the officiating clergy; cyclical prayers for the Communion (which helps creates a common identity and concern within the Anglican Communion) were replaced with ad-hoc prayers centred only on the immediate needs and tastes of the congregation. There was nothing Anglican, not even Low Church, in the liturgy of the diocese. Only the cathedral and one other parish ministering to white foreigners retained Anglican forms of worship.

Needless to say, Archbishop Carey, who in the early 1990s had jurisdiction over the diocese before it became an independent province, did not meet with these concerned local Anglicans when he visited, neither did he seriously consider the several dangers they were articulating in their modest Asian ways. Instead, the focus was on how the local church had grown. That was to be celebrated, of course. However, it should come as no surprise that neglect at cultivating a regard for Anglican liturgy in Singapore would also mean that there would be scant respect for an Anglican approach towards theology, biblical hermeneutics, episcopal collegiality, or the *via media*. In fact, while it appears that the Province of Southeast Asia has staked a claim in the leadership of the Anglican Communion, and would very much like to lead it, it has very little use for Anglicanism (in theology, ecclesiology, hermeneutics, liturgy, music, history) except, of course, for what is actually at stake: the allegiance of the *minds* and *hearts* of the majority of Anglicans in the world. These people, of course, are in the global 'South'. And western liberals, in charge of the leadership of the Communion, but too afraid or tired to make a stand for Anglicanism (might they be called 'racist'?), succumbed to what looked easy. Which is to say, 'we'll include everything (because that's Anglicanism), but we won't care (out of laziness) if who or what we include care at all about inclusion'.

We are not saying that there are limits to inclusion. Inclusion is inclusion, and all are one in God's eyes. But inclusion as a political litmus test is not the same as connection. The former is an ideology, the latter an ontological fact. Astrologers and astrophysicists should certainly find ways to connect with each other (perhaps go bowling together?). But for them to be *inclusive* of each other by issuing joint statements about the universe? Beyond agreeing on the names of the planets, their views of what the universe *means* are entirely divergent. Astrologers belong to the magical level of development (Spiral Dynamics Stage 2), while astrophysicists are at the rational level of development (Spiral Dynamics Stage 5 or 6). Liberals need to give up the holy grail of *dialogue* (and its spawns, the joint communiqué, the commissions of studies, etc.) as the equivalent of connection. Inclusion and dialogue have become political agenda items masquerading as a united common life. However, if the bishops were interested in *common life*, in *connecting*, then they might consider rolling up their sleeves to work together – conservatives and liberals – in a soup kitchen for the homeless, and forget tea at Lambeth.

Why did Synthetic-Conventional Anglicans in the US and Canada progress, while Synthetic-Conventional Anglicans in Singapore regress? In Southeast Asia, faith development was not supported internally by the leadership, nor externally by historical circumstances. Internal to the diocese, the leaders were not interested in progression. Yap Kim Hao, who was then Secretary General of the Christian Conference in Singapore and a bishop in the Methodist Church, was asked by the then Archbishop of Canterbury's Secretary, Terry Waite, to provide some international ecumenical experiences for the new bishop Moses Tay, since Tay had only just completed his basic external degree in theology. Kim Hao extended an open invitation to him to attend ecumenical meetings, but Tay never participated. Ecumenism is a sign of more mature faith development, because ecumenism requires the cultivation of paradox – a simultaneous questioning of one's position while requiring faithfulness to one's position. Ecumenism, by bringing different, divergent and even opposing parties together, forces one to individuate (i.e. to think for oneself), while at the same time, requiring one also to be more connected to the other. This increase of both individual autonomy and interconnection, of more ambiguity with more faithfulness, and the increased ability to deal with greater and more nuanced complexity, are the signs of developmental maturity.

Externally, historical circumstances mitigated against the maturation of faith development in Southeast Asia. More than the stress of industrialisation or the anxieties of being a rich minority race (Christians in Southeast Asia are disproportionately minority ethnic Chinese, who also happen to be relatively more wealthy), it was the Cold War that shaped the Christian churches – Anglican or otherwise – in the region.

In the protracted fight against communism throughout Singapore and Malaysia in the 1950s and 1960s, civic groups, inclusive of religious ones, that agitated for social justice or civic concerns were inaccurately tarred as Marxists or communists. Labour unions were often crippled or co-opted. In the 1960s, when the danger of communism was perceived to be the greatest, the Social Gospel movement and the ecumenical movements were either marginalised or purged by the state. As late as 1987, the Singapore government arrested a group of Catholic lay men and women organising for the rights of Filipino domestic workers for allegedly being part of a Marxist conspiracy. As such, over time, the form of Christianity that survived and thrived, whether Protestant or Catholic, was socially conservative and compliant towards the state, and, with economic growth, preached a prosperity theology. But most weakening to the faith was the substitution of a scrupulous personal morality for liberation and justice. Injustice, prejudice, discrimination – the sins of groups rather than of individuals – became almost foreign concepts in the province.

Singaporean Christians, if Catholic, had been steered away from any kind of liberation theology that had followed Vatican II; and if Protestant, had never heard of Reinhold Niebuhr or Martin Luther King, or sometimes it seems, the gospels (since Paul is more often quoted). Collectively, they drank from that other well that was drawing in foreign direct investment dollars – American 'right wing' Christianity. It is therefore no wonder that the political agenda of this form of Christianity – with its standardised loyalty list – would come to dominate: opposition to homosexuality, feminism, evolution and abortion; support of biblical literalism and the State of Israel; and a belief in Satan and the Apocalypse.

Homosexuality in Asian cultures and changes afoot

In writing this essay, we have tried to rectify the impression of Singaporean Christianity as a kind of monolithic front – everyone conservative and anti-gay. The Rev. Yap Kim Hao is a straight man, a former bishop of the Methodist Church in Singapore and a pastor with the Free Community Church (FCC). Singapore's first all-inclusive church with a sizeable lesbian, gay, transsexual and bi-gender (LGBT) congregation, FCC has many heterosexuals and parents of gay and lesbian worshippers. In its Faith Statement it declares:

> We believe that God desires to affirm the worth and dignity of every human being regardless of religion, ethnicity, gender, sexual orientation, economic status or physical or mental ability. All people on earth have an equal claim to life, liberty and justice. Therefore any ministry of outreach must affirm human dignity with authentic respect for human freedom.[15]

FCC grew from many streams, including *Safehaven*, a gay and lesbian Christian Fellowship that Lee Tuck-Leong helped organise in the late 1990s, which itself was preceded by *Sanctuary*, the first LGBT Christian Fellowship that Leng Lim started in 1992.

Some of this positive growth of a dignified, self-respecting, self-affirming and God-loving gay and lesbian Christian church has come about, ironically, with help from the homophobic Mythic-Literalists. *Choices* was a programme started by Exodus International that worked to change gay people into straight, or at least celibate, ones. Sponsored by the Anglican Church of Our Savior in the mid-1970s, it actually served to bring gay Christians out of the closet. But at one point, *Choices* went overboard with a graphic poster showing handcuffs, and the slogans 'Gay but not happy' and 'You Can be Free'. As a result, a significant number of participants left the programme and, with much courage, founded an independent Christian group, *Safehaven*. This group then evolved into the Free Community Church.

As authors, we have also wanted to describe the changes taking place in Singapore. On 4 July 2003, Goh Chok Tong, then Prime Minister, announced that the Civil Service would not discriminate against homosexual persons and included a statement that caught the gay community by surprise. He said, 'Let us let the [homosexual issue evolve] and in time the population will understand that ... we are born this way, and that they are born that way, but they are like you and me.' This was the first time that respect for the dignity of homosexual persons, *qua people*, was clearly articulated by a member of the conservative ruling party. The public media took the cue and turned homosexuality into a highly significant national debate that lasted more than a month. In an interview with the BBC's *Out in Asia* programme which aired on 13 November 2003, then Deputy Prime Minister Lee Hsien Loong (in 2005 the current Prime Minister) made a comment which articulated a Kohlberg's Moral Stage 3 and 4 consideration of group norms:

> These are social mores and norms, a balance which is set not so much by the Government, as by the expectations of the public, and this is a multi-racial, multi-religious public and some segments are very conservative and traditional in their views, and we have to accept that. As you say, homosexual people are not harassed or intimidated or squeezed in Singapore. But neither do we encourage homosexual lifestyles to be publicly flaunted or legitimised or presented as being part of a mainstream way of life.

But more encouraging was the measured tone taken by Singapore's religious leaders, Christians being the exception. A top religious leader of the Muslim community – the Assistant Mufti – called on Muslims to take the middle road, not to condemn gays. The General Secretary of the Singapore Buddhist Federation was reported in a national paper as saying, 'People have different likes and dislikes. Of course, as a religion, we do not think that homosexuality is right. But we should still respect them and try to help them as much as possible. We would extend them a hand of compassion.' In a further interview given to a group of gay Buddhists, he clarified that the Buddhist Scriptures say nothing about homosexuality and he was merely reflecting the general opinion of the Buddhist population, who were mostly Chinese-speaking and who felt homosexuality was somewhat unacceptable.[16]

Predictably, The National Council of Churches, representing the Protestants, issued a statement which called for maintaining the status quo – maintaining the nineteenth-century colonial sodomy laws that prescribe imprisonment and continuing the prohibition against the formation of homosexual civic organisations. Later that year, a small group of Christians from the *Love Singapore* organisation, associated with the former Bishop of Singapore, Moses Tay, led by Yang Tuck Yoong, a lay Anglican minister, and the Rev. Derek Hong from the Anglican Church of Our Savior, lobbied extensively through the local media and local churches. Derek Hong, at an evening service on 19 July, preached that the devil was trying to undermine the very social fabric of the nation. He promised to mobilise churches in Singapore to stand up against the gay issue. He envisioned Singapore as a nation of righteous Christians, free from the contamination of the gay lifestyle.

However, it is possible that the above account of the Singapore government's view of homosexuality is too prematurely positive. More recent actions have indicated a move back, possibly because Christians in society and within the bureaucracy have exerted pressure. But in some ways, certainly, both the government and secular society have become more open to gay people. The irony is that the secular government, often regarded as authoritarian, has been able to be more accommodating to gay people, while the Christian community, though equally authoritarian in leadership, is unable to move forward. While the state does not feel threatened by the gay community and acknowledges that they have a contribution to make to society with their creative talents, authoritarian church leaders feel more threatened. Why? It is because the secular authoritarian leadership embraces the future (out of economic prag-matism) while the religious leadership, which is also authoritarian, hugs the past (out of a need to be 'on the right side of things').

The push back from the Singapore church is a defensive reaction to the ever-increasing secular recognition and even acceptance of homo-sexuality as a common (if not as yet natural) human condition. For four years, Singapore has hosted the 'Nation Party', the largest lesbian and gay party in the Asian region, which drew 6,000 visitors in 2004. Singaporean gay people have established their own Pride Centre, which is used as a counselling space, library and activity centre. Gay and lesbian visibility in Singapore's commercial districts and city centre is comparable to many cosmopolitan cities in the world. Indeed, the culti-vation of 'bohemian' enclaves in different parts of the island-nation has been part of government policy to remake Singapore into an attractive cosmopolitan society, with the capacity to attract 'innovative foreign talent' to service its economy. However, the political schizophrenia towards the gay issue remains: the government recently banned the Nation Party for 2005 – it's being held in Thailand – purportedly because HIV infection rates have increased.

In writing this essay, we have also wanted to challenge the often-held conception of gay culture as foreign to Asia. A huge body of literature in sociology, anthropology, history and the performing and poetic arts shows the existence and acceptance of lesbian, gay, bisexual and trans-gendered people across Asia. LGBT people have existed and exist across Asia, from the islands of Indonesia, to Peninsula Malaysia, to China and Japan, and it was with the coming of western missionaries that their roles and positions received approbation.

Nevertheless, I wonder what would change from knowing this? The Mythic-Literalists would only see this as further evidence of pre-Christian depravity. Liberals might derive some intellectual interest. But might gay Asian Christians find encouragement and affirmation in knowing about an indigenous, native and proud gay Asian heritage?

What we have discovered over the years of walking our own spiritual journeys and counselling LGBT people is that no amount of progressive biblical exegesis, no amount of same-sex blessing rites, no amount of civic liberties or celebrative gay histories, can eradicate the core spiritual issues of self-hate, internalised shame, guilt and fear for LGBT people who come from a Mythic-Literal Christian heritage. Yet the path out of self-hate, internalised shame, guilt and fear is rather simple:

> Choose not to. Choose life instead. The experience of choosing is no different than the kind of choice many gay Christian converts make when they accepted Jesus as Lord and Saviour at an altar call. CHOOSE DIFFERENTLY. CHOOSE A NEW LORD.

As Moses said to the Israelites: choose LIFE that you might live (Deuteronomy 30:19). Guilt, shame, fear and hate are emotions culti-vated by authority figures for the express purpose of *control*. They are emotions generated when we were at lower levels of development, to get us to conform to their wishes. Unable to challenge these authority figures because we depended (or might still depend) on them, we internalised the abuse. Guilt, shame, fear and hatred belong to lower levels of faith and moral and consciousness development. They are hindrances to building a loving and vibrant resurrected life.

Take guilt for example. If one has committed a wrong, say by hurting another human being, either intentionally or unintentionally, then the healthy emotional response for this failure is not guilt or shame, but remorse and sorrow. Remorse allows one to feel the pain of the other, while shame and guilt is still a narcissistic fixation on one's own interiority. Sorrow and remorse also allow for the courage to make restitution. Humility might also come into play, as one then takes stock of how one might act more morally the next time. But guilt and shame only create grovelling.

When authority figures – familial, political and religious – can get a handle on one's sexuality and instil guilt, shame, fear and self-hate, then control is established. So whether it is secular commercial gay culture with its message that one is never going to be beautiful or desirable enough, or a pathological religious culture that gay people are never going to be lovable enough to God, or a family culture that a lesbian or gay child is not going to be filial enough, or a society that refuses to enshrine rights because LGBT people are never normal enough – this shame about not being enough is created by others. *But, its daily implementation is outsourced to gay people to do to ourselves.* Hence, we pay for the accoutrements of secular gay culture with its body-perfection fetish, and tithe to homophobic church leaders – all with the vague hope that we might become enough. In this sense, we, as LGBT people, are partly the cause of our own misery.

To honour oneself, one must see oneself as God sees us – cherished, whole, creative, blessed, unique, lovable in mind, body (including sex) and soul. There is no original sin; there is only the original refusal to see oneself as blessed and enough. The fundamental choice in front of gay, lesbian, bisexual and transgendered Christians is to choose to love – self, other and God. It begins with simply saying no to shame, guilt, fear and self-hate. To do this is to develop and grow up into the full stature of Christ.

The future of the Anglican Communion

In a *closed system*, power lies with the leader and the organisation and there is an emphasis on hierarchy and security, with people playing clearly defined roles. The few leaders manage for the good of the whole. An army is an example. In an *open system*, power orientation lies with the collective, and there is an emphasis on adaptation, participation, consensus and commitment, with people in teams following the rules of process rather than formal leadership. Leadership balances the good of the whole with the individual. A co-operative business or store with many stakeholders is an example.

Theological issues aside, the ordination by Archbishop Yong Ping-Chung (Archbishop Tay's successor as Primate) and Archbishop Kolini of the two Americans to the episcopacy – contravening centuries of church practice and process honouring diocesan borders – was an exercise of closed power. Processes, both local and global, were tossed aside, simply because the leaders said so. In the doctrinal formulations, it is the few leaders who decide, while other voices from the ground up are silent or silenced. The advantage of a closed system is decisiveness; the shadow side is the tyranny of monarchy.

On the other hand, the ordination of Gene Robinson to the episcopacy was a result of an open process – local church committees chose him as a candidate; elected members of the New Hampshire Diocese elected him; and his ratification by the province was again through a broad representation of elected lay people, priests and bishops. When the Episcopal Church in the USA is confronted with new challenges, study commissions are convened. Over time, theology is adapted in response to pastoral needs and tradition, and a careful balance struck between groups. Thus, Presiding Bishop Allin, who personally opposed women's ordination, continued to preside over the province, because of his commitment to open process. The advantage of the open system is inclusion; the shadow side is the tyranny of process and the endless talking and compromises that so frustrate everyone.

The Anglican Communion itself, in contrast to the Roman Catholic Church, is a relatively open system, hence our ability to be a big umbrella for everyone – a *via media* community. The question is what should an open system do with a group (for example, the Mythic-Literalists) within it that not only wants to be closed (which it is entitled to do; after all, armies exist within democracies, for the greater good of those open systems), but rejects the overarching open system by which it is sustained? (Military coups are generally fatal to civilian democracies, and eventually corrupt the military itself.) But more to the point, if Anglicans believe that the spiritual life is endless warfare between Good and Evil, we should rationally opt for a closed system. (After all, would you trust a military that operated on consensus?) But if Anglicans believe that whatever it is that has needed to be won has been won through Christ and, as such, the life of discipleship is simply 'loving God with our hearts, minds and souls, and our neighbour as ourselves', and that what 'God requires of us is to do justice, love kindness and walk humbly with your God' (Micah 6:8), then we must choose an open power system and reject the closed.

NOTES

1. The most comprehensive summary of Kohlberg's six stages is at http://faculty.plts.edu/gpence/html/kohlberg.htm. A shorter summary can be found at http://www.nd.edu/~rbarger/kohlberg.html.

   The third level ('Post-conventional') of moral thinking is one that Kohlberg felt is not reached by the majority of adults. Its first stage (stage 5) ('Social Contract') is an understanding of social mutuality and a genuine interest in the welfare of others. The last stage (stage 6) ('Principled Conscience') is based on respect for universal principle and the demands of individual conscience. While Kohlberg always believed in the existence of Stage 6 and had some nominees for it, he could never get enough subjects to define it, much less observe their longitudinal movement to it.

2. A summary of Robert Kegan's five levels is found at http://www.lios.org/Resources/ReadingRoom/linkages32b.php.

3. Ken Wilber, *The Collected Works of Ken Wilber* (Boston: Shambhala Press, 2000), v. 7, pp.7–13.

4. Bill Torbert, 'Seven Transformations of Leadership', *Harvard Business Review*, April 2005.
5. James Fowler, *Stages of Faith: The Psychology of Human development* (New York: HarperCollins, 1995).
6. *The Analects of Confucius,* 4:20. See http://afpc.asso.fr/wengu/ wg/wengu.php?]=Lunyu&no=20.
7. See also Chiu's account of the event in chapter 6, 'The Spiritual Gifts', in Michael Harper (ed.), *The Bishops' Move* (London: Hodder & Stoughton, 1978), an anthology of the charismatic experiences of six bishops in the 1970s.
8. Fowler, *Stages of Faith*, op. cit., p.149.
9. http://www.carmelcom.com/aboutus.html. Kehilat HaCarmel is a Messianic congregation in Israel.
10. The Rev. Titus Soo, 'Catch the Foxes for us!' St Andrew's Cathedral, Singapore, website, although it does not appear to still be linked.
11. http://www.covpubs.org/oon/archives/000316.html. John Hines at the General Convention, 1970.
12. Fowler, p.182.
13. Fowler, p.201.
14. Ken Wilber has succinctly critiqued the failings of postmodern liberalism in his integral philosophy. See *A Brief History of Everything* (Boston: Shambala, 2000), and *The Marriage of Sense and Soul* (New York: Random House, 1998).
15. See http://www.freecomchurch.org/01-principles.htm.
16. Au, A. (2003). Reflections on a meeting with The Venerable Shi Ming Yi. Retrieved 22 June 2005, from Yawning Bread website: http://www.yawning bread.org/arch_2003/yax-338.htm.

Chapter 6

THE STRUGGLE TO BE HUMAN: A REFLECTION ON HOMOSEXUALITY IN INDIA

Aruna Gnanadason

Reflections on human sexuality – a taboo topic

For the church in India, issues relating to human sexuality are still by and large a taboo topic. The churches have been reluctant to address the manifold ethical challenges as well as the potentials and gifts offered by the human body. The churches would neither affirm the beauty of the body and the God-given gift of pleasure that it offers nor will they recognise the extent of the use and abuse of the human body and our sexuality. Dealing with human sexuality has been largely relegated to the entertainment industry and media, to the scientific community, and to powerful patriarchal forces in the family and in the social structure of Indian society such as the caste hierarchy with its underlying principles of pollution and purity associated with the body. The distorted attitudes to human sexuality have given rise to multifarious cultural practices of discrimination and even violence against women, children, sexual minorities and other oppressed groups such as the Dalits in India.[1]

While discussions on human sexuality *per se* are not easy, the Indian church has had even bigger difficulties in dealing with issues related to homosexuality. As this essay will demonstrate, the organised presence of the gay and lesbian community in India has been attempting to conscientise the society for some decades now. Additionally, in the recent past, a significant attempt was made by the National Council of Churches in India (NCCI) to initiate a series of seminars to open up the discussion. An issue of the official journal of the NCCI called the *National Council of Churches Review* was devoted to the discussion so as to encourage the churches to address the issue.[2] This was followed up by two Study Institutes on Human Sexuality, initiated by NCCI for church leaders. The institutes have included as speakers, representatives of the gay and lesbian community, transvestites and carriers of the HIV/AIDS virus who personally testified to their struggles and challenged the church to respond pastorally.

The church has for so long tended to ignore the gay and lesbian community, including gays and lesbians in its own body. The challenge for the churches in India to respond came from elsewhere. As the second

Study Institute described it:

> We also meet at a significant moment in time when the global
> churches are not only struggling with these issues but are also
> expressing them differently. For example, the issues surrounding
> the consecration of a gay Bishop, the ordination of gay/lesbian
> priests and pastors, and the solemnizing of same-sex marriages.
> The rapid development in information technology has also enabled
> openness and offered a new space in relation to human sexuality
> discourses. This has led to the breaking of the '*culture of silence*'
> with regard to human sexuality.[3]

Provoked by the controversy in the Anglican Communion around homosexuality, the bishops of the Church of North India held conversations
regarding the topic in 2003. They recognised the need for a pastoral
response from the church. However, no report of this discussion is available and repeated attempts to get some more information regarding this
discussion in the CNI have been unsuccessful. The United Evangelical
Lutheran Church has begun discussions with its member churches, but
this too is yet unrecorded. The reluctance to put this down on paper is
indicative of the difficulties the church has in addressing this issue.

The gay community speaks out

Asian lesbian women participating in the World Council of Churches-
organised regional consultation on violence against women in Bali,
Indonesia in 1994 challenged the women gathered. They called on us to
listen – with compassion and justice – to the struggles that they experience in a society that has systematically denied them their rights and
even their existence. It was the first time that I had heard Asian women
articulate so clearly their conviction that we cannot ignore this issue any
longer. If we are to be serious about speaking of violence against
women, then the violence that is perpetrated against lesbian women
needs to be addressed. What the Bali meeting pointed to was that sexual
violence is rife in Asian societies, women's sexuality has been com-
mercialised and commodified and this is often legitimised by religion.
But within that scenario, violence against lesbian women needs particular attention. Compulsory heterosexuality is demanded in a context
where women's fertility is controlled within a patriarchal system that
places a glorified emphasis on motherhood. The final Declaration of the
Bali Consultation acknowledged this complex reality:

> The family, along with the state today, has sought to control
> women through rigid definitions of sexuality and to appropriate
> for itself reproductive rights and control over her body. Violence

and subjugation have been woven into institutionalised forms of religion whose patriarchal tenets have marginalised and domesticated the female and the feminine, shackling her and legitimising violence against her. Social and legal codes of justice have either been blind to crimes against women, such as wife battering and prostitution that have in fact received tacit social approval, or have seen violations like sexual assault and rape as acts of individual aberration and deviance *and has even rendered some totally invisible, as in the case of homophobia.*[4]

Lesbian women in Asia pointed out that homophobia is rampant even within feminist circles. Their struggle to assert their identity and claim their right to a life of security is not acknowledged even by progressive groups, because issues relating to sexuality are so often hidden from public discussions. However, there is some change as homosexual men and women get organised and articulate more clearly their demands for justice. Here, I will focus on the Indian reality, though references will be made to other Asian contexts.

A hostile atmosphere for the homosexual community

That homosexuality is widespread in India is generally accepted – it is not unusual to see two men in close embrace or two women with arms around each other in public places. (In fact, it is often more difficult for a heterosexual couple to publicly express their affection for each other!) However, there is a lack of credible data or well-researched statistics available on the number of homosexual men and women in the country. If we go by the generally accepted formula which places ten per cent of sexually active adults, in any given society, as practising homosexuals, there must be over 80 million homosexual men and women in the country. But then, in the Indian context, there is a large percentage of adults who would engage in both heterosexual and homosexual relationships. Unwritten family codes force most to hide their homosexual identity or express it only surreptitiously. A majority of homosexual men and women are content to lead a double life. They dutifully get married, as is demanded of them due to social pressure, and act out their parts as husband or wife – dropping their mask only when they are among people of their own sexual preference. They are expected to project a veneer of being 'normal' – what happens outside the public eye is ignored. In an article on Calcutta's homosexual men and women, Soumitra Das writes:

> Most homosexuals, however, feel there is no need to make a song and dance about an entirely personal matter. 'Under no circumstances, do you discuss your sexual preferences with your family. So why should homosexuals do it?' asks a senior teacher of a

public school. He is sure he won't lose his job if he chooses to 'come out', but a 'stigma will be attached'.[5]

It is this stigma that is attached to those who have the courage to 'come out' that forces many to pretend to be heterosexual. Frequently, when parents realise that their children have homosexual tendencies, they reject them or even worse try to get them 'cured'. Largely forced by such familial pressures, a large number of the country's seemingly hetero-sexual population is indeed suppressing its true sexual identity. Tragically this has led to a life of misery and in some cases to suicide, in a society that prefers silence on this issue. Rather than supporting a person who wishes to 'come out', by giving him or her a way in which to cope with his or her sexual orientation, so as to be true to themselves, parents would dismiss homosexuality as a 'passing phase'. They would quickly get the young person married so as to avoid the 'scandal' that this knowledge could involve. This often leads to a destructive hetero-sexual marriage. That the married relationship is not working is ignored both by the couple and by the family, so as to keep up the facade.

A Delhi-based doctor, whose research centres on homosexual men and women, says that the prevalence of bisexuality is far greater in India than in the West. He attributes this to the lack of stigma attached to bisexuality before the British colonised India. Since then, according to him, 'we are conditioned by Victorian mores.'[6] It is also recognised that in the country's bigger cities homosexuality is hidden away more efficiently than in the smaller villages where individuals are sometimes tormented because they are forced to live double lives or face being ostracised.[7]

One study available on the issue is *Less Than Ga: A Citizen's Report on the Status of Homosexuality in India*, prepared by the AIDS Bhedbhav Virodhi Andolan (ABVA) in 1991. This group of activists working to overcome discrimination against people with AIDS decided to focus attention on the rights of homosexual men and women. They did this because they saw that, 'the emergence of AIDS as a major public health crisis has had a devastating effect on gay people in most parts of the world ... Though there is no inherent link between AIDS and homo-sexuality, it has become more necessary than ever before to understand the status of homosexuality in our society.'[8]

After interviewing a wide spectrum of people – political leaders, artists, social activists, medical professionals, ordinary men and women on the streets and others – they conclude that much of the stigma attached to the issue in India is related to the fact that:

> Homosexuality challenges widely held assumptions about mas-
> culinity and femininity, about the way men and women relate to

each other. Not surprisingly, its existence is either vigorously denied or subjected to abuse and ridicule. The fact that many gay men and lesbians feel obliged to conceal their sexual orientation makes it difficult for them to assert their civil, political and cultural rights, as individuals and as members of a sexual minority. Neither the government nor civil rights groups even acknowledge that homosexuality exists, let alone address gay people's experiences of discrimination.

Whether it is blackmail or physical violence, verbal abuse or police harassment, forced heterosexual marriage or denial of homosexual marriage, gay people, *as gay people*, live like second-class citizens, unable to obtain fair treatment because of their 'wrong' sexuality. The question of the human rights of gay men and women is not about whether or not people approve of homosexuality or the concept of gay identities. Rather, it is a question of equality under the law and under human rights covenants, like the International Covenant on Civil and Political Rights, to which India is a signatory.[9]

There is also the fact-finding report about Bangalore City, organised by the Peoples Union for Civil Liberties, Karnataka Branch, in 2001. The report, 'Human Rights Violations Against Sexual Minorities in India', explores every dimension of the issue.[10] It underlines our worst fears of the extent of discrimination and humiliation experienced by gays, lesbians and transvestites at the hands of the law and the police. But their experiences of violence extend into society – in the family, by the medical establishment, in work places, in household spaces, in public spaces and in popular culture. Those from low-income/non-English-speaking backgrounds and transvestites face the worst kinds of discrimination and humiliation, according to the report.

Organised voices of resistance and support

There have been some significant efforts by homosexual men and women to organise themselves to raise their voices against the discrimination they experience. Most major cities in India have now got an organised group attempting to draw attention to the varied and rich forms of homosexual life that do exist in India. They try to expose the forms of violence that exist by law and in the everyday life of people who choose to openly live their homosexuality. Groups such as SAKHI (Companion) in Delhi, DOST (Friend) in Bombay, 'Freedom' in Gulbarga, 'Fun Club' in Calcutta and 'Friends India' in Lucknow are some groups that have focused attention on providing a safe space for homosexual men and women to meet and discuss the multifaceted oppression they experience. They also develop strategies for joint action.

Homosexuality an accepted way of life in India's past

'Homophobia and not homosexuality is new to Indian culture,' says
Vinay Chandran of the Bangalore-based charitable trust, Swabhava.[11]
Therefore, perhaps the most important contribution these groups have
made is to expose the historical facts to validate such a claim. There has
been present, since ancient times, an acknowledgement of homosexual
love and same-sex contact. The *Kamasutra* is the first literary classic in
the world on matters of sex. The sage Vatsyayana authored it in the
fourth century CE. The *Kamasutra* is not an original work – it is a com-
pilation of the rules of love as written in the *Kama Shastra*, a treatise on
life, which dates back to the fourth century BCE or earlier. According to
Vatsyayana, the various works belonging to the *Kama Shastra* had
become difficult to access. For this reason he undertook to collect them
and summarise them in his *Kamasutra*, which became a classic in that
genre. In the *Kamasutra*,

> Lesbianism is described in detail, as well as the inversion of roles
> by a dominating female. Male homosexuality forms an integral
> part of sexual life and various homosexual practices are described
> in detail. Transvestite prostitutes play a role in public life, and their
> presence at weddings and religious ceremonies was considered a
> symbol of good luck down to our own times.[12]

The *Kamasutra* contains an entire chapter, *Auparishtaka*, on homosexual love. The *Shushruta*, a treatise on medicine some two thousand
years old, describes treatment of possible injuries incurred during homosexual lovemaking! Eighth-century CE temples dedicated to the Lord
Shiva, in Bhuvaneswar, Orissa, and the Khajuraho Temple, a ninth- to
eleventh-century masterpiece in Madhya Pradesh, both contain
explicitly carved stone icons of homosexual love. Indian sculptures
representing the various sexual positions, group sex and homosexual
practice are found in many temples because, according to legend, they
protect the temples from lightning. The *Kamasutra* teaches that 'the
final aim of sexual pleasure is spiritual', and that 'like ethics and
prosperity, sexuality is one of the bases of civilisation'. It also unlinks
sexual pleasure from procreation, emphasising that procreation is not the
aim of sexual love, 'amorous ecstasy is assimilated to mystic experience,
to the perception of the divine that is supreme enjoyment'.[13]

According to A. A. MacDonell, Emeritus Professor of Sanskrit in the
University of Oxford, 'The contents of this work [the *Kamasutra*],
appear to us in the most part indecent, but it must be borne in mind that
the Indian is much more outspoken on sexual matters, than we are.'

Quoting this passage, the ABVA Report concludes: 'It is a shame that a Westerner has to remind us about our traditional sexual openness whereas we continue to vigorously deny it.'[14]

Another strand of India's ancient past that is referred to is found in the *Puranas* (pre-Aryan religious texts), which affirm the vision of sexual dualism. Giti Thadani, an independent researcher from New Delhi, elucidates this stream of philosophy where,

> Importance was not attached to the 'male–female couple' but on the notion of the *yoni*, which signifies 'the womb, the infinite source', the symbol of which was the triangle. The triangle consists of two points of 'light' represented by female twins, symbols of fusion, and of a third point, which is the earth. The notion of twins or *jami* also signifies, in various texts, 'homosexuality' ... Sexuality was based on pleasure and on fertility, but not on progenity (the practice of passing over the children to the man). Phallic discourse only appeared with progenic sexuality. So the first notion of 'heterosexuality' appeared later, under the terminology of *a-jami*, that which is not *jami* which is not paired, fused as it is in the notion of 'homosexuality'.[15]

Muslim culture

There is a view often expressed that homosexuality, and particularly sodomy, was introduced into India by Muslims. But the texts quoted above, among others, indicate that the practice of homosexuality had existed as an accepted way of life for centuries before the Mughal invasions. Under Muslim rulers, however, homosexuality entered Indian court life. Muslim nawabs and Hindu aristocrats kept harems of young boys in the sixteenth century. Babar, the Mughal ruler, wrote romantically about his famous love affair with a boy, Baburi. There are records of homosexual love in the culture of Delhi between 1739 and 1741.

In Islamic Sufi literature, homosexual eroticism was a major metaphorical expression of the spiritual relationship between god and man and much Persian fiction and poetry used gay relationships as examples of moral love. Although the Koran and early religious writings do make negative references towards homosexuality, Muslim cultures were in fact very tolerant. The classical works of Arabic poetry and prose, from *Abu Nawas* to the *Thousand and One Nights*, treat homosexual men and women and their sexuality with respect. The Arabic language contains a huge vocabulary of homosexual erotic terminology. According to John Boswell, the association of homosexual feelings with moral looseness appears to be a comparatively recent phenomenon.[16]

If Indian society had permitted same-sex eroticism for centuries, when did the intolerance against homosexuality begin? The patriarchalisation of Indian religions, which came several centuries after treatises such as the *Kamasutra* were expounded, could be the origin of the intolerance. Homosexual activists would claim that hostility towards homosexuality has its roots in patriarchal religions that glorify marriage as the only norm for family life. A personality is said to be incomplete without a hetero-sexual relationship. Sex, according to religious teachers like Manu, is purely for the procreation of a son. So in a rigid patriarchal system there is no place for homosexuality. The pressure was placed particularly on lesbians, as a woman's sexuality is to be kept under rigid control. Jaya Ramanathan, in an article in *The Pioneer* writes:

> Sexuality, any kind of displayed sexuality, in Indian women, is an anathema to society and is meant to be strictly under wraps. A total departure from 'normal' inclination is not only unacceptable, but is seen as an aberration, something to be treated, medically, psychologically or even violently.[17]

While a son's declaration of his homosexual tendencies is received with consternation, the daughter's declaration is often suppressed because parents believe they could ignore her claim by getting her married. A women's crisis centre in Madras has found that a large number of women who come to them for intervention in failing marriages seek help because of the inability of the couple (either of whom are homosexual in orientation) to have a 'normal' sexual relationship. Male homosexuals find that the women they are forced to marry are no longer willing to silently allow their 'strange behaviour' and this of course jeopardises the marriage relationship.

The legacy of British intolerance: unjust legal sanctions
The ABVA Report would trace intolerance to the fact that the 'erstwhile British rulers found [homosexuality] to be repugnant and declared it a crime in the Indian Penal Code (IPC)'.[18]

It is important to note that this piece of legislation, which was drafted by the famous British legal expert Lord Macaulay during the British Rule of India, *does not criminalise homosexuality as such; it crimina-lises sodomy, without actually mentioning the word sodomy.* A man having anal sex with his wife is as guilty as a man having anal sex with another man. It is section 377 of the IPC that is interpreted as a sanction against homosexuality, though the law does not clearly indicate it. Section 377 forbids 'carnal intercourse against the order of nature', with man, woman or animal, and provides a jail term of ten years to a lifetime for a violator.

Lesbianism has been rarely brought before a court of law in India and this is not covered by section 377. According to Jeffrey Weeks, lesbian acts are not outlawed because of 'the secondary position accorded to female sexuality in general. It is not so much lesbianism as female sexuality which society denies.'[19] The ABVA Report quotes many examples of lesbians who have committed suicide because they were not permitted their relationships. The question we have to ask ourselves is whether we are going to remain silent as more and more women, coming particularly from non-urban backgrounds, die before Indian society will acknowledge that lesbianism exists in all sections of our society. Lesbians who wish to live together, let alone get married, have on occasion had to face legal prosecution at the behest of parents or family.

Ironically, the sodomy law is almost never enforced and not more than a few men have been prosecuted in the almost fifty years of India's independent history. But homosexual men and women still want the law repealed because it makes them vulnerable to extortion and blackmail by both policemen and hustlers in public parks. Section 377 may not be enforced but it infuses fear among Indian homosexuals who feel insecure anyway, because they know that their sexual orientation arouses the loathing of the heterosexual majority. Frequent arrests of gay men by the police have reinforced the fear.[20] Such attitudes are based on the centuries-old misconception that homosexuality and sodomy are one and the same thing.

Attacks against gay people in public places of urban areas are extremely common. Gay men and lesbians more often than not do not report crimes against them. The reasons seem to be that violence and other forms of human rights violations against them often result in intense feelings of shame, as if somehow they have brought the assault upon themselves. This sense of self-blame is, of course, not unique to gay victims of crime, but is exacerbated in that many gay men and lesbians have not arrived at an acceptance of their own sexuality.[21]

India is one of the few countries that keep this archaic law on sodomy in its law books. 'In July 1990, Hong Kong decriminalised adult consensual homosexual acts. India, Pakistan, Malaysia and Singapore are the only Asian former colonies that still have sodomy laws.'[22]

Responses of the medical profession

The position of the medical establishment has not always been very helpful – it has unfortunately taken an ostrich-with-head-buried-in-the-sand approach! One of India's top scientists, Dr A. S. Paintal, until recently Director of the Indian Council of Medical Research, insists that homosexuality is alien to Indian culture. Employing a strange brand of logic, he claims 'there is no homosexuality in India, because there is a law against it.'[23] Yet another interesting view came from the Directorate

General of Health services. In their magazine, *Swastha Hind*, they claim with great authority:

> ... a good percentage of our young people do not lead a loose sex life. Sexual promiscuity is a relatively unknown term for many. Many young people come to know of homosexuality only after reading about or seeing photos and pamphlets about AIDS. We should exercise caution that we do not overeducate them as instead of controlling, we may then arouse their curiosity and lead them to unsafe sex practice.[24]

Such unscientific views come from a country which boasts of ancient sages and scientists such as Varahamihir, an astronomer and *ayurved* (practitioner of the ancient Indian system of medicine, *Ayurveda*), who was counted as one of the 'nine gems' of the court of the monarch, Vikramaditya. He had written approvingly about lesbian love in his *Brihatjaka* (550 CE).

But in modern times too we have doctors such as Modi, whose *Textbook of Medical Jurisprudence and Toxicology* (1983, 3rd reprint) is a worldwide authority. He writes, 'A homosexual component exists in everybody, so in this sense it is universal; but it varies qualitatively in different individuals. It exists in all levels of society.' Professor M. P. S. Menon, Head of the Department of Medicine, University of Delhi, gave his views on homosexuality in a written communication to ABVA:

> I do not think homosexuality is a cause of AIDS. Homosexuals and heterosexuals are prone to developing sexually transmitted diseases equally. If homosexuality or heterosexuality degenerates into intimidation, coercion and use of force, both become illegal. Sex acts with mutual consent, with proper care to avoid receiving and transmitting diseases should not be considered a crime. Using minors as passive agents should be made punishable. Sex acts as a means of earning wealth, positions of power etc. are reprehensible, whether they are heterosexual or homosexual.[25]

As Dr Menon prescribes, and most homosexual activists would concur, the issue is not homosexuality or heterosexuality, it is a commitment to safe sex, devoid of the use of violence or force, and faithfulness to one's partner that are the norms for all relationships. In a society in which heterosexual relationships have so degenerated, where women, particularly, are vulnerable to many forms of abuse at the hands of their male partners, and where the commodification and commercialisation of sex have become institutionalised, it is indeed immoral to target homosexual love for attack.

The silent church: a theological response

The Indian church, as mentioned earlier, has by and large been silent on this issue, as it is on all matters concerning human sexuality. Drawn into the vortex of western patriarchal theology and inherited church structures, the Asian/Indian church has lost its cultural roots, influenced strongly by its history as a minority among great religious faiths. Such a consciousness has rendered the church incapable of providing a holistic view of human sexuality, whatever form or expression it takes. In fact, in the Bali Asian Consultation, referred to earlier, violence against lesbian women in the church was also referred to.

Women theologians in India, influenced by their Asian sisters, are now beginning to speak out more clearly about sexuality. Asian women theologians have had to struggle not only against a patriarchal church and society, but have also had to contend with what the male liberation theologians themselves have not fully understood – what patriarchal violence does to women. While almost all statements made by Asian theologians would refer to the oppression of women, it is only in passing, as one would speak of one of the marginalised groups in a society. It is only very recently that Asian feminist theologians have been able to highlight the violence women experience in Asian society and how that violence is institutionalised in the family structure, in religion, in cultures and in all aspects of our societies. The docile, subservient image of Asian women persists in the minds of men and this has been the root of much of the oppression – in particular in the profits of the multinational prostitution industry. Asian women now speak of an alternative theological paradigm drawn out of their experiences as Asian women in struggle. They affirm that sexuality has to be discussed as a theological concept if the church is to provide a word of comfort to Asian women:

> Sexuality is too often seen as the antithesis of spirituality. As a group we affirmed that human sexuality is part of spirituality and condemned the distorted view and practices which have led to the oppression, victimisation and impoverishment of Asian women ... What has liberation spirituality to say and do about sexuality in the Asian setting?[26]

Kwok Pui Lan urges us to go a step further. She writes:

> Many of us today would not be comfortable discussing sexuality and few would try to imagine what the gospel according to the prostitutes would be ... While some lesbians are trying to break the taboo and talk about passionate love and relationships among women, many women have yet to find a language to speak about the pleasure of the body, female sexuality and the power of the

erotic because the yoke of 'compulsory heterosexuality' is still
heavy upon us.[27]

Conclusion

In their struggle to find justice and acceptance, homosexual activists
demand that the legal and political climate be made free. They demand
that civil rights legislation be enacted that will protect their life and
liberty. They claim their right to safety and security, and urge that the
overt and covert forms of violence they experience be regarded as
violations of human rights. But they also demand their right to live their
lives in privacy, without the hostile and negative attitudes that follow
them in their everyday lives. Can the church provide that space for an
alternative lifestyle and new forms of caring family life?

The World Council of Churches has initiated a space for ecumenical
conversations on contemporary ethical challenges such as the sometimes
difficult to address issues surrounding human sexuality. The VIII
Assembly of the WCC in Harare described this space:

> Issues of personal and interpersonal ethics must also be addressed.
> The WCC should offer space and direction for conversation and
> consultation enabling member churches to discuss these difficult
> issues – including human sexuality – which cause division within
> and among its member churches. This conversation must build on
> a shared theological and hermeneutical reflection.[28]

The Assembly further urged the WCC 'to engage in a study of human
sexuality, in all of its diversity, to be made available for member
churches'. It is in pursuit of this mandate that a Staff Group and a
Reference Group have been formed by the WCC General Secretary to
prepare for a follow-up and reporting to the IX Assembly to be held in
Porto Alegre, Brazil in 2006.

Will the churches in India be ready to contribute to this study and to
change their attitudes, as also their theological and pastoral responses to
the gay and lesbian community in their midst? Will they be ready to
create a sensitive and compassionate environment for understanding and
open dialogue? This is indeed the challenge before us.[29]

NOTES

1. The Indian social structure is built on the caste system of graded subjugation.
   Four main caste groups form this structure: the Brahmins or the priestly caste at
   the top, followed by the warrior caste, then the merchant class and at the bottom
   the *shudras* or the working classes. Outside this structure are the Dalits who are
   considered 'unclean' and polluting and therefore for centuries have even been
   treated as untouchables. They continue to face discrimination and violence

simply because they are Dalits. Mahatma Gandhi called them *harijan* – children of God – a title they have rejected because it does not challenge the structure. They have chosen to use the title Dalit, a name given to them by their leader Ambedkar. He gave the 'oppressed' class a new identity to protest their socially and religiously sanctioned pollution codes that have been responsible to a large degree for the discrimination they experience.

2. *NCC Review*, Vol. CXXI, No. 4, May 2001.
3. 'An Epistle on Human Sexuality to the Churches in India', from the Second Study Institute on Human Sexuality jointly organised by the National Council of Churches in India, with the Student Christian Movement in India, the Indian Society for Promoting Christian Knowledge, the United Evangelical Lutheran Church in India HIV/AIDS Desk and the Church's Auxiliary for Social Action with the assistance of International Services Association (INSA), in Bangalore, India, 24–26 September 2003.
4. The Bali Declaration of the Asian Regional Consultation on Violence Against Women, held in Bali, Indonesia, organised by the World Council of Churches, the Christian Conference of Asia and the Asian Women's Human Rights Commission, 1–6 August 1993 (emphasis added).
5. Soumitra Das, 'Sad to be Gay', Miscellany Section, *Sunday Times*, 18 April 1993.
6. Swati Chaturvedi and Navneet Sharma, 'The Angry Young Men and Women', Miscellany Section, *Sunday Times*, 10 January 1993.
7. Manjunath Chinmayee, 'Homosexuality in India, where tradition still rules', 8 June 2003, greatreporter.com. Accessed 25 September 2004.
8. *Less Than Gay, A Citizen's Report on the Status of Homosexuality in India*, AIDS Bhedbhav Virodhi Andolan (ABVA), New Delhi, India, November–December 1991, p.1. It was surprising to note that the word 'gay' is often used in India to refer to both homosexual men and women. Perhaps this usage reflects the deep-seated patriarchal attitudes in India, which have penetrated even movements for justice – such as that of the gay and lesbian movement.
9. *ibid.*, p.67.
10. 'Human Rights Violations Against Sexual Minorities in India', Peoples Union for Civil Liberties, Karnataka Branch PUCL-K, Bangalore, 2001.
11. Quoted by Manjunath Chinmayee, op. cit.
12. Alain Daniélou (trans.), *The Complete Kamasutra: The First Modern Translation of the Classic Indian Text* (Rochester, Vermont: Park Street Press, 1994), p.10.
13. *ibid.*, pp.10, 17 and 34.
14. *Less Than Gay*, ABVA Report, p.50. The quotation is from MacDonell's *India's Past: A Survey of her Literatures, Religions, Languages, and Antiquities* (Miami: University Press of the Pacific, 2004).
15. Quoted in *Less Than Gay*, ABVA Report, p.51.
16. J. Boswell, *Christianity, Social Tolerance and Homosexuality: Gay People in Western Europe from the Beginning of the Christian Era to the 14th Century* (Chicago: University of Chicago Press, 1981), quoted in *Less Than Gay*, ABVA Report, p.56.
17. Jaya Ramanathan, 'Asian Homosexuals: No Longer in the Closet', *The Pioneer*, 22 November 1992, Delhi.
18. *Less Than Gay*, ABVA Report, p.31.
19. Jeffrey Weeks, *Against Nature*, 1991, quoted in *Less Than Gay*, ABVA Report, p.29.
20. Arvind Kala in *The Pioneer*, 1 December 1992, Delhi.

21. *Less Than Gay*, ABVA Report, p.71.
22. *Trikone*, July–August, 1990, quoted in *Less Than Gay*, ABVA Report, p.43.
23. Interview with ABVA, October 1989.
24. *Swastha Hind*, December 1988.
25. *Less Than Gay*, ABVA Report, pp.47, 42, 43.
26. 'Final Statement of the Asian Theological Conference (ACT III)' in Virginia Fabella, Peter K. H. Lee and David Kwang-sun Suh (eds), *Asian Christian Spirituality Reclaiming Traditions* (Maryknoll: Orbis Books, 1992), p.8.
27. Kwok Pui Lan, 'The Future of Feminist Theology: An Asian Perspective', in *Voices from the Third World*, XV(1), June 1992, p.157.
28. Excerpts from the Programme Guidelines Report, Harare Assembly.
29. An earlier version of this chapter appeared in *In God's Image: Journal of Asian Women's Recource Centre for Culture and Theology* 20:3 (September 2001), 22–30.

Chapter 7

A SPIRITUALITY IN CHRIST THAT HUMBLES
AND TRANSFORMS

Duleep de Chickera

The election of Gene Robinson, a gay priest, as Bishop of the Diocese of New Hampshire in the US had just been announced. Earlier the Canadian Anglican Diocese of New Westminster had authorised a public rite for the blessing of same-sex unions. Human sexuality was becoming a controversial issue in the worldwide Anglican Communion.

It was against this backdrop of events that a reporter from a Sunday newspaper in Sri Lanka sought the views of various leaders, including me, on homosexuality. Carefully choosing my words, I suggested that just as heterosexual persons had the right to define their sexuality, so should homosexual persons have the right to define theirs. I went on to correct a popular misconception in Sri Lankan society that all paedophiles are homosexual, and finally condemned paedophilia and licentiousness in both heterosexual and homosexual persons.[1]

In this statement I had qualified the Anglican position on human sexuality in relation to the Sri Lankan context (1998 Lambeth resolution 1.10 required pastoral care for homosexual persons, and this could only be done if they identified themselves) and commented on certain prejudices that prevailed in Sri Lankan society in the area of human sexuality. Since the topic of human sexuality was generally taboo (with exceptions in academic, medical and pastoral groups), I was aware that I was treading on sensitive and controversial ground. But as a Christian leader I had a duty to voice an opinion and bring such ethical questions onto the socio-religious agenda and also help facilitate discussion and debate on these very issues that concerned the identity and orientation of human beings and our attitudes to each other.

The response to my comments was somewhat unexpected. A mixed group of Christians and persons of other faiths wrote or telephoned in appreciation of these views, and that they were expressed by a religious leader. Some were pleased that the topic had been addressed, and others pleasantly surprised that a voice from religion spoke from such a perspective. Others engaged in a discourse with me, disagreeing with my opinion that homosexual persons had a right to define themselves, but yet remaining open. A few, three or four I recollect, criticised me publicly in the media. They were all Christians. No doubt sincerely, they had concluded that I had endorsed homosexuality. They went on to take exception that I, as a Christian leader, had done so in the light of Scripture and the teaching of the church which they claimed condemned homosexuals and homosexuality. They were silent on my clarification regarding paedophiles and my condemnation of licentiousness regardless of one's sexual orientation.

Understanding the Scriptures

Soon I was to learn that these views were similar to those expressed in other parts of the church and that any resolution of this crisis would require a review of our understanding of biblical interpretation. With this in mind I suggest three approaches for consideration.

The impact of text on text

At times texts seem to give contradictory teaching or direction. I recall the story of a cardinal responding to a criticism that one of his priests was outside God's grace because St Paul in Romans condemns homosexuality as sin (Romans 1:26–27). Acknowledging the sexual orientation of the priest concerned, the cardinal nevertheless described him as one of his finest and most caring, creative and sensitive priests. Without doubt he was able to see in this priest, more than in most others, the qualities of love, joy, peace, patience, kindness, generosity, faithfulness, gentleness and self-control: all gifts of the Holy Spirit also enumerated by the same St Paul (Galatians 5:22).

How does God's word condemn him who is also filled with God's Holy Spirit, was the question that emerged through this dialogue. The cardinal's reply highlights this tension between texts and also suggests the need to be cautious about total dependence on select texts. Perhaps the way forward may be to look for guidance from the other two approaches as well, and to work for consensus this way, rather than rush into conclusions based on select texts only, incompatible with the ethos of wider biblical teaching.

The impact of theme on text

Overriding biblical themes or motifs, consistent through the whole Bible, such as grace, love, mercy, salvation, freedom and so on, must impact on select texts if biblical teaching on ethics and morality is to be adequately interpreted. We have this example in Christ when he met the misuse of select texts on the Sabbath, murder, adultery and so on through the broader framework of the priority of humans and the value of human relationships in God's design (Mark 2:27–28; Matthew 5:21–22, 27–28).

Consequently the literalism of a select text must be subject to interpretation in terms of the wider character, expectation and designs of God. This again seems to be Paul's argument in Galatians when he refutes those who advocated circumcision (mutilation of the body), clearly defendable with select texts, in the light of the new freedom and culture (liberation of the person) that Christ brings humans, and for which at the time of writing there was little written scriptural endorsement (Galatians 5:1). The oral tradition was just evolving by the grace of the Holy Spirit.

The impact of context on text

Anglicans believe that revelation and inspiration by the Holy Spirit, who inspired the written word, continue beyond the biblical manuscript. This is why tradition (the accumulation of the church's experience and practice through interaction with God's world, much of it through trial and error) and reason (knowledge, thinking and advancement which when tested and approved in the light of God's design, become gifts of God meant to be taken cognisance of by the church) are also contextual vehicles for doing theology and discerning the purposes of God. As the Spirit speaks and challenges the church through its context, an impact is made on the frail and sinful church's understanding of the Scriptures.

Consequently the church has known and advocated change through the guidance of the Holy Spirit with regard to certain restrictive texts. These include the stance on ordained women, in spite of St Paul's oft-quoted exhortation that women should be submissive, silent and restricted in teaching and authority over men in the church (1 Timothy 2:11–12.); the accepted model of gender equality in marriage, in spite of St Paul's clear definition of male hierarchy (Ephesians 5:21–24); and the church's positive position on non-violent resistance to injustice, in spite of several Old Testament texts that clearly describe God as being pro-war and violence (Exodus 15:3; Zechariah 12:6, 9).

Such instances should not be seen as a contradiction of the text but a fulfilment of God's purposes, which build on and widen the scope and application of biblical teaching. So Christ declares that he has come not to abolish but to fulfil the law and the prophets, and goes on to deepen and humanise our understanding, especially when and because we tend to use texts to exclude humans and exploit God's purposes and design for our own limited agendas (Matthew 5:17). This was clearly one of the recurring conflicts that Christ had with the Pharisees.

To continue still further, this method of the impact of context on the text also allows usury, widely condemned in the Bible (so that Israel, surrounded and threatened by other nations, would remain a closely knit exclusive people) to be practised by today's church, caught up in a very different socio-economic ethos. And it is this method that has motivated a shift in the thinking of today's church, placed in the context of an egalitarian society, from the embarrassing stance Paul takes on the then culturally acceptable concept of slavery and the status of slaves (Colossians 3:22ff; Ephesians 6:5ff).

Prejudice and stereotyping

For us in Sri Lanka, biblical interpretation alone is not the challenge. Through the many extended conversations and discussions that followed my newspaper statement, I came to realise a massive hidden prejudice in Sri Lankan society. While there was reason to earlier suspect such a prejudice, the extent to which it prevailed and the extremism of the prejudice came as a surprise.

Most of this prejudice sees homosexual persons as simply immoral. At best they are weak persons who have succumbed to a lesser lifestyle. Abnormal, deviant and sinful were the other adjectives used to describe them. Since it was assumed they were what they were by choice, reformation and return into the heterosexual camp also by choice was the solution. Those who needed help could obtain it from counsellors and doctors and clergy. These no doubt were the views of mostly hetero-sexual persons.

In fairness to those who expressed these views, there was very little first-hand knowledge or friendship with homosexual people. This is because the majority of homosexual people in Sri Lanka, and for that matter in South Asia, are compelled to remain hidden, and suffer in their silent world for fear of being grossly misunderstood or ridiculed, or for the embarrassment that sympathy and undue attention could bring. For various reasons, such as religious stereotyping which influences the psyche, the lack of adequate education and awareness and the reluctance of adults to discuss these matters with their children, there is little space for a more open approach to understanding the concept of homo-sexuality or the homosexual person in the Sri Lankan perspective on human sexuality.

This perspective stereotypes the individual and reduces one's ability to reconcile homosexual orientation with other responsible and healthy social lifestyles. Such persons being helpful colleagues, conscientious citizens, loving siblings or aunts and uncles, gifted sportspersons, creative writers, musicians or artists and so on are lost sight of under this overriding label. In fact, there tends to be disbelief if and when the homosexual identity of such a person is revealed, since she or he seemed 'so normal'! There is also, because of this perspective, a reluctance to critically listen to and benefit with discernment from the unfinished debate in the world of behavioural and medical sciences on whether the cause of homosexuality is nature or nurture. The perspective seems to cloud all else. It is this mentality that has even prevented an attempted amendment to the clause that criminalises homosexuality in the penal code of the country established by the British colonial rulers in the nineteenth century.

Understanding the homosexual person: a case study

My mind goes back to my first serious encounter with a homosexually oriented person, almost twenty-five years ago. He was a young student and I a young priest. We had a very close relationship of trust. In the early stages of his struggles I failed to understand him and kept suggesting that he would soon begin to be attracted by girls and that he was no different from his adolescent peers. As time passed I sensed that I was wrong. My young friend was clearly showing a preference for friendship with males. I prayed and read and consulted a psychiatrist friend who helped me understand that some people were oriented this way. This indeed was my first serious introduction into the hidden world of homosexuality. Before this, I, like most others of my generation, thought that homosexuality was a passing phase in the lives of some boys and young men and they soon grew out of it. Seminary and theological training had done little to change this mindset. Beyond educating me and suggesting I remain close to my young friend, my psychiatrist friend was unable to help us further. Consequently I resolved to walk with my young friend and extend pastoral care to him. From time to time we spent many agonising hours talking about his frustrations of not being able to visibly manifest his orientation, and praying together. He was a committed Christian. His frustrations soon centred on questioning God and my role became an increasingly difficult one, trying to justify God's love, plan and purposes, which I soon felt were becoming empty words. My questions soon connected with his.

It was when he began to talk about migration to a more open society in the global North that I was finally able to convince him that his parents had to be told. This turned out to be one of the most disastrous decisions we ever took. His parents reacted furiously. They were convinced that he was irresponsible and simply playing around. He could not be different because he was their son and should buckle down and change this nonsense, for if word got around, this would bring disgrace to the entire family. Typically the question most feared was family reputation at the expense of understanding what their son was saying about his sexual identity.

The tragedy of this story is that in addition to his inner struggles of sexuality my young friend now carried a strained relationship with his family. He soon moved out to live on his own and the company he kept became more and more questionable. Around that time I left the island for studies abroad and our communication was reduced to occasional letters. Very gradually we lost touch with each other. Soon afterwards I received the shocking news that he had died a violent death.

Dialogue towards a shared agenda

Though often not the case, the church in Sri Lanka has recently been more ready to address the issue. Ever since the tensions spilled over, the Diocese of Colombo has systematically studied these developments and concerns. Clergy conferences, area deanery meetings, Diocesan Councils and Joint Standing Committee meetings with our sister Diocese of Kurunegala have spent time trying to understand the sensitivities, rationale and tensions of fellow Anglicans around the world in the light of God's purposes. Our two dioceses together responded to the questionnaire preceding the Windsor Report and thereafter welcomed the Report itself. We particularly appreciated the moratorium on the blessing of same-sex unions, the episcopal ordination of practising gay priests and provincial interference in the jurisdiction of other dioceses, as measures that would provide space for reflection, understanding and healing without worsening the situation.

In a letter to the Archbishop of Canterbury following the Primates' response to the Windsor Report, we questioned whether the request that the Anglican Church of Canada and Episcopal Church voluntarily absent themselves from the Anglican Consultative Council was prudent. We wrote:

> We consider it unfortunate that the recommendations contained in the Windsor Report have not been followed in letter and spirit by all the parties. We believe that the acceptance of the Commission's unanimous recommendations and a continuing dialogue on the issues causing division in the light of the Anglican way of Scripture, tradition and reason is the only way that all of us in the Anglican Communion can walk together. We believe that excluding any church within the Anglican Communion from any of the Instruments of Unity is not the way of reconciliation and healing. It will only pave the way for an impaired or broken Communion. The Primates should be taking the lead in reconciliation and healing. Within their Provinces, we have no doubt that there is a variety of views on the very issues that divide us. All such voices should be freely heard in this ongoing discussion. The bonds of affection within our Communion should be celebrated and nourished, however strongly we disagree with the scriptural understanding of another.[2]

The letter was a call for continuing dialogue until a reconciliation is reached which will provide space for all without hurting the sensitivities of some.

The need of the hour is therefore clearly for people to remain in dialogue, asking questions and offering insights from the Bible, tradition and reason. Competent and experienced pastors and counsellors, theologians and those from the world of medicine and the behavioural sciences must be heard, and a culture in which homosexual persons will reveal their orientation and share their experiences, at least within trusted groups for a start, must in this way be created.

The recent emergence of an openly gay group in Sri Lanka is a welcome opportunity for dialogue. One lesson that our protracted ethnic conflict has taught throws light on this dialogue. As it was wholly improper and misleading for Sinhalese to define Tamil aspirations, for Tamils to define Muslim aspirations, and for oppressors to define the aspirations of the afflicted and so on, it would similarly be improper and misleading for heterosexuals to even attempt to define homosexual aspirations and identity.

Our immediate task is to facilitate this dialogue and reconciliation process through a shared agenda. The churches of the North first dominated this agenda and it now appears that the churches of the South could well take over. Bearing in mind this unfair and unnecessary two-way swing in dominance, such a shared agenda in which all voices will be given space and respect becomes imperative for both the local as well as the world church. Such a shared agenda should promote dialogue in the following areas:

(1) homosexuality and sin in the light of the Lambeth resolution that describes it as being incompatible with the Scriptures;

(2) the identity and aspirations of homosexual persons in the light of testimonies of changed lives and continuing medical and psychiatric research, including restorative therapy;

(3) the distinction between those who choose a homosexual lifestyle and those who find themselves with a homosexual orientation and the ensuing consequences;

(4) a spirituality in Christ that addresses disrespect for and violations of directions given by the Instruments of Unity (Archbishop of Canterbury, Anglican Consultative Council, Lambeth and Primates) as well as respect for all God's creation, especially when there is consensus among these voices;

(5) a spirituality in Christ that discerns the promptings of the Holy Spirit and strengthens communion as we continue to address this extremely grave responsibility of understanding,

interpreting, and reflecting human sexuality as a people of God.

If the church can play this modest pastoral role in this sensitive task, it would be one of the more constructive repercussions of the world-wide Anglican conflict on human sexuality. We trust that through this first step, fortified through prayer and consultation, based on our resilient Anglican spirituality, the future will carry rich experiences and lessons for all. There cannot be a better way of reflecting unity in diversity, and being humbled and transformed as co-workers with Christ for healing and transformation of all, in God's world, torn and divided, but for the present only.

NOTES
1. 'People often make the mistake of associating paedophilia with homosexuality. Paedophiles could either be heterosexuals or homosexuals. Paedophilia, meaning the sexual abuse of children, should be condemned without reservation and strong preventive action taken. But homosexuality is something entirely different. People must be allowed to define their own sexuality. Although to most people heterosexuality must seem the natural way to define themselves, there will be others who may wish to define themselves as homosexuals. Just as it is with heterosexuals, people who define themselves as homosexuals must also be received with dignity and respect. However, in both types of sexuality, licentiousness cannot be condoned.' *The Sunday Times*, 13 February 2003.
2. Excerpts from 'A Joint Letter by the Bishops of the Church of Ceylon', dated 30 March 2005.

Chapter 8

SEXUALITY AND THE CHURCH'S UNDER-STANDING OF AUTHORITY: A RESPONSE FROM JAPAN

Renta Nishihara

Sexuality and the Nippon Seikōkai

There has not as yet been much discussion of sexuality in the Nippon Seikōkai (Anglican Church of Japan; NSKK). Compared with the discussion surrounding women's ordination to the priesthood, it would not be an exaggeration to say that it has hardly begun. The first reason for this is that there are almost no people in holy orders who have 'come out' as clearly belonging to that sexual minority. Secondly, in Japanese society as a whole there is not yet any clear trend toward an understanding of minorities like the homosexual community. Moreover, the church in Japan tends to be even more conservative than society as a whole, with the result that there is little realisation of the existence of homosexual persons in the church. For such reasons, the theme of homosexuality and the church, which represents the greatest point of conflict within the Anglican Communion today, seems to the NSKK like some far distant issue. At the ecumenical level, in the largest denomination, the United Church of Christ in Japan, there are a number of pastors who have 'come out' as homosexual persons, while associations of sexual minority Christians like 'The Wind of Christ' are engaged in a variety of activities.

However, even in the kind of NSKK I have described, in 2004 there was an epoch-making event. A young priest on the active list of the NSKK (let us call him 'Priest A') 'came out' to the church where he served as a member of the sexual minority known as *sei-dōitsusei-shōgai* (transgendered). The diocese to which he belonged, beginning with the bishop and standing committee, has actively supported his coming out and accepted it. Before coming out formally at a meeting of the full parish vestry, he awaited an opportunity to come out to his church committee (vestry executive). At that time, both the diocesan bishop and the author, who was a member of the standing committee, were present. There I read out a message to the congregation, whose edited text reads as follows:

There is a term in English, 'sexual minority'. It is difficult to translate, but one might paraphrase it as follows: 'In a society which sees a clear division between male and female and recognises only sexual relations between those two, it applies to those who find such relationships difficult and whose sexuality takes a variety of forms.' This 'definition' includes those whose orientation can be called homosexual, but also includes asexual, bisexual, transsexual, transgender, transvestite, intersexual ... So there are people who represent a truly wide variety of types of sexuality. At the same time, there are limits to the term, 'sexual minority'. Apart from those mentioned above, there are many, many people whose sexual orientation is not firmly established, or to whom those categories do not apply. In any case, there is no doubt that it is an illusion to believe that in this world there can only be a clear, heterosexual, division between 'male' and 'female'.

In a society that fails to understand this reality, there are few individuals who will – or can – 'come out' by stating publicly that they belong to such a sexual minority, so it is difficult to know exactly what proportion of the population they represent. However, there are studies that state that they constitute at least 3 per cent of the population, and at most about 10 per cent. As Christians in Japan number less than 1 per cent of the population, the probability of meeting a member of the sexual minority on the street is far greater than that of meeting a Christian! I have heard more than a few people around me say in effect, 'I've never met a member of the sexual minority, and of course there is no one like that among my friends. So it's a matter that really has nothing to do with me.' I'm sure that there are many more people who think like that. Yet actually, in any region, in any social relationship, in any generation, around 10 per cent of the people will always belong to that sexual minority, so it would be unreasonable to say that one had never met one.

As a matter of fact, to put it even more precisely, every one of us possesses a different sexuality. Sexuality consists not only of two kinds, male and female, but if there are 100 people there will be 100 kinds of sexuality. In other words, there is no one who has the same kind of sexuality as I. Sexuality is diverse, and we exist as various shades (gradations) of it. For that reason, when we come to know for certain that the sexuality of each one is only one variety among many, then the term 'sexual minority' will have lost its meaning.

Actually, however, our society does not understand the pain and suffering experienced by those who have acknowledged that they belong to the sexual minority. Given such a society, we need to be aware that there are people who are forced to deny their identity, hiding it and covering it up.

'To live as oneself': that should be the natural right granted to every person without exception. There are those who choose the way of 'coming out' *in order that* they may find themselves. This is what Pastor Aika Taira of the United Church of Christ, who came out as a member of the sexual minority, had to say: 'Coming out is much more than opening up one's secret self. Confrontation with one's real self involves an act of building a completely new structure of relationships, often at the cost of great sacrifice.' I sincerely hope that you will understand what Rev. A said to you recently, precisely in this sense. At the same time, the act of coming out is not possible unless one has profound confidence in those to whom one speaks. It is above all because Rev. A loves the people of this church with all his heart and trusts you that he has been good enough to reveal his story to you.

Well then, how should we in the church think about this? For example, we are told that the Scriptures strictly forbid homosexual acts as sinful and in general see any talk of sexuality as taboo. As a result people in the sexual minority find themselves in a situation that is even harder for them to bear than in society at large.

Although it is true that Rev. A is not homosexual but transgendered, it does not matter what kind of sexuality it is, one would hope that we in the church would strongly affirm that *every human being* is an irreplaceable creation by God. The position that we can never forget is actually stated in the text of the Anglican–Roman Catholic Joint Statement, *The Gift of Authority* (1999), as follows: 'Human beings were created by God in his love with such diversity in order that they might participate in that love by sharing with one another both what they have and what they are, thus enriching each other in their mutual communion' (§27).

With the presence of Rev. A, this church, our diocese, and the entire NSKK have been granted a rare opportunity to become a fuller communion. I hope and pray with all my heart that you in this church, as forerunners in this kind of fellowship, will guide our steps.[1]

In the end, this church was able, by and large, to deal positively with Rev. A's coming out. Naturally, it is not clear whether everyone understood it completely. And there were a few members – but only a few – who expressed feelings of rejection. However, all things considered, the important thing is that a priest came out publicly, in church, as a member of the sexual minority, and the church accepted it, while the diocese also supported it positively. There is no doubt that for the NSKK as well this was a big step forward.

Sexuality and the church's understanding of authority

There is an important point to consider when one is talking about the subject of the sexual minority in a context like Japan's. It is not sufficient to express it in terms like human rights or problems of discrimination. One needs to make one's point from the standpoint of the church's understanding of the Gospel and, even more important, from its understanding of authority. For that reason, when I introduced the subject in my statement above, quoting from the ARCIC joint statement, *The Gift of Authority*, I discussed how it might be possible from the standpoint of the church's authority to locate the question of the sexual minority.

Now, coming to the main subject, I shall try to reflect on some of the main points of the recent discussion. To do so I shall make use of the ARCIC statement, *The Gift of Authority: Authority in the Church III*, the report of joint conversations between Anglican and Roman Catholic Churches.[2] I am confident that such a venture will be a contribution from our context here in Japan. *The Gift of Authority* was published as the fruit of work done at ARCIC-2 (The Second Anglican–Roman Catholic International Commission). It was occasioned by an observation by Robert Runcie, former Archbishop of Canterbury, that no society or church can escape the need for some kind of authority. But in fact it is not a question of whether authority is necessary or not – rather, what kind of authority, and how or by what means it is exercised.[3] Certainly this has to be a serious question for both society and church in our age.

In particular, the church today is continually being asked to clarify its guidelines from a position that will be both responsible and clear, not only with regard to the sexual minority, but to many other questions such as medical ethics, ecology, and so forth. When faced with these questions, who will make judgements about their nature and determine what is good or bad? When judging or determining, what will be the basis? Without doubt, that basis will be the *authority* of the church. At times we are apt to confuse *authority* with *power*. We need to be careful to note that authority and authoritarianism mean completely different things. We might describe *authority* as a guidepost for a traveller seeking the truth.

In the context of ecumenical discussion, it is surely *The Gift of Authority* that has so clearly recognised this understanding of authority. It is already twenty-five years since the Anglican and Roman Catholic Churches began the discussion of authority in their international meetings aimed at unity. Mary Tanner has noted that *The Gift of Authority* has become an important text, not just for the two Communions, but for the whole ecumenical movement as well.[4] In truth, it is not too much to say that the influence of that discussion has not remained with the two churches, but has been a meaningful one for wider ecumenism.

Points at issue in *The Gift of Authority*

I would like to take the various points raised by *The Gift of Authority* in order. The document is made up of sixty-three paragraphs in all, with the main subject beginning with paragraph 7. This first part is entitled 'Authority in the Church'. The main theme here is God's 'Yes' to humans and their response to God, 'Amen', taken from Paul's image in 2 Corinthians 1:18–20, where he writes, 'For in [Jesus Christ] every one of God's promises is a "Yes". For this reason it is through him that we say the "Amen", to the glory of God.' The argument unfolds on the basis of this understanding.

Creation and redemption are the expression of God's 'Yes' to human-ity, and God's deeds in the processes of creation and redemption represented God's invitation to humanity to answer 'Amen'. The sending of Jesus was God's 'Yes' to humankind, nothing less than God's affirma-tion of human nature. And at the same time, in Jesus' humanity we can see the perfect response, humanity's 'Amen' to God's purpose. Through the work of the Holy Spirit in us, we are enabled, with Christ, to say 'Amen' to 'God's purpose'.

Accordingly, we can begin to understand the purpose of 'Authority in the Church' when we see it from the standpoint of 'God's "Yes" to humanity'. Authority in the church exists in order that those who believe may continually remember God's 'Yes' and to draw out the 'Amen' which is their response to God. To put it another way, *authority* is nec-essary for the church to maintain a faithful relation with God. Authority exists to preserve the relationship and communion between God and humankind. In that sense, 'The Gift of Authority' affirms the fact that authority is a gift granted by God to the church. 'Authority' is the 'gift' that God has given to us in order that the church may always hold fast to God's purpose of creation and redemption and may faithfully respond to that purpose.

The second point in the first part is the key word 'local'. The place where God's 'Yes' to us, and our 'Amen' to God, become real is 'the local church'. The foundation of our faith is built up through the local community. Baptism is the sacrament of the local church. And the faith of each individual is nourished within the life of the faith community in a local area. At the same time, however, the local church is never an isolated entity. Transcending time and space, every local church is related to the universal church. Accordingly, the task of each individual Christian is to carry out God's 'Yes' within the local community, but also in communion with all the other churches. In this way, each Christian becomes connected within the life of the whole universal church. Though the response of the individual Christian is made primarily within the local church, at the same time it is also part of the response of the church as a whole.

The third point has to do with the passage of time, whose key word is 'tradition'. The life of the church is portrayed as the transmission of what was delivered to the apostolic community: something that transcends the generations (§14). However, tradition is more than a set of propositions. It is the very life of the church itself. Faith and sacrament, teaching, how one lives as a Christian: these and much else the church receives as tradition, living within it and handing it over. So the church is defined as the community that is invited to receive the tradition with faith and hand it on. On the other hand, *The Gift of Authority* makes an important point which is that, when faced with new situations, this tradition must be received in new ways: '[The church] must continue to be free to receive the apostolic Tradition in new ways according to the situations by which it is confronted' (§24).

'Within Tradition the Scriptures occupy a unique and normative place and belong to what has been given once for all' (§19). The expression 'within tradition' would not please those Anglicans who believe that the Scriptures exist apart from, and above, tradition. However, according to *The Gift of Authority*, the Scriptures themselves 'bring together diverse streams of Jewish and Christian traditions' (§20), and one can discern in them a process where the community receives the faith and passes it on. The process of receiving and re-receiving has existed from the history of the formation of the scriptural canon. Consequently, the fact that the message of the Gospel recorded in the Scriptures can be re-received within the context and controversies of a given period does not in any way threaten their primary position. The understanding that the church is always involved in the process of receiving and re-receiving and is a 'community of continual interpretation' is an extremely important element for Anglicanism.

John Henry Newman clearly pointed out that doctrine continually develops. The theology of the development of doctrine and the understanding that the church is a community of constant interpretation are the two sides of one coin. At the same time, it must be said that for Anglicanism the question is always lurking as to who is to judge whether a development is legitimate or not.

In this regard, the meaning of the text of paragraph 27 of *The Gift of Authority* is extremely important. For how one reads it will naturally determine our response to the various moral situations with which we are faced:

> In the rich diversity of human life, encounter with the living Tradition produces a variety of expressions of the Gospel. Where diverse expressions are faithful to the Word revealed in Jesus Christ and transmitted by the apostolic community, the churches in which they are found are truly in communion ... As God has created diversity among humans, so the Church's fidelity and identity require not uniformity of expression and formulation at all levels in all situations, but rather catholic diversity within the unity of communion.

The Gift of Authority reinforces this statement by concluding this paragraph with a quotation from an earlier published ARCIC report, *Church as Communion*:

> Human beings were created by God in his love with such diversity in order that they might participate in that love by sharing with one another both what they have and what they are, thus enriching each other with their mutual communion.[5]

God has in creation endowed human beings with variety and blessed it. There is nothing more important for our theology of the church than this. There can be no dynamism in our ecclesiology unless we take this standpoint as the point of departure. It is no exaggeration to say that the very foundation of Anglicanism's confidence in its diversity is here.

Here the question of 'authority' is once more raised. That is to say, it is a question of who is to describe the nature of this variety, also, who is to define its limits? Because previous ARCIC statements have been criticised for continuing the division between bishops, clergy and laity, *The Gift of Authority* may give the impression that it speaks of the bishops alone as the ones authorised to make such judgements, but actually such is not the case. *The Gift of Authority*'s answer to this question is stated in paragraph 28: 'The people of God as a whole is the bearer of the living Tradition.' The Holy Spirit works through the whole 'people of God'. It is not just bishops, clergy or theologians who have the authority to judge matters to do with tradition or variety. It is the duty of all to discern such matters. Every person possesses the *sensus fidei* which is defined as follows: 'This *sensus fidei* may be described as an active capacity for spiritual discernment, an intuition that is formed by worshipping and living in communion as a faithful member of the Church.' 'When this capacity is exercised in concert by the body of the faithful we may speak of the exercise of the *sensus fidelium*' (§29).

The first section ends the description of the variety of offices in the church with the image of a 'symphony' in which each among 'the whole people of God' have a part to play. When the whole body – bishops, priests, theologians, laity – play together, then for the first time a harmonious symphonic work is born. Each one has a special responsibility within the exercise of the church's authority (§30). Within the symphony, the episcopal office is connected above all with 'the ministry of memory'. It is a special office, maintaining the principal theme of the symphony as it 'remembers' the dynamism of God's 'Yes' and our 'Amen'. 'The ministry of memory' reminds the church of God's approval of humanity through creation and redemption. And it shoulders the work of reminding the church of the 'Amen' that is its response to God's call:

> Through such ministry the Holy Spirit keeps alive in the Church the memory of what God did and revealed and what God will do to bring all things into unity in Christ. In this way, not only from generation to generation, but also from place to place, the one faith is communicated and lived out. (§30)

The important point is the relation and balance between the *sensus fidelium* borne by the whole people of God and 'the ministry of memory'. Only when there is a mutual relationship between each will the 'symphony' be realised: 'The bishops, the clergy and the other faithful must all recognise and receive what is mediated from God through each other' (§30). It can be said that this basic assertion reveals a truly inclusive understanding.

The Gift of Authority affirms the above ecclesiology with the words, 'Anglicans and Roman Catholics can agree in principle on all of the above' (§19). However, at the same time it supplements this statement with the condition that both churches must 're-receive' everything, beginning with 'Tradition': that the church is local, and also universal; that the church is called to live dynamically within a tradition that is passed on from generation to generation; that though the Scriptures represent the norm, the church is required to receive and re-receive the tradition; that the church be characterised by a rich diversity; and that the whole people of God bear the responsibility for discovery of the truth and for the continual preservation of faithfulness toward God. When we re-receive this kind of understanding, it is certain that we can accept 'authority' as a 'gift'.

The second section (paragraphs 32–50) is entitled 'The Exercise of Authority in the Church'. One key word, 'synodality' stands out in this second section. Derived from the Greek *syn-hodos* (walk a path together), *The Gift of Authority* describes it as follows:

> The term synodality (derived from syn-hodos meaning 'common way') indicates the manner in which believers and churches are

held together in communion as they do this. It expresses their vocation as people of the Way (cf. Acts 9:2) to live, work and journey together in Christ who is the Way (cf. John 14:6). They, like their predecessors, follow Jesus on the way (Mark 10:52) until he comes again. (§34)

Synodality means more than just structure. What the term expresses is the outward aspect of the church's life. Like 'symphony', we have here a fertile image that emphasises being together. At the same time, synodality is an expression of the dynamic motion in the church's life. All who believe are a people on a journey together, so it is as if synodality was an expression of the people as they walk together within tradition, transcending time and space.

Paragraph 53 records an important understanding, in particular for Anglicanism:

> The Lambeth Conference of 1988 recognised a need to reflect on how the Anglican Communion makes authoritative decisions. At the international level, Anglican instruments of synodality have considerable authority to influence and support provinces, yet none of these instruments has power to overrule a provincial decision, even if it threatens the unity of the Communion. Accordingly, the Lambeth Conference of 1998, in the light of *The Virginia Report* of the Inter-Anglican Theological and Doctrinal Commission, resolved to strengthen these instruments in various ways, particularly the role of the Archbishop of Canterbury and of the Primates' Meeting. Alongside the autonomy of provinces, Anglicans are coming to see that interdependence among local churches and among provinces is also necessary for fostering communion.

The elements that *The Gift of Authority* continually emphasises are 'collegiality' and 'synodality'. If the Anglican Church is to be a communion, no one diocese or province can by itself fulfil such things as its mission. Synodality requires community between local dioceses and churches. Throughout the history of all our churches – including the Roman Catholic Church – down to the present, the office of the diocesan bishop, in a variety of ways both personally and collectively, has supported synodality. In recent years there has been a noticeable trend toward strengthening the authority of the Archbishop of Canterbury and the Primates' Meeting.[6]

It could be said that such a trend is a natural one in order to consolidate the unity of the Anglican Communion. However, strictly speaking, theologically the only level at which Anglicanism can 'decide something' is the diocese or the province. This has been our heritage from the English Reformation of the sixteenth century onwards. It can be said that it is a fundamental principle of Anglican ecclesiology that the national church is the basic unit. As the 1998 Lambeth Conference also declared, '[We recommend] that, *while not interfering with the juridical authority of the provinces*, the exercise of these responsibilities by the Primates' Meeting should carry moral authority calling for ready acceptance throughout the Communion.'[7] The autonomy of the province (diocese) is preserved as a holy doctrine.

The Archbishop of Canterbury or the Primates' Meeting can only interfere if there is an emergency situation in the concerned province that it has been unable to solve or there is a condition of confusion resulting from the absence of episcopal oversight. Indeed, there have been incidents where the Archbishop of Canterbury has intervened on moral grounds in the Anglican churches of Sudan and Rwanda. However, even if such interventions might be justified on moral grounds, Anglicanism needs always to be aware that they cannot be justified from the standpoint of its theology and practice of the church.

At its very end *The Gift of Authority* extends its discussion to recognition of the primacy of the Bishop of Rome as a support to the cause of church unity. In order to do so its description of the balance between a universal structure and the authority of the diocese is rather cautious. Paragraph 56, 'Issues Facing Anglicans', expresses this balance as follows:

> Is the [Anglican] Communion also open to the acceptance of instruments of oversight which would allow decisions to be reached that, in certain circumstances, would bind the whole Church? When major new questions arise which, in fidelity to Scripture and Tradition, require a united response, will these structures assist Anglicans to participate in the *sensus fidelium* with all Christians? To what extent does unilateral action by provinces or dioceses in matters concerning the whole Church, even after consultation has taken place, weaken *koinonia*? Anglicans have shown themselves to be willing to tolerate anomalies for the sake of maintaining communion.

I would like to point out that this expression is, strictly speaking, the raising of an issue, and that *The Gift of Authority* has not come to any kind of conclusion.

We have outlined the main points of *The Gift of Authority*. One should probably note that the whole document is set in the context of the re-reception of the universal supremacy of the Bishop of Rome. At the same time, it ought not to be unprofitable to consider the various ethical issues the Anglican Communion is facing at present over against the basic principles about which *The Gift of Authority* speaks.

The meaning of the Diocese of New Hampshire decision

We have already seen how 'God's "Yes" to humanity' represents the most important keynote for *The Gift of Authority*. God proclaims the divine 'Yes' to all people. And it is to that God that we respond 'Amen'. There is not a single person on this earth to whom God has proclaimed a 'No'. *The Gift of Authority* points to the fact that, at the least, Anglicans and Roman Catholics are in agreement on this one fundamental principle. Among those 'persons', there can be no doubt that people of the sexual minority must be included.

The Gift of Authority furthermore declares that 'Human beings were created by God in his love with such diversity in order that they might participate in that love by sharing with one another both what they have and what they are, thus enriching each other in their mutual communion.'[8] God in creation bestowed variety on human beings and blessed that variety. There is nothing more important for our church than that understanding. The net that those who fish for people use is one that encircles all human beings in their variety, and from that net not a single person will spill out or escape. This is really simple, but it is a most important truth of the Gospel. It is not impossible at all to understand the emergence of Bishop Robinson as a happening that is symbolic of a church's communion that is founded on the richness of the variety of its members, the net grasped by the fishers who fish for people. Although the discussions of the 1998 Lambeth Conference did not assent to the ordination of homosexual persons, it did acknowledge the existence of members of the sexual minority within the communion of the church. So there was a strong emphasis in the discussion on recognising the need for pastoral consideration of gays and lesbians. The present discussion following the consecration of Bishop Robinson concerned the problem of the place of homosexual persons in the episcopate and not, as voices of moderation were heard to emphasise, about expelling the sexual minority from the community of the church. At the same time if, as *The Gift of Authority* stated, the episcopal office is 'The ministry of memory which reminds the Church of God's approval of humanity through creation and redemption', then one could also say that Bishop Robinson is, above all, a fitting person to bear the special office of episcopacy. *The Gift of Authority* uses the image of a symphony to describe the variety of offices in the church. In a symphony *every person* is given his or her part to play. The decision of the Diocese of New Hampshire to give the conductor's baton to a member of the minority raises an important question concerning the actualisation of the church's synodality.

The core criticism levelled against Bishop Robinson's consecration is that it goes against biblical teaching, so that the ordination of homosexual persons, and above all to the episcopate, contravenes the church's tradition. *The Gift of Authority* states clearly that tradition, 'under new conditions', needs to be received 'in new ways'. Concerning the Scriptures, it says that it is possible to re-receive the gospel message recorded in the Bible in accordance with the conditions and controversies of the age. This in no way threatens the primary position of the Scriptures: 'In the rich diversity of human life, encounter with the living Tradition produces a variety of expressions of the Gospel.' In this context, when we consider the present episcopal consecration, there is no way that we can think of it as a contravention of scriptural teaching and the church's tradition. Rather it presents us with the possibility of grasping its meaning as a re-reception of Scripture and tradition.

If the decision of the Diocese of New Hampshire is seen as a problem, the problem must reside in the gap between the key words 'local' and 'universal'. In other words, it is the question of whether the local action of that diocese is to be seen as having universal meaning. If the Anglican Church is a communion, it is not possible for one diocese or province by itself to fulfil the mission of the whole. The Diocese of New Hampshire and the Episcopal Church were responsible for explaining to the Anglican Communion how they understood the meaning of the synodality which, according to *The Gift of Authority*, needs the association of local dioceses and churches. At the same time, it would be necessary to make the same criticism of those provinces who so quickly after that consecration pronounced the 'liquidation' of one province and one diocese. Judgements from any of those dioceses are nothing more than the judgement of a single local body, but they are actions that break down the unity, the synodality, of the Anglican Communion.

In such a situation one might say that the trend toward the strengthening of the functions of the Archbishop of Canterbury and the Primates' Meeting is an inevitable progression. Nevertheless, we must affirm once more what *The Gift of Authority* carefully asserts that even the Archbishop of Canterbury or the Primates' Meeting do not have the authority to deny the decisions of a particular province or diocese – in this case the Diocese of New Hampshire in the Episcopal Church . Just because of this situation, Anglicanism should not do away with the principle that the only level where decisions can be made is the diocese, or else the province. Because in one sense that is Anglicanism's lifeline.

Response of the Nippon Seikōkai to the Windsor Report

Like other provinces, the Nippon Seikōkai was asked to respond to the Windsor Report upon its release by the Lambeth Commission on

Communion in October 2004. The NSKK House of Bishops met in February 2005 to prepare a response, both for the Commission and for the Primates' Meeting in Northern Ireland later that month. The NSKK House of Bishops showed considerable awareness of the issues of unity and diversity that I discussed earlier in this chapter, exemplified by *The Gift of Authority*.

The NSKK bishops' response was in ten paragraphs. The first three noted the background to the Lambeth Commission on Communion and the Windsor Report, noting that the NSKK had already expressed its regret to the Episcopal Church and Anglican Church of Canada (Diocese of New Westminster) for the actions they took despite concerns expressed by Lambeth 1998 and Primates' Meetings. However, the NSKK bishops' statement went on in its fourth paragraph to declare its opposition to any direct authority ('practical directions') being exercised by the Communion against provinces or dioceses dissenting from the views of the majority:

> However, it should be enough for the Anglican Communion as a whole, or the Archbishop of Canterbury, to urges churches (dioceses) concerned with those kinds of resolutions and actions to reconsider their stand. There is no need to enumerate (Section D of Windsor Report) the kind of 'advisories' (practical directions) that have no precedent in the history of the Communion. Similarly, it should also be sufficient just to urge reconsideration of their actions on the part of those bishops who have intervened in the legitimate resolutions and actions of autonomous provinces.[9]

The fifth paragraph of the bishops' statement endorsed the call of the 1998 Lambeth Resolution 1:10 to listen to the experience of homosexual people:

> At the same Lambeth Conference, which passed the resolution to refrain from the ordination of homosexual persons, the bishops of the Communion urged us to commit ourselves to listen to the voices of homosexual people. The NSKK sincerely hopes that every province and diocese of the Communion will understand the importance of this resolution and act upon it.

The sixth paragraph then tackled the issue of unity and diversity, so much a part of *The Gift of Authority*:

> At this time the NSKK wishes particularly to emphasise that element of the Anglican tradition which seeks all possible means to recognise the diversity which emerges in the process of the indigenisation (inculturation) of the Gospel.

Following this theme, the seventh paragraph puts forward a solidly
contextual view of the interpretation of Scripture and hermeneutics:

> Moreover, while the NSKK believes in the authority of the
> Scriptures, we understand that the *text* of Scripture was formed
> within a particular historical and faith context. Accordingly, we
> believe that, in a context which differs both in history and the
> expression of faith, we are actually permitted a variety of ways of
> interpreting Scripture.

In light of the previous two paragraphs, the bishops go on in the next two
paragraphs to argue against one single view of human sexuality and
basing the unity of the church upon it:

> ... we cannot think that the church can have only one absolute view
> of human sexuality. While recognising the authority of the Bible,
> there is every possibility that in the process of working out its
> message, differences of time and culture may be reflected in the
> understanding of human sexuality. We would like to think of the
> series of decisions and actions of ECUSA and ACC in this light. (§8)
> ... [The] NSKK does not think that unity can be manifested
> only if we take the same interpretation of Scripture and the same
> theological standpoint concerning our basic understanding of
> human sexuality. (§9)

Finally, in their last paragraph, the bishops reject the proposed Anglican
Covenant, arguing that the proposal's references to the diversity of
'moral values' and the 'vision of humanity' within the Anglican
Communion 'appear to imply a variety whose considerable latitude
ought not to be limited by such a covenant'.[10] The bishops assert that the
kind of codified pledge proposed in the Covenant is contrary to
Anglican tradition. The NSKK bishops' overall response to the Windsor
Report reaffirmed the basic Anglican principle of 'unity in diversity' and
represented the expression of an important position in the light of the
present authoritarian trend of the Anglican Communion.

However, I deeply regret the extremely biased conclusion of the
Primates at their February 2005 meeting in Northern Ireland, which
urged the Anglican Church of Canada and the Episcopal Church to withdraw voluntarily from attending Anglican Consultative Council meetings until the Lambeth Conference in 2008. At the very least, if the
Primates cannot affirm a 'unity' based on the kind of principles contained in the NSKK response, the Anglican Communion will surely be
unable to avoid breaking up, not only structurally but also theologically.

In conclusion

'Will the Anglican Communion break up?' With the consecration of Bishop Robinson and the events that have followed, many in the media, both church and secular, both here and abroad, are stirring up people's feelings. However, I rely on what *The Gift of Authority* says: 'In order to maintain communion, the members of the Anglican Communion have tolerated a variety of irregular practices.' If the Anglican Communion is able to share the principles enunciated by the NSKK, it ought to be possible for it to surmount this present problem as well.

The only key to untangling a complex relationship such as that between ecclesiology and morality is a hermeneutical process in which we learn how to receive, then re-receive, an understanding of Scripture and tradition. In that sense, the 'ecumenical hermeneutic' proposed by the World Council of Churches is worthy of study as a most useful approach. Christopher Hill, in his response to *The Gift of Authority*, emphasised the need within Anglicanism for a 'hermeneutic of trust'.[11] Surely the task facing the Anglican Communion is to accept what has happened in New Hampshire with a 'hermeneutic of trust'.

NOTES

1. Francis Renta Nishihara, Chubu Diocese, Nippon Seikōkai, 20 April 2004.
2. *The Gift of Authority: Authority in the Church III* (New York: Church Publishing Inc., 1999).
3. R. A. K. Runcie, *Authority in Crisis? An Anglican Response* (London: SCM Press, 1988), p.22.
4. Mary Tanner, 'Authority: Gift or Threat?' in Peter Fisher (ed.), *Unpacking the Gift: Anglican Resources for Theological Reflection on* The Gift of Authority (London: Church House Publishing, 2002), p.15.
5. The reference is to §35 of *Church as Communion*.
6. This trend can be seen in Resolution III-6 of the 1998 Lambeth Conference.
7. 1998 Lambeth Resolution 3.6(c). Author's emphasis.
8. *The Gift of Authority*, §27, quoting from *Church as Communion*, §35.
9. The full text of the English translation of the NSSK Bishops' Statement on the Windsor Report may be found at: http://www.rci.rutgers.edu/~lcrew/dojustice/j264.html.
10. The reference is to Part III, Article 10 of the proposed Anglican Covenant.
11. Christopher Hill, 'An Ecumenical Hermeneutic of Trust' in *Unpacking the Gift*, op. cit., p.75.

Chapter 9

MUSLIM ATTITUDES TO HOMOSEXUALITY

Stuart E. Brown

Introduction

This essay has a dual purpose. First, I intend to survey various perspectives regarding homosexuality current among Muslims today, and I then hope to develop an assessment of the possible impacts which any endorsement or recognition of homosexual preferences on the part of any group of Christians may have on intercommunal relations. Of course, these internal observations stem from an awareness that there are individual Muslims who have experienced some form of homosexual attraction, and any consideration of the experience of the Christian community is necessarily of secondary interest and importance in the debate within the Islamic *ummah* (community). To some, it may come as a surprise that it is possible even to refer to such a debate, but the existence of several associations of gay Muslims provides sufficient evidence for sober reflection and ample encouragement for thoughtful examination.

Basic dogma

> Indeed, you approach men in your lust rather than women, and you are a people exceeding all bounds. (Q. 7:81)

Any consideration of the attitudes of contemporary Muslims to homosexual tendencies and behaviour must begin, as with any other topic, with the relevant verses of the Qur'ân, pausing only to note that Muslims take the Arabic text of the Qur'ân as a verbatim message from the Creator, a clear guide to the believers. In this case, there are only nine passages to study, and they all refer to Lot's confrontation with the people of a city which the Qur'ân does not name, but which sounds quite like Sodom and Gomorrah mentioned in the Book of Genesis. The Qur'ân's treatment of the incident is both more elaborate and more precise than the Bible's, leaving no room to argue that the real issue could be hospitality or anything else but sex between men. Given Lot's apparent displeasure, it seems ironic that the Arabic language has used his name to coin the terms *liwât* (for the act) and *lûtî* (for the person).

The collections of *ahâdîth* (statements attributed to Muhammad) indicate that the Prophet strongly disapproved of homosexual acts: 'When a man mounts another man, the throne of God shakes'; 'Kill the one that is doing it and kill the one to whom it is done.' He is also reported to have equated *musâhaqah* (lesbian activity) with adultery, and implicitly subject to the same penalty (stoning or whipping). Male homosexuality, however, was considered a distinct offence with its own special punishments. Abû Bakr, the first *khalîfah* or successor of the Prophet, burned a man convicted of *liwât*, whereas Alî, the fourth *khalîfah* and Muhammad's son-in-law, chose to have one man so condemned thrown from the highest minaret of the local mosque. These were cases of the 'active' partner in the coupling; the 'receptor' was usually burned. In any case, the result was always death, and the means were seldom chosen for a quick or merciful loss of consciousness.

Through most of Islamic history, in virtually every corner of the Muslim world, the death penalty continued to be the officially preferred sentence for persons convicted of homosexual activity. For a typical opinion from a recognised authority, I mention the work of al-Dhahabi, a scholar who lived in Damascus in the thirteenth century (seventh of the *hijri* calendar) and wrote a compendium on the seventy greatest sins (entitled simply *al-Kabâ'ir – The Great Sins*). Polytheism and murder head the list, but homosexuality ranks eleventh, right after adultery and before usury or the oppression of orphans, and well ahead of embezzlement and blasphemy. Today, in this fifteenth century of the *hijri* calendar, there are still seven countries which execute offenders for such misdeeds. In August 1992, Iranian police arrested ninety gays and lesbians at a private party, and all were condemned to die. More recently, in February 2001, a lesbian couple was sentenced to death in Somalia, and in April of the same year six men were executed in Saudi Arabia after being found guilty of 'deviant sexual behaviour'. These few examples are by no means an exhaustive catalogue.

Such accounts indicate that, even when the direst consequences could be expected, there have been people in Islamic societies who engaged in homosexual encounters in spite of the risks. Several Muslim mystics have written of their love for God in terms that seem to evoke erotic heterosexual relationships, and a few others have described their *sûfî* exaltation in phrases suggestive of homosexual attraction and fulfilment. Many judges have tended to pronounce lighter sentences than official policy or received doctrine would require. Homosexual comportment has been condoned among youths who were strictly denied any heterosexual forms of indulgence, and many visitors to Islamic lands have written copiously of observing widespread homosexual practice, especially among slaves and eunuchs. An older contemporary of Dhahabi's, the Tunisian judge Shihâb al-Dîn al-Tifashi, edited a volume (*Nizhat al-albâb – The Diversions of the Hearts*) on the sexual practices of his own society, including several reports of male or female homosexuality.

Some students of the Qur'ân and the *sunnah* (normative practice or exemplary behaviour attributed to Muhammad) have argued for more tolerant exegesis and more gentle interpretation. One of the few areas open for dialectical nuance in the study of the Qur'ân concerns the relative importance to be given to verses which could in theory be seen in competition with each other in their application in various circumstances. In practical terms, one could ask how the verses against homosexuality relate to those verses which Muslim reformers quote in support of human rights or social reform. In adopting such a tactic, gay Muslims and their friends must embrace the whole strategy of modern revision, given that the repression of homosexual conduct and the execution of its adepts have for so long enjoyed such a solid consensus of legal experts in every part of the Islamic world. The proponents of openness and tolerance can hope for progress only if they insist with other reformers on the advent of a new era of individual study (*ijtihâd*) and a radical re-examination of the Qur'ân in the light of contemporary science and circumstances. I now turn to an overview of a few of the contexts of this discussion.

Contemporary opposition

As Gay Muslims, we know too well the discrimination, homophobia, hatred and outright rejection that exists in our communities toward gay, lesbian, bisexual and transgendered (GLBT) people. Men and women who are GLBT face tremendous pressures, including marriage, and if our homosexuality is discovered, we are isolated and ostracised not only from our friends, families and communities, but more importantly, from the religion we love so deeply.[1]

Although many countries have abandoned the death penalty, homosexual behaviour remains illegal in most Islamic societies and in most multi-faith regions with large populations of Muslims. While legal sanctions vary, from severe lashing and jail time to fines or public humiliation, most gay Muslims can expect to suffer extreme forms of ostracism, such as interdiction from most forms of employment or expulsion from family structures. This is true even in those few havens where homosexuals are free from prosecution, whether this is because they are in a western state with no law against their lifestyle, or because their government has tempered its zeal in pursuing them (as has been the case recently in Cameroon, for example). The merest suspicion can prompt officials to adopt a range of regulations, such as the Nigerian government's ban on dreadlocks and facial jewellery in junior soccer tournaments or the president of Guinea's ordering all the players on the national team to get proper haircuts.[2]

Denial of the company of one's closest family or exclusion from an inheritance may be the mildest reactions of a Muslim family to any relative who adopts a gay identity or lifestyle. One Jordanian man reported to Amnesty International that his family had thrown him down the stairs, and while he was in hospital with a broken leg and a shattered jaw, one of his brothers shot him in the ankle. The brother was not prosecuted for this assault, because the police understood the incident to be a 'family matter'.[3]

A Mauritanian man was granted political asylum in the USA because he had informed his father of his orientation, and his father had threatened to kill him if he came home.[4] In April 2002, a gay Muslim was murdered in the Nigerian state of Jigawa.[5] Besides the lack of income which is the logical consequence of family and economic ostracism, people who are excluded from their societies are often deprived of health care, especially if they suggest that they suffer from any complaint associated with homosexual activity.

In the relative freedom of the United States, a group of gay Muslims began to correspond online and, eventually, to plan a series of meetings. The group, which took the name Al-Fatiha, meaning 'the beginning' or 'the opening' and the title of the first *sûrah* of the Qur'ân, gradually expanded to include members in several states as well as Canada, Australia and western Europe. This affirmation of the presence of a significant number of persons who considered themselves to be gay and Muslim, attracted new members and sympathetic enquirers. It also attracted the hostile attention of many conservative Muslims, some of whom assumed the duty of disrupting al-Fatiha's meetings and threatening physical harm to anybody attending. Persons known to have been involved with the organisation are generally not welcome at mosques or within the general Muslim community.

Gay Muslims

As I have suggested, the many incidents of punishment and persecution dramatically confirm the presence of homosexuals in every part of the Islamic world, for it seems self-evident that nobody would invite such hardship and calumny on a whim or a jest. Available evidence suggests that the incidence of homosexual tendencies or preferences in Muslim societies is approximately the same as in any other human community. While there have been certain contexts in which homosexual activity could be condoned, the general attitude of Muslim communities has been hostile and persons found to have engaged in homosexual acts have faced the most severe penalties. The advent of the Internet and its relative anonymity has given those homosexual persons with the requisite financial and technical means a new avenue of contact.

The web page for Salaam Canada offers a list of 'Queer Organizations and Groups', mostly in Iran and the Arab world.[6] In Indonesia, Dr Dede Oetomo (an associate reader in linguistics at the University of Airlannga in Surabaya) founded a gay group, which had some five hundred persons on its mailing list in February 1999, according to information he posted himself on a Dutch web page.[7] Alliance Rights Nigeria claims a membership of over eight thousand, although it is not clear how many of these would be Muslims, as there are no Muslim names among the persons whose stories are available on the web page.[8] For many years, a group of Muslim homosexuals has operated in Kano and other northern cities, under the name of *dan Daudu*. The website *Behind The Mask* gives information on most African countries; understandably the information varies greatly in terms of date and detail, but it does identify several organisations. For example, Groupe Andligeey in Senegal (which names both its president, Serigne M'Bodji, and its treasurer, Mohamed Tiam), has received grants from the National AIDS Program.[9]

Information is more accessible in Europe and North America. A typical group of gay Muslims in Europe would be Kelma, a solidarity group for gays of North African origin living in France. While Kelma sponsors some social gatherings and discussion groups, many of its members prefer to remain strictly anonymous, for fear of the usual cultural penalties, such as exclusion from one's family and the ostracism of other North Africans. Kelma is reluctant to engage in campaigns of any sort, as its members wish to avoid attention. The group exists primarily to offer encouragement and solidarity to individuals who are generally very insecure; similar organisations among other Muslim minorities in several parts of Europe have adopted parallel policies.[10]

Even Al-Fatiha began very discreetly, with an anonymous enquiry on the Internet in 1997: 'Is there anybody out there like me? Is anyone out there a gay Muslim?'[11] The founder, Faisal Alam, was soon identified by diligent Muslim researchers, and he went public with his efforts for Al-Fatiha, which from the beginning has waged a double 'jihad' (struggle), urging mainstream Muslims to acknowledge that gays have a valid claim to membership in Islamic society, and trying to explain the merits of Islam to the general homosexual community. In February 2003, Al-Fatiha staged a major convention in Toronto, in spite of the evident risks. Many participants faced expulsion from their families, exclusion from their mosques and even surreptitious physical assault, if their involvement, and especially their orientation, were to become known in their home communities.

Several cities in North America now have relatively open associations of gay Muslims, like Salaam, which sponsors e-mail discussions and advertises support groups meeting at its own community centre on Church Street in Toronto, as well as rallies, parties and other occasions. Sami, the leader of Salaam, is one of relatively few gay Muslims who claim to have come to terms with their situation. He affirms that he has 'found peace' and that he is loyal to Islam, which to him is a religion of 'love, hope, tolerance and peace'.[12] Like-minded persons, who understand that they must use their courage in mutual support and in affirming their more hesitant colleagues, have launched the Gay Muslims Listserv, which claims adherents in twenty countries in its efforts to gain acceptance for homosexuals within Islamic society and for Muslims in interfaith gay groups.[13]

Let me close this section with an extended quotation from Faris Malik, one of the more articulate advocates of the gay Muslims' position:

> Is gay sex permissible? When two consenting adults love each other and want to share their love physically, one can reasonably doubt its supposed 'sinfulness', but this is a very personal matter best left to the individual conscience. Love and relationship are healing and can help people become psychologically healthy and content – sin does just the opposite. There are many benefits to love and healthy sexuality, and none at all to its opposite. Refusing queer Muslims the right to love and be loved is, to some of us, a much larger 'sin' because its consequences are so destructive all the way around. Even so, there are some of us who take a much more conservative view and refrain from sexual activities. Ultimately it is up to each gay person to decide how best to reconcile their sexual needs with what the Qur'ân teaches, and to examine their own behaviour and motives and determine the purity of their own intentions.
>
> Should gay and lesbian Muslims leave Islam? No, they should not. They should not let ignorance and homophobia drive them away from their adherence to Allah. We must learn to embrace what Allah has decreed for us, accept it, be at peace with it – and move on.[14]

Toleration

In the same article, Malik reminds us that, throughout history, 'Islam has been very tolerant of homosexual love and has even tolerated many forms of homosexual sex.' He also insists that all the verses of Qur'ân have always been open to a broad range of interpretation. We have noted that the *dan Daudu* group has existed for several years in northern

Nigeria, and this presence strongly indicates an elementary level of
tolerance on the part of the surrounding society, which is overwhelmingly Muslim. Similarly, in Indonesia, Oetomo observes that homosexual behaviour is much less reprehensible than adultery, although it is
the duty of every Muslim to marry eventually and to abandon any homosexual interests at the time of marriage. He also mentions a number of
local cultures remarkable for the intensity of homosexual activity,
especially in religious schools, claiming that local Muslims have always
known of this activity and condoned it, pointing to several examples
from traditional literature to support his case.[15]

One Islamic country with no legal sanction against homosexuals is
Turkey, where an association called Lambda holds weekly meetings and
several individual homosexuals have their own web pages. One transsexual, Demet Demirel, even stood as a candidate for political office,
and Turkish gays see their role and status more in the context of
European social and political values than in terms of Islam; for example,
they note that Turkish women could vote before French women, and
they consider themselves as part of the European movement for gay
rights.[16]

In some western societies, Muslim leaders have joined in general condemnations of gay-bashing and other forms of outright discrimination.
Muhammad Yusuf, chairman of the British Organisation of University
Imams, helped organise a letter to the *Guardian* protesting against
homophobia, because of his conviction that 'all forms of
fundamentalism, whether fundamentalist Islamic or fundamentalist
evangelical are abhorrent to the values of Britain's multi-faith and
multicultural society.'[17] Similarly, the president of the Canadian Islamic
Congress, Mohamed Elmasry, eschewed overt persecution of homosexuals even as he affirmed the classical repugnance against their
activities: 'It is clear that homosexuality is forbidden and if someone
wants to insist on doing it, that is their personal decision. They will be
held accountable in the end.'[18]

Once again, it is appropriate to include a few extended excerpts from
a single article in an attempt to capture the flavour of this growing
tendency among Muslims in western societies to express more tolerance
for homosexuals in the broad context of human rights:

> Gays and lesbians wishing to marry face a gauntlet of opposition
> and we, as a heterosexual Muslim couple, can empathize with their
> pain.
>   ... As practising Muslims, we acknowledge that no faith,
> particularly Islam in its traditional interpretation, permits same-
> sex marriage or condones homosexuality. However, neither does

faith allow hate and bigotry to be camouflaged as a quest for religious purity.

Most Canadian Muslims reject the notion of same-sex marriages and they are perfectly entitled to their beliefs, if, indeed, the issue is one of belief. But we think the position taken by religious leaders attacks the basic humanity of gays and lesbians. Dehumanizing 'the other' is the first step to setting them as targets of bigotry and hate. Invoking religion to accomplish this task is shameful.

... If gays and lesbians wish to pursue their own path in life, who are we to place obstacles in their way? If their choices are contrary to that of the Divine, only the Divine can be certain. Let us find God in our kindness and compassion instead of hate and self-righteousness. For isn't God the most merciful and the most compassionate?

Only God knows whether we are right in standing up for our gay friends, but we do so in all sincerity (and with the hope that no one should shower grief over the happiness sought by another human being). Let us learn to live and let live.[19]

In the closet

Given the risks of coming out, it is hardly surprising that homosexuals in many Islamic societies, from the Arab world across Iran and Pakistan to Malaysia and Indonesia, prefer to keep their orientation a secret from their neighbours and their kinfolk, limiting their communication to relatively secure Internet links. Discretion is not the only motive for such secrecy, however, because many gay Muslims share the general attitude of their fellow-believers towards homosexuality.

On the one hand I want to have intimate relations with people of the same sex; on the other hand I am ashamed as well as afraid I have sinned against God. While I am just a lay person who lacks understanding of the complexities of religious law concerning gay people, I have heard a little about them, where the gist is that engaging in intimate relations with people of the same sex is a great sin. That is so horrible. It means that gay people are great sinners. But when I reflect on it a bit more, why does God create gay people, when no one in the world is willing to live as such?[20]

The fact that most African languages have words for 'homosexual' shows that this tendency has been known in traditional societies, even before the colonial period, and we have already noted the existence of various groups of gay men in countries from Nigeria to Indonesia. Young people with homosexual feelings who are reluctant to take the overt action of joining a group like *dan Daudu* must keep their thoughts very much to themselves, and they usually conform to accepted societal norms in terms of participating in expected forms of heterosexual inter-action. The leader of Alliance Rights Nigeria estimates that 40 per cent of Nigeria's gays are married and continue to have sex with male part-ners, thus putting their wives at risk of HIV infection.[21] When they can, gays from traditionally Islamic societies try to emigrate to more tolerant western environments; an example is Cheikh Traore, the son of a Mauritanian father and a Nigerian mother who left Africa in 1997 and has since worked in London as an AIDS educator.[22]

When Faisal Alam started the Gay Muslims Listserv, he had to wait for seven months before anybody else would post a message, because others feared being discovered. They were right to be cautious, as 'Alam himself was outed when some orthodox Muslims infiltrated his Listserv. They made copies of his messages and distributed them in mosques in New York.' Al-Fatiha has since installed an elaborate security system, requiring an initial telephone interview and frequent checks.[23] Even those who use the facility show their own concerns for discretion in their comments and requests, such as the man who advertised for a 'lesbian friend and maybe marriage' in the hopes of concealing his gay relationship (already four years old) from his family.[24]

The situation of Imam Abdallah has been especially delicate, as he has completed the necessary courses to qualify as a religious leader in the United States. In order to pursue his studies, Abdallah concealed his orientation in the hopes of gaining recognition and engaging other lead-ers in open debate. Since graduating in 2002, he has counselled some gay Muslims and performed some same-sex marriages, but conducts most of his outreach online.[25] Meanwhile, more than one gay Muslim has wondered, in the shadows, whether straight Muslims 'think they are confused because there is something wrong with their sexuality or their lustful desires' in a context where 'the Muslim community is ready to hug progressive, conservative, liberal and all other kinds of Muslims but not Queer Muslims . . .'[26]

Alternative options: therapy or apostasy?

'Honestly, I do feel that it is very wrong,' said Sheikh Mustafa during a web chat. Mustafa is a gay Muslim living in Singapore. 'Islamic teach-ing prohibits gay activities. I'm trying to be straight to be close to Allah. I'm praying very hard.'[27] This 'solution' is familiar in Christian circles, based on the same underlying assumptions about God's preference for people and the implicit power of prayer to elicit a change of orientation. Other remedies developed within the Muslim community also have their counterparts among Christians, such as the website called straightway.org.uk, which offers advice to Muslims who wish to avoid homosexual temptations and 'follow Allah's guidance above your own desires'.[28]

As noted, some Muslims argue for new interpretations which would permit homosexual activities within the limits of a revised *sharî'ah*, while some gay Muslims try to be straight. Others adopt a third course and leave Islam. Arslan Durrani, who lives in Oakland, is a gay who has renounced Islam, and dismisses those who claim to be gay Muslims as 'a bunch of hypocrites', attempting without success 'to reconcile their homosexuality with spirituality'.[29] Danial, the Pakistani gay mentioned earlier, has also concluded that it is impossible to be a good gay Muslim, 'so you make some changes in your belief; now you believe in God but you do not believe in the religion'.[30]

Once again, the most elaborate and explicit rationale for this option comes from a person writing in the relative freedom of the Untied States. Here is another extended quotation, given to capture the full timbre of the repudiation, in a piece entitled 'The New and Improved Sulayman X':

> It is time for me to come clean and confess that I can no longer consider myself a Muslim. Despite years of effort, I can find no way to reconcile Islamic teaching on homosexuality (and sex, in general) with my own reality of being a gay man. In fact, I cannot, in conscience, accept Islamic teachings on sex: I do not believe in polygamy; I do not believe it is moral to force one's female slaves into accepting your sexual advances (among more intelligent people, this is known as rape); I do not believe each person must be straight and married and make babies; I do not believe Paradise will be filled with beautiful babes ready to service you for eternity; I do not believe a Muslim husband has the right to 'lightly beat' his wife; I do not believe anyone should be stoned to death for adultery, much less that homosexuals should be killed 'wherever you find them'. All of this is repulsive to me, and sticks in my throat like broken glass.
>
> I have tried – believe me, I have tried – to separate out the Arabic cultural nonsense from the real Islam, to look at the broad picture, to ignore questionable verses in the Qur'ân, to ignore my own doubts about a God that, time and again, reportedly destroys this and that community for whatever reasons (including the community of Lut).
>
> The point is this: I cannot worship a 'god' that created me as a homosexual being, and then will destroy me for being what he made me to be. This is utter nonsense.[31]

Some fine distinctions

In most Muslim societies, there is strong evidence of widespread homosexual activity among unmarried adolescents. The generally accepted
way to avoid any stigma is to grow up into a 'normal' married person,
and to become a parent. This is clearly suggested by such early writers
as Tifashi, and by people in our day in as widely separated areas as
Pakistan and Nigeria. Even among married men, there has been a tradition, so to speak, of sexually exploiting men who are in some way
dependent or subservient, and men who are thought to be very wealthy
or powerful are also assumed to have access to many *dan Daudu*.[32]
Jurisprudence has also established a general principle which distinguishes participants in homosexual acts (other than intercourse): 'Ghalib
Dhalla explained that it depends on who is administering the sexual act:
"If I get blown, I'm not gay."'[33]

Here again, a lengthy excerpt from one articulate source will demonstrate a general observation. In this case, I refer to an essay entitled
'Good Dogs and Homosexuals',[34] which itself depends on a book by
Arno Schmitt and Jehoeda Sofer, *Sexuality and Eroticism among Males
in Moslem Societies*.[35] The book's primary focus is a set of the experiences of some sociologists and transplanted European gay men in
several Islamic countries of the Mediterranean.

> In these cultures, there is much homosexual sex among men, but
> as in ancient Rome, it mainly features the exploitation of stigma-
> tized 'soft boys' or men called *zamel* in Morocco, for example,
> who allow themselves to be penetrated and are therefore held in
> mild or virulent contempt by 'real men' who consider themselves
> normally heterosexual and perform only a single 'homosexual' act
> regarded as dominant. And much to the surprise of most westerners,
> most of the dominant participants are actually just what they claim
> to be.

The essay continues with the further observation that this apparently
acceptable homosexual activity by men who are 'normally' straight has
obscured or distorted any observation of more authentic gay love in
societies where the law still sanctions serious penalties for genuine
homosexual relationships. Furthermore, say the authors, the formidable
obstacles imposed in most Islamic societies to any heterosexual
indulgence outside marriage creates the social circumstances which
sociologists elsewhere have observed in other female-deprived groups of
men, like naval vessels, military camps or, most notoriously, prisons. It
is easy to concur with the writer's conclusion that much of the apparently
homosexual activity in these rarefied contexts results from a combination of power relationships and otherwise unquenchable lusts. These

classical Islamic situations also have an obvious impact on the women, who are also insulated from heterosexual contact, but in a different way.

> Female–female sex, in such an atmosphere, becomes implausible, and conspicuous lesbian relationships are mostly precluded by parental marital arrangements and other limits on women's freedom. If such relations arise in a single household, among a man's wives, they are probably easy to conceal completely.[36]

Another masterful study is Sami Aldeeb's *Sexuality in Islamic Law*.[37] This work offers many similar remarks, with a more extensive list of examples, including several cases of outright exploitation, such as schoolteachers abusing their students. Once again, the general contention is reinforced, that stable, loving relationships between two men (or two women) are virtually impossible to sustain in Islamic societies. Even in more liberal polities, any gay or lesbian couple who claimed to be Muslims would soon be denounced or expelled by the local Islamic community. Where the imams oppose violence and endorse modern notions of tolerance, such Muslims would still run a constant risk of surreptitious attacks on their persons and their property. There are exceptions to every rule, of course, like Oetomo and his partner in Indonesia or the *dan Daudu* couples in northern Nigeria, but they tend to prove the rule.

The interfaith dimension
While most traditional Islamic societies condemn homosexual activities and punish offenders with sentences ranging from humiliation to ostracism and even death, it is possible to argue that much of the reproof lies in the local culture. Thus, Arab Christians generally share the range of opinions expressed among Arab Muslims. In most African milieux, Muslims and Christians are in general agreement, whether in a relatively liberal context like South Africa's or a stridently proscriptive setting like Nigeria's. Most Muslims in western Europe and North America, while expressing personal distaste or affirming Islamic prohibitions, will argue for tolerance on the grounds of human rights. There is certainly a widespread reluctance to admit the possibility that a person could be both an active homosexual and a pious Muslim, but there is also a general recognition of the place of gay lifestyles in a plural society.

Both in North America and in Europe, gay persons claiming to be Muslims seek to articulate their faith in dialogue with homosexuals of other beliefs. These people have thus accepted a daunting double challenge. It is still an uphill struggle to persuade their fellow Muslims to accept them and their activities; it is equally arduous to sing the praises of their creed in a homosexual company which is well aware of the constraints imposed by the broader Muslim community and its leader-ship. Evidence is more difficult to collect in conservative societies, but there are strong indications that gay Muslims in places like Indonesia or Nigeria interact with their Christian counterparts in an atmosphere of shared repression and mutual encouragement.

Muslims are little engaged in the current debates about sexuality which have excited Christians in local contexts, like the proposed revision of the marriage canon in some Anglican dioceses or the risk that the Anglican Communion could disintegrate. On a national or regional scale, Muslims and Christians in dialogue are apt to share common cultural values to a sufficient degree that there will be an unspoken con-sensus. Whether this tacit understanding leans towards tolerance in the name of human rights or towards disapproval in keeping with local social conventions, participants will be sufficiently in tune with one another to avoid distraction from their more immediate agenda of social or theological concerns. In international meetings, Muslims and Christians are both apt to represent broad ranges of attitudes that will, on balance, have little effect on either the participants or the programme, given that the people who join such discussions are already used to tolerating major differences of doctrine on a vast range of topics from polygamy to priesthood.

Conclusion

In exploring the interrelationship of Islam and homosexuality, this essay has shown that there are Muslims of homosexual tendency in every part of the Islamic world, and that these people generally face serious diffi-culties in responding to their circumstances. The Qur'ân and the *ahâdîth* have a strongly negative attitude towards gay practices, although some individuals hope to develop a more indulgent exegesis. While it is pos-sible in western societies to affirm that one is both gay and Muslim, the persons who do so are usually excluded from most mosques and often expelled from their families and any other Islamic associations. In tradi-tional societies in Africa and Asia, homosexual activity has long existed on the margins, in certain limited situations, and many Islamic countries still have laws providing severe social and physical penalties for persons convicted of homosexual activities.

Because Muslims are in general agreement with their neighbours of other faiths on questions of tolerance and social norms, Christian debates about sexuality will have very little impact on interfaith dialogue, either in local forums or global gatherings. The agenda of inter-religious discussions will continue to focus locally on matters of contention, like the scope of the application of *sharî'ah* in the various states of northern Nigeria or the content of religious curricula in public schools in Europe and North America. Whether Islamic jurisprudence anywhere can develop a case for condoning or affirming homosexual practice remains a very distant prospect. Although there will certainly be groups of persons claiming to be gay and Muslim, they will continue to live on the margin of Islamic society for the immediate future. However the internal Islamic debate develops, interfaith dialogue will continue around the issues which commend themselves to the mainstream Muslim and Christian leaders in their several places of meeting.

NOTES

1. gaymuslims@yahoo.com; www.geocities.com/WestHollywoodheights/8977.
2. *Maclean's*, 11 October 2004, p.14.
3. *Toronto Globe and Mail*, 20 May 2004.
4. www.geocities.com?WestHollywood/3273/lnews1.html.
5. http://www.mask.org.za/Sections/AfricaPerCountry/abcnew/nigeria/nigeria_in ex.html (22 April 2002).
6. http://www.salaamcanada.org/links.html.
7. http://www.isim.nl.
8. http://www.sodomylaws.org/world/Nigeria.ninews010.html, 7 May 2004.
9. http://www.mask.org.za/Sections/AfricaPerCountry/senegal/html, January 2001.
10. http://www.kelma.org/pages/documents/association-homosexuel.php.
11. Kelly Cogswell, *Gay Muslims in the Post-Attack World*. http://www.thegully.com/essays/gaymundo/011027_gay_muslims.html.
12. http://www.salaamcanada.org/intro.html.
13. http://www.us.net/epf/pages/muslims.html.
14. http://www.well.com/user/queerjhd/aboutqj.html, 10 January 2003.
15. Dede Oetomo, 'We've Got to Live Life as Gay People', 1 February 1999; http://www.isim.nl.
16. http://www.kelma.org/pages/documents/turquie_gay.php. Interview with Philippe Blacher, 3 December 1997.
17. http://www.web.net/~jharnick2/aaa/muslimsu.html.
18. He was so quoted in an article by Stephanie Levitz, 'Canada's gay Muslims unite to celebrate their faith and their sexuality', http://www.recorder.ca/cp/national/030618/n061865A.html.
19. Tarek Fateh and Nargis Tapal, 'Do foes of gay marriages simply fear joy itself?' *Toronto Star*, 13 September 2003.
20. Anonymous letter quoted in Oetomo, op. cit.
21. http://www.sodomylaws.org/world/Nigeria/ninews010.html, dated 7 May 2004.
22. 'One Face of Gay Africa: Long Road Home', 4 December 2004; http://www.thegully.com/essays/africa/021204_traore_gay_afr_AIDS.html.
23. Lakshmi Chaudhry, 'Virtual Refuge for Gay Muslims', *Wired News*, 8 May 2000.
24. Quoted in Heidi Dietrich, 'To Be Gay and Muslim', 9 April 2002; http://www.allternet.org/story/12817.
25. Levitz, op. cit., 10 February 2003.
26. In the words of a Pakistani gay, who gives his name only as Danial, 20 May 2004, http://danial.pixelsndots.com/archives/000026.html.
27. Quoted in Dietrich, op. cit.

28. http://www.narth.com/docs/muslims.html. Updated 19 September 2004.
29. Dietrich, op. cit.
30. op. cit., 30 May 2004.
31. http://www/well.com/user/queerjhd/sxnonviolentlyhappy.htm.
32. Eric Beauchemin, 'The Nigerian Closet', 11 January 2002, in http://www2.rnw/en/features/humanrights/gays02011.html.
33. Dietrich, op. cit..
34. http://www.sympatico.ca/ross.fraser/Richard7.htm.
35. New York: Haworth Press, 1992.
36. ibid.
28. http://www.groups.yahoo.com.group/sami/files.

Chapter 10

MARCHING OR STUMBLING TOWARDS A CHRISTIAN ETHIC? HOMOSEXUALITY AND AFRICAN ANGLICANISM

Kevin Ward

Homosexuality as an issue within Africa

Before the 1990s homosexuality was hardly a topic within the ethical discourse of African churches. When addressed at all, it was widely understood as a marginal issue for Africa. In contrast, there is a long-standing and wide-ranging debate about the compatibility between Christian and African understandings of heterosexual activity and marriage. In this regard, all Christian churches in Africa have been faced with a dilemma. While seeking to enunciate clear moral standards of conduct, they have had to accept the reality that there is often no internal consent with those standards, even among their own membership, let alone in the wider society. The churches have a long history of conflict with traditional African cultures over issues of polygamy, marital infidelity and the position of women. The churches have also been rightly critical of modern social and economic trends which have loosened the stability of family life, and which have encouraged promiscuity and transient relationships. At times they have been less than honest in acknowledging that some of these problems have been exacerbated by Christianity itself, in encouraging increased mobility, delayed marriage, and more individualistic understandings of human relationships. In the face of modern threats to stable family life, the churches have often made a tactical alliance with traditional African cultural values, which, for all their defects, have been seen as providing certain guarantees for stable human relationships. Thus, for example, churches have often upheld the principle of bride price, and sought to ensure that traditional norms have been complied with before agreeing to a church wedding. In the last twenty years, awareness of AIDS as a major problem has added urgency to the sense of crisis in sexual relations in many parts of Africa.

Compared with these enormous issues, homosexuality appeared to be a very minor 'problem', seen by African Christians and African nationalists alike as 'unAfrican'. Where there was evidence of same-sex relations it was easily dismissed as an aberration, something to be explained away as a result of contact with the outside world. Thus the presence of homosexual activity at the courts of the Kabaka of Buganda or the Mwami of Rwanda could be put down to Arab influence; while homosexual relations in South African mines could, with some justification, be seen as a deleterious consequence of the system of migrant labour. Evidence of homosexual desire and activity in traditional cultures was passed over in silence or dismissed as trivial.

Post-apartheid South Africa

An increased focus on homosexuality came about quite suddenly in the mid-1990s and had two distinct causes. The first was the series of events which brought about the end of apartheid in South Africa, the democratic elections of 1994 and the making of a new constitution in 1996. In the violent, final years of the apartheid system, gay and lesbian campaigning groups had begun to emerge among both blacks and whites. Activists in the struggle returned after many years in exile. They were alert to the connections between the struggle against racial discrimination and the advancement of the rights of sexual minorities. The issue of sexuality was included in the discussions about the transition to a democratic South Africa and the new constitution outlawed discrimination on the ground of sexual orientation.[1]

The general climate of freedom in the new South Africa fostered for the first time a sense of being liberated to express gay identities. Both Desmond Tutu and Njongonkulu Ndungane, successive Anglican Archbishops of Cape Town, had taken prominent roles in the liberation struggle. They have been supportive of the extension of human rights and dignity to gay and lesbian people.[2] On the other hand, leaders in other parts of Africa were decidedly unhappy about the direction in which South Africa was going, dismissing homosexuality as a symptom of a degenerate western culture which Africa would be best to reject.

The Anglican debate

The other series of events that focused attention on homosexuality in Africa was the preparations for the Lambeth Conference of 1998. A large number of African Anglican leaders participated in the second 'Anglican Encounter in the South', which met in Kuala Lumpur, Malaysia, in 1997. The meeting was chaired by the Archbishop of Nigeria, Joseph Adetiloye, and came out with a strong statement about the incompatibility of homosexual practice and biblical teaching. It acknowledged the need for 'sensitive pastoral care', but this was in the context of an acknowledgement of sin and repentance.[3] Other preparatory meetings within Africa alerted more church leaders to the issues.[4] Notoriously, this issue dominated the 1998 Lambeth Conference, with African bishops taking a robust stance against any change to what they saw as traditional Christian teaching. Events since 1998 have only intensified that resolve on the part of African bishops outside South Africa to resist such changes. Both on their own initiative and in collaboration with 'orthodox' sections of the church in the North, African Anglican leaders have denounced 'revisionist' tendencies as subversive of biblical Christianity and the integrity of the Anglican Communion.[5] Archbishop Peter Akinola of Nigeria and, in Uganda, Archbishops Livingstone Nkoyooyo and Henry Orombi, clearly envisage a fracture of the Communion on this issue.

The voice of Nigeria and Uganda

As leaders of Anglican churches claiming 17 million and 8 million members respectively, the voices of the leaders of Nigerian and Ugandan Anglicans cannot easily be ignored. By comparison, the Church of the Province of Southern Africa, with its 2 million members, is much smaller both in absolute numbers and as a percentage of the total Christian communities in those countries. Both Akinola and Orombi have considerable experience in the West. Peter Akinola trained at the Virginia Theological Seminary in the United States. Henry Orombi did a degree at St John's College, Nottingham, in England, and was attached to Holy Trinity, Brompton, a centre of charismatic Anglicanism. Both are articulate and understandably resent the charge that they are acting as the mouthpiece of northern conservatives, though they would acknowledge a strong sense of common identity with evangelical and charismatic forms of Anglicanism in the North. They represent important strands of spirituality, nurtured over many years, within their own churches.

Orombi comes from the East African Revival tradition known as the Balokole, with its emphasis on repentance, public confession of sin, a strict moral ethic, honesty and openness and fearlessness in denouncing sin within the church. One of the crucial characteristics of the Balokole movement, which began in the 1930s, has been its loyalty to the Anglican Church – even when it might have been tempted to form its own purer form of evangelical Christianity.

The Anglican Church in Nigeria shares with Uganda an evangelical heritage imparted by the Church Missionary Society. In the 1920s and 1930s, the Yoruba heartland of Nigerian Anglicanism also experienced spiritual revival. But, in contrast to the Balokole movement, many revivalists left the Anglican Church to establish a number of independent churches – the *Aladura* or praying churches. Partly in reaction to these schisms, Nigerian Anglicans tend to be conservative about their evangelical heritage, particularly in worship and liturgy, much more so than the churches of East Africa. Unlike the Anglican churches of East and

Southern Africa they have resisted the ordination of women. In the 1960s, during a time of great disturbance during the civil war, many young Nigerian Anglicans were influenced by the charismatic spirituality that they encountered in high schools through the Scripture Union. Some left the mission-founded churches to become leaders in the new Pentecostal or charismatic churches. But many stayed within the Anglican Church and are now in positions of leadership.

The charismatic/Pentecostal movement is a major new force in Christianity throughout Africa. Although Anglicanism in Africa remains distinctive, it is being radically transformed by its influence.[6] African charismatic Christianity is characterised by its global networking, its utilisation of technology, its participation in a worldwide youth musical culture, and the influence of conservative American theological literature, which is distributed much more effectively and cheaply than traditional Anglican/Protestant theological or devotional literature. But, it is also strongly assertive of African identity and leadership, and can be outspoken in its criticism of the colonial legacy and of forms of neo-colonialism. For example, Archbishop Akinola's initial comment on the Windsor Report was that it 'fails to confront the reality that a small, economically privileged group of people has sought to subvert the Christian faith and impose their new and false doctrine on the wider community of faithful believers'.[7]

One characteristic of the new charismatic Christianity is that it engages much more directly than older forms of Protestant Christianity with African beliefs in the power of the spirit world, but uncompromisingly denounces those spirits as demonic, and negated by the power of the Holy Spirit. While there is little evidence to suggest that this new Christianity was any more focused on the dangers of homosexuality than the older churches before the 1990s it is clear that the spiritual warfare can easily be extended to the 'demon' of homosexuality too.[8] The globalisation of charismatic Christianity implies awareness that there are global lifestyles which are identified as anti-Christian.

A variety of homosexual practice has always been present in Africa for as long as there have been human communities on the continent. An awareness of homosexuality as a defining expression of a person's nature and identity is a relatively new phenomenon. The demand for recognition of this new identity is even more recent. Like Pentecostalism, gay identities are shaped by participation in a global culture and are almost unimaginable without that participation. Yet both Pentecostal and gay identities struggle to assert their 'Africanness', and to receive public recognition as 'authentic' African modes of being. Outside of South Africa, neither society nor church is yet ready to accord that status as far as homosexuality is concerned.

The problem of church discipline in the Church of Uganda

The current global Anglican crisis has served to stifle real debate about homosexuality as a Christian ethical issue for African Christianity. This is the more regrettable because it gives a false impression that everything to do with sexuality is cut and dried, done and dusted, in the church in Africa. But this is far from the case. The experience of African Christians is overwhelmingly that there are no easy answers to questions of human sexual relations, that neither rigorous nor permissive stances can of themselves resolve the intractable mystery of human love, desire and community. In the face of that mystery, Anglicans have always been reluctant to foreclose the issues. Even when they have insisted on clear-cut and difficult standards of personal morality, and the shaming of those who do not keep those standards, they have recognised that there must be some room for tolerance, that the arena of sexuality is not one of compulsion but of freedom. The strict standards of the church are consistently tempered by the pastoral need to care for those who do not keep the standard. But beyond that, there is the common sense of the community that, whatever the teachings of the church, there is more to life than morality. People find themselves in situations and relationships which preclude them, in practical terms, from finding satisfactory solutions which precisely fit the approved pattern of Christian discipleship. The Anglican Church has traditionally recognised this, implicitly, if not in its public teaching.

To take the Anglican Church of Uganda as an example, although smaller in overall numbers than the Church of Nigeria, it has perhaps the largest proportion of Anglican adherents anywhere in the world – 40 per cent of the total population.[9] Inevitably there have been longstanding tensions between the church's role as a folk church representing the community as a whole, and its desire to be the gathered community of Christ's faithful people over against the wider community. The Balokole tradition, from which the great majority of the bishops come, manifests an uncompromising, straight-talking, undeviating witness to the demands of Christian discipleship, critical of the church's seemingly inexhaustible attempts to compromise. Bishops tread a delicate path between their commitment to Revival values and their recognition of responsibilities, as bishops, to the whole body. The Church of Uganda as a whole embodies a more flexible and tolerant attitude than the Balokole. Polygamists, and those living in marriages not sanctioned by the church, may be denied Holy Communion, but they are certainly not excluded from the church community as such.

The reality is that only a minority of Anglican Christians in many parts of Uganda are communicant members of the church. The main reason for their status as non-communicants is that their marriages or their relationships are not recognised as holy matrimony. For many years the Church of Uganda had a strict baptismal policy by which only children born 'within wedlock' could be baptised; given the low rate of church marriage, this effectively disqualified the majority of children. In 1973 a new canon on baptism was introduced which opened baptism to all. Many Balokole lamented the dilution of the standard. But even Balokole are divided between the demands of strictness and of inclusiveness. Attempts to admit to Communion all members of the church, even if their marriages were not in order, have been resisted. Indeed many Christians willingly assent to their exclusion, recognising that the church has, and ought to have, standards which they cannot fulfil, but still wanting to remain part of the church, and still overwhelmingly accepted as such by the Christian community at large. Even strict Balokole reluctantly accept them as 'Christian', even if they are '*abebafu*', sleeping Christians. While at first the AIDS pandemic did carry with it a stigma, and it is still felt improper to talk openly of people dying of AIDS, there has been a strong shift in the public teaching of the church away from denunciation of sexual offenders to a care and compassion for those living with AIDS; and a greater recognition of the need for societal change rather than putting the emphasis entirely on individual sin and guilt.[10]

Attitudes to homosexuality in Uganda

As Sylvia Tamale, a Ugandan lawyer and academic, puts it, 'The HIV/AIDS Pandemic has in many ways flung open the doors on sexuality. In particular, it has forced into the open the myths and secrets in relationships and identities that are often silenced or taken for granted.'[11]

Tamale's study shows that in Uganda there are networks of people who recognise themselves as gay and lesbian, operating in rural as well as urban settings, among the poor and uneducated, as well as in professional classes. They tend to be concerned with support and self-protection rather than with campaigning for acceptance and esteem. This is partly because of the strength of anti-gay sentiment which surfaced in 1999 when President Museveni spoke out against a supposed gay marriage in Kampala and in 2003 when Sylvia Tamale and a section of Uganda's women's movement approached the Equal Opportunities Commission to encourage them to consider seriously the status of homosexuals. The group was urged not to jeopardise its gains for the rights of women by getting involved in this unpopular subject. One of the deeply unfortunate aspects of the present situation in Uganda is that colonial laws criminalising male homosexual behaviour, never much used in colonial times and forgotten for most of the thirty years of Uganda's independence, have been given a new prominence. The profession of a gay identity, once tolerated as mildly eccentric, is now dangerous and liable to life imprisonment.[12]

During this time, the Church of Uganda was involved in its own high-profile conflicts, first over the condemnation of Bishop Christopher Senyonjo, retired Bishop of West Buganda, for his support for Integrity, a newly formed Ugandan Anglican lesbian and gay organisation. After the fall of Amin in 1979, Senyonjo had achieved some notoriety in the church for asking the question of whether the church needed to take a more understanding attitude to polygamy, given the large number of widows in the aftermath of war. He was also seen as dangerously liberal in his attitude to the old gods of Buganda – the Balubaale – whom, he argued, might be considered as having an angelic rather than a demonic status. But perhaps the most important reason for the virulence of the church persecution of Integrity was its links with the American Episcopalian organisation Integrity. The abrasive style and lack of deference of its campaigners on visits to Uganda have been taken as examples of a neo-colonial, patronising style and the assumption that Integrity is little more than a proselytising arm of an American gay mafia.

Certainly the House of Bishops showed no sympathy for Integrity Uganda or for Bishop Senyonjo. They characterised homosexuality as unscriptural and anti-human. The perception that Integrity Uganda was overly dominated by its American backers, at least in its rhetoric and modus operandi, was not wholly without foundation. It illustrates the importance of the Ugandan movement's developing in accordance with its own needs, but also highlights the problem of 'extroversion' – the need for a weak and struggling local organisation to find international backers.

The ill-will created by the dispute between Senyonjo and Archbishop Nkoyooyo has had its ramifications in the 2004 spat between Archbishop Orombi and Louie Crew, a prominent member of the Episcopal Church of the USA and founding member of Integrity USA. Crew had a few years earlier antagonised Orombi's predecessor, Archbishop Nkoyooyo. Crew had brought up the issue of Uganda's treatment of gay people when he was part of an Episcopal Church delegation gathered in Kampala to discuss ways of helping the Episcopal Church in the Sudan. In 2004, Crew pointed out that the Church of Uganda was claiming to have cut off all ties with the Episcopal Church for its ordination to the episcopate of Gene Robinson, but did indeed continue to receive financial help. This provoked Archbishop Orombi to decide on a radical cutting of all the ties with the Episcopal Church:

> One of the hallmarks of the East African Revival . . . is 'walking in the light'. On 20 November 2003 the Church of Uganda broke

communion with ECUSA until it repents of its actions in approv-
ing and consecrating as bishop a man in an actively homosexual
relationship. Furthermore, we have taken the position that, as a
result of broken communion, we will not take any financial gifts
from ECUSA.[13]

Accordingly a number of dioceses had decided to withdraw their request
for grants from the United Thank Offering of Episcopal Women.
Archbishop Orombi talked of working with the 'faithful remnant of
Anglicans in America'.

The African proverb 'When the elephants fight the grass suffers'
seems appropriate in understanding the effect on the lesbian and gay
community within Uganda. Despite claiming a pastoral role in relation
to homosexuals, there seems little willingness to tolerate within the
church those who are open about their identity. The attempt of Bishop
Senyonjo to provide counselling and support services at his small
'clinic' in Bukoto, a suburb of Kampala, is neither recognised nor supported by the church. Almost certainly gay people are members of the
church – as long as they are not open about their sexuality. Indeed, those
who are in married relationships or those who have not married and are
not living with partners of the other sex, are more likely to be able to par-
take of Holy Communion than many heterosexuals, whose partnerships
may not be sanctioned by the church. But the impossibility of openness
or honesty cannot be regarded as a satisfactory solution for a church
whose revival tradition puts such a great store on 'walking in the light'.

The traditional position of the Church of Uganda, with its toleration
of two tiers of membership, is difficult to defend theologically. Yet it has
enabled an inclusive church to thrive. It has created a church which has
some claims to take discipleship seriously and yet one which is not simply the gathered community of the saints. It provides a forum in which
the casual believer can be confronted with the demands of the Gospel.
However, the idea of a church consisting of some, the minority, who are
'saints' and the rest who are 'sinners', must be seen as unsatisfactory in
so far as it fosters spiritual pride and complacency. The Balokole, with
their emphasis on honesty and humility, are less likely than most to be
guilty of pride and complacency as individuals. Nevertheless, as a movement, the Revival finds it difficult wholly to overcome its sense of
superiority with regard to ordinary Christians. Ordinary Christians may
reciprocate these attitudes. The Balokole are often resented for their dis-
dain for, and lack of participation in, many of the traditional rites which
bind the wider society together and give it savour.

The present problem for gay people is that they feel rejected by both
groups. Within the Revival, a genuine struggle to understand their sex-

uality is unlikely to receive sympathy and support unless the outcome is predetermined as a renunciation of homosexuality. On the other hand, Sylvia Tamale's researches seem to suggest that there is hardly more sympathy among ordinary Christians, or in society as a whole, at the moment. Heterosexual transgression may be widely tolerated but homosexuality is despised and feared. Moreover, homosexuality has become entangled in the popular mind with issues of child abuse and 'violation'. Women's campaigning groups have put these issues on the agenda in recent Ugandan thinking.[14] On the other hand newspapers like *New Vision* and *Monitor* have a good record for sane and rational discussion on gay issues, critical of both political and religious leaders for a disproportionate moral outrage.

In the light of the lack of sympathy among Anglican church leaders, gay people may increasingly go elsewhere. The gay support groups described by Tamale may emerge as religious communities in their own right. Contemporary Uganda is no longer dominated by the old duopoly of Anglican (Protestant) and Catholic. Catholics are as clear in their condemnation as the Anglicans, though in a less frenetic way, and are less likely to regard the presence of gay people as a provocation. The new Pentecostalism is no more sympathetic to gay people than the Anglicans but Pentecostalism is diverse in organisation and doctrine and it is certainly possible to conceive of Pentecostal-like Christian fellowships emerging which are hospitable to gay people.

The South African experience: pastoral care

It would be incorrect to assume that because the political climate in South Africa is so liberal and the hierarchy of the Anglican church generally so supportive, the situation for gay and lesbian people is a welcoming one. The growing evangelical and Pentecostal movement in South Africa is deeply upset by the liberalism of the constitution, and a Christian political party, so far with little success, tries to roll back some of the human rights gains in the area of personal morality (gay rights and abortion, as well as unease about the abolition of the death penalty).[15] But that discrimination against homosexuals and other sexual minorities is illegal is of great importance in promoting toleration and recognition. The supportive stance of the Anglican Church (irrespective of the still unresolved issue of the ordination of gay people) allows the church to have a ministry to gay people. But there are South African Anglicans who are disturbed by the warm support for gay issues of the hierarchy and who have formed Anglican Mainstream Southern Africa to promote what they see as a more orthodox position:

It seems to many that over the past few months, there have been frequent pronouncements in the media by people perceived to be speaking on behalf of the CPSA, which clearly advocate support for full acceptance of homosexual practice as a valid option for Christians . . .

We fear that, by appearing to condone one aspect of sexual immorality, the church will lose the right to speak with authority on other moral issues, and our relationship with other Christian churches in Southern Africa and the world will be compromised.[16]

The Open Letter is deliberately phrased in a moderate way, emphasising an absence of homophobia, a willingness to engage in discussion, and a concern for justice – illustrating the different sensibilities operating in Southern Africa in comparison with Nigeria or Uganda.

Busangokwakhe Dlamini has worked for many years as an activist and counsellor of gay people in the Kwazulu-Natal Midlands area. This was an area much affected by the violence between rival Africa National Congress and Inkatha gangs during the 1980s, a time of social disruption and the disintegration of many traditional values and also the forging of new patterns of relationship and community. Young people who had previously felt guilty of homosexual inclinations and who tried to conform to their family and society's expectations now found it both necessary and easier to identify themselves as gay. As Dlamini shows, gay people often remain puzzled about the nature and implications of their sexual orientation. They have little more than the 'negative stereotypes that pervade contemporary society' and are frightened and isolated. They need reassurance and encouragement, especially from their families who may themselves feel confused and disorientated. Dlamini urges the church to challenge the 'normative assumptions' which pervade society, to 'ferment new values for a new community', 'new symbols for living as Christians':

> The patterns of Christian living are as demanding as the older ones. It is precisely because the same principles underlie all true discipleship that basic Christian communities now have a greater opportunity to cherish and nourish those individuals and groups who are involved in new patterns of Christian living. If this is to happen, then, the church and congregations must become inclusive not exclusive; open to new ideas and not closed to the different just because they are unfamiliar.[17]

The need for biblical and theological debate

As yet the churches in Nigeria and Uganda have not really begun to give serious thought to how the church can actually help gay people and their families. Even from a theologically conservative perspective this ought to be done. It may not satisfy those who wish for a profound revolution in the churches' thinking. But it would at least show that the church was not content simply to denounce homosexuals as subhuman or as peculiarly sinful. In the rhetoric about the apostasy of the American Episcopal Church, homosexual practice has been likened to a new form of slavery. If this is more than blatant polemic, there needs to be serious study of ways in which sexuality can become enslavement – a research which is likely to show that this is as much, if not more, a problem of heterosexual practice. There must also be serious engagement with the links (so clear in South Africa, less so elsewhere) between racism, homophobia and enslavement.

Equally there needs to be serious biblical study, from within an African context, on homosexuality. Archbishop Akinola properly rejects arguments that biblical teaching can be ignored and that the Bible is 'only for primitive people'. Yet it has to be recognised that the application of the Bible to contemporary ethical issues is not straightforward; that there has always been room for difference of opinion on what the text says and how it is applied in a particular context. This does not preclude the church from making statements about the limits of appropriate faith and practice, and for insisting on compliance. But it must also make provision for principled questioning of those beliefs and practices. The old Reformation principle applies here – *Ecclesia semper reformanda*. Not to engage in critical enquiry is to make an idol of the church. Even when the present crisis within the worldwide Anglican Communion has been resolved, or the Communion has fractured, this task must be undertaken within African Anglicanism. This is why the witness of the Church in South Africa is important for the rest of the Anglican Communion on the continent.

One particular pastoral issue presents itself to be of very great importance and is alluded to in Dlamini's studies. This is the intense traditional African emphasis on children as central to human worth and the continuity of society, an emphasis which is prominent in the Bible too. Many gay people have as a great difficulty as their families and friends in coming to terms with a sexuality which cannot be legitimated in terms of children. Yet the biblical message is one of hope for the 'barren', of the grace of God which transcends the natural. Christianity has been crucial in spreading less instrumentalist views of human relationships and it is of great importance that gay people also hear this message of human worth.

A number of urgent issues emerge from the present situation. The first is the need for amendment of laws which criminalise homosexual behaviour between consenting adults. The South African experience

shows that, until this happens, the toleration of homosexual people is not
likely to make much headway. The church also needs to make good its
claim to welcome all people, regardless of their sexuality. *Carte blanche*
denunciations of homosexuality and of people who are homosexual are
likely to be simply counterproductive. Even a church which teaches the
incompatibility of sexual activity outside marriage acknowledges large
groups of people for whom it is difficult or impossible to achieve
Christian marriage. But homosexuality has not yet been included in this
category of states of life which, while not ideal, are nevertheless
tolerated within the community. The present sense of crisis within the
Anglican Communion has inhibited the expression of even mildly
exploratory or dissenting views among African Anglicans outside South
Africa. A climate of theological enquiry needs to be fostered, in which
issues of homosexuality can be integrated into the more general
discussion of sexuality in Africa.

The Quiet Violence of Dreams

Important aspects of the African experience of being gay are encapsu-
lated in the novel, *The Quiet Violence of Dreams* by a black South
African writer, Sello Duiker.[18] It tells the story of a young student,
Tshepo. Confused about his gay identity, committed for a time to an
asylum, misunderstood and abused by others as he tries to make a life
for himself, he eventually experiences an inner liberation which mirrors
the transformations taking place in South Africa. He discovers in
Johannesburg the vitality of Africa as a whole in the Nigerian,
Senegalese and Congolese migrants who have flocked there and who are
as unwelcome as gay people have been in the past.

> I don't care for purists. They are dangerous and full of lies ... I
> don't care for people who want to prescribe what it means and
> doesn't mean to be African ... I am who I am ...
>
> The nature of change is violent. It goes without saying that
> blood will be spilled. But there is the sunnier side to consider, the
> sunnier side of fresh beginnings ...
>
> When I look at the children I work with, mostly black, with
> some coloured and white faces, I sense that God can't be one story.
> He is a series of narratives. And He is watching.
>
> I am leaving behind life as I know it. Great changes await us. All
> the hatred and disappointment is falling away. We must think of
> each other, about how we fell, and what we will do to comfort each
> other. I am tired of pointing fingers, of assigning blame.[19]

Tshepo's experiences take him far from conventional Christianity. But
his experience is a powerful one for all the churches if they want to

speak the Good News to the great diversity of men and women of different peoples, ethnicities and sexualities in a new Africa.

NOTES
1. See Sheila Croucher, 'South Africa's Democratisation and the Politics of Gay Liberation', *Journal of Southern African Studies* 28:2 (Oxford: Carfax, June 2002), pp.315–30.
2. See, for example, Tutu's foreword to Paul Germond and Steve de Gruchy (eds), *Aliens in the Household of God: Homosexuality and Christian Faith in South Africa* (Cape Town: Philip, 1997).
3. Kuala Lumpur Statement, 1997.
4. For example, a Great Lakes Conference in Kampala, Uganda, in June 1998.
5. The contrast between 'orthodox' and 'revisionist' has become the language of choice for conservative leaders in the 'north' in their discussions of the events surrounding the ordination of Gene Robinson as bishop.
6. For a discussion of the complexities and variety of this phenomenon, see Paul Gifford, *Ghana's New Christianity: Pentecostalism in a Globalising African Economy* (London: Hurst, 2004).
7. Statement on Windsor Report, 19 October 2004, http://www.americananglican.org.
8. Neither Gifford's recent study on Ghana nor a recent PhD dissertation on the development of charismatic Christianity in the Igbo region of Nigeria would suggest that homosexuality as such was seen as a great issue before the late 1990s. See Richard Burgess, 'The Civil War Revival and its Pentecostal Progeny ... among the Igbo People of Eastern Nigeria 1967–2002', PhD dissertation, Birmingham University, 2004.
9. The 1991 Population and Housing Census, Uganda, in David Barrett *et al.*, *Uganda Christian Encylopedia* (Oxford: Oxford University Press, 2001), Vol. I, p.762.
10. For a discussion of Ugandan issues on marriage, see my article, 'Same-Sex Relations in Africa and the Debate on Homosexuality in East African Anglicanism', *Anglican Theological Review* 84:1 (Winter 2002), 81–111.
11. Sylvia Tamale, 'Out of the Closet: Unveiling Sexuality Discourses in Uganda', *Feminist Africa,* Issue 2 (2003). See http://www.feministafrica.org.
12. Amnesty International, *Breaking the Silence: Human Rights Violations Based on Sexual Orientation* (London: Amnesty International, 1997), p.89.
13. Statement from the Archbishop of the Church of the Province of Uganda, 23 September 2004. See http://www.americananglican.org.
14. A. M. Tripp and J. C. Kwesiga, *The Women's Movement in Uganda* (Kampala: Fountain Press, 2002).
15. Anthony Balcomb, 'From Apartheid to the New Dispensation: Evangelicals and the Democratization of South Africa', *Journal of Religion in Africa*, 34 (Leiden: Brill, 2004), 1–2.
16. http:///www.anglican-mainstream.org.za: 'An Open Letter to the Bishops of the CPSA from Anglican Mainstream Southern Africa, November 2004'.
17. B. D. J. Dlamini, 'Contextual and Theological Factors Influencing Pastoral Ministry with Families of Gays in the Black Society of Kwazulu-Natal Midlands'. This is work being undertaken for the PhD degree at the University of Kwazulu-Natal at Pietermaritzburg.
18. K. Sello Duiker, *The Quiet Violence of Dreams* (Cape Town: Kwela Books, 2001).
19. ibid., pp.438, 455–6.

Chapter 11

KENYA REFLECTIONS

Esther Mombo

In the current constitution of Kenya sodomy is a crime. During the review of the constitution a clause on sexual freedom in the draft constitution raised a storm when it came up for debate. The Penal Code indirectly touches on homosexuality as an unnatural offence and states:

> Any person who has carnal knowledge of any person against the order of nature or b) has carnal knowledge of an animal, c) permits a male person to have carnal knowledge of him or her against the order of nature is guilty of felony and is liable to imprisonment for 14 years with or without corporal punishment.[1]

The two key phrases in the above provision are 'carnal knowledge' and 'against the order of nature'. From this one would assume that what Kenyan law is really concerned about is not 'homosexuality' as such, but anal intercourse in both the heterosexual and the homosexual contexts. While the legal aspects of homosexuality may be left for the law courts to interpret and decide, homosexuality is still one of those things that people do not talk about openly. Yet the general public's silence on homosexuality does not mean that this sexual style is non-existent in Africa, as popular opinion would have us believe. The truth is that homosexuality exists in Africa even in the most sacred echelons.

I have taken the liberty of quoting below the testimony of a college student in Kenya. I have personally talked with him and have his kind permission to cite the true episode. I am the 'Academic Dean' in the story. The student's story is as follows:

> Some bishops shout loudly that homosexuality is western. I wonder how much they truly know about homosexuality. Homosexuality is not western or African. It is a human issue. I too used to think that homosexuality is western until I went through the following experience.
>
> When I joined college, I was young and green. Most members of the community welcomed me. At the halls of residence, my neighbour was very helpful. He talked to me and was willing to give me information I needed. He was a good speaker and to me a very disciplined man. He did his work well and always attended all

the services of worship including revival meetings and he played a
key role in these meetings. I got to know him and I learnt that he
was involved in ministry having had earlier training.

One day my friend asked me to accompany him to the city so
that he could show me places that I did not know. I accepted the
invitation. We left the college in the middle of the day and we went
to the city. We went to several places and he introduced me to some
of his friends. It was getting late and I wondered when we would
return to the college. He assured me that we would return or stay
in the city and return the following day to college. We had our
evening meal and were not able to return to college. He told me
that he would get a place for us to sleep. He hired a room and we
went to stay. When we went to the room, and it was time to sleep,
I realised what my friend was up to. I was shocked and afraid, and
wondered what was going to happen to me. My friend argued with
me but whatever he said, he could not convince me to have an
affair with him. I was angry and wanted to escape but he had
locked the room and hidden the key. Like a prisoner I stayed the
night and was glad to see the morning. In the morning we went
back to the college and I was very angry. I wanted to share with
someone because I thought the college must know who this man is
and if they saw me with him they will conclude I was the same.

I shared with a priest who listened to me but did not help me
much. I went to share with one member of the college administration who also did not help me. I then chose to speak to the
Academic Dean. For over four hours I shared my experience and
we sought for ways of dealing with the issue because it was a
sensitive one. In my anger, I wanted to stand up in the college
chapel and denounce this man so that it is known that I am not
associated with him, and also to ensure that he does not do this to
anyone else at the college. The dean talked me out of this but
helped me to understand the situation. I did not understand why
she was sympathetic and understanding and she helped me to see
that denouncing Jim in public would not help him or me either.

After meeting with the dean, I went to my room and slept until
the following day. I was feeling better although the matter was still
in my mind. The dean had told me that it will take a while before
I could look at the matter differently. True, any time I heard people
talk on the issue I was angry. Since I had shared with more than
one person the matter got to be known. Some people wanted to use
the issue to punish Jim and they threatened me. But when I told
them that I had already shared with the Academic Dean they feared
what she would do. Other members of staff asked me and I

narrated the story as it was. But I did not wish to punish Jim. He continued with his studies, he remained friendly to me but I feared him. I wondered what he was doing to others who did not know his nature. He finished his studies and left. But even if I met him today, I would not feel free to associate with him. Now I understand what his nature was and am able to discuss the matter freely.

I was still haunted by the episode and wondered whether I was the only one who had gone through this experience. Through some research I discovered that my next-door neighbour in the hall had been through a similar experience. He had been taken to the city and taken to the same spot but a fight broke out and he escaped. He did not make the matter public because he did not want to be associated with him in case students thought he was of the same group. But because Jim was a very good preacher, my neighbour invited him to go and speak to a youth group in his home church. They had to share a house and a fight broke out too in this house because Jim made passes to him. When they returned to the college my neighbour decided not to associate with Jim anymore.

I would wish to let those who are denying the issue of homosexuality to be African to stop and think. If they wish to deal with it, they better see it as a human issue and know that they are talking about real people who are right around us.

From the above episode it becomes evident that homosexuality is not a western issue but a human issue. In these reflections, I wish to look at three areas. First what I have already noted above, that homosexuality is a human issue. Second, if we are going to use the Bible on this issue, we should use it as a whole, not in part. Finally, I shall discuss the reactions from some sections of the church leadership that Africa should not be critiqued; rather, I argue that Africa should not be taken as divine.

Homosexuality is a human issue

Homosexuality transcends cultures and continents. It has been there since the history of humankind began. Writing in 1972, John S. Mbiti observed:

> Fornication, incest, rape, homosexual relations, bestiality ... All constitute sexual offences in a given community ... African people are very sensitive to any departure from the accepted norm concerning all aspects of sex. This is a fundamentally religious attitude, since any offence upsets the smooth relationships of the community, which include those who have already departed. For that reason many of the offences must be followed by a ritual cleansing after physical punishment otherwise misfortune may ensue.[2]

Those who argue that homosexuality is 'not African' might just be wanting to sweep the issue under the carpet. For Mbiti homosexuality was not really absent in African societies; only it was considered a 'sexual offence'. Others besides Mbiti have also documented homosexuality in Africa.[3] Alice Walker in her *Possessing the Secrets of Joy* seems to be lenient on this issue. In a West African context a character advises Tashi, the heroine of the novel, who has recently been circumcised, to try anal intercourse as 'boys do it all the time'. Thus, while there may not be precise words for homosexuality in African languages, one cannot argue that homosexual sexual preference was totally alien to African societies.

Homosexuality in Africa can be considered at two levels: verifiable data and not-so-verifiable data. The *first* category is that of verifiable data. We know what happened among the gold-miners in South Africa, how these men living away from their families entered into same-sex bonding. In the words of Kevin Ward, 'male–male sexual relationships became institutionalised'.[4] We also recall the behaviour of Kabaka Buganda and how he sexually harassed his pages. Ironically, at that time it was the western missionaries who laid their life on the line to protest against a rather shameful episode of homosexuality in Africa. A few years ago there was the famous trial of the Rev. Canaan Banana, the former president of Zimbabwe, on charges that while in power he had sexually harassed his own aide-de-camp. Banana denied the charge and was eventually acquitted. A few years ago the *Standard* newspaper in Kenya carried the story of a young man, Kamau, who had 'married' an old white man in Britain and how he (Kamau) proudly introduced himself as '*mama wa nymbani*' (mother of the house). Jonah Anguka in his infamous book *Absolute Power* has narrated his own ordeal in a Kenyan prison, giving a graphic picture of ongoing homosexuality in our prisons. According to Anguka, there are two classes of homosexuals in the prisons – *mtoto* (wife) and *mende* (husband).[5]

Our purpose in the above quick run of qualitative data is twofold. First, it is to show that homosexuality is not all that foreign to Africa. Second, it is to show that somehow the known episodes of homosexuality in Africa appear largely of the negative type. The kind of affectionate bonding in the stories of Kamau and the South African miners is apparently usually not there. The picture of homosexuality in Africa brings to mind the picture of a predator Kabaka, or a depraved prisoner, or a rogue college senior, who sees nothing beyond satisfying his own lust. This factor could offer another reason for the generally negative response to homosexuality by the African church.

Then, of course, there is data that cannot always be verified. Such data is available on the Internet. I searched the Internet using such codes as 'gay', 'flirt' 'Africa', 'M4M', 'MSM', 'Homosexual', 'F4F', 'FSF',

'W4W' and 'WSW'.[6] Following are some of the indicators of the possible prevalence of homosexuality in Africa. According to the Google search engine, 316,000 'hits' for 'Men Seeking Men Kenya' were returned. There were 360,000 returned for 'Women Seeking Women Kenya'.

The website known as 'AdultFriendFinder' claims listings on the Kenyan homosexuality scene for 'Men Seeking Men Kenya' (313 listings), 'Men Seeking Couples' (2 men) (24 listings), 'Women Seeking Women' (203 listings) and 'Women Seeking Couples' (2 women) (52 listings). Another meta-search engine called 'Gay Crawler' offers to roll out eleven 'directories' at the disposal of the searcher for homosexuality in Africa. Several other websites, for example, 'GayEgypt.com', 'Metrodate.com', 'Expatriates.com', 'eGay.com', and 'GayUniverse .com', claim to contain listings on homosexual persons in various African countries. Finally, there is the website 'SMS.ac' which has a 'Flirt' section. It contains a 'Men Seeking Men' directory for some twenty African countries. Each of these countries contains profiles in excess of at least 100 men seeking men in Africa.

The above data might seem overwhelming to 'prove' the presence of homosexuality in Africa. However, such a conclusion would require the following caveats: (1) most of the above websites are commercial and not academic, hence their objectivity and accuracy cannot always be established; (2) the 'hits' obtained from search engines are based merely on electronic matching of words and might not necessarily be indicative of homosexuality as a concept in Africa; (3) it is probable that many subscribers to these 'lists' might be expatriate residents in Africa, and not native Africans; and (4) as we noted earlier, the accuracy of information on the Internet cannot be easily verified. For example, there is virtually nothing to stop a 67-year-old heterosexual man posting a notice on the Internet posing as a 21-year-old woman, and soliciting same-sex partners. However, even with the above caveats on homosexuality-specific websites, our original argument still remains: homosexuality is not just a western or African issue, it is a human issue.[7]

We need the whole of the Bible

The debate on the homosexuality issue has brought to the surface a fundamental difference of approach to biblical authority. The question often asked by bishops who speak publicly on this issue is, 'How can the Americans do what they did and still claim to be following the Bible? How do they even begin such a conversation?'

The Bible is always quoted as being against homosexuality and, yes, there are portions of Scripture that are used for that. But in most cases the application of biblical passages is selective and arbitrary. For example, there would be quick condemnation of homosexual priests on the grounds that they are 'unbiblical'. True enough, but if we are trying to apply the biblical directives to priests, then should we not apply the entire biblical code rather than only those passages that apply to homosexuality alone? For example, Leviticus 21:1–24 provides a complete code for priests. It commands that:

- Priests should not trim their sideburns or their beards.
- They should not marry non-virgins, widows or divorcees.
- They must only marry within the clan.
- They should not be blind or lame or have a limb too long or too short.
- They should not have an impaired leg or hand.
- They should not be hunchbacked.
- They should not be too thin or small.
- They should not have deficient eyesight.
- They should have no skin disease and no physical defects.

We all know that if the church applied the above biblical strictures at the time of ordination, we would lose about 80 per cent of our priests for one reason or another! How do we decide that these regulations that are explicitly for ordination are not relevant today, but the prohibitions about homosexual acts are? If we have chosen certain aspects because of changing times, then the criterion should apply to both. Why should we single out the prohibition against male-to-male intercourse in the Holiness Code while ignoring other stipulations in the same Holiness Code, for example, the mixing of grain or fibre, various dietary regulations, etc? What about other sins, for example, the sins of adultery, lies, pride, gluttony, excess wealth, indifference to the poor and inhospitality?

In fact the Bible condemns sin in both the heterosexual as well as the homosexual contexts. In other words, the Bible condemns both heterosexual and homosexual lust. In one interpretation, it was this lust that motivated the perverted men of Sodom to want to gang rape Lot's male visitors. God justly answered them with fire and brimstone (Genesis 19:1–14). It was perhaps this lust of men having sexual intercourse with other men that the author of the Book of Leviticus saw as an 'abomination' worthy of death (Leviticus 18:22 and 20:13). It was this lust that would motivate men to lie with male prostitutes in Canaanite temples, and pay them wages for their sexual services. The God of Israel sternly rejected the offering of such shameful wages earned by unscrupulous Israelite youths in the flesh market (Deuteronomy 23:17–18). It was perhaps because of this lust that Paul and his disciple Timothy included the 'male prostitutes' (Greek, *arsenokoitai*) in their lists of shame (1 Corinthians 6:9–19 and 1 Timothy 1:9–11). Paul summarises this position in his famous condemnation of men who were 'consumed with passion for one another' in Romans 1:18–32. This, in summary, is the biblical condemnation of homosexual lust.

Having condemned homosexual lust, the Bible also condemns hetero-sexual lust – the sins of adultery, fornication and rape – in equally strong terms. Indeed the Ten Commandments, having made no reference to homosexuality, still condemn adultery, which is a heterosexual sin. As Malcolm Macourt observes, 'Almost 90 percent of all murders commit-ted in England are, in one form or another, heterosexual crimes of passion.'[8] Thus, heterosexual persons cannot escape God's judgement simply because they are not homosexual.

The Bible here condemns both homosexual and heterosexual lust. This then leads me to put forward another point as concerns the Bible on the gay issue: we do not need only some selected parts of the Bible, we need the whole of the Bible.

For Christians the purpose of the Bible is fulfilled in the single task of revealing Christ and his salvific work. In this the Bible is a priceless asset for every Christian. It also contains divine guidance for successful human conduct. In that, it is priceless to Christians and non-Christians alike. However, the use of the Bible entails the temptation that at times we might be choosing what to follow in it just to suit our own tastes. We might claim to follow the Bible, but need to remember that merely following the Bible does not make one a Christian. As far as following the Bible is concerned, many non-Christians have surpassed even Christians. Mahatma Gandhi is a celebrated example of this group. And what about the times of Jesus? Throughout the four Gospels, Jesus is at odds with the 'Bible-believing' people of his day – the Pharisees, the Sadducees, the doctors of the law, the experts in the Scripture. Indeed it was these grey-bearded and long-robed religious leaders of the day who quoted their Bible in part and delivered the Lord of Life to be crucified.

In the context of our argument this means that mere Bible-quoting to further our own interests does not solve the problem we are trying to solve. In fact, one may be forgiven for saying that this kind of sectarian Bible-quoting creates more problems than it purports to solve. Look at the Garden of Eden, for example. How did Satan start his drama of tempting our first parents? Did he not start with quoting the Word of God: 'Did God indeed say … ' (Genesis 3:1). If indeed the term *theology* (or *theos-logos*) can be translated as 'God-talk', then the first theologian was none other than the devil himself! And what about the Temptation of Christ? Once again we meet the devil, that old deceiver, in the garb of a Bible-wielding street preacher. 'It is written … ' Three times he quotes the Scripture carefully selected to justify his own attempt at tempting the Son of God. And three times Jesus reminds

Satan, 'It is *also* written ... ' The Bible needs to be quoted in full, not in part. So the devil quotes one part of the Bible. Christ completes the exercise by quoting the other part. And this drama of Bible-wielding, Bible-quoting continues right in our times. Sometimes it is Christ who is quoting the Bible. Other times it is the devil. Our problem is that just by looking at those quoting the Bible we cannot tell who is who. Perhaps all we can say is that quoting the Bible to justify our own choices is devilish, quoting the Bible to understand the truth and the whole truth, and to expedite God's love and salvation to the whole of humanity, is divine.[9]

Africa using numbers to break up the Anglican Communion

At times it appears as though African Christianities are taking the world by storm in terms of numbers. This argument is used to bulldoze the Anglican Communion into giving in to various African demands. Bishops of Africa, Asia and Latin America represent one-third of Anglican Communion members world-wide. These bishops threaten to sever relations with dioceses that authorise same-sex blessings.

Since the consecration of Bishop Gene Robinson, there have been calls from some provinces to sever relations with the Episcopal Church. Sometimes the issue of numbers is used and at other times it is the issue of Africa being more Christian. On the issue of numbers it has been observed by Andrew Walls that:

> Perhaps one of the two or three most important events in the whole of church history has occurred within the lifetime of the people not yet old.
>
> It is nothing less than a complete change in the centre of gravity of Christianity, so that the heartlands of the church are no longer in Europe, decreasingly in North America, but in certain parts of Asia and ... Africa.[10]

Philip Jenkins in his *The Next Christendom: The Coming of Global Christianity* writes:

> We are currently living through one of the transforming moments in the history of religion worldwide. Over the past five centuries or so, the story of Christianity has been inextricably bound up with that of Europe and European derived civilizations overseas, above all in North America. Until recently the overwhelming majority of Christians have lived in White nations, allowing theorists to speak smugly, arrogantly, of 'European Christian' civilization. Conversely, radical writers have seen Christianity as the religion of the 'West' or, to use another popular metaphor, the global North.[11]

Jenkins like Walls also observes, 'Over the past century ... the center of gravity in the Christian world has shifted inexorably southward, to Africa, Asia, and Latin America.'[12] No doubt there is a marked growth in Christianity in Africa. But what type of Christianity are we talking about here? It has been observed that most of the African Christianities tend to be overtly conservative and biblicist. But that is only 'overtly'. On the outside, African Christians appear to espouse and conserve biblical dicta. There is a great show of uncompromising moral concern. Inside, however, African Christianities suffer from what Desmond Tutu calls a form of 'religious schizophrenia'. With part of himself, the African Christian is compelled first to lip service to Christianity, as understood, expressed and preached by the white man; but with another ever-greater part of himself, a part he has been ashamed to acknowledge openly, he has felt that his African-ness has been violated.[13]

Most African Christians seem perpetually to oscillate between a strongly conservationist, cruci-centric theology, on one hand, and the indefatigable hold of African culture on the other. Thus, from the inside most African Christianities are inhabited by ordinary talk – big mortals, ordinary people making extraordinary claims. Mercy Amba Oduyoye, in an unpublished paper, has used the analogy of an onion for African Christianities. The onion can have a glossy silk skin on the outside but when one starts to peel it, it is rotten and has a hollow centre.

It has also been noted that, 'taking leave of God is now possible without taking leave of the church. The church has so embraced numbers and outward form of religion without transformation – resulting into a schizophrenic religiosity where doctrine is not always translated into practical matters of ethics.'[14] If this is a true analysis of African Christianity, then it cannot have the moral (or even logical) authority to point fingers at other forms of Christianities, which to Africans appear to be faulty. The homosexuality issue should help us to examine the forms of Christianity that we hold dearly and critique them from inside. There is no perfect Christianity in any given areas. We are living under the grace of God, and this should help us to judge ourselves more than we judge others.

So when does homosexuality become sin?
Most of the comments that have come from African church leaders on homosexuality are based on the argument that it is a sin. Some have even argued that unless the homosexual persons and those who support them 'repent', the church will not have fellowship with them. If one believes that homosexuality is a sin, then it should not be a sin only to bishops but to all – laity and ordained. It cannot be sin for one group and not sin for the other. A man can be openly gay and a priest, but if he wants to

become a bishop it is a problem. Why? If it is wrong to be a gay bishop, then it is equally wrong to be a gay priest.

The consecration of Gene Robinson has become a peg on which some bishops wish to hang their frustrations. There are those from the North seeking alliances from the bishops of Africa and elsewhere, possibly because they have failed to get hold of the leadership in the Episcopal Church. They then expect to use the loosely structured Anglican Communion to expel or discredit the leadership and synodical structures of the Episcopal Church and the Anglican Church of Canada. The methodology used to collect support can be questioned, because it gives one-sided views on homosexuality. Some of the views treat homosexuality as an illness, or disobedience to God, which, once acknowledged and prayed for, will be cured.[15]

Some of the African bishops, too, seem to be serving more in the parishes in the Episcopal Church than being at home in their own dioceses and parishes. The homosexuality debate has come in handy for them to avoid problems at home, which they claim are the priority but do nothing about them. Issues of poverty, HIV/AIDS, theological education, women and children are being pushed under the carpet while the flag of homosexuality is being flown high. I have wondered and continue to wonder why issues of genocide, for example, have never become Communion-breaking, while homosexuality is being used to break apart the Communion. We sometimes believe that other fires are easier to put out than our own.

Sexual sins tend to be at the forefront of our issues, but they may not be what is most important in our communities and before God. The woman caught in adultery was not condemned but pardoned by Jesus. Though he charged her to 'sin no more', he told the crowd to put down their stones. When will the church put down its stones? Sexual issues require much prayer, counselling and compassion. The reasons why people are gay should not be trivialised because this is violence.

The church has failed this part of the population because it has demonised and criminalised them. They have gone underground, or hidden their behaviour. Now there is a major concern about men on the 'down low', which means covertly homosexual. What is frightening is that homosexual persons are forced to hide their identity, to marry wives and then to live with a double sexual life.

> Socially, it seems, the Kenya gay man is a gypsy-nomad, forever condemned to shifting from place to place, leaving sniffles and scandals in their wake. The homosexual/gay community mostly remains invisible behind the straight façade of mainstream hetero-sexuality. Like a stream running crooked underground beneath

plain terra firma. Like all groups that feel marginalized, the city's gay community is both close-knit and underground lot, paradoxically operating in the open but with some secrecy, like eyes behind sunglasses.[16]

The homosexual community is inclusive of both lay and ordained persons. In places where they have tried to come out in the open, they are put under discipline or transferred to new places, if not forced out.

Conclusion

This paper is a reflection from a Kenyan woman on the ongoing war of words on homosexuality. I have indicated that homosexuality is a human issue and not an issue of particular people. There are those who argue that the Bible condemns homosexuality, and I have noted that if we are going to use the Bible on this issue, then we should use it wholesale and not in a piecemeal way. The church must provide a safe space, free of condemnation, where we will listen to those who are of the gay and lesbian communities. Though we might not agree, theologically, it is important that we are able to listen. After all, there are many things we do not agree on theologically and we have continued to interact with one another at most levels of the Communion. By listening to each other we are able to get rid of some phobias that we (most of us) harbour and it will increase understanding. I believe we would have less violence committed against homosexual persons if the church takes a stand. Demonstrating the love of Christ with our neighbours is always our first priority. Such a loving approach will open new understanding and provide a way to live with those who might be hiding their sexual identities and living in a world of fear.[17]

NOTES
1. Laws of Kenya, Penal Code, CAP. 63, ch. 3, §§162–3.
2. John S. Mbiti, *Love and Marriage* (Nairobi: Heinemann, 1973), p.218.
3. See Robert M. Baum, 'Homosexuality and the Traditional Religions of the Americas and Africa', in Arlene Swindler (ed.), *Homosexuality and World Religions* (Valley Forge, PA: Trinity Press International, 1993); and Stephen O. Murray's entry on 'Africa Sub-Saharan', in Wayne R. Dynes (ed.), *Encyclopedia of Homosexuality* (New York and London: Garland Publishing Inc., 1990).
4. Kevin Ward, 'Sexuality, Homosexuality and the African Church', *Crucible,* 2003. See also his chapter in this book.
5. John Anguka, *Absolute Power: The Ouko Murder Mystery* (London: Pen Press Ltd, 1998).
6. Men for Men or Male for Male; Men Seeking Men; Female for Female; Female Seeking Female; Women for Women; Women Seeking Women.
7. C. B. Peter, 'The Church and Same Sex Unions', paper presented at St Paul's Limuru Theological Society, 2004.

8. Malcolm Marcourt, 'But what about the Partner?', *Search* 27:3 (Autumn 2004), 225.

9. Peter, op. cit.

10. Andrew F. Walls, 'Towards Understanding Africa's Place in Christian History, in J. S. Pobee (ed.), *Religion in a Pluralistic Society* (Leiden: Brill, 1976), p.180.

11. Philip Jenkins, *The Next Christendom: The Coming of Global Christianity* (Oxford: Oxford University Press, 2002), pp 1–2.

12. ibid., p.2.

13. Desmond Tutu, 'Black Theology and African Theology: Soul Mates or Antagonists?', in John Parratt (ed.), *A Reader in African Christian Theology* (London: SPCK, 1987), pp.47–8.

14. J. Galgalo, 'Challenges Facing Theological Education in Africa', unpublished paper presented at the Conference of Africa Theological Initiative, Uganda Christian University, November 2004.

15. See, for example, Leanne Payne, *The Broken Image: Restoring Personal Wholeness through Healing Prayer* (Grand Rapids: Hamewith Baker Books, 1996), pp.124–5.

16. 'Behind the veil of homosexuality', *Sunday Standard*, 5 September 2004.

17. These reflections have been enhanced with the work of C. B. Peter, with whom I wrote a paper in *Search*. We have reflected together on this issue and the life of the church in Kenya in general.

Chapter 12

HOMOSEXUALITY AND THE CHURCHES IN NIGERIA

Rowland Jide Macaulay

> But as many as receive him, to them he gave the right to become children of God, to those that believe in his name. *John 1:12*

> Jesus declared, 'For God so loved the world that he gave his only begotten son, that whosoever believes in him should not perish but have everlasting life.' *John 3:16*

Introduction

It is ironic that when asked to make a contribution to a powerful subject, the entire world seems to come to a standstill. Yet when we look around us, we can tell that things are not right, that basic human rights are violated, resulting in the oppression of gays and lesbians. From my personal experience, knowledge and circumstances, I am able to make a small contribution on this issue.

The concerns in this article are the relationship between homosexual persons and the reactions of the churches and Christian organisations in the Federal Republic of Nigeria. The discussion to follow may alarm many people but to others it will be unsurprising. It must be acknowledged that more and more gays and lesbians living in Nigeria suffer greatly because of the slow pace of enlightenment, prejudice within Nigerian culture and insufficient education on sexual orientation.

The prohibition of homosexuality is not only confined to legislation but it is also strongly affirmed within the culture. As far as Nigeria is concerned, homosexuality is an abuse of traditional values. This chapter addresses the reality of the lives of gays and lesbians in Nigeria in the twenty-first century. Where same-sex relations are frowned upon, many are in secretive same-sex relationships, even in cases where they are married to the opposite sex. This reality reflects the diversity and depth of the cultures of Africa.

The Federal Republic of Nigeria

Nigeria was under British control until 1 October 1960, when it gained independence. The Yoruba were mainly in the southwest, the Ibo in the southeast, and the Hausa and Fulani in the north. From 1960 to 1965 Nigeria had a parliamentary democratic system of government similar to that of Great Britain but it came under military rule in January 1966 when the civilian government was toppled in a coup. The country remained under military rule until 1 October 1979, when a new civilian government based on the presidential system was inaugurated. Nigeria came under military rule again on 31 December 1983 when the civilian government was overthrown in a coup. President Olusegun Obasanjo, who came to power in 1999, is now in his second term in office in a democratic government.

The British colonials who settled in Nigeria first introduced Christianity to the country. Today Christianity is the most popular religion in the southern part of Nigeria. On every street and corner there is a church; it is trendy to be part of a local Christian assembly. However, there are consistent religious tensions in the Islamic North with the spread of *sharia* law. There are also border conflicts in the southeast with Cameroon and violent crime throughout the south.

There are also great conflicts on the issues of sexuality and the law. According to articles 214, 215 and 217 of the Nigerian Penal Code, homosexuality and other kinds of 'carnal knowledge against the order of nature' carry a penalty of fourteen years imprisonment. Any person who attempts to commit any of the defined offences is guilty of a felony and liable to imprisonment for seven years. This law has existed for a long time, and yet homosexuality is a reality in Nigeria. This legislation needs urgent review and repeal.

How Nigerian tradition reacts towards homosexuality

Nigerian tradition and culture is less likely to accept gays and lesbians; homosexuality is seen as a condition that brings shame to our society. In Nigeria, like most countries, gays are active members of society: they are the rulers, the politicians, the doctors, nurses, choirmasters, students, pastors, intercessors, ushers, the legal practitioners, parents, bankers, police, accountants, traders and many more, all involved in their communities and churches. However, their sexual orientation is not to be made known in relation to their public and community responsibilities; the shame is far too much to bear, hence the total silence. This silence of homosexual persons on matters that adversely affect their sexual orientation and their existence in Nigeria cannot change the attitude of the people, the church or the government. But if action is taken, the tide can turn to facilitate actions that will bring recognition, education and awareness to the existence of homosexual people in the country.

Gays and lesbians in Nigeria cut across all levels of education, social status and wealth. In Nigeria I found that some gays and lesbians I came in contact with are independent, confident and unequivocal on their sexual orientation; however, about 90 per cent are married. Some express their singular unhappiness and associate it with their marriage – a firm duty, inescapable, to please their families and society, and to produce offspring. Thus, an open gay or lesbian lifestyle cannot be allowed.

Parents of gays and lesbians in Nigeria

Being born homosexual in African culture is not something that you will understand as a child. Nigerian society has made it a taboo because it cannot deal with the increasing demands of gays and lesbians. If homosexuality were determined in the physical features and identifiable at birth, many Nigerian parents would bury their homosexual child before it has the chance to live. Homosexuality is seen as the influence of sexual corruption and immorality from the West. Parents in Nigeria will seldom accept that their child is gay. Even those who have come to terms with the knowledge will continue to pray for a change.

Some parents believe homosexual persons have become members of a cult. It is commonly said, 'I would rather have the corpse of my child than accept him or her as homosexual.' In cases where the parents or family know their child's sexual orientation, they will take further steps to seek counselling, prayers, exorcism and binding the spirit of homosexuality.

Gay parenting in Nigeria

Since the law is against the practice of homosexuality, it will be another struggle to assuage negative attitudes to the issue of gay parenting and to bring about its understanding and acceptance. The welfare of the child will be in question, in conjunction with the strong and fast rules on morals held by the infallible culture of Nigeria.

The definition of a complete family in Nigeria is a man, his wife and many children; same-sex parenting will not be tolerated. Neither the law, nor the churches nor the cultures of Nigeria acknowledge gay and lesbian relationships. Seldom and never without good cause would you find two men living together and raising children in Nigeria. This would be ideal. However, the culture is so rigid and it is given to understanding that men, homosexual or not, remain dominant while women are sub-servient. The chance of an upbeat, sympathetic and frank portrayal of gay and lesbian parenting issues cannot at this time be pursued, but there is a need to heighten public awareness and debate and to tackle the social taboo surrounding the general issue of same-sex parenting.

There is still much misunderstanding of gay men and lesbians who want to become or who already are parents. I hope that by confronting the laws with articulate stories we may bring some sense and under-standing to the issue. As we begin to understand gay parenting, we can go on to improve public awareness of the issue of homosexuality, and show that gay men and lesbians have put a lot of love, effort and deter-mination into starting and continuing families and have the right to be treated like anybody else.

The battle of homosexuality in Nigeria today is met with rigour, dogmatism and rejection in society. Commonly, if a person is discovered or known to be homosexual, her or his immediate family will be first to reject that person. The trauma is enormous. In Nigeria most children will live with their family until they get married. The system is often too rigid – you grow up, you are sent through school, college and then university and then you get married and have children; the lives of homosexuals in Nigeria are not fully developed.

Most gays and lesbians in Nigeria that I spoke with are in denial and dire straits; they have experienced their love in same-sex relationships from a young age, most before puberty. The majority have had their first same-sex encounter before the age of fourteen. Most associate their feel-ings with strange behaviour and think they are in need of psychiatric help; this situation is regardless of religious belief – the phenomenon is not confined to the Christian faith. The enforcement of laws against homosexual practice will require hard evidence for arrest and prosecu-tion. Known homosexual persons in the face of adversity will deny their sexual acts and orientation.

Homosexuality, though widely practised, still remains the most secretive lifestyle in Nigeria. The activities around gays and lesbians are always coded and the government has made no provision to repeal its legislation, which makes homosexuality a criminal offence. Homosexual persons caught in any sexual act become the subject of public ridicule; the enforcers of the criminal justice system or civil law do not challenge this treatment, though unlawful. Homosexual persons can be arrested or imprisoned without trial, for this is a very grey area for both the victims and the government. There are no specialist lawyers on the issues of homosexuality in Nigeria. Cases cannot be prosecuted or proven successfully in a court of law.

Nigerian culture has a strict element of training. You are expected to do what you are told or taught – for example, you are taught from an early age that you must get married.

The Nigerian Christian views on and reactions to homosexuality

The attitude of the churches to homosexuality is highly conservative, with all the best intention; the church is not prepared to engage in

discussion of the issue for the liberation of homosexual people at any
level. However, I agree with the comment,

> God does not condemn homosexuality. What God condemns is
> abusive and violent sexuality, lack of mutuality, any kind of co-
> ercion. This is what I wish the church could get on with – how to
> form a loving and responsible sexual ethic, not just for gays, not
> just for straights, but for everybody.[1]

None of the churches in Nigeria supports openly the practice of
homosexuality; they are not prepared to bless a union of a same-sex
relationship and there are no known openly gay couples. The life of
homosexual persons, for those who practise, must be simple and discreet
with the knowledge of their sexuality remaining amongst a small
number of associates and friends.

If you are openly gay and profess that you are a Christian, this
assertion will be seen as a serious commission of sin that cannot be forgiven; homosexuality, as far as the churches in Nigeria are concerned, is
an unforgivable sin against the Holy Spirit. The churches in Nigeria
believe that homosexuality defies the country's rich culture and its practice makes the individual an outcast. Openly gay and lesbian people are
compared and referred to as 'dogs'. Active homosexual persons are seen
as disobedient and traitors; they are seen as having sold out to another
culture. They are seen as having denied their family values, the plain
teaching of the Scriptures and the moral consensus of the church, all of
which forbid homosexuality.

Nigerians and the Nigerian church have no agenda to take a more
redemptive view of homosexual practice. Nigerians have made their
conclusion based both on ignorance and on a culture deprecating homosexuality, such that they can never accept homosexual persons; and the
church claims that it is not possible for Christians to have a same-sex
relationship. Assumption of homosexual practice is not acceptable in the
quest for civilisation.

Peter Akinola, Anglican Archbishop of Nigeria

Archbishop Peter Akinola, in one of his many remarks, 'cannot imagine
two men in a sexual relation, even this does not happen in the animal
kingdom'. Others have echoed this remark; they continue to deny the
existence of same-sex relationships. Emphatically, educators of Nigeria
are ignorant, stupid or ill-informed of the social strata of homosexuals
in its population.

Such was the furore of the response to the existence and appointment
of gay bishops in the USA and United Kingdom. Peter Akinola continues to speak against the appointment of such clergy, saying that homo-

sexuals are lower than beasts; his views on homosexuality are such that he ranks it alongside polygamy, incest, adultery and bestiality. From his stand in Nigeria, these words will further increase and fuel the church's hatred and continued denial of gay and lesbian citizens of Nigeria. Contrary to the Archbishop's views, Dr Neil Sheppard writes, 'actually, there is a large and increasing body of scientific evidence of same-sex relations throughout the animal kingdom, which does not exclude man.'[2]

Conservative Christians in Nigeria

Conservative Christians in Nigeria continue to exert pressure from within the church. They are the lead members in church management and financial support; as stakeholders, they continue to assert conservative dogma and disregard the human rights of gays and lesbians. They exercise either 'strong' or 'moderate' influence on what happens in the church. Conservative Christians are those who are rigid and narrow in their understanding and interpretation of the Scriptures; they take a literal approach and not a liberal or wider interpretation. They believe that homosexuality is a sin, not in the will of God and forbidden by the Bible.

Conservative Christians have been increasingly irritated with what they regard as an ambivalent attitude towards gay rights by the churches, especially the Anglican Communion. Whether they can deliver on their threats is another matter. As fundamentalists, compromise does not come easily to conservative Christians, particularly on social and welfare issues for lesbians and gays. Conservative Christians often state, 'God loves everybody, but not sinful behaviour or the sexual practice of homosexuals.'

The messages of the churches in Nigeria also confirm the Nigerian cultural beliefs; the issue of homosexuality in the church is not an easy question for many Christians, as Scripture still plays a big part in Christian ethics. The church is careless and does not see the need to extend the rights of lesbians and gay men, who are not visible in Nigeria. If there were to be any appreciation or taking into account of gays and lesbians, it would send the conservative Christians into a frenzy.

Homosexual persons in Nigeria are no different from homosexual persons in other parts of the world; gay and lesbian Christians in Nigeria worship a loving God, and that loving God leads us into the truth: 'And you shall know the truth and the truth shall make you free' (John 8:32).

The churches in Nigeria are ill prepared to challenge the view that 'homosexual behaviour is abnormal behaviour according to the clear and consistent teaching of Scripture from the Book of Genesis to the end of the New Testament.' This is based on my experience and discussions with Nigerian clergy, which confirm the stubborn and dogmatic approach of the churches in Nigeria to this issue. The Nigerian churches

are biased against homosexuals; the lack of understanding and the fast
rule of Nigerian culture have meant that the strong conservative views
will always be upheld. The criminality of sexual orientation is also a
barrier to the liberation of gays and lesbians.

It has always been the claim of the church that homosexuality is contrary to the clear teachings of Scripture and would cause great distress
within the community. However, the church has forgotten the pain of the
individual who has to live through rejection and prejudice. Gays and
lesbians in Nigeria lack self-esteem; very few gays and lesbians are open
and the fear of 'coming out' is just too much. The churches in Nigeria
are regarded as sanctuaries, but not a place for homosexual persons to
run to in time of trouble. The churches are bent on adhering to the teaching that marriage is primary, that sex should only be within marriage and
that homosexuality has no place. Embracing homosexuality is seen as an
omission; it is believed that by taking such steps towards homosexuality,
those individuals have placed themselves outside the traditional
Christian values of Nigeria.

The nation and government's reaction to homosexuality

'Coming out' in Nigeria as gay or lesbian is not an option; there are no
social or welfare systems to support such individuals. 'Coming out' in
Nigeria? You might as well sign your death warrant.

Homosexuality means a difficult life in Nigeria. 'Coming out' is a
difficult decision for a young person to make. 'Coming out' as gay or
lesbian means leaving home, which means having your own financial
support; but this is usually not an option in a country where unemploy-
ment is high and where there is no state financial support, social welfare
or housing projects.

It is a great concern for many homosexual persons, knowing that this
is a very difficult choice to make in a country such as Nigeria. Those living abroad or in exile are very aware of their good fortune. Being out and
open, any form of exposure, through gossips or snide remarks, usually
leaves the victim bewildered and has heavy repercussions. This may
even culminate in strange behaviour, depression or even suicide.

Secret gay Christian organisations are emerging, but this is what the
Nigerian people associate with occultism. This association is slowly
becoming a serious problem as the church fails to understand the need
for sexual liberation. The groups can only survive with a small and
closely trusting membership. They cannot operate an open-door policy
or advertise their existence, and they cannot use the media such as
television, radio, newspapers or billboards. Socially, there are no official
businesses or meeting places for gays and lesbians; however, there are
organised parties, events and underground circles, which meet the needs

of a selected few.

The best word around and on the street for gays and lesbians in Nigeria is to be secretly homosexual; being open is not an option. Nigerian society is not prepared to face the problems and human rights issues of homosexual persons. Living as an openly gay man in Nigeria is a personal choice but the dangers can be overwhelming if you are not secretive. The lack of government support has also meant that the church will always take its stand in opposition to a gay life. Archbishop Akinola's view does not surprise me, as there are many more echoes of his voice in Nigeria; if the church or any hierarchy takes a silent approach they will be seen to support or advocate homosexuality. The lack of an integrated view of the predicament of gay and lesbian Christians is a serious matter for Nigeria.

Homosexual persons in Nigeria include the elite, who are more aware of the human rights issues and their breach by the Nigerian government. The church is wrongly relied upon to be the outspoken institution against the violation of human and gay rights.

Nigerians believe that heterosexual relationships form the basis of the decency in African culture. Politicians and the church echo this view, as they ignore many attempts to become inclusive or socially aware of homosexual practice. The activities of homosexual persons are seen as a taboo; though frustrating and demeaning, it is pointless to talk of having an open homosexual lifestyle.

Gays and lesbians of Nigerian parentage residing in the United Kingdom tell me in personal interviews that they would not consider living in Nigeria as openly homosexual persons. There are no remedies for cases or issues concerning homosexual persons. There is no official body they can turn to in case of human rights abuses such as homosexual rape, homophobic violence or sexual harassment. There is no reliable government department in Nigeria that would take seriously the complaints of gays and lesbians in Nigeria and would deal with them without prejudice.

Traditionally, homosexuality is associated with an evil spirit, a demon that must be cast out of the person. With traditional medicine the gay or lesbian person will be taken to a traditional herbalist or local healer who will attempt rituals and give medicinal potions to cast out or remove the homosexual spirit. Christians harbour hatred against homosexuals; it is unbelievable that in the church Christians will impose fasting and prayer and subject their victim to days of exorcism.

The dangers homosexual persons will encounter in Nigeria

As a result of the psychological, sociological and religious context, the future of gays and lesbians in Nigeria is filled with uncertainty. Most crimes against homosexuals in Nigeria are not reported. For example:

Crime and blackmail
Homosexual persons in Nigeria suffer a great deal of rejection and the violation of their basic human rights; they are also frequent victims of crime. The prevalent crime against homosexuals is blackmail. Once the criminals know you are gay they will extort you, either sexually or financially. Due to an inefficient police force, untrained in matters concerning homosexuality, it is impossible to guarantee the safety of a homosexual person against criminal behaviour in Nigeria. Due to the lack of security, homosexuals are vulnerable and are often easy targets or prey to criminals and the media.

Homosexual rape
Though uncommonly reported, there are instances of male homosexual rape. However, the victim has no recourse to bring the perpetrator to justice, as the attempt to do so will probably be ineffective.

Isolation, loneliness and rejection
Openly gay individuals also run the danger of being isolated and lonely; whether the individual chooses to leave home or 'come out', the consequences often outweigh the benefits, as the family unit in Nigeria is one of the strongest units of its culture. There are no organisations, or church or government bodies, that look into the needs of rejected gays and lesbians. It will take a long time before we can find an advocate or a louder voice for homosexual persons in Nigeria.

An understanding of the psychological needs of gays and lesbians is far from the narrow list of the Nigerian Department of Health's priorities. A case of loneliness, rejection or isolation may often culminate in a mental disorder and these patients are often sent to a general psychiatric ward at a government mental institution.

Homosexual prostitution
There is evidence that the practice of homosexuality is increasing for many different reasons. One cause is the economic situation, causing people to become gay prostitutes. The lifestyle may be taken on for the short or long term. The benefits of a gay sexual orientation, when used for prostitution, are primarily economic advancement. Most of those who get involved in gay prostitution are the breadwinners of their families; they give themselves to whoremongers and are not likely to give up the trade. On the other hand, criminals also use gay prostitution to target vulnerable subjects, which often leads to a catalogue of unreported blackmail. The true sexual orientation or identity of the gay prostitute is not always conclusive; in any case, gay prostitution will remain secretive.

Death

Many homosexual persons have taken their own life or been killed in the process of being 'outed'. The pain becomes too much if discovered at a young age, with no one to turn to such as professional organisations or even the church. It may be impossible to survive the trauma of living in a homophobic society. Exposure, or the lack of care, often leads to the breakdown of an individual's psychological wellbeing, which may lead to a mental breakdown or even suicide.

Unsafe sex

As a result of little education on sexual practices, sex between men where protection is pursued is frowned upon, resulting in the transmission of HIV. Generally, sex between men and women is seen within the African communities as acceptable. However, gay sex resulting in the transmission of HIV is regarded as a punishment for homosexuality.

HIV/AIDS

HIV/AIDS amongst Nigerian gays and lesbians has been an issue for decades. The church has frustrated attempts to deal with this issue. Looking back in history at the outbreak of HIV/AIDS, the level of ignorance within the church community was high. Churches said, 'Christians cannot get HIV/AIDS' as it was thought that the disease was always associated with homosexuals. HIV/AIDS was dubbed a 'homosexual disease' and a punishment for sodomy. While other nations, especially in the West, were busy taking care of themselves and coming to some understanding of the new epidemic, Nigeria and the churches turned a blind eye, raising their voices louder and louder in messages of gloom and doom. It emerged that the infection crosses cultures regardless of sexual orientation. Homophobia, as a result, came at a price, as many people suffered and a lot more died just because of ignorance, resentment and stigmatism. This homophobia no doubt perpetuated the increase of HIV/AIDS. In Nigeria today, a lot more people are dying of HIV/AIDS according to the World Health Organisation's finding in 1998–2001, but the fate of homosexual people in Nigeria as a group is not known because they cannot be identified or accounted for in the findings. They are victims of society's cruel culture and old-time family traditions.

Discrimination

The rejection of homosexual persons in Nigeria also contributes to stigmatism and unsafe sexual practices. Homosexuals are more likely to be discriminated against on the grounds of sexual orientation in employment, including the military. Those who are visibly effeminate are more likely to be tortured or physically and verbally assaulted. There is a lack of sexual education and understanding of the need to express sexual orientation, which has led to many unattractive situations. The sex education required for homosexual persons is no different to that needed for heterosexual persons. Without the government's support and the acceptance of the church, unsafe sex and discrimination will continue to cost lives.

Public display of affection

Due to the cultures of Nigeria, gays and lesbians are unable to show affection in public without prejudice. It is the same for heterosexual persons; they too are unable to enjoy the freedom to show affection outside their home. Displays of affection between members of the opposite sex are usually met with abusive words. Overtly effeminate guys and butch girls are usually noticed and regarded with suspicion. Ironically, holding hands and cuddling in a public place is not a serious misdemeanour, but this is not an acceptance of homosexuality.

My personal experience

Born to Nigerian parents, I am an ordained minister, a lawyer and a poet. I spent my teenage years in Nigeria, where I first experienced my sexuality, although in great fear – fear of being caught, fear of sin, fear of committing an abomination. I grew up with a lot of guilt in my heart. I often prayed for forgiveness, sanctification and purification.

I grew up with my father who is a Christian leader. We love each other so much, but the culture and tradition of my tribe, the Yoruba, meant that no matter how successful I became, how great a child I was, homosexuality is not part of the culture.

I was married and divorced with a child; the marriage broke down because of my confession of the truth, that 'I am gay'. By this time I was in fear that I would lose my life and my family. For many years, I lived a double life, safeguarding any revelation of my sexual orientation. It became a secret that would haunt me for many more years.

I was 'outed' at my local Pentecostal church among heterosexual friends; it also became a revelation at work. This was painful and difficult for me to deal with; it has been even more painful to deal with my family, as they are embittered towards me. Having no one else to turn to, I turned to the Lord; only then did I make peace with God and begin to understand that my pain and anguish was for a reason. I understood that I was to be the voice for those who suffered a similar predicament.

My purpose at this present time is to reach out to other gays and lesbians suffering persecution – to offer some hope and to let them know they are not alone. It is not my intention to be a martyr, but simply to stand up and be counted. I am ready to persevere, to speak up and pay the price for what I believe.

The homosexual population in Nigeria

Over the past ten years I have spent more and more time in Nigeria. Each time there have been new discoveries of the homosexual populace, who consist of persons from all kinds of backgrounds, from students to government officials, from young adult to middle-aged men and women. My observation is that there are several rings or circles of unsuspected homosexual people; these are sexually active men and women, some in multiple relationships with men and women. However, I have concentrated on the relationship of the churches and homosexual people in Nigeria.

The way forward

There is an immediate need for gay and lesbian Christians to meet, and to look at and discuss the urgent needs of gay and lesbians Christians in Nigeria. In the twenty-first century there is the need to push for a sexual reformation that will make Nigeria a more peaceful and loving place – not only by including gays and lesbians in the government and church programmes, but also by viewing all forms of sexual expression between committed adults as an 'original gift of God'. I believe the following is the way forward:

1. Sitting on the radical edge of gay theology, it is right to call for churches in Nigeria to abandon the concepts of a 'sexual norm' or 'normality' and accept gays and lesbians as people made in the image of God, whose sexuality is a divine blessing.
2. An increasingly vocal gay movement, within the church and led by Christians, will create an impact on Christianity in Nigeria.
  3. I hope for a debate that many Nigerian gay rights advocates will engage in intensely, offering a general reading of Scripture from a gay perspective, advocating that homosexuality is not a sin but a blessed characteristic of humanity.
4. Gay Christians in Nigeria have so much cultural baggage around sexuality, so much shame that outlives the pleasure. It is time that Christians across the board reconnect with their lovers, their community and their God.
5. Church leaders owning and accepting the work of bringing gays and lesbians to God must preach the true Gospel of Jesus Christ, which is LOVE.
6. There is a need for more HIV- and sexuality-awareness seminars and for new gay Christian fellowships that will transcend the issues

of pain and extend the good news of welcome to gays and lesbians who really need the love of God.

7. Nigerian gays and lesbians are still very far behind in the global social structure (they do not exist anywhere else). They are not identifiable in business ownership, politics, church leadership and are less likely to adopt children. Although educated, the ignorance and neglect from their communities, societies and families has created a serious disadvantage. Time and again they cannot fight back against a ruthless system; this situation must be turned around.

8. The messages that work well are continuous campaigning, education and training, including literature that looks deep into the issue of stigmatisation and that challenges homophobia.

9. The main point of concentration will be to promote sexual awareness and the freedom of same-sex relationships, to encourage monogamous relationships and to educate society.

10. Homosexual persons in Nigeria do not have the same legal protection and rights as homosexual persons in Europe and North America. This situation needs to change.

11. We need to ensure that all anti-gay legislation is repealed and that gays are protected under the new laws and powers.

12. Having more political leaders who are openly gay would create role models and assist with understanding the struggles of gay and lesbian Nigerians.

13. There is a clear need for research and open debate on the needs and existence of homosexual persons in Nigeria.

14. We should encourage and create systems for gay Nigerians to support each other; they need to discuss ways to reconcile their sexuality with their faith and create a liberal perspective.

15. Good and positive media must be developed and used to raise these issues in strong cross-cultural and political debates.

16. The stigma of homosexuality is so bad that HIV/STI-preventative measures, such as condoms and relevant sex education, must be freely available or affordable.

Bear one another's burden, and so fulfil the law of Christ. *Galatians 6:2*

It shall come to pass in that day that his burden will be taken away from your shoulder, and his yoke from your neck, and the yoke will be destroyed because of the anointing oil. *Isaiah 10:27*

NOTES

1. Robert Goss, Professor of Religious Studies at Webster University, St. Louis, in

an article in the *Washington Post*, August 2003.
2. Sheppard referred to an article 'The Animal Homosexual Myth', by Luiz Sérgio Solimeo. See http://www.narth.com/docs/animalmyth.html.

Chapter 13

THE CHURCH OF UGANDA AND THE PROBLEM OF HUMAN SEXUALITY: RESPONDING TO CONCERNS FROM THE UGANDAN CONTEXT

Kawuki Mukasa

Take a second look

In August 2004, an open letter to Archbishop Henry Orombi of the Church of Uganda touched off a storm whose impact reached down to Anglican communities at the local level in this small but densely populated country. The letter was written by Louie Crew, a member of the Executive Council of the Episcopal Church of the United States of America (ECUSA).[1] In this letter, Crew launched a thinly veiled attack on Orombi and the bishops of the Church of Uganda, accusing them of duplicity in their public relations campaign against the Episcopal Church. He was particularly troubled by what seemed like a serious breach of ethics on the bishops' part: that they claim, on the one hand, to be in a state of 'broken communion' with ECUSA while, on the other, continue to accept financial aid from the American church. 'It is not fair', he wrote, 'to claim you are turning down support when you are actually seeking it on the sly.'[2] Crew confessed that he took no pleasure in lecturing church leaders on matters of integrity and transparency. 'But I am not underwriting anyone's hypocrisy,' he wrote.

Such incendiary remarks produced a predictable and perhaps inevitable response from Archbishop Orombi. Since, at the very least, his personal integrity was now being questioned, he took it upon himself to ensure that every loophole by which ECUSA funding might find its way into the Church of Uganda was closed. All applications submitted after the consecration of Bishop Gene Robinson in November 2003 would be affected. The ban would also cover funds already approved but waiting to be transferred, or instalments yet to be sent. Indeed, the church was even turning down funding that had already been received.

For those who were directly affected by Orombi's decision, it was little comfort to be reminded that he did the right thing and that he took the only course of action he could with integrity. The reaction of one young clergyman I met is typical. He was to leave for the United States in August 2004 on a full scholarship for three years. His family would join him in January 2005. Unfortunately, because of a family emergency, he had to ask for and was granted permission to delay his departure until October 2004. He would later deeply regret that decision. Just as he was wrapping up his family affairs and getting ready to leave Uganda for the United States, he was informed that his scholarship had been cancelled and his plans to travel to the United States suspended indefinitely. It was a devastating blow for this young man. He kept asking himself why: 'Why am I paying for the sins of someone I don't even know?'

The question symbolised in my view a dynamic that is likely to creep into the collective consciousness of the Church of Uganda as the implications of its decisions assume more concrete forms. As the state of 'broken communion' begins to have a tangible impact on people's lives, the need to take another look at the issues arises. People seek to examine more critically what is at stake and to determine whether or not the stand they have taken is indeed well thought out and justified.

In the interest of facilitating such a second and perhaps more critical examination of the issues behind the 'broken communion', I conducted interviews with a number of bishops, clergy and laity in the Church of Uganda.[3] The interviews covered a wide range of issues related to the problem of human sexuality and in particular the current controversy in the worldwide Anglican Communion. I wanted to look beyond the mounting stress caused by the strained relationships to the real concerns of the Church of Uganda with respect to the problem of human sexuality.

My thoughts in this chapter arise from the need for a more critical look at the issues. I am confident that if we keep listening to one another, the Holy Spirit will eventually bring us to a place where God's grace in all of this conflict will become evident. It is in that spirit that I offer the following reflection.

Responding to concerns from the Church of Uganda

As far as I could gather from the people I interviewed and from the statements of church leaders I have reviewed, the position of the Church of Uganda on the current controversy may be characterised in terms of three basic objections. One is moral, the second relates to the perennial struggle against neocolonialism and the third to the concern for a proper confession of the faith. Let us take a closer look at them one at a time.

The moral objection

The objection that is often immediately raised is the claim that homosexuality is totally incompatible with African values and morality. It is fundamentally un-African, contradicts the structure of the African extended family and violates the sanctity of gender roles upon which the stability of African communities rests. These assumptions are so strongly and deeply imbedded in the psyche of the general public that they elicit little critical examination. In other words, there appears to be no need to argue their validity. People are simply satisfied with making these assertions in absolute terms so that it is self-evident that such relationships are not to be included in the definition of a good and acceptable lifestyle in the context of our cultures.

But what does it mean to say that homosexuality is 'fundamentally un-African'? How does it contradict the structure of the African extended family or violate the sanctity of gender roles? Most of my interviewees were unwilling or unable to probe deeper into these claims. Those who did, however, emphasised the communal character of African (and in this case Ugandan) cultures and how morality must be defined in terms of the collective stability and welfare of the community. A person's identity does not spring from their individuality. It arises from the community to which they belong: the extended family, the clan. An individual's behaviour reflects the integrity of the community to which they belong. On the other hand the community's esteem is reflected in the stature and morality of its members.

A man who is unable to have children leads a very miserable life. There is nothing he can do as an individual to compensate for this glaring emptiness in his life. No achievement can remove the sense of inadequacy that will follow him to the end of his life for being unable to contribute to the stability of his clan and society. Indeed, his sense of inadequacy and shame will extend beyond him to his family: his parents, brothers and sisters, aunts and uncles. They will all share the pain of their male relative's inability to affirm himself in this basic manner.

Yet, if a man cannot have children because of an illness or some other involuntary reason he may win sympathy from the wider community. But the one who wilfully decides to be childless will be looked upon with contempt. He will be seen as thumbing his nose at the community, saying: 'I don't care about my roots. I don't care about my family. I have no interest in sustaining my clan into the future. I am here for myself and myself alone.' This kind of attitude has no place in a culture that elevates the community over the individual.

Since homosexuality cannot lead to reproduction, a man who makes the choice to be in this type of relationship (and it is understood to be a choice) pursues sexual gratification without responsibility or sense of obligation to the community. He is making a choice not to have children and therefore opting for a morally bankrupt lifestyle. It is in this regard that homosexuality is said to be a contradiction and danger to the extended family structure.

Here we also reckon with a worldview that assumes cosmological unity and the ordered interdependency of every element in the universe.

For decades now, researchers in what may be described as African philosophy and religiosity emphasise the aspect of interdependency and the basic unity of the cosmos as part of the African worldview.[4] But this unity is held in a delicate balance that is very easily and often disrupted by human behaviour. African customs and practices do provide adequate means of redressing any minor interruptions to this cosmological harmony and restoring balance. Switching gender roles, however, is a disruption of seismic proportions because it makes a mockery of what the Supreme Being has designed. Having two men or two women live together as husband and wife forces at least one of them to function in the role of the opposite sex. This is what opponents mean by violation of the sanctity of gender roles.

The claim that homosexuality is fundamentally un-African springs from these concerns. They are part of the siege mentality that has characterised the African experience over the last two centuries: the continuing anxiety that we are losing our authenticity and gradually becoming disconnected from our roots. Before I respond to these claims, it may be helpful to present the substance of the second objection, since the critique of neocolonialism arises directly from this sense of being under siege.

The neocolonialism objection

When he finally responded to Louie Crew's open letters, Archbishop Orombi described the tone of those letters as 'condescending and imperialistic'. It was a smart move on his part to slip in these two loaded words. By that one stroke Louie Crew's concerns were recast as a problem of *neo*colonialism: the continuing economic and cultural domination of Africa by the western world. In this territory, Orombi's allies were limitless.

Crew underestimated the context in which he was making these inflammatory remarks. At a time when African underdevelopment continues to be blamed on western imperialism and African poverty is explained in terms of economic dependency, his remarks were bound to invite precisely the kind of response they did.

By describing Crew's attitude as imperialistic and yet maintaining a degree of civility in his own response, Orombi skilfully accomplished at least two things. First, he was able to present himself as a responsible African leader standing firm against western imperialism. In North America, he might be dismissed as posturing. In Africa he would come across as a defender of African interests, alongside Kwame Nkrumah, Julius Nyerere and other highly regarded leaders of postcolonial Africa. Secondly, Orombi managed with those two words to place the debate on homosexuality in the context of the widely endorsed struggle to preserve

African authenticity. The claim that homosexuality is fundamentally un-
African is strongly reinforced in this regard. So now, in the face of what
would appear to be the intention of western imperialism to impose
homosexuality upon us, is it not time to revisit the quest for the true
African personality? That is the question implied in the neocolonialism
objection represented here.

'African personality' and 'negritude' were part of the ideological
framework in which the new African intelligentsia attempted to redefine
Africans away from any assumptions created by European colonisation.
A key aspect of this reconstruction was the search for the authentic
African. Who were we before the invasion of Europeans? How much of
that original heritage can we recover and apply to the rebirth of the
African personality in the postcolonial era? These questions came with
great expectations that traditional African values and culture would
easily become part of contemporary African lifestyle. However, such
expectations also came with serious contradictions, not least of which
was that the African elite – the social grouping that was to embody the
new authentic African personality – was itself already held hostage by
the western consumer culture. Despite political independence, Africa
was still firmly under the economic and cultural grip of western imperialism. A new form of colonialism, fuelled by economic control, was
frustrating the emergence of the authentic African.

The neocolonialist objection begins with the assumption that homosexuality is fundamentally un-African. It then proceeds to frame the
problem in terms of western cultural imperialism enabled by economic
control. From this perspective, the goal of western imperialism is to
frustrate the development of authentic African values and to impose a
morally bankrupt lifestyle upon our people. It is therefore important to
resist this kind of influence even at the price of economic hardship.
Financial aid in itself is not wrong.[5] But when such aid forces us to
accept a way of life that contradicts our values, it must be rejected.

Responding to the moral and neocolonialism objections

When my daughter was fourteen, she asked me a question that continues
to illustrate for me the limits of our knowledge about reality and truth
with respect to our environment. She came to me one day and said,
'Dad', and I replied, 'Yes?'

'So, it is *like* mandatory that public buildings now must have *like*
ramps for the physically challenged, right?'

'Yes, that is correct,' I said.

'Well, so what would people *like* do back then?'

'What do you mean?' I asked.

'*Like* the physically challenged,' she said. 'What would they *like* do?'

'Well . . .' I started giving some sort of answer but then realised that I had none. I didn't know.

'Well?' she asked.

'I don't know', I said. 'I really don't.'

The truth was that I already had enough data (because of my longer experience) to answer that question. What I needed was a moment to reflect on that data in order to present a meaningful narrative about reality with respect to public buildings as my daughter and I experience it. If I had taken that moment, I might have shared a narrative that said something like this: 'Once upon a time the reality was that public buildings had no ramps. Buildings had steps leading from point "A" to point "B" and the physically challenged would seek assistance from others to be carried upstairs. It was normal and absolutely fine. Then one day someone said, let there be ramps. And there were ramps: a new reality, a more inclusive reality, the reality that you and I have come to know and take for granted. This too is normal and absolutely fine.'

Researchers in a variety of disciplines now agree that we are not passive recipients of objective truth and reality out there. We are active participants in the construction of reality as we know and experience it. We interpret our environment, we give meaning to the events we experience, we share those meanings and develop a collective understanding of what is real and true which we then package in some form of narrative and communicate to the next generation.

The narratives that our particular community or society develops about our environment will be presented as objective truth or reality. We might even attempt to communicate reality in absolute terms, that is to say, supposing our representations to be absolutely true. Narratives, however, are at best a macroscopic view of reality. Narratives cannot fully reveal the creative processes behind the reality in question in all its complexity. A narrative will capture only certain aspects of the collective experience that can be meaningfully communicated at any given time. At some point it may be necessary to add new dimensions to the meaning of the experience and therefore to our understanding of reality. In that case the narrative in question will be revised to account for the new information.

Suppose my daughter had posed questions about the shift from the old to the new reality regarding public buildings. To accommodate her need to know I would have had to adjust my narrative so that it incorporated an interpretation of the events that led to the change. This would have added new dimensions to the meaning of the experience. The revised narrative would now present a reality that elevates current practice over what used to be, thus justifying the change as progress.

All this suggests that truth and reality as we know them are always tentative. They are fluid, they develop and grow as we raise more questions and share more information. The apostle Paul was making the same observation when he said, 'what we see now is but like a dim image in the mirror' (1 Corinthians 13:12a). He was saying that reality (as we know it) is a representation. It is a dim reflection, constructed from our collective effort to integrate and make sense of the data accumulated from our environment.

Now, the narratives of postcolonial Africa fulfil at least two functions. On the one hand they are narratives of liberation. They react to the dehumanisation and demonisation of Africa in colonial discourse. The goal of African narratives in this regard is to deconstruct the truth-claims of colonial discourse about Africa and to clear the ground for the reconstruction of an authentic African identity. At the same time, however, in the very process of constructing a new postcolonial African identity, these narratives of liberation also fulfil a stabilising function. They bring different aspects and configurations of the new identity into a cohesive whole that is deployed as the truth about Africa. In this regard they are harmonising narratives or narratives of order.

The assertion that 'homosexuality is fundamentally un-African' must be understood as a fragment of a harmonising narrative. It is part of a narrative or group of narratives that attempt to construct an authentic African identity. As such it is grounded in a rich foundation of post-colonial discourse that is aimed at deconstructing the negative assumptions about Africa formed under colonialism. We have already observed the connection between such narratives and a wide range of claims in postcolonial discourse. The effort to rediscover the authentic African worldview is one such claim. The notion of African community and the structure of the extended family is another. Definitions of morality grounded on the collective stability of the community, the idea of sacrosanct gender roles and the vision of a new African personality may also be added. These are the discursive reconstruction of African identity from which harmonising narratives on the problem of human sexuality in Africa are derived.

It is important to understand that rooted in such a solid foundation of constructive discourse the claim that homosexuality is fundamentally un-African cannot be easily dismissed. Indeed, we must concede that it is true. In other words, it does in fact reflect reality as known within certain socially constructed parameters. The people who hold strongly to this view are not naive, nor are they out of their minds. They are simply responding to a set of socially constructed realities and notions of what is true and wholesome. Having said that, it is equally important to remember that we are not dealing with absolute truth here. This is (as indeed with any other known reality) tentative truth, open to growth as we collect more data from our environment and integrate more dimensions of meaning to our collective experience. The harmonising narratives of postcolonial Africa must remain flexible and open to revision as our understanding of the reality around us changes.

Within the constructs of a new postcolonial African identity, there is room for marginalised voices to be heard and new narratives of liberation to be embraced. The dominant narratives of order in contemporary African cultures will no doubt resist any alternative voices. They are, after all, narratives of stability. Their objective is to limit dissent and to present a coherent reality of the African experience today. But we Africans, perhaps more than anyone else, must understand the oppressive capacity of such a grand ordering of reality. We know how such all-embracing definitions of morality and totalising narratives of right and wrong thrive on silencing alternative voices. They do not reflect the complexity of the lives that people actually live. It is in this regard that the hard-line position of the Church of Uganda on the issue of homosexuality must be challenged. The church needs to take a more critical examination of its position, understanding that we do not yet have all the answers and that certain dimensions of truth are still hidden from our view. The claims we make about our experience and who we are must remain open to new insights from sources hitherto unknown.

The moral and neocolonialism objections sketched above arise from the assumption that the narratives of contemporary Africa represent the absolute and immutable truth about Africans today. I am suggesting that they are, in fact, a macroscopic view of the realities they endeavour to communicate. For this reason it is important to avoid taking a dogmatic stand on reality as they present it, recognising that what we see now is but a dim image in the mirror. We must be sensitive to the voices on the margins of our society that are yearning to be heard. We must be ready to listen to the alternative experience of life that such voices represent and the reality they attempt to communicate. Recognition of the stories from the margins can only enrich our quest for the true African personality reflected in our communities. On the other hand, stifling those voices and denying the reality they represent will impoverish our effort to understand who we are at this point in our history.

The concern for a proper confession of the faith

The third and perhaps most compelling African objection to homosexuality relates to the concern for a proper confession of the faith. This is especially critical because it concerns people's most inner experience: their spirituality and faithfulness to God. It points to the very core of their existence. Its implications transcend the petty anxieties of this world to connect with matters of eternal life or damnation. There is therefore (in some people's minds) no room for games here. We have to be absolutely obedient to God's will.

For the leadership of the Church of Uganda the will of God with respect to human sexuality is simple and clear. According to the Holy Scriptures, 'Male and female God created them' (Genesis 1:27). Homosexuality is sin. It is a deviation from God's will and intention. There is no room for compromise and there are no grey areas. The proper response to sin is repentance. The only question is whether we choose to live in obedience to God or not.

A wide range of biblical references is cited to support this position. The Genesis story of creation cited above is one example. Here, the male/female union is presented as a reflection of God's image. 'So God created humankind in God's own image. In the image of God they were created. Male and female God created them' (Genesis 1:27). From this teaching we may draw the conclusion that homosexuality violates God's image. The leaders I spoke to also appeal to the story of Sodom and Gomorrah for evidence of God's wrath upon the practice homosexuality (Genesis 19). They point to the clear condemnation of homosexuality in Leviticus 18:22 and 20:13. They quote Paul's condemnation of homosexual behaviour in Romans 1:26–27 and his urging to suppress the desires of the flesh by living in the Spirit (Galatians 5:16–26). In light of all this evidence from Scripture, it is clear from these leaders' perspective that homosexual unions are not compatible with a life of faithful and obedient service to God.

Here, we come face to face with the hermeneutical problem at the centre of this controversy, namely how we understand the authority of the Bible and how we read the holy Scriptures. The question is whether in relation to common human experience, we should read the Scriptures (and doctrine) prescriptively or dialectically? The leaders I interviewed would seem to hold the view that the Bible prescribes a code of conduct for the faithful to follow in every situation. In this regard faith is approached from dogma to life. We take doctrinal principles from the Scriptures and apply them prescriptively to particular situations or contexts. Anything in human behaviour that does not fit the stipulations of these principles must be rejected.

Even if we grant that this is the most appropriate model for practising the faith, it will be impossible to apply it consistently in any given cultural context. As much as there are practices from the holy Scriptures that are compatible with the customs of a given cultural setting, there will be others that are not. The incompatible practices will then have to be circumvented or somehow explained away. Once that happens, the prescriptive model is already violated. Perhaps this is why Paul warns against subjecting ourselves to the law, for then we are 'obligated to obey the law in full' (Galatians 5:3).

The Church of Uganda has on occasion applied principles that are not immediately consistent with biblical practice, in order to resolve pressing social issues in its mission field. Its praxis on the issue of polygamy, for example, has evolved, driven primarily by the dynamics of society. The problem of children born out of wedlock and their place in the church, the consumption of wine in Christian homes and the question of traditional rites of passage are some of the issues where church praxis is shaped primarily by questions arising from society rather than principles to be applied directly from the Scriptures. All this leads to the observation that even with the best of intentions, it is not possible to employ the prescriptive model consistently in any cultural setting. Biblical and doctrinal principles themselves arise from particular cultural contexts and will carry the limitations of the social settings from which they developed. A different model of reading the Scriptures and appropriately applying biblical authority in multiple settings needs to be articulated.

In the last three or four decades we have seen a proliferation of alternative models of confessing the faith, models that have drawn attention to the inadequacy of the dogma-to-life approach. What these new models have in common is a commitment on the part of the confessing subject to articulate the questions that are of the greatest significance for them from their unique experience. The starting point for living the faith shifts from dogma to the circumstances of the subject. The questions arising from there lead to a critical examination of the dominant ideological structures that explain the prevailing realities. This critique provides a tentative explanation of the particular set of circumstances as well as some options for action. It is at this point that we engage doctrine, the biblical witness and church tradition. The purpose of this exercise is not to simply apply doctrine to the circumstances in question. It is to reinterpret the faith in light of the prevailing realities.

From this perspective, the proper confession of the faith is that which connects intimately with people's real lives and enables us to experience God's grace and God's special gift of revelation for us in our particular set of circumstances. Our confession of the faith is corporate but the meaning and significance of that confession will have a particular dimension because it springs from our unique experiences. Since I am not living my neighbours' experience, I must trust them to develop their own understanding of the faith we confess and what it means in their special situation. It follows that there will be differences in the way we encounter God's grace and how we practise the faith. For that reason we must avoid the tendency to idolise doctrine and instead refocus our attention on the blessings from the multiple testimonies of God's people from every walk of life.

NOTES

1. See Louie Crew, 'An Open Letter to Archbishop Henry Luke Orombi and Other Bishops', 25 August 2004, http://www.andromeda.rutgers.edu/~lcrew/natter/msg00077.html.

2. Louie Crew, 'Uganda has not Returned UTO Money', 8 September 2004, http://www.newark.rutgers.edu/~lcrew/rel.html.

3. I spoke to five bishops, fifteen clergy and ten lay people.

4. See for example J. N. K. Mugambi and A. Nasimiyu-Wasike, *Moral and African Issues in African Christianity: Exploratory Essays in Moral Theology* (Nairobi: Initiatives Publisher, 1992).

5. The Church of Uganda (including Archbishop Orombi himself) continues to solicit funding from the United States, except now from what are considered to be 'safe' sources. The partnership between the Church of Uganda and the Diocese of Pittsburgh is a good example (see the *Pittsburgh Tribune Review*, 26 November 2004).

Chapter 14

PUTTING RIGHT A GREAT WRONG:
A SOUTHERN AFRICAN PERSPECTIVE

David Russell

The Holy Spirit continues to guide and lead the church of Christ, in spite of all our fallibilities, our questionable assumptions and prejudices. In our age, there are encouraging signs that the Spirit is leading the church to 'put right a great wrong', by repenting of her attitude towards and treatment of homosexual persons. In the tradition of the church, the attitude of Christians towards homosexual persons has been cruelly rejecting and judgemental. The church has been guilty of grave sin against this group of God's people for centuries. Archbishop Desmond Tutu in his foreword to the book *Aliens in the Household of God* writes:

> One would have expected that the church of Jesus Christ would reflect those attractive characteristics of its Lord and Master. Alas, this has not always been the case, for the church of Jesus Christ has caused him to weep yet again, as it has been riddled with racism, sexism, and heterosexism.[1]

In recent times, the church has begun confessing her sins of destructive prejudice. The official teaching is now stressing God's welcoming love towards all people. Alas however, too many church members (perhaps a majority) are still guilty of a cruelly prejudiced attitude towards homosexual persons, 'just for being who they are'.

While preaching God's love for all people, the dominant tradition still asserts that any and all homosexual practice in sinful. It is this issue that will be addressed in this chapter, believing that we still have a way to go in 'putting right a great wrong'. I shall focus on presenting a view that Christian moral norms in the area of sexuality and sexual behaviour should be applied equally to all human relationships, whether hetero-sexual or homosexual.

We are all aware of the highly charged, and at times alas, even bitter debate that is raging in the Anglican Communion (let alone in other churches) around the issue of the morality of homosexual practice. Those Christians holding the traditional position (expressed by the majority of bishops at Lambeth in 1998) have been shocked and even scandalised by the movement to bless same-sex unions in church. They regard this as contrary to a right understanding of the Scriptures, as well as against sound Christian theology and anthropology. Nevertheless, the plea of Danie, an 'ordinary' black South African, needs to be heard and responded to: 'Who says I can't be a Christian and gay? My faith is the same as yours. I am not different to you. Don't treat me differently. I've been born in the image of God. See me as a child of God.'[2]

South Africa: a particular context

All discrimination outlawed

There are particular historical, political and social factors which make South African society more open to debate on these issues than is the case in societies to the north in Africa. The long struggle for liberation against apartheid culminated in the forging of one of the most progressive and enlightened democratic constitutions in the world, with a strong emphasis on human rights. The Bill of Rights (Chapter 2.9.3) outlaws discrimination against anyone on a range of issues and specifically includes sexual orientation. This provision was included in the very first draft. However, a number of gay and lesbian rights groupings, aware of negative traditional attitudes, campaigned vigorously to ensure that it remained included. Many of the individuals in these groupings were well-known and committed members of the majority party, the African National Congress (ANC). They took care to meet with the leaders of all the political parties in the Constitutional Assembly. In the end only a miniscule party of conservative Christians voted against its inclusion in the Bill of Rights. Some parties abstained, but the overwhelming strength of the ANC ensured its inclusion.

The outlawing of discrimination on these grounds (among others), was endorsed 'from the top' by the country's hugely revered leadership – headed by Nelson Mandela – a national and international icon. This has had its impact on social attitudes. In addition, the courts began to deal with cases and hand down judgements in keeping with these newly established rights of homosexual persons. This process continues. It is only a matter of time before the Constitutional Court will open the way for same-sex marriages (or the legal equivalent).

It has become commonplace for the issue of homosexuality to be raised as a matter of human interest in TV talk shows and dramas and in the press. There is still a long way to go but attitudes are undergoing a slow but steady organic change. This context is in stark contrast to neighbouring countries like Namibia and Zimbabwe where the government leadership has voiced very negative views on the issue, to a degree that embarrasses many Christians holding the traditional position.

Professor Njabulo Ndebele, vice-chancellor of Cape Town University and one of South Africa's eminent men of letters, refers to the extreme language of certain church leaders, as 'prejudice that is akin to the blindness of bigotry. Such attitudes cannot define our future.'[3]

Turning then to the churches, they (essentially the English-speaking ones) had been clear in their condemnation of the cruel and inhuman apartheid system, and spoke strongly in defence of human dignity and fundamental rights. When the time came for constitution-making in the early 1990s, there was broadly based support for the human rights emphasis and the basic values of the liberation leadership. Enough of hateful discrimination; everyone was disowning it now! Thus, though all the mainline churches and other faiths remained committed to their traditional teachings on human sexuality, there was little inclination to fight against the inclusion of this particular clause at this juncture. Furthermore, Archbishop Desmond Tutu prophetically wrote a letter to the Constitutional Assembly (16 August 1995) encouraging its inclusion. He was supported in this by the Presiding Bishop of the Methodist Church of Southern Africa, Bishop Stanley Magoba, who had served time on Robben Island with Nelson Mandela and others.

The liberation leadership was intent on establishing a secular state based on justice and human rights. There was fortunately no temptation to provide any 'theocratic underpinning', as in some Islamic states today, or in some 'Christian states' in the past. The highly significant clause in the Constitution outlawing discrimination on the grounds of sexual orientation was due to the progressive views of the liberation leadership, evolved in the crucible of the freedom struggle.

Homosexuality – not just a 'western' phenomenon

Those who assert that homosexuality is only a 'western thing' are either in a state of denial or are revealing their level of ignorance. This is a myth which is fast collapsing. As Professor Welile Mazamisa of the Religious Studies Department of Cape Town University puts it, it is as old as humanity itself.[4] And again, in the words of John Matshikiza, one of Southern Africa's best known journalists: 'the gay phenomenon exists everywhere – much to the chagrin of those who would piously claim that being gay is a European-imported disease.'[5] The truth is that it has been so repressed that people did not acknowledge or even recognise it. And where it might have emerged, it was, and still often is, responded to with violent rejection. However, visit the Good Hope Metropolitan Community Church in Cape Town and you will find a lively charismatic congregation of whom the overwhelming majority is black. The 'spread' of gays and lesbians in South Africa is across the rich and varied ethnic make-up of our population.

Homosexual persons still the victim of cruel prejudice

The Rev. Nothemba, leader in a local charismatic congregation, has a horrendous story to tell: 'When I came out in 1997, I was raped by four men. I was told that I was demon-possessed.' Another group of gays and lesbians from an 'African township' spoke of their experience: 'Most are still in the closet. If you come out you'll lose friends and be isolated. Things have improved; it was once worse. There is still a danger of being raped.' And then Thandi, a black South African studying for the ministry, shares her view: 'Because of some texts in the Bible, Christians have persecuted gays and lesbians. But there is more than one way to interpret the Scriptures.'[6]

The Church of the Province of Southern Africa

The Church of the Province of Southern Africa (CPSA) has had a definite role in shaping the peculiarly South African context concerning attitudes to homosexuality. It is important to remember that the CPSA, apart from the dioceses in South Africa, includes the Dioceses of Swaziland, Lesotho, Namibia and Angola, as well as two dioceses in Mozambique, not forgetting the Diocese of St Helena. This makes for a rich diversity both within our episcopal leadership, as well as among our members. The CPSA fully reflects the radically multicultural nature of society here in Southern Africa. In this way we are a kind of microcosm of the Anglican Communion.

The majority of our members still support the traditional teaching of the church on this issue. However, in keeping with society as a whole, a significant minority of our members are of homosexual orientation, but because of the high degree of prejudice and rejection, which they still experience, they do not yet feel free to 'come out'. Nevertheless, change is slowly taking place, and there are a small number of 'gay-friendly' congregations. This fact is generally known and accepted. At this level at least, tolerance does prevail. More significant perhaps is the fact that as long ago as 1993 the Diocese of Cape Town elected a gay priest, Father Merwyn Castle, to be Bishop Suffragan; his election was accepted with virtually no fuss. He is a greatly loved and respected leader in our church, a person of humble dignity, and an example to the flock.

We, as the CPSA, believe that we have 'an experience to share'. It arises out of our particular history, and in the way we have dealt with conflict and differing convictions. In the last two decades, we have been extraordinarily blessed in having remarkable leadership, first under Archbishop Desmond Tutu (another national and international icon), and then under Archbishop Njongonkulu Ndungane who has also played a significant role both nationally and internationally in church affairs, and more widely in society at large. They are both competent theologians, nurtured in and committed to the solid mainstream of our Anglican tradition. They are both deeply orthodox.

Under Archbishop Desmond's leadership, the bishops evolved a way of handling divisive issues in the church community. We perhaps forget now how deeply divided Anglicans have been over the issue of the ordination of women. Those who were against it quoted Scripture and appealed to the long tradition of the church. In the context of deeply held differing convictions on this issue, Archbishop Desmond encouraged and fostered a spirit and ethos of mutual respect and acceptance among the bishops. We held on to one another, focusing on our oneness in Christ, acknowledging our diversity, and determined to seek God's way forward together. God indeed blessed us, and brought us through our differences in a wonderful way. It was a spiritually enriching process.

It is this very approach that Archbishop Njongonkulu has sought to promote, as we respond to and handle the equally emotive and divisive issue of homosexuality that has come unavoidably to the fore. This is how we have worked together collegially as bishops. Thus the Bishop of Swaziland, Bishop Meshack Mabuza, explains in a statement to the people of his diocese that 'as Bishops and provinces we differ on the present issue, but we are conscious of the importance of remaining a united communion.' He shares his own position, namely that he 'has yet to be convinced' by arguments for change concerning the issue, and further states that 'in our own culture as Swazis, the issue of homosexuality is unacceptable even though it does exist in our midst.' However, he identifies with the Bishops' Statement (September 2003) that in spite of differences, 'we are of one mind in our desire to dialogue [and] are particularly determined to ensure that members of both homosexual and heterosexual orientation and practice are included in such dialogue . . . believing that this is how Jesus would want us to handle this divisive and as yet unresolved issue.'[7]

Then again, the Bishop of Namibia, Bishop Shihala Hamupembe, writes to the people of his diocese, expressing his conviction that whatever we may think about the actions of other provinces, it is nevertheless 'fundamental to our life as Provinces in the Anglican Communion, that we respect the autonomy of each Province and respect the integrity of the processes in each Province'. He then goes on to point out 'that there is a great deal we still have to learn concerning the gift and mystery of human sexuality', and that 'the Anglican Communion is renowned for its diversity, and this is perhaps its major strength . . . The Diocese of Namibia and the Province of Southern Africa are committed to on-going dialogue and listening within the Anglican Communion.'[8]

The bishops are commending this non-combative model to the church. We must help Christians who have uncritically imbibed the mindset and prejudices of the past to challenge themselves and each other. People need to be both encouraged and even 'prophetically prodded', to think and reflect and to try and hear what the Spirit may be saying through the experience of sisters and brothers in Christ.

Called to bridge-build

Some have said that the CPSA is out of step with the rest of Africa, with the implication that we ought to 'get into step'! They have gone further and expressed the view that the leadership of the CPSA is out of step with their own grassroots membership, with the implication once again that it should get into step. The question is: What step? Of course, we should be fully in touch with the views of our sisters and brothers in other provinces, as well as those of our own members – listening and recognising that the Spirit speaks through all God's people. However, questions remain: Should our leadership not be challenging? Is there no place for prophetic leadership? Is not the Spirit longing to cleanse the people of God from the appallingly prejudicial dehumanising attitudes towards homosexual persons that are still all too pervasive? Is it really sufficient for people to quote particular verses from Scripture and some-how fancy that the final and absolute word has been said, ending all searching and questioning debate? Do we not need to dig deeper into the Scriptures to discern the mind of Christ?

Surely it is precisely around this issue that we need to be helping our members to delve more deeply and discerningly. It is part of each person's spiritual journey and growth in Christ to be freed from demeaning prejudice and discriminatory attitudes and practices, and to recognise that no one has easy answers to all questions raised by our expressions of God's gift of sexuality.

It is in this way that the CPSA, arising out of our particular historical context, is called to help build a bridge across the disturbing divides within the Anglican Communion. We certainly do not 'have all the answers'; we too are divided. However, we want, humbly and without presumption, to respond to this calling to be a reconciling bridge, as the churches of the world grapple with this question as never before. God is surely yearning for our provinces in Africa and worldwide to find and engage with one another. Let us trust in God's power to lead us.

Embracing the convictions we share in common

No one involved in this debate is unaware of how deep the divisions go. Nevertheless, we need to remind ourselves and each other of how much we share in common. Much more than divides!

We are all committed to Jesus as our Saviour and Lord, and to seeking his mind and heart in these matters, as in all things.

We accept the Holy Scriptures as the authoritative text of our faith. We recognise, as Anglicans, that the Scriptures need interpreting, and further that Christians have always interpreted them in different ways, aware of our fallibility.

We believe that God loves all people regardless of their sexual orientation.

We are all committed to upholding and furthering the moral values of our faith, and condemn the sins of promiscuity, paedophilia and adultery, along with all the other sins of pride, hate, lust, greed, dishonesty, envy and malice!

Thus, though we may disagree deeply on *how* we interpret the Scriptures, and in some of our understandings of the purpose and right expression of God's gift of sexuality, let us hold on to one another, and rejoice in the 'much more' that we have in common.[9]

Interpreting the Scriptures

The Holy Spirit leading the church in discerning

In all matters of Christian moral teaching, we as Anglicans search the Scriptures, and seek to interpret them under the guidance of the Holy Spirit. We seek to listen to God in the experience of his people, the believing community. We seek to relate our faith (our teachings and traditions) to new insights revealed by the Spirit. The Spirit is alive and active in this dynamic.

The process of interpreting, questioning and reinterpreting the Scriptures is central to the Scriptures themselves, and was fundamental to their unfolding. We think of the classic drama of the Book of Job, questioning the assumptions of the deeply rooted orthodoxy of Judaism concerning the mystery of human suffering.

Jesus initiated in Paul a radical conversion, bringing him to a fundamentally new way of understanding the meaning of the Hebrew Scriptures. Again, we read in Acts 10 how the Spirit led Peter in a dream through an agonising break with the time-honoured sacred traditions of his forebears with regard to the teachings of the Jewish faith concerning foods appropriate to eat. It is a dramatic and moving story: at first Peter stubbornly resisted this 'new word' from God but the Spirit persisted and the radically new insight prevailed. This process has continued in the believing community down the ages – the Spirit leading God's people into deeper truths of the Gospel of Jesus Christ (John 16:12f).

Changing interpretations on major issues

We know well the familiar list of examples of where the church has moved significantly in her teachings and understandings of Scripture in important areas of life and faith. We can all cite numerous texts concerning the institution of slavery, the status of women, the prohibition against divorce and remarriage and other issues. We would neither dare nor wish to uphold the institution of slavery today, though the texts in support of it are formidable. We would be shocked to hear the subjugation of women justified today from many passages of the 'written word of Scripture'.

Perhaps the most significant and radical 'departure from Scripture' which we Anglicans have made is in the matter of remarriage after divorce. The teaching of Jesus is very strict and clear about the permanence of marriage yet the CPSA and other provinces allow for the remarriage of divorcees for a range of reasons. In spite of the strong biblical teaching and the long-standing traditional teaching of the church, we have for pastoral reasons come to the conviction that the Holy Spirit has led us in this direction. There can surely be no question that the church has indeed come to very different understandings concerning the meaning, and 'authority for us', of certain texts. We need to recognise and accept that in a number of instances the church no longer teaches what is 'stated in the written text'.

This fact must be applied without prejudice when we come to consider the conviction being shared with the church in our time by sincere members, namely that the Spirit is leading the church to accept faithful same-sex partnerships. At the very least it should be recognised in principle that this may be true. It is most encouraging to note that the respected conservative writers of the booklet, *True Union in the Body?*, do indeed concede this: 'in principle, of course, Christian Tradition might be in need of correction and development in this area.'[10]

Interpreting the Scriptures in the Anglican tradition

We all agree that the Scriptures are our authoritative text. However, the mainstream Anglican tradition has always been wary of a 'proof-texting' approach to Scripture. This can lead to ridiculous contradictions such as 'letting women speak in church, when the Bible tells us not to'! The Scriptures need to be interpreted by the believing community under the guidance of the Holy Spirit and looking to Jesus Christ as our way and truth. Jesus is the key to all interpretation of Scripture. This process involves interpreting the Scriptures in terms of the core values of the Gospel, and whatever promotes goodness and holiness, wholeness and humanity. It is these that provide the objective criteria for authentic interpretation as we seek the mind of Christ on a particular issue.

The essential problem is how we are to discern and distinguish between those teachings of Scripture which were 'of the times' and those which are 'for all times'. It is now clear that there are some teachings in the Bible which reflect the cultural attitudes and outlook of the age in which they were written and which are not intended by God to bind us today: 'Christians need to discern what are the anchor points of their tradition, and what can be rethought in changing circumstances.'[11] For example, in the Old Testament we no longer feel bound by much that is contained in the Jewish Holiness Code. And in the New Testament, we treat texts referring to the institution of slavery and some of the teachings about women as simply reflecting the mindset of the times.

Authoritative interpretation of Scripture is done corporately, in the Body. In addition, according to Anglican tradition, it should be done under the authority of 'those having oversight'. There are, however, times when God speaks through prophets and confounds the 'guardians of orthodoxy' and the accepted orthodoxy of the time. This was at times how doctrinal teachings and traditions evolved. There can be no sure and infallible way of authoritatively interpreting Scripture. The church of God can and does 'get it wrong' at times; nevertheless it is our joyful conviction that the Holy Spirit is guiding the church of God, in spite of our frailties and blindness of heart.

Human sexuality – evolving understandings

The divide in the Anglican Communion concerning the issues of human sexuality revolves essentially around two areas of focus: (1) the Scriptures and what they require – how to interpret them; and (2) our understanding of God's intention and purposes in making us sexual beings. What is God's purpose regarding the sexual dimension of our being human? For a start, obviously, for the procreation of the species. Is this the only purpose that God had in mind? We would all now say, of course not. Yet for a long time, perhaps for the greater portion of the church's history, this was somehow the dominant message. The church of God and the 'guardians of orthodoxy' have moved a long way in their teaching about God's purposes for this gift and profound dimension of our humanity.

God's gift of sexuality for loving relationship

The gift of human sexuality is clearly not just for procreation; it is for so much more as well. Anglicans are familiar with the moving words of the Marriage Service:

> The union of husband and wife in heart, mind and body is given for their mutual comfort and help in prosperity and adversity. It is given that they may know each other with delight and tenderness

in acts of love. It is given that they may have children and bring them up in the knowledge and love of the Lord'.[12]

The gift of human sexuality is for loving relationship, building companionship and expressing intimate joy and tenderness.

The debate in the churches during the last century around the use of contraceptives is instructive here. An early Lambeth Conference (1908) said no, in a seemingly final way. However, by the time they met in 1930, the bishops had come to view the matter entirely differently, and decided yes! This shift was confirmed again at Lambeth in 1958. Why this shift? Our church was coming to recognise and affirm the significance of the relational aspect of the gift of our sexuality. There was a gradual shift in the mindset of the people of God. A conviction emerged and grew that the Holy Spirit was leading the church into a deeper understanding of God's purpose in giving us this gift of our sexuality. It was now recognised that sexual intercourse with one's spouse need have nothing necessarily to do with procreation as such; indeed, the gift of sexuality might find expression in a way that deliberately excluded the intention to procreate. It is fully appropriate to enjoy this gift of God simply and solely for the expression of loving relationship with one's spouse. This became in time the teaching of the Anglican Church.

Why not for homosexual relationships also?
In recent decades we have been confronted with the question: why should this teaching concerning heterosexual relationships not be applicable to faithful same-sex relationships? It is this issue that divides the Anglican Communion, and the CPSA is struggling with it too. In September 2003, our Provincial Standing Committee, comprising bishops, priests and laity, affirmed the following in a resolution:

1. The CPSA has declared that homosexual orientation is not, in itself, sinful. It is not clear what forms our sexual orientation. Are we born that way (nature)? Is it our early life experience (nurture)? Is it a combination of several factors?
2. What is now being debated by many Christians is whether sexual intimacy between people of the same sex is right or wrong. The church has always taught that the holy place for sexual intimacy is in the context of a life-long, faithful marriage relationship between one man and one woman. Some are now arguing passionately that gays and lesbians should be affirmed in same-sex relationships that are faithful, monogamous and committed.
3. We believe that as we seek further understanding we need to listen to people of all orientations as we seek the heart and mind of Jesus Christ in this and all things.

In considering the position of those who argue that 'gays and lesbians should be affirmed in same-sex relationships that are faithful, monogamous and committed,' we begin with the CPSA's declaration that 'homosexual orientation is not, in itself, sinful.' Though this statement is now widely accepted as a 'given' in the debate, it is still significant in our Southern African context. The extremely negative way in which some Christians talk about homosexuality would suggest that they regard the very orientation as somehow sinful. There were bishops at the Lambeth Conference who argued with a kind of angry conviction that homosexuality was unchristian, wicked and sick – a condition to be cleansed of in a moral and spiritual, let alone psychological, sense. They were manifestly disgusted, not even wanting to discuss the matter. In the light of such unexamined prejudices, the CPSA's simple statement that the orientation is not in itself sinful becomes an important assertion.

However, there remains a much larger constituency in our Communion which believes that while homosexual orientation may not in itself be sinful, it is nevertheless a disorder which needs to be healed. Homosexuals, they believe, are somehow sick, and need to pray for healing. Is not this in essence the position of those who argue that homosexual practice is sinful, and who, therefore, believe that the blessing of same-sex unions is fundamentally contrary to the Gospel? There are further implications here which need to be drawn out.

Homosexual persons placed in an inhuman situation

Homosexuals are actually trapped in a psychologically and morally intolerable situation. For the heterosexual it is perfectly natural and healthy to find a person of the opposite sex attractive. Sexual desire in heterosexuals is a God-given aspect of one's make-up, needing control of course, but otherwise fine and good. For the homosexual person, however, same-sex desire is by this argument, as it were by definition, disordered, unnatural, wrong and therefore by implication, virtually sinful. 'You are sick, not fully or properly human to have such thoughts and desires. Having such desires means that you should not accept yourself as you are! You must change, you must be healed.'

In his book *faith beyond resentment*, James Alison speaks of 'the great annihilation of being which accompanied same-sex desire throughout the monotheistic world and beyond'. Elsewhere he refers to 'the profound "do not be" which the social and ecclesiastical voice speaks to us, and which forms the soul of so many gay people'.[13]

It is becoming clear that it is not helpful to make too significant a distinction between the orientation and the expression of it. How can a person be and yet not be who they are? We must be 'who we are' in the expression of our sexual orientation. The implication of the traditional

position is that God is in effect saying to people of homosexual orientation: 'You are not. I didn't create you. I only create heterosexual people.
You are a defective heterosexual. Agree to be a defect, and I'll rescue
you. But if you claim to be, then your very being is constructed over and
against me, and you are lost.'[14] This is utterly devastating. It is inhuman.
Does the church not need to revisit her traditional teaching and
approach? What is the Spirit saying to the church in our time?

Affirm gays and lesbians as they are

Why should it be assumed that being homosexual is necessarily a
disorder, a type of sickness that requires healing? Why can it not be
accepted that some people grow up differently? What is so terrible about
this condition that those so orientated are encouraged to seek 'healing'
at all costs? Why the annihilating pressure to insist that all homosexual
persons need to change? Why can't this minority be accepted as
different, and affirmed as they are?

There have been those who, after a period during which they have
identified themselves as homosexual, do indeed change and actually
settle into a heterosexual orientation. For some this happens naturally.
For others it might be a painful struggle arising out of psychological
problems which might beset anyone on their journey to wholeness.

Having recognised this, however, it is another matter altogether
dogmatically to assume and assert that all homosexual persons can and
should go on the same journey. We have questioned above such sweep-
ing assumptions, which have led to such destructive prejudice and
treatment of homosexual persons in the history of the church. The vast
majority of homosexual persons do not change, either because they see
no reason to do so or because they might have tried to change but found
it just 'didn't work'. Concerning this overwhelming majority, why not
accept that God accepts them as they are? Does God really want them to
change their orientation? God is not disturbed by a person's sexual
orientation. Why are people so disturbed by difference and not accepting of diversity? God looks to the heart and longs to help us to grow in
likeness to Jesus Christ. It would surely be cruel and seriously misguided
to suggest that in order for people of homosexual orientation to grow in
likeness to Christ they need to change their orientation. We repeat once
again the question of this chapter: why should not the traditional moral
norms in the area of sexuality and sexual behaviour be applied equally
to all human relationships, whether heterosexual or homosexual?

The way ahead – dialogue in the Spirit

The booklet *True Union in the Body?*, referred to above, produced in
2003 by a group from the conservative wing in our Communion, may

actually be pointing us in a positive direction, as we struggle to handle our divisions while holding on to one another. 'It is important', they say, 'that the Church respects (and engages in serious dialogue with) individual Christians who see loving and committed same-sex relationships in our culture as lying outside the scope of these passages of condemnation.'[15] They go on to make what is surely a significant 'concession', coming as it does from respected conservative bishops and theologians: 'Strong opposition to the public conferral of legitimacy on same-sex unions does not necessarily entail the exclusion of all Christians who enter such unions in the sincere belief that they are an acceptable pattern of Christian discipleship. Here there is room for a generous inclusivity in the name of Christ.'[16]

This position implies that in this matter the writers are suggesting that respect should be given for freedom of conscience. This, of course, would certainly not be applied to any member who was a practising adulterer, paedophile, thief or fraudster! The implication is surely that, in the case of committed same-sex relationships, we are dealing, even from their conservative perspective, with an ethical 'grey area', in which it is appropriate to suspend judgement, as we listen and dialogue and research further. Could not this inclusive position be accepted by the bishops of the Anglican Communion as the common ground and basis from which to continue the dialogue, holding on to one another, as we seek the heart and mind of Christ in this matter?

We have come through to a place of deeper awareness and sensitivity and would not now deny that in the tradition of the church the attitude of Christians towards homosexual persons has largely been cruelly rejecting and judgemental. Surely then the appropriate starting point for our dialogue in the Spirit is confession and repentance. We need to be healed of those prejudices which have been so destructive. We as a church need to pray for the grace to ask our lesbian and gay sisters and brothers in the Body for forgiveness. Here lies our challenge. This is the redeeming way. In God's loving time, we will find each other and rejoice with each other in our shared journey to wholeness in Christ.

NOTES

1. Paul Germond and Steve de Gruchy (eds), *Aliens in the Household of God: Homosexuality and Christian Faith in South Africa* (Cape Town: David Philip, 1997). This book is a milestone for South African writing on this subject. The twenty-six chapters include impressive analyses, as well as moving life stories by various contributors.
2. 'Created in the Image of God', video produced by Inclusive and Affirming Ministries (IAM), Cape Town, 2003. This is an excellent presentation of the issues in the South African context.
3. Prof. N. Ndebele, 'Gays, the Church and Progress in Human Consciousness' in

The Gateway, St George's Cathedral, Cape Town, Advent 2003, p.13.

4. 'Created in the Image of God', IAM video.

5. *Mail and Guardian*, 21 November 2002.

6. These stories are all from 'Created in the Image of God', IAM video.

7. Statement on Homosexuality issued by the Rt Rev. Meshack Mabuza, Bishop of the Anglican Church of Swaziland, 6 November 2003.

8. Press Statement. The Rt Rev. Shihala N. Humupembe, Bishop of the Diocese of Namibia (CPSA), 5 November 2003.

9. See 'Discussion Document on Human Sexuality' issued by Archbishop Njongonkulu Ndungane, Archbishop of Cape Town, January 2003.

10. *'True Union in the Body?* 'A contribution to the discussion within the Anglican Communion concerning the public blessing of same-sex unions', commissioned by Archbishop Drexel Gomez, Archbishop of the West Indies (2003), p.27.

11. *Being Human: A Christian Understanding of Personhood Illustrated with Reference to Power, Money, Sex and Time*, Report of the Doctrine Committee of the General Synod of the Church of England (London: Church House, 2003), p.80.

12. *An Anglican Prayer Book 1989*, Church of the Province of Southern Africa, p.461.

13. James Alison, *faith beyond resentment: fragments catholic and gay* (London: Darton, Longman & Todd, 2001), pp.xi and 39. The writers of *Some Issues in Human Sexuality*, a discussion document from the Church of England House of Bishops, 2003, do not do justice to Alison's theological position. He is not denying that we exist in a moral universe (in this sense, in a 'natural moral order') under God. He is raising questions around our 'certainties' about what is 'natural'. He is asserting that our *assumptions* as to what constitutes God's creative order are necessarily and creatively provisional. The living Spirit is enlightening us.

14. Alison, op. cit., p.202.

15. *True Union in the Body?*, p.25.

16. ibid., p.34.

Chapter 15

DEHUMANISATION FROM THE PERIPHERY

Julius Powell, Jr

Introduction

This chapter examines the perceived source and cause of homophobia in Jamaican society and the wider Caribbean culture, the negative impact a position of intolerance by the church has had on the gay community and the nature of identity politics. In a press briefing marking the 2003 Synod of the Anglican Diocese of Calabar in Nigeria, Bishop Tunde Adeleye declared, 'In one of my sermons in the cathedral, I did mention that [homosexuality] is immoral, sinful and unacceptable to both human beings and animals. Those who wish to practise it must be far less than animals. We have no apologies.'[1] If these words represent the conservative view of the church in Africa and the global South, then the homophobia experienced by gays and lesbians of African descent should come as no surprise. Having experienced the horrors of slavery and colonisation, gays and lesbians of African descent in the Anglican South are being dehumanised from the periphery.[2]

'Colonialism and imperialism, in theory, aimed to set up respectable, loyal and profitable European outposts overseas, and to impart European (generally Christian) virtues to "savages" and "heathen"; in this design, homosexuality had no place.'[3] This is the premise for the high level of homophobia in the Caribbean – which is reinforced through church teaching and anti-sodomy laws. The denunciation of the election, confirmation and consecration of Gene Robinson as Bishop of New Hampshire in a statement of thirteen 'Primates of the Global South', a last vestige of British colonial imperialism, reflects this thinking – causing one to ask whether it is possible to decolonise the Caribbean and African churches from a theology of oppression.[4] The continuous attacks by Archbishop Drexel Gomez of the Church in the Province of the West Indies (CPWI) reaffirms the oppression of a significant section of the church – a group that has contributed to the mosaic that makes us Catholic. I shudder to think that our Primates and Metropolitans see homosexual persons as animals, a dehumanisation reminiscent of how occidentals justified their plunder of the new world.

It is apt to describe the view posited by our southern brothers and sisters in the words of Paulo Freire: a 'dehumanization, which marks not only those whose humanity has been stolen, but also (though in a different way) those who have stolen it, is a distortion of the vocation of becoming fully human.'[5] Although 'conservative Christians' tend to focus on 'hate the sin, not the sinner', the opposition of the thirteen southern Primates to the consecration of an openly gay man as Bishop of New Hampshire supports a culture of violence and homophobia against the gay and lesbian community in the Church in the Province of the West Indies.

Ministers perpetuate a culture of violence

At the age of six, I knew I was different. I can recall my mother asking, 'What would you like to be when you grow up?' I replied in earnest, 'A fireman!' Mummy said to me, 'You have no ambition! Is there nothing else you would like to be, like a doctor or lawyer?' I thought about it for a while and then said, 'I want to be like Reverend Steadman.' At six years old your local parish priest can have a lot of influence; but aware of my own life experiences, I left this issue of responding to the *call* and being *faithful to ministry* in the back of my mind for another twenty-two years.

I decided in 1996 to apply to the Diocese of Jamaica as a candidate to the priesthood, having struggled with my sexuality and my thoughts of the church's perception of me. I thought heavily about the progressive approach to the ordination of women in my local diocese and province and felt that the time was right to make a personal commitment to full-time ministry.

As a candidate to the priesthood, I met with the bishop's chaplains, telling them I wanted my ministry to focus on issues affecting gay, lesbian and bisexual persons, as well as persons living with HIV/AIDS. The then Bishop of Montego Bay commented, 'Oh! Why would you want to do that?' I realised that though I could dish out the standard response to ministry, I did not. But in the process of discernment I thought it would be a long journey; but I had already come to the realisation that God made us (gays and lesbians) in his image and likeness. The bishop's chaplains preferred instead to shroud themselves in a 'Victorian veil of silence' and ignore the issue of my sexuality. The diocesan bishop approved my candidacy but I had no idea of the backlash that would ensue as a result.

At my local parish church, the curate, a female priest, was enraged. In her conversations with me two weeks prior to my entering theological college, she made it clear that she was leading a delegation to protest the diocesan bishop's decision to accept my candidacy to the priesthood. She wanted answers to several questions, for example, 'What type of sordid and decadent sexual behaviour would I be engaged in with other male students at the United Theological College?' 'Could I be trusted to have any interaction with young boys in the church if I managed to "escape" and become a priest?' 'If there were visitors to the rectory, would I acknowledge the presence of a male partner?' 'Would I indulge in sexual orgies in the rectory?' She felt that, as a gay eucharistic minister licensed to assist with the chalice, every time I took up the chalice during the Mass God would strike me down with lightning! And she made it clear that she would never take Communion from me knowing that I was a homosexual person.

With these questions before me, I wondered if the Anglican Church could be true to its own heritage. The words of my curate seemed harsh, especially against the backdrop of my coming full circle and accepting the validity of her ordination and the right to include women in ordained ministry. I had a hard time believing that it was my curate, one of the first women to be ordained in the local church – a process that I recall took twenty-five years – who struggled most with my sexuality. I thought that of all the people, she would understand oppression. Facing ostracism from my family and having my house stoned at night by local residents, I took my curate's pastoral advice seriously and withdrew my application to the priesthood.

As a homosexual person who had received the gift of the Holy Spirit through baptism and confirmation, I wondered why the 1662 Book of Common Prayer reassured the faithful that clergy are but vessels, called by God to celebrate the Eucharist on Jesus' behalf. Why is Article 26 not prominent in today's liturgical consciousness? I also wondered, what happened to Jesus' commandment, 'the greatest of these commandments is love'? Article 26 of the Thirty-Nine Articles, speaking of clergy presiding at the sacraments, states: 'Neither is the effect of Christ's ordinance taken away by their wickedness, nor the grace of God's gifts diminished from such as by faith, and rightly, do receive the Sacraments ministered unto them; which be effectual, because of Christ's institution and promise, although they be ministered by evil men.'[6] Because of the institutionalisation of homophobia in the Church in the Province of the West Indies (CPWI) one could argue that maybe half the battle was won.

There appears to be a tacit understanding of the presence of homosexual persons in lay ministry, but an obvious rejection of their full participation as ordained ministers. It is this next step to the priesthood that triggers a sense of fear in the 'evangelical' arm of the church, that homosexual persons cannot become 'good' role models: a rejection which in some way contradicts the call of the Samaritan woman, Mary Magdalene, Judas Iscariot or Zacchaeus the tax collector. In fulfilling its purpose as a vehicle through which social justice issues are channelled, the church in a modern society needs to take responsibility for engendering change and embracing diversity.

Culture of violence

In order for me to articulate the structural and cultural issues of homo-sexuality, I must examine and explore the effects that the culture of violence and homophobia in Jamaica has had on gays and lesbians there.

In August 1997, the Commissioner of Corrections in Jamaica announced a proposed condom distribution programme within the island's prisons to stem the rising HIV infection rate among male prison inmates and warders. The outcry over this proposal culminated in a general strike of prison warders and a three-day insurrection of hundreds of prisoners claiming that the programme assumed they were all homo-sexual and, in addition, encouraged homosexual activity in the prisons. By the time the armed forces could quell the rioting, sixteen prisoners, suspected to be homosexual (the perceived 'targets' of the programme), were brutally murdered and set on fire, while over fifty others were severely injured, all at the hands of fellow inmates.

Extreme scenarios like these colour my experience of living in Jamaica, fuelling my inner drive, passion and motivation to frame a response to the exclusion of lesbian, gay, bisexual and transgender (LGBT) persons from the Anglican church in the Caribbean. The thir-teen 'Primates of the Global South' in their understanding of ministry demonstrate a lack of tolerance towards the practical and systematic inclusion of these minorities and the richness and diversity that LGBT peoples can bring to enable a deeper experience of the image and likeness of God.

> People living with HIV/AIDS and men who have sex with men face numerous human rights abuses that constitute barriers to obtaining necessary medical care. Among these are discrimination by health workers who forced them to wait extended periods of time to be seen, treated them in an abusive or degrading manner, provided inadequate care, or denied them treatment altogether. Health workers also routinely violated their privacy by disclosing confidential information about HIV status and sexual orientation.[7]

The church, and by extension the wider society, lacks the capacity for assessing and evaluating the overall infrastructures and the efficacy of prevention messages targeting lesbian, gay, bisexual and transgender persons living with HIV and AIDS. The continued opposition to homo-sexuality in the CPWI prevents it from critically looking at its own policies to determine an effective response to the growing numbers of new HIV infections in their various dioceses. Similarly, a religious fundamentalist view of Christianity prevents the Caribbean church from analysing the various policies, agencies and support systems within governmental and non-governmental structures that affect gay and lesbian populations living with HIV/AIDS.

Popular culture and societal norms

Dancehall culture and reggae have evolved from the euphoria of love and peace, espoused by stalwarts like Bob Marley, to the current phenomenon that promotes the murder of homosexual persons. 'Dancehall lyrics have a long history of violence: Seminal artist Buju Banton's 1992 hit "Boom Bye Bye" urged listeners to burn, shoot and pour acid on gay people, and Beenie Man's (Anthony Moses) current underground hit "Weh Yuh No Fi Do" says gay men should die.'[8] In one of Beenie Man's songs, 'That's Right', he sings; 'We burn out Chi-Chi man and then we burn out sodomite and everybody bawl out, say, "Dat right!"'[9] 'Chi-Chi man' and 'sodomite' are Jamaican patois for a male homosexual person and a female lesbian respectively. Jamaican popular culture and societal norms have long reflected the position that homosexuality is sinful, harmful and degrading. In the wider Caribbean, similar attitudes inform public discourse on the issue and in the Commonwealth Caribbean, homosexual sex is an outlawed and prosecutable offence. For these reasons I became involved in 1998 with the then fledgling Jamaica Forum for Lesbians, All-Sexuals[10] and Gays (J-FLAG) – the only political organisation on the island advocating the decriminalisation of homosexuality and the recognition of human rights for lesbian, gay, bisexual and transgender people. J-FLAG reports:

> Jamaica's intolerance of homosexuality is so acute that it has gained international notice, through the lyrics of gay-bashing songs like 'Boom Bye Bye', and the hostility to our gay visitors, which they have reported to international organisations like the International Lesbian and Gay Travel Association. It is not only the international gay community that has been incensed by such incidents, but also persons of heterosexual orientation who value human rights and justice. Some boast that intolerance towards the gay and lesbian community is 'part of our culture', and that protection of homosexuals from discrimination is, likewise, counter-cultural and even anti-nationalistic.[11]

Oddly enough, Jamaica has a long tradition of recognising and respecting individual rights and freedoms in the international arena. It should, therefore, make every effort to protect the human rights of its citizens whose sexual orientations differ from the norm against verbal and physical abuse. The repeal of the 1861 'Offences against the Person Act', which criminalises acts of homosexuality with ten years imprisonment at hard labour, would be a step in the right direction.

As a last resort, it is essential for gays to have recourse to rebellion against tyranny and oppression, to ensure that our human rights are protected by the rule of law. We wish to share a vision of a world in which every person enjoys all of the human rights enshrined in the Universal Declaration of Human Rights and other international human rights covenants. As with the numerous cases of extra-judicial killings by the Jamaica Constabulary Force, there is an absence of evidence and court documents in Jamaica to support the claim that the human rights of Jamaican gays and lesbians are protected. The perception is not only in England that Jamaica is homophobic! It is a global perception – of a high level of arrogance and a putrid Victorian wall of silence, which permeates the whole society. Having discussed the perception of Jamaica's homophobic culture at international conferences in Brazil, Trinidad and Dominica, I know that many share this view.

It would be good if Jamaica could give consideration to the Constitution of the Republic of South Africa, in force since 7 October 1997, which declares that the state may not unfairly discriminate directly or indirectly against anyone on one or more grounds, including race, gender, sex, pregnancy, marital status, ethnic or social origin, colour, sexual orientation, age, disability, religion, conscience, belief, culture, language and birth.

Jamaicans are still stuck in a world defined by the 1861 Offences against the Person Act. The country remains a closed society, which does not understand the importance of difference and has no positive concept of 'the other'. The end result is that homophobia is institutionalised into the *very structure and function of society*, which includes church, state, family, the individual, politics and the economy. For the purposes of this discussion we will examine only two specific elements of institutionalised homophobia: state and church.

Institutionalised homophobia
One cannot enter into discussion of the perceptions that impede HIV/AIDS prevention and community mobilisation efforts without examining the issue of homophobia in the church and how cultural barriers influence this homophobia. I am committed to changing the social structure of society and I am encouraged by this debate to work aggressively to redefine the concept of institutions like the church and family. These institutions have become agents of oppression rather than agents of social change. Homosexual behaviour challenges the patriarchal role of men in Caribbean society and family as is evidenced by the retention of sodomy laws in all the territories.

Because men and women have very well defined roles in the Caribbean they are more affected by socio-cultural contexts. The gay male is seen as a threat to the traditional Caribbean man, and their feminisation in a culture of machismo precludes any open expression of homosexuality, resulting in their penalisation and the brutal condemnation of homosexual persons.

There are many advocates in support of Archbishop Gomez's intolerance toward gays and lesbians. For example, Roman Catholic bishops in the Caribbean have protested against recommendations that Jamaica decriminalise homosexual acts. Monsignor Richard Albert, one of the most prominent Roman Catholic priests in Jamaica, spoke on behalf of the Caribbean bishops when he was quoted by the national newspaper, the *Daily Gleaner*, declaring, 'There is an obvious consistency in the Old and New Testament salvation history about the moral unacceptability of homosexual relations.' The bishops spoke out after a government-appointed committee on human rights reform recommended that homosexual acts in private between consenting adults should be decriminalised. Former colonial power Britain has been urging Commonwealth Caribbean governments to liberalise anti-gay laws.[12]

The source of the intolerance 'it is felt is cultural, that we are a Christian country and that our homophobia finds justification in the Bible. But I think that if we aspire to be a non-theocratic society then we should not be using the Bible to make moral laws.'[13] My involvement in J-FLAG and Jamaica AIDS Support (JAS) allowed me to channel my energies into a *new ministry* – working for community-based organisations geared towards removing intolerance towards homosexuality and doing the type of social change and social justice programmes the Gospel of Jesus is presumed to be about.

The call for Anglicans to join the thirteen 'Primates of the Global South' in their 'repentance for failing to be sufficiently forthright in addressing this issue [of homosexuality] in the past' is nothing but hypocritical! The Primates' statement only goes one step further to reinforce the institutionalisation of homophobia in the wider Anglican and Caribbean society, and begs a deeper understanding of the impact of discrimination on gays and lesbians in Jamaica.

The impact of discrimination on gays and lesbians

The local gay rights advocacy group in Jamaica, J-FLAG, believes that,

> Acts of discrimination are usually due to ignorance, lack of respect, intolerance and fear, to name a few. They are often exhibited through acts of physical, emotional, mental and verbal abuse. Other manifestations include (but are not limited to) hiring procedures, access to services and social interaction.[14]

J-FLAG holds the position that support of *any* form of discrimination is support of *all* forms of discrimination. J-FLAG believes that 'any act of discrimination meted out to an individual known or alleged to be homosexual or bisexual is profoundly unjust. Moreover, discrimination is a violation of human rights as outlined in the Universal Declaration of Human Rights as well as the Jamaican Constitution.'[15] It is terrible to see that Archbishop Gomez does not recognise acts of discrimination, which are experienced by lesbian and gay parishioners in Jamaica and worldwide, as an important human rights issue around which to *unite* the 'Primates of the Global South'.

When Archbishop Gomez and other members of the church support the exclusion of lesbian and gay people from participating fully in the ministry of the church, it reinforces a culture of violence and encourages the homophobic attacks for which Jamaica is famous worldwide. There are documented interviews with surviving partners and families of over fifty members of the gay community in Jamaica dating back to 1981. A common link between most survivors is the knowledge that their loved ones were murdered purely on the basis of their perceived sexual orientation. The causes of their deaths generally demonstrate violence and vengeance, with victims' having their throats slashed or being stabbed many times. What has served to justify the murder of homosexual persons is that their deaths are followed by a public sense of relief – a notion that has been reinforced by a fundamentalist view of religion and homosexuality. 'In April 2000, a man was allegedly refused police protection which he requested after he received death threats. The man fled his home after his partner was chased by a mob into a church and killed.'[16] He later died after being shot seven times on the steps of a church on Holy Saturday.

> The night before Lawrence O.'s interview with Human Rights Watch, a friend of his was robbed and stabbed in front of him. The police came to the scene, retrieved the knife, and left without investigating the incident or assisting the injured man in obtaining medical care. 'The guy [the assailant] told the police that we were battymen. So the police just left. The police should have done something. [My friend] was cut and he was bleeding ... They looked at us and said, "you are all battymen". Then they took the knife [from the assailant] and told him to go.' Tonya Clark, a nurse with Jamaica AIDS Support in Kingston, said that a JAS client who had suffered a head injury had been denied services twice in the week prior to her interview with Human Rights Watch. In June 2004, Gary T. was beaten and suffered a head injury. He first went to the police, who referred him to the hospital with a form to be completed with details of his injury. After Gary T. told the nurse that he had HIV, she tore the form up and told him to leave. A JAS

social worker returned to the hospital with Gary T., where they again refused to treat him.[17]

The church in the Caribbean has been noticeably silent at the diocesan and provincial level on these murders, which in my mind raises doubts about the sincerity of the 'repentance' of the thirteen 'Primates of the Global South'. The repentance, which they so vigorously seek, is nothing short of repentance for being 'both human and less than human'.[18] It is interplay of power being exercised over a minority group, in much the same way that women were subjugated and excluded from participating in and exercising their right to vocations in ordained ministry.

What the Primates have offered is a passive form of discrimination, one that occurs by failure to act, not meeting the needs of particular groups, often with the justification of providing equal treatment for all, but instead failing to meet the special needs of some.[19] 'Discrimination refers to any form of distinction, exclusion or restriction affecting a person, usually, but not only, by virtue of an inherent personal characteristic, irrespective of whether or not there is any justification for these measures.'[20]

In January 2005 Dr J. Peter Figueroa, Chief of Epidemiology and AIDS for Jamaica's Ministry of Health, commented:

> A number of underlying social factors that affect HIV/AIDS prevention and treatment on the island include poverty, marginalization, stigmatization, and population movements. These social factors were driving the HIV/AIDS epidemic in Jamaica. Currently in Jamaica there are an estimated 22,000 persons living with HIV/AIDS in Jamaica where men accounted for 46.9 per cent of the annual AIDS cases in 2003.[21]

It is generally accepted that a variety of factors force the gay and lesbian community to remain hidden from the general public and from the church community in particular. These factors include the stigmas attached to and the discrimination resulting from homosexuality and infection with HIV/AIDS, and the lack of a broader approach to sexuality and knowledge of HIV/AIDS. It is widely believed that the continued hiding of the gay population from the general public and from the church community at large creates a barrier to a better understanding of sexuality, HIV/AIDS prevention and community mobilisation efforts. The effect of the politics of HIV/AIDS on the gay community, stigma, silence, discrimination, denial and lack of confidentiality all undermine prevention, care and treatment and increase the impact of the epidemic on individuals, families, communities and nations.[22]

Identity politics

The church has long held the view that sexual orientation is a learned behaviour. It is necessary to consider other constructs. One possible alternative is 'identity politics'. 'Identity politics typically concerns the liberation of a specific constituency marginalised within its larger context. Members of that constituency assert or reclaim ways of under-standing their distinctiveness that challenge dominant oppressive characterisations, with the goal of greater self-determination.'[23]

Identity politics is a critical issue for oppressed groups. The position of the 'Primates of the Global South' should continue to embrace and affirm various definitions of sub-groups of 'Men who have Sex with Men' (MSM) in their struggle to liberate themselves from a culture of homophobia, violence and cultural ostracism from the wider church community. MSM are a living example of the fluidity in the conscious-ness of this population and the context within which their opinions are shaped. This information helps to inform us in our response to commu-nity mobilisation efforts – a strategy the church could employ to increase its membership and address the paucity of priests and large number of parishes without clergy. It is this recognition of identity that is lacking within the politics of dominance perpetuated by mainstream society.

Jamaican popular culture continues to reinforce negative stereotypes of the gay community through daily bursts of homophobia heard on radio, and through popular music such as hip-hop, reggae and now calypso. Henry Louis Gates describes this experience poignantly: 'Much of black suffering stems from historical racism; most gay suffering stems from contemporary hatred.'[24]

Experiencing hatred and contempt by the dominant mainstream church community traumatises gays and lesbians. This hatred and con-tempt is displayed on a daily basis under the guise of *culture, morality, traditional teachings of the church*, and the *fundamental right of freedom of speech*, which often serve to trample the human rights of gays and emasculate their efforts to fully participate in ministry. In essence it can be equated with a form of religious evil.

In a study I conducted among 'African American Young Men who have Sex with Men' (AAYMSM)[25] in 2002, 55.6 per cent of the total number of respondents said that the statement by Ice Cube, 'Real niggers ain't gay', is not an African American belief,[26] which shows that AAYMSMs are not *unplugged* from the mainstream African American community. Further analysis of the results within the AAYMSM community rejects and condemns the statement made by Ice Cube, reiterating that it is not the position of the larger African American society. The research showed that because AAYMSMs are overly concerned about how they are perceived by society, they appear to be mindful of what images and opinions are diffused about them through the media. They also appeared to be making a statement as to where AAYMSMs stand and to claim their place within the black community.

A Caribbean gay identity in my view is still fragmented, and where it exists, it is at best constructed around an identity congruent to nation states – with Caribbean homosexual persons extracting only what is important from an individual country perspective. Community organisers in movements such as J-FLAG espoused views to deepen the levels of integration in advocating for human rights reform. Because the Jamaican homosexual community remains resolute in their nationalist outlook, there is no appropriate reaction to the call for more participation of homosexual persons in the church. The fear of being known also makes it impossible for any meaningful cohesion of a political identity among this community. And, especially in the case of Jamaican homosexual persons, any construct of community and identity based on sexual orientation is remote and at best repugnant.

'There may be ways in which a homosexual identity can be contemplated ... within the Christ-given human identity that admits of no division.'[27] The time is now for gays and lesbians in the Caribbean church and across the Anglican Communion to rethink the politics of identity in much the same way as mainstream gays and lesbians in the African American community in the United States and the Diaspora have done. bell hooks suggests that any critic exploring the radical potential of postmodernism as it relates to racial difference and racial domination needs to consider the implications of a critique of identity for oppressed groups.[28] The consecration of an openly gay man as bishop should not be seen as rebellious and erroneous but as a deeper understanding of a homosexual identity, which is just as legitimate as an identity based on race, class or national consciousness.

The church's mandate

The task of the leadership of the Anglican Communion is to challenge the Communion to create a new understanding of liberated 'national consciousness'[29] within the autonomous dioceses and to embrace the ideal of securing employment and the basic necessities of life for all. The various 'South' dioceses should not see the issue of homosexuality as something being imposed by the more affluent and decadent 'North' but the expansion of their own 'national consciousness'. The 1963 Anglican Congress described Anglican life in communion at the time as 'mutual interdependence and responsibility in the Body of Christ'.[30] The encouragement by the thirteen 'Primates of the Global South' of the 'Network of Anglican Communion Dioceses and Parishes' as a 'hopeful sign of a faithful Anglican future in North America' only further impedes the church from being One. The Primates should be concerned with healing rather than placing the full weight of their office behind a move to add one more group to the list of churches that are out of communion with Canterbury. As the Windsor Report states:

> Communion is, in fact, all about mutual relationships. It is expressed by community, equality, common life, sharing, inter-dependence, and mutual affection and respect. It subsists in visible unity, common confession of the apostolic faith, common belief in scripture and the creeds, common baptism and shared Eucharist, and a mutually recognised common ministry. Communion means that each church recognises that the other belongs to the One, Holy, Catholic and Apostolic Church of Jesus Christ, and shares in the mission of the whole people of God. It involves practising a common liturgical tradition, and intending to listen, speak and act alongside one another in obedience to the gospel. In communion, each church acknowledges and respects the interdependence and autonomy of the other, putting the needs of the global fellowship before its own.[31]

The 'Primates of the Global South' should seek to encourage and nurture the diversity of cultures, which exist in the church today. As Samir Amin notes:

> Cultural diversity is a fact. But it is complex and ambiguous. The forms of diversity inherited from the past, however legitimate they might be, are not necessarily synonymous with diversity in the construction of the future, which should not only be admitted but also advocated.[32]

The role of the 'Primates of the Global South' should be to embrace concepts of the *other* and *difference*, for example, by facilitating problem-solving meetings to work with gay and lesbian Anglicans to plan and chart their own course out of poverty and oppression. I hope that gay and lesbian Anglicans will come to recognise that their sexual orientation and the stereotypes associated with them are labels that the greater society has placed on them and do not essentially hinder their own actions toward self-actualisation.

Coming full circle

It is ironic that at the time of my 'scandal' and 'outing' in the church in Jamaica, my curate suggested that I go to the Episcopal Church in the United States, where I could find solace and enter the priesthood. I had no idea that seven years later I would be actively participating in the life of the Body of Christ in the Episcopal Church tradition. My experience in the Jamaican church left deep wounds and scars still visible years after the fact. It was the spiritual conviction of a fellow church member at the Church of St Mary the Virgin, Molynes Road, in Kingston, Jamaica, who took time to comfort me, that nurtured me back into the fold. Three years later in 2000, with her help, I was able to visit with my curate as she lay in bed, stricken with breast cancer. As I listened to her apology and her request for me to be a pallbearer, I recalled her characterisation of me years earlier. I wondered then if I could truly trust the church to share the gift of the Holy Spirit.

I served for four years on the executive board of the National Council of Anglican Youth Fellowships, the governing body of 200 youth programmes in the Diocese of Jamaica and the Cayman Islands. During my tenure I interacted with nearly 250 Anglican churches in the Diocese of Jamaica and in each church I met at least one gay male actively participating in the leadership and governance of the local church. The Bishop told me, 'You are not the first to come to ministry and you certainly won't be the last!' I would much prefer an openly gay bishop as Chief Shepherd than a closeted homosexual suffering from internalised homophobia and self-hatred. I chose not to remain 'simply quiet' about my sexual orientation (not that it was being broadcast on CNN) but to declare and develop my interest in a ministry reflective of my sexual orientation. I have come full circle in answering the encouraging call to strengthen my vocation. I have sought to better understand the Christian ethos and have responded in accordance – just as I AM.

Conclusion

My objective in the long term is not only to suggest structural improvements but also to ask the Caribbean church to critically examine the need to refocus its energies on the legal and cultural foundations of homophobia and homophobic violence that often mitigate the process of recognition, provision and care for afflicted lesbian, gay, bisexual and transgender persons at the institutional level as well as at the community level. The Caribbean church fails to recognise the impact its current attitudes towards homosexuality have on how policy decisions are made as they relate to HIV/AIDS in the Caribbean. These attitudes continue to reinforce negative stereotypes of homosexual persons, especially each time the church fails to include such persons in the sacred ministry.

The church fails to recognise the hurt and pain experienced by gays and lesbians because it has chosen to adapt to a culture of violence and hatred towards sexual minorities. To repeal the anti-gay legislation, a legacy of British colonialism, more work needs to be done in the wake of institutionalised homophobia and acquiescence of the church in supporting these laws. My hope is that with this issue on the agenda for debate, the Primates of the Anglican Communion will begin to focus their energies to assure homosexual persons that they have a rightful place in the body and life of the church of Christ. We can help the 'Primates of the Global South' in this time of crisis. It is possible to create collaborations to work effectively to create democracy in our church by incorporating the ideals of pluralism and cultural diversity; by developing an understanding of inclusiveness; by ensuring that all members are committed to the wider church and its objectives; and by ensuring full participation by all members of both sides of the divide.

NOTES

1. 'Behind the Mask: Mind, Body and Spirit Christianity', accessed 26 September 2004 from http://www.mask.org.za/SECTIONS/mind%20body%20spirit/christianity_11.htm.

2. The term periphery is defined as the countries and regions that do not have local control of the process of accumulation, which is mainly shaped by external constraints. See Samir Amin, *Delinking towards a Polycentric World* (London: Zed Books Ltd, 1990), p.10.

3. Robert Aldrich, *Colonialism and Homosexuality* (London and New York: Routledge Taylor and Francis Group, 2003), p.4.

4. 'Thirteen Global Primates State "ECUSA has Separated Itself"', Anglican Communion News Service #3773, 9 February 2004.

5. Ana Maria Araujo Freire and Donaldo Macedo (eds), *The Paulo Freire Reader, Pedagogy of the Oppressed*, Ch. 1, 'The Fear of Freedom' (London and New York: Continuum, 2000), p.45.

6. *Book of Common Prayer* 1662, Article 26 of the Articles of Religion, 'Of the unworthiness of the Ministers, which hinders not the effect of the Sacraments'.

7. 'Hated to Death: Homophobia, Violence, and Jamaica's HIV/AIDS Epidemic Findings of Human Rights Watch's Investigation'. Accessed 8 May 2005 from http://hrw.org/reports/2004/jamaica1104/7.htm#_Toc87670799.

8. Bill Werde, 'Reggage Boycott', *Rolling Stone*, 11 November 2004, 30.

9. Kelefa Sanneh, 'Dancehall's Vicious Side: Anti-Gay Attitudes', *New York Times*, 6 September 2004.

10. 'All-Sexual' is a term used in the Caribbean Forum of Lesbians, All-Sexuals and Gays (C-FLAG) network to indicate that it considers all sexual behaviour to be part of a sexual continuum in which classifications such as 'gay', 'lesbian' and 'bisexual' often cannot be rigidly applied. See http://www.jflag.org/misc/allsexual.htm.

11. J-FLAG Parliamentary Submission, accessed 25 October 2004 from http://www.jflag.org/programmes/parliamentary_sub.htm.

12. 'Caribbean Bishops Oppose Jamaica Proposal on Gays', Reuters, 18 December 2001. Accessed 26 September 2004 from http://www.sodomylaws.org/world/jamaica/janews006.htm.

13. Julius Jerome Powell, Jr, 'A Culture of Intolerance: Insights on the Chi Chi Man Craze and Jamaican Gender Relations', radio interview with Gregory Stephens, Spring 2002. Accessed 4 October 2004 from http://www.jahworks.org/music/interview/jflag_interview3.html.

14. Jamaica Forum for Lesbians, All-Sexuals and Gays: Position Paper on Discrimination, 5 June 2001.

15. ibid.

16. Amnesty International, *Jamaica Killings and Violence by Police – How many more victims?* AI Index: AMR 38/003/2001, April 2001, 40.

17. 'Hated to Death'. Accessed 2 January 2005 from http://hrw.org/reports/2004/jamaica1104/index.htm.

18. Eugenia C DeLamotte, 'Sexuality, Spirituality, and Power', in Eugenia DeLamotte, Natania Meeker and Jean O'Barr (eds), *Women Imagine Change: A Global Anthology of Women's Resistance from 600 BCE to Present* (New York and London: Routledge, 1997), p.6.

19. New South Wales Anti-Discrimination Board, *Discrimination – The* Other *Epidemic: Report of the Inquiry into HIV and AIDS Related Discrimination*, 1992, cited in T. Bruyn, 'HIV/AIDS and Discrimination: A Discussion Paper', Canadian HIV/AIDS Legal Network and Canadian AIDS Society, Montréal, 1998. Downloaded from http://www.aidslaw.ca/Maincontent/issues/discrimination/discussionpapers/DISCtoc.html.

20. UNAIDS, *Protocol for the identification of discrimination against People Living With HIV* (Geneva: United Nations, 2000), p.7.

21. Julius Powell, *Hated to Death! Jamaican Government Responds to Human Rights Watch Report*. Pulse Spring 2005, p.14. Accessed 8 May 2005 from http://www.gmad.org/images/Pulse_14.htm.

22. Joint United Nations Program on HIV/AIDS, *World AIDS Campaign 2002–2003, A Conceptual Framework and Basis for Action: HIV/AIDS Stigma and Discrimination* (Geneva: United Nations, 2002).

23. Cressida Heyes, 'Identity Politics', in Edward N. Zalta (ed.), *The Stanford Encyclopedia of Philosophy* (Fall 2002 edition), accessed 31 October 2004 from http://plato.stanford.edu/archives/fall2002/entries/identity-politics/.

24. Henry Louis Gates, Jr, 'Backlash', in Eric Brandt (ed.), *Dangerous Liaisons: Blacks, Gays, and the Struggle for Equality* (New York: The New Press, 1999), p.28.

25. The term 'Youth' (between the ages of 18 and 24) includes Blacks, Continental Africans and youth of African descent living within the Diaspora who identify as either gay, bisexual, transgender, same-gender loving, or men who have sex with men, as well as those who do not wish to be identified in any category but are engaged in sex with men.

26. Julius Jerome Powell, Jr, 'A Study of the Challenges perceived by African American Young Men Who Have Sex with Men (AAYMSM) that increase their risks of infection and transmission of HIV/AIDS and that hinder their efforts at Community Mobilization, Education, and Prevention', October 2003, p.23.

27. Oliver O'Donovan, 'Homosexuality in the Church: Can There Be a Fruitful Theological Debate?' in Timothy Bradshaw (ed.), *The Way Forward? Christian Voices on Homosexuality and the Church*, 2nd edn (London: SCM Press, 2003), p.30.

28. bell hooks, *Yearning: Race, Gender and Cultural Politics* (Boston: South End Press, 1990), p.26.

29. Frantz Fanon, 'The Pitfalls of National Consciousness', Ch. 3 of *The Wretched of the Earth* (New York: Grove Press, 1963).

30. The Lambeth Commission on Communion, *The Windsor Report 2004* (London: The Anglican Communion Office, 2004), p.13.

31. *The Windsor Report*, p.25.

32. Samir Amin, 'The conditions for an alternative global system based on social and international justice', document for World Social Forum, Mumbai, 2004. Accessed 14 October 2004 from http://netx.u-paris10.fr/actuelmarx/m4aminm.htm.

Chapter 16

DO NOT JUDGE ... ONLY COMPREHEND: THE ANGLICAN COMMUNION AND HUMAN SEXUALITY

Pedro Triana

> Let us therefore no longer pass judgement on one another, but resolve instead never to put a stumbling block or hindrance in the way of another. I know and am persuaded in the Lord Jesus that nothing is unclean in itself; but it is unclean for anyone who thinks it unclean. *Romans 14:13–14*

Since Lambeth 1888, with the beginning of the discussions on polygamy, human sexuality has been a point of debate in the Lambeth Conferences up to today. Nevertheless, the Lambeth 1998 resolution on homosexuality, which unambiguously declares this sexual expression as 'incompatible with Scripture', the planned appointment of Jeffrey John as Bishop of Reading in England, the election and consecration of Gene Robinson as Bishop of New Hampshire, and, more recently, the declarations of the 74th General Convention of the Episcopal Church in the United States and of the 2004 General Synod of the Anglican Church of Canada, which approve or look benevolently upon the blessing of unions of people of the same sex, have unchained opinions so diverse that they threaten the very integrity of Anglicanism. Without doubt, never before has the Anglican Communion been involved in such a heated debate as on this area of human sexuality.

As a theologian and biblical scholar, Anglican and Cuban, I shall try to make some very personal reflections, evaluations and notes within the spirit of diversity and comprehension that has been historically characteristic of Anglicanism. I want to emphasise that these notes are mostly along ethical, pastoral and ecclesiological lines. And I shall particularly emphasise the ecclesiological aspect, because without question the debate on the sexual direction of the Anglican Communion has gone beyond healthy discussion and debate, arriving even at internal divisions within some provinces and recriminations and threats of excommunication towards other provinces. Therefore, if a consensus is not reached, we could arrive at the disintegration of our own Communion. Therefore, in my reflection, I want to call attention to the lessons that we as

Anglicans, but particularly as Christians in the beginning of the twenty-first century, need to draw out from this debate.

Bible, tradition and reason

I do not intend to repeat all that has been said in terms of hermeneutical and biblical, theological, ethical, psychological, clinical, biological and cultural studies on the theme of sexual orientation. All these studies have exhaustively established that homosexuality is neither a sin, nor a crime, nor a disease.[1] Since this debate is founded on a biblical basis, from my position as theologian and Bible scholar, I would like to emphasise some hermeneutic aspects. The official declarations of Anglicanism claim that:

- 'The Holy Scriptures of the Old and New Testament [are] the revealed Word of God';
- the Bible inspired by God is 'the last criterion of [Jesus'] teachings and the main guiding source';
- 'Holy Scripture of the Old and New Testaments, "[contain] all things necessary to salvation" and [are] the rule and ultimate standard of faith.'[2]

Certainly all these affirmations and declarations must also be seen in light of the formulations of Richard Hooker, considered one of the greatest Anglican theologians of all time. Hooker puts in place the three pillars of Anglican theological thought: the Scriptures, reason and tradition.

Even though Anglicanism has always considered the Bible as central, the character and function of its authority has never been clearly expressed and defined. This is because Anglicanism, although maintaining that the creeds 'may be proved by most certain warrants of Holy Scripture' and that the church 'hath power to decree Rites or Ceremonies, and authority in Controversies of Faith; and yet it is not lawful for the Church to ordain any thing that is contrary to God's Word written',[3] separates itself from the *sola scriptura* position of the most rigorous reformers, introducing tradition as a standard of judgement and discernment. The introduction of tradition as a hermeneutical criterion allows the practice of the church (tradition) to influence how the Scriptures themselves were and must be read. Finally, the other pillar within the interpretative process enunciated by Hooker, reason, guided by the Holy Spirit, cannot be excluded from the process.

On the basis of the hermeneutical principles expressed above, I would like to emphasise, after seeing how the Scriptures are being 'used' or, more precisely, 'wrongly used' to legitimise the marginality, exclusion and condemnation of people of a homosexual orientation, that we cannot use the Bible as a simple book of questions and answers for our own time, or as an ethical and moral prescription book.

The Bible, the great North American preacher, Phillips Brook, wrote, 'is like a telescope'. If we look through the telescope we see the world through it, but if we look at the telescope, we only see the telescope. For that reason the Bible is something through which we look, to see what is further on; but when we only look at the telescope we only see something written. The great preacher wants us to realise that the Bible is not a written code that kills, but a vehicle of the Spirit that gives life (see 2 Corinthians 3:6); the Bible is for seeing across and beyond itself. For that reason the Bible must always be interpreted through tradition, reason and Christian experience before it is known as revelation.

Therefore, today we have to place a very high value in the process of interpretation on the information provided by other sciences like archaeology, sociology, history of literature, economics, psychology, and the empirical sciences in general. The biblical writers lived in a world completely different from ours. Different ethical and moral cultures and conceptions separate us. It is necessary to recognise, therefore, that due to the distance of centuries, the biblical writers did not think in the same terms or have the same questions that we have today. And in the case of sexuality, the Scriptures were not put forward to respond to the actual questions on sexual ethics that we have at the moment.

And I emphasise all the above because it happens that the literalistic approach is the one that dominates most analyses of the only five biblical texts that express opinions on sex between men,[4] in order to 'prove' that homosexuality is 'contrary to the Scriptures'. Nevertheless, the best and most up-to-date contemporary biblical criticism has widely established that the Bible 'takes no direct stand on the morality of homogenital acts as such nor on the morality of gay and lesbian relationships as we conceive them today'.[5] Also, biblical exegesis has clarified that not even Jesus said anything on homosexuality when he came face to face with a person, who according to the customs of the time, it seems, maintained an affective homosexual relationship with his slave (Timothy 8:5–13; Luke 7:1–10).[6] In short, when using reason as a hermeneutical principle we cannot go to the Bible to condemn people of homosexual orientation.

On the other hand, biological and psychological studies have already established – and here also we find the hermeneutical principle of reason – that people do not 'choose' to be homosexual. Perhaps if it were simply a matter of 'choosing' a form of sexual expression, moral approval or condemnation could be made. But people 'do not choose' to be gays or lesbians, they 'recognise themselves' or 'find that they are' gays or lesbians. Already in this case we must consider, as Richard Harries points out, other parts of the Bible where we see the attitude of Jesus towards the marginalised, the excluded and the victimised of his time. Bishop Harries affirms, in addition, that the implication this has in our days is that all Christians, both heterosexual and homosexual, must meet and be united in the Body of Christ, respecting the points of view of one another and together recognising our common loyalty to Christ, because the Bible is not interpreted in a world outside time and history. We must interpret and apply the Bible in our own time, in the same way as those who wrote it did it for their own time.[7] Therefore, as William Countryman also comments, 'To deny an entire class of human being the right peaceably and without harming others to pursue the kind of sexuality that corresponds to their nature is a perversion of the gospel.'[8]

Prejudice, intolerance and discrimination

For many centuries the attitude of all the churches to human sexuality has been negative. Speaking in general terms, sex has been understood as the way to procreate but not as a source of pleasure. Nevertheless, today it is understood that we can use our sexuality without thinking about reproduction. Nor is sexuality only and necessarily the sexual act. For that reason, the churches have been accused of being secretive and repressive towards sexuality. And although this affirmation could seem exaggerated, the people who express themselves in this manner have not always been completely mistaken. For some, the only way to sin is through the genitals.[9] And it is not an exaggeration when the churches are blamed for being secretive and repressive of sexuality because, in practice and without doubt, in the discussions on homosexuality, the church has been the main institution that has legitimised discrimination against people of homosexual orientation.

Abel Sierra Madero, investigator of the Fernando Ortiz Foundation, when reflecting on homophobia in our Cuban culture, affirms:

> When we learn to identify and to socially recognise these people as such, we will have begun somewhat to re-vindicate the homophobic and discriminatory attitudes that have marked our historical past. Our 'sexual nation' has tried to exclude homosexuals. But a nation is not constructed on the basis of segregation, exclusion and discrimination, for it would be condemned to failure.[10]

And when we see these reflections on sexual orientation beginning in the secular world, debating with a problem that is complex, thorny and still not solved, but trying to understand it from the viewpoint of our present time, and, on the other hand, when we see the intolerant, discriminating and excluding attitudes of the churches, ears deaf to the psychological and genetic studies; with biblical texts manipulated and un-contextualised to justify intolerance and prejudice, I ask myself: have we perhaps forgotten the attitude of our own Jesus towards the discriminated, the excluded and the marginalised of his time? Certainly, as Bishop John S.

Spong has affirmed, the church 'cannot claim to be the body of Christ if it fails to welcome all whom Christ would welcome'.[11]

Therefore, it is distressing and alarming, that because of the discriminating and excluding principles that accompany the debates and discussions on sexual orientation, a great 'scandal' has broken out in the Anglican Communion. And many of us ask ourselves: why do we not react with this same energy against the great problems that threaten our world? Why is it that in our Communion there has not been a global reaction, and as strong as the one that focuses on sexual orientation, against the genocide in Afghanistan and Iraq, and against the Palestinian people? Why do we not react with as much vehemence against state terrorism, the problems with peace and systemic violence, neo-liberal globalisation or the sustained and systematic destruction of our ecosystem that jeopardises life for future generations?

Taking again the ideas of a priest from our Episcopal Church of Cuba, Canon Pablo Odén Marichal, we could say that the poor – either heterosexual or homosexual – do not have the time to discuss, nor are they interested in discussing, the sexual conduct of people, nor are they concerned about what others do with their sex, because they are completely engrossed in their fight for survival: what to eat, where to live, where to find work, how to clothe themselves, how to educate their children, how to keep their family healthy. Do we stop on our path to ask whoever struggles to feed the hungry, or to give water to the thirsty, or to clothe the naked, if he or she is homosexual or heterosexual?[12]

Being Anglican, including in Cuba

I certainly believe, as I have expressed, that this debate has strong and deep ecclesiological implications because it has much to do with 'being Anglican' and the so-called 'spirit of Anglicanism'. For that reason, I also think that what today most threatens Anglicanism and its pertinence and relevance as part of the church of Jesus Christ is not that it does or does not ordain gays or lesbians as bishops, presbyters and deacons, because it has always ordained them – but until now it has not been said and has been hidden for fear of repression and marginality. Rather, the real danger, as is so evident in the points of view, interpretations, and ethical, biblical and theological approaches to this problem, is an affirmation of the intolerance, prejudices and conservative positions within our Communion, and therefore, an increasing loss of the inclusive and free spirit that has historically characterised Anglicanism.

And when I have affirmed that I write these notes within the spirit of diversity and comprehensiveness that has historically characterised 'being Anglican', I mean the diversity and plurality understood as a unity of faith and adoration, already reaffirmed in Lambeth 1968 during the controversies over the ordination of women; and the comprehensive-ness, also defined in Lambeth 1968, as an attitude learned by Anglicans through all the controversies of their history, which demands com-promise with a fundamental and tolerant mutual recognition of our differences, without the need to break Communion. Comprehensive-ness, which does not necessarily mean compromise, but implies that the apprehension of the truth is something that grows, and that we will only be able 'to know the truth' gradually.[13]

But if we review the debate on human sexuality in our Communion, we see that since Lambeth 1888 it has been a point of discussion and conflict. Polygamy, divorce, birth control, premarital sexual relations and sexual abuse have been subjects of strong debate and heated discus-sion, as well as of diverging and contradicting positions. But, as has already been expressed, never before in Anglicanism have discussions on human sexuality encountered such a polarising subject as when debating the question of sexual orientation.

This subject appears for the first time in Lambeth 1978. The resolu-tion of this Conference proposes the need for a deep and dispassionate study on homosexuality, taking seriously the teaching of the Scriptures as well as the results of scientific and medical research. It also encour-ages a pastoral approach and dialogue with people of homosexual orientation. With regards to the debate on sexual orientation, the Lambeth 1978 Report stated, 'Today we do not expect everyone to con-form to a norm – a sort of average humanness – but rather to rejoice in variety; so the status and rights of homosexuals are being reconsidered.'

The Report continues:

> Homosexuality has rarely received understanding either in Church or in society. Despite much research there is still considerable dis-agreement about its nature and causes. It is commonly referred to as a deviation, yet many homosexuals do not believe they are abnormal. They do not ask for sympathy, but for recognition of the fact that their homosexual relationship can express mutual love as appropriately for the persons concerned as a heterosexual relation-ship might for others. The majority of Christians would not will-ingly agree with this attitude. We assert however that an adequate understanding of, and response to, homosexuality will not be found until society as a whole and Christians in particular, can approach the subject compassionately and without prejudice.
>
> Questions relating to homosexuality are admittedly complex, and we note that these questions are currently the subject of seri-ous study in some parts of the Anglican Communion. There are other places (e.g. in the Church of Africa) where homosexual

behaviour has not emerged as a problem. This fact indicates the
need for further study as to the possible relationship between
homosexuality and environment. There is also particular need for
further study of the Scriptural evidence such as Romans 1:18–32
which depicts homosexual behaviour as one of the manifestations
of the fragmentation of life in a fallen world.

It is the responsibility of every local Church to become such a
warm-hearted, Christ-centred, eucharistic fellowship, that people
of every temperament and tendency might find their true unity and
fellowship within the total family of Christ, where all are sinners,
but all can find the grace and forgiveness of Christ in 'his accepting community'.[14]

Lambeth 1988 fundamentally reaffirms the declaration of Lambeth
1978, but also recognises that there is much confusion with regards to
human sexuality and calls attention to the need to develop a more
extensive study on the subject. Also, it urges to take into account the
socio-cultural factors giving rise to different attitudes in the provinces of
the Communion. Lambeth 1998 again expresses interest in the pastoral
care of people of homosexual orientation.

If we balance Lambeth 1978 and 1988, we would have to recognise
that in both Conferences the subject is treated with realism, moderation
and pastoral understanding and certainly within the Anglican spirit of
comprehensiveness, tolerance and respect for diversity. Neither Lambeth
1978 nor 1988 risks hasty or absolute judgements. They deal with the
theme of sexual orientation within the Anglican spirit of drawing near
the subjects being discussed with a dialectical approach, that is, using
the interrelationship of Scripture, reason and tradition.

In neither Lambeth 1978 nor 1988 do we see a de-contextualisation
of the Scriptures, rather, simply an appeal to take their teachings 'seriously'. Also, when asked to make a deep and actual study, both
Conferences exhort us to consider tradition and the importance of the
socio-cultural aspects, as had previously been done with subjects like
polygamy, divorce and premarital relations; in addition they exhort us to
take reason into account, when declaring the need to consider biological,
genetic and psychological research. However, we must say with Richard
Harries that one of the main criticisms that must be made of these resolutions is that they always talk about people of homosexual orientation
as 'they' or 'others', or 'strangers'. So it seems as if Christian heterosexual or homosexual people are not the united Body of Christ, called to
mutually respect the points of view of each other within the Christian
spirit of love and brother/sisterhood.[15] With Lambeth 1998 the discussion on sexual orientation already takes on another spirit. In my opinion,

the resolution on homosexuality of Lambeth 1998, when it 'reject[s] homosexual practice as incompatible with Scripture' and 'cannot advise the legitimising or blessing of same-sex unions nor ordaining those involved in same-gender unions', separates itself completely from the moderate, sensible, comprehensive, pastoral and dialogical spirit of the two previous Conferences.

Lambeth 1998 does not call any more for the serious study of the Scriptures, nor to consider biological, psychological and genetic research, nor to take into account the cultural factors, nor to continue the studies in the different provinces of the Communion. In Lambeth 1998 the Scriptures are de-contextualised and are not used, but 'wrongly used' to justify exclusion and marginality, in this case, of homosexual people, using texts removed from their cultural and religious contexts, turning its back and having deaf ears to the best and most up-to-date hermeneutical principles of contemporary biblical studies. But this false and wrong approach to the Scriptures – fundamentalist, conservative and literalist – is highly dangerous, because it could be also used today to justify other exclusions and marginalities, for example, the marginalisation of women – if certain texts from Paul are removed from their context – and especially contribute to legitimise false political messiahs, who use a religious disguise to threaten peace and inter-human solidarity. In my opinion, Lambeth 1998 seems to take us back to the time in which isolated biblical texts were used to justify the exploitation of our American indigenous peoples, or the slavery of the hundreds of thousands of black people who were uprooted from their African homes to build the wealth of the colonisers.

Nor, in Lambeth 1998, when discussing the theme of homosexuality, do we see the traditional Anglican appeal to tradition, much less to reason. There is no more comprehensiveness; there is no more respect for diversity, no more respect for the cultural plurality of our Communion. There is no longer anything to discuss, no longer anything more to study; already, everything has been said. Lambeth 1998 dogmatically closes any study on the subject, closes the dialogue. And I ask myself, does this approach comprise the Christian and Anglican spirit?

And when we weigh Lambeth 1998 we certainly could also ask ourselves: what is left of a church that has been recognised as 'broad church', 'the most extensive house and the most expandable church in Christianity', 'the church of integration and reconciliation'? What is left of 'mutual responsibility and interdependence in the Body of Christ', proclaimed in the 1963 Toronto Anglican Congress, affirming the mission of the church to the world from our plurality and cultural diversity? And this loss, in my opinion, has been most lamentable and constitutes the true danger for our Communion. Because the foundations and the precedent have now been laid, so that the spirit of intolerance and the abandonment of respect for diversity and Anglican plurality will begin to affirm itself, not only when discussing the subject of sexual orientation, but other controversial subjects as well.

In the case of the Episcopal Church of Cuba, the first time the church dealt with homosexuality was in 1995. The Diocesan Synod passed a very brief resolution 'not authorising the ordination of persons engaging in homosexual practice as deacons, presbyters or bishops'. This resolution passed without any serious study about human sexuality and was surrounded by much prejudice. The resolution dealt only with the ordination of persons to the ordained ministry. After much debate, the introduction of the phrase 'homosexual practice' at least opened the way for a more moderate position, avoiding an open condemnation of persons of homosexual orientation. But for ten years the Episcopal Church of Cuba continued without analysing deeply the issue of human sexuality.

Recently, after the Lambeth 1998 debate on human sexuality, the church was challenged to reassess its position on the debate, and a new resolution was passed in the 95th Synod of the Episcopal Church of Cuba in February 2005. There was a period of study before the Synod but it was not a serious, deep and complete study of the issue in all parishes and missions; and even in the Synod itself there was still a lack of information, many things needing clarification and strong prejudices to be overcome. The resolution was entitled 'Human Sexuality' rather than 'Homosexuality' and is at least more explanatory than the 1995 resolution. It tries not to enter into anathematisation and condemnation, and Scriptures are not used to condemn homosexuality.

The new resolution reaffirms the resolution of the 1995 Synod in not authorising the ordination of persons engaged in homosexual practice, but at least the Cuban cultural context is taken into account: 'according to the biblical models for leadership and our cultural way of interpreting and putting into action the church's mission, this leadership would be [adversely] affected if it is exercised by persons engaged in homosexual practice.' The use of the word 'practice' leaves the possibility for a celibate homosexual person to be ordained. The resolution also does not approve 'same-sex unions through rites of the Church' and it affirms that that 'the ideal of Christian marriage is the life-long union between a man and a woman'. But regarding Scripture, the resolution takes a certain distance from Lambeth 1998, because Scriptures are not used to justify a condemnation of homosexuality. The resolution goes on, 'the Scriptures clearly teach us that God loves all human beings and also that Jesus Christ declared himself as having come to save the world rather to condemn it.' Ending with two positive remarks, the resolution 'plainly rejects any manifestation of homophobia and hatred towards persons of homosexual orientation as something which would constitute the sin of lack of love', and 'assures persons of homosexual practice [*sic*] that the Church is committed to listening to their experience, reiterates that God loves them and that all baptised persons, regardless of their sexual orientation, are full members of the Body of Christ'. One notes that the resolution uses the word 'homophobia' (Spanish, *homofobia*), a term rejected in the 1998 Lambeth debate by conservative bishops who felt that it reflected a form of gay ideology.

Having reflected on Lambeth 1998 and how the Episcopal Church of Cuba is handling the matter of human sexuality, I want to look again at some remarks by Canon Pablo Odén Marichal. He says that nobody thinks that either Jeffrey John or Gene Robinson was the first homosexual bishop to be consecrated. Perhaps they are only the first ones to admit it openly and publicly before they were named or consecrated bishops. Indeed, it is impossible to say, even approximately, how many gay or lesbian bishops, presbyters and deacons there are in the Anglican Communion, whether celibate or not.

Marichal continues that it could seem that for the church the sin is not that these clergy (including bishops) are homosexual or lesbian but that they admit it publicly. It seems that what offends is not that they are homosexual, but that they admit it. Therefore, the conclusion would be: to lie is not a sin; the sin is to tell the truth. While everything is within the shadow of the scope of secrecy there is no problem: if I pretend not to know it, nor others know that I know it, the church does not know it and God does not know it.

Lambeth 1998 speaks of not ordaining 'those involved in same-gender unions'. But in relation to this subject the comments of Canon Marichal are also sharp: are we going to demote from the ministry those homosexual and lesbian clergy who, from fear of not being ordained or through the pressure of discrimination at the time of their ordination, did not confess their homosexuality and today comprise the active ordained ministry of the church? We know it or we imagine it, but indulgently we keep quiet, because they are our friends, or they are good people or they are very able. Then, are we going to let them stay? And if we let them stay, why say yes to the ones who arrived first, hiding their homosexuality, and then to those who do not hide it, later say no? Was the concealment of the fact worth more than honesty?

Certainly these questions must make us seriously think about where intolerance and lack of vision can take us. And we could ask many more questions. Could it be that we are going to affirm a double moral standard with relation to the subject of sexual orientation? And what pastoral word will we have towards gays and lesbians who every Sunday sit in the pews of our churches? Will they be treated as 'the others', 'the

218 OTHER VOICES, OTHER WORLDS

strangers', part of the excluded ones of today whom Jesus in his time would have invited to the banquet of his kingdom (Luke 14:15–24)? Or could it also be that we are going to incite a 'witch hunt', and now also of 'wizards', in the style of the heresy trials of the medieval inquisition? In relation to this area, the North American theologian Rosemary Radford Ruether notes, 'Although heresy is no longer an official category of crime, contemporary views of homosexuality still preserve much of this classic Christian paranoia.'[16]

And we are not deceived: the subject of homosexuality is a reality, a fact. We have as many heterosexual and homosexual people in the ordained ministry as in the pews of our congregations, but all of us together are one in the Body of Christ. And all the parts of the Body are worthy and deserve respect and consideration (1 Corinthians 12:12–30). Then with the intolerable, excluding and marginalising attitudes, what are we trying to silence or ignore?

To be Christian and Anglican today

It has been said that we do not live in a time of changes, but in a change of times. Our world is made more plural and diverse. And as Anglican Christians we must live up to the new times. In the middle of widespread violence, of excluding and exploiting globalisation, of the devastation of our natural home, the churches, and religions in general, have a responsibility to contribute towards developing a culture of peace, solidarity and reconciliation. But certainly to be able to contribute towards the creation of such a culture of peace, solidarity and reconciliation, we must first learn to live that culture within ourselves, avoiding that religious and personal intolerance which is a source of divisions, conflicts and exclusions in civil society – and then we can turn our attention to the serious problems that affect us.

The lesson that as Anglicans we must take from all this debate on sexual orientation is that it has become imperative that we rethink our ecclesiology. Thus, we must rethink what it means 'to be Anglican', to recover what to my understanding could possibly be lost: 'the spirit of Anglicanism'. To go on to think seriously about the great problems of humanity, we will let each province of our Communion assume its options, in this case on sexual orientation, according to its cultural characteristics, without rejecting or excommunicating each other.

For that reason, when the tendency towards anathematisation and demonisation of 'the other' is on the rise, it becomes imperative, as part of the recovery of 'being Anglican', that we recover and assume in its true sense one of our more respected principles: the *via media* or middle way. This principle, having its origins in the thinking of Richard Hooker, was recovered in the nineteenth century by the Oxford Movement in the midst of the serious and deep tensions that the Church of England lived between the Protestant and Roman sides of its heritage. And from that moment in history the *via media* was affirmed as a fundamental principle of Anglican unity and identity.

But the *via media* is not, as some simplistically think, being a 'bridge-church', because the Oxford Movement reacted as much against Rome as against the Protestants with their Puritan heritage. The *via media* is not a display cabinet for those outside, nor a way to convince others that we are very moderate; because we cannot be moderate towards foreign and in-house extremists. The *via media* is a movement towards unity, but it is not a commitment to reconcile two discrepant parts – *rather it is a method for understanding diversity within ourselves*, with respect and ethics; it is to be ample and flexible, respectful and ethical towards other persons and their ideas.[17]

Finally I shall finish with an anecdote that is pertinent to the theme that we have been developing:

> A western man was placing flowers on the tomb of a relative, when he sees a Chinese placing a plate of rice in the neighbouring tomb. The western man goes to the Chinese and asks him, 'Excuse me, Sir, but do you really think that the deceased will come to eat the rice?' 'Yes,' the Chinese responds, 'when yours come to smell the flowers.'

The moral of the story is that to respect the choice of others is one of the greatest virtues that a human being can have. People are different, act differently and think differently.

NOTES

1. See John Boswell, *Christianity, Social Tolerance and Homosexuality: Gay People in Western Europe from the Beginning of the Christian Era to the Fourteenth Century* (Chicago and London: University of Chicago Press, 1980); Daniel A. Helminiak, *What the Bible Really Says about Homosexuality* (San Francisco: Alamo Square Press, 2000) (Spanish edition, *Lo que la Biblia realmente dice sobre la homosexualidad* [Barcelona/Madrid: Editorial EGALES, 2003]); and James B. Nelson and Sandra P. Longfellow (eds), *Sexuality and the Sacred: Sources for Theological Reflection* (London: Mowbray, c.1994) (Spanish edition, *La sexualidad y lo sagrado* [Bilbao: Desclée De Brouwer, 1996]).
2. 'The Chicago Quadrilateral', 1886; 'The Declarations of Faith and Order' of the 1949 General Convention of the Episcopal Church; and Lambeth Conference, 1888, Resolution 11 ('The Lambeth Quadrilateral'), section (a), citing Article VI of the 'Articles of Religion'.
3. Articles VIII and XX of the 'Articles of Religion'.
4. Leviticus 18:2 and 20:13; Romans 1:27; 1 Corinthians 6:9 and 1 Timothy 1:10. Although the story of Sodom and Gomorrah (Genesis 19) has been used many times, the actual text refers to having sex with 'angels', 'messengers' from God.
5. Helminiak, op. cit., p.132.

6. Helminiak, op. cit. See Helminiak's section on 'Jesus and the Centurion's Slave Boy', pp.127–30. This is part of Ch. 8, 'Other Supposed References to Homosexuality', pp.117–30.
7. Richard Harries, 'Presentation on Human Sexuality', in James M. Rosenthal and Nicola Currie (eds), *Being Anglican in the Third Millennium: The Official Report of the 10th Meeting of the Anglican Consultative Council: Panama, 1996* (Harrisburg: Morehouse Publishing, 1997), pp.60–1.
8. L. William Countryman, 'New Textament Sexual Ethics and Today's World' in Nelson and Longfellow (eds), op. cit., p.34. The essay was originally published in Countryman's *Dirt, Greed and Sex* (Philadephia: Fortress Press, 1988).
9. Jorge A. León, *Apuntes para una teología de las sexualidad*, Psicopastoral, Cristianet.com, 2001.
10. Abel Sierra Madero, 'La policia del sexo – La homofobia durante el siglo XIX en Cuba', Sexología y Sociedad, 9:21 (April 2003).
11. Helminiak, op. cit., 'Prologue', p.12.
12. Pablo Odén Marichal, Rector of the Episcopal Church 'Fieles a Jesús', Matanzas, Cuba ('Faithful to Jesus' Episcopal Parish, Matanzas, Cuba), and Professor of the Ecumenical Theological Seminary, Matanzas, Cuba, 'La sexualidad humana en la Communión Anglicana – Abriendo la Caja de Pandora en torno a un debate' (distributed electronically).
13. *The Lambeth Conference 1968* (London and New York: SPCK and Seabury Press, 1968).
14. *The Lambeth Conference* (London: CIO Publishing, 1978), pp. 64–5. Archbishop Desmond Tutu chaired the section on 'What is the Church for?' that produced this report.
15. Richard Harries, op. cit., pp.55–66.
16. Rosemary Radford Ruether, 'Homophobia, Heterosexism and Pastoral Practice', in Nelson and Longfellow (eds), op. cit., p.388. The chapter was originally published in Jeannine Gramick, *Homosexuality in the Priesthood and the Religious Life* (New York: Crossroad, 1989), pp.21–35.
17. See 'La vía media' in 'Carta Pastoral', Parroquia de Fieles a Jesús, Matanzas, Cuba, 28 December 2003 and 4 January 2004 (distributed electronically).

Chapter 17

PRACTISING SEXUAL THEOLOGY:
UNDRESSING SEX, PLEASURE, SIN AND GUILT
IN COLONISED MENTALITIES

Mario Ribas

Introduction

Since the 1998 Lambeth Conference, practising or non-practising gayness within the Anglican Communion has become the key element for the acceptance or non-acceptance of gay people within its midst, especially in the ordained ministry.[1] The intention in this paper is to explore the implications of this point of view, which is directed towards, in one way or another, the avoidance of sexual intercourse. My analysis will take into account issues of power and hierarchy, sin, pleasure, guilt, colonialism and the class system, within the church, other institutions and society itself.

Practising and non-practising gayness and disciplinary measures

The demand that gay persons should not be 'practising' normally implies that they should not be active in same-sex acts. Gay persons are expected to deny their own need for intimacy with someone of their own sex, and live a life of celibacy or chastity. I would maintain that celibacy or chastity here is imposed as a discipline to maintain hetero-patriarchal structures and paradigms. The alternative represents a challenge to this power construction, as it does not conform to the established worldview of the body and sexuality. This discipline is imposed as a power tactic that, according to Michel Foucault, has three functions or characteristics: 'low exteriorisation, relative invisibility, and little resistance'.[2]

The imposition of the practice of 'celibacy' (or, more recently, 'chastity') as a way to demand sexual abstinence of all those who do not fit into the heterosexual paradigms can be seen as a pre-conceptualised reduction of gayness into same-sex intercourse only. It does not recognise the whole complexity of humanity that determines one's sexuality; instead it determines one's humanity by imposing control on genital organs only. This concept of celibacy results in a theology in which the starting point is the denial of the bodily functions, going against the principles of incarnational theology; indeed, it becomes a theology of dis-incarnation. This theology ignores gay consciousness and gay people's awareness of their bodies, which can be of great help in the process of building an embodiment theology. It goes, instead, in the opposite direction, leading gays and lesbians into annihilation through their genital organs.

To be gay is much more than just practising sex with someone of the same gender (if, indeed, gayness can be defined by the practice of same-sex acts, as there are many men who engage in such acts and do not see themselves as gay). It is, in broader terms, an expression of sexuality that cuts across and breaks gender barriers (how they are formed, their prescriptions and hierarchy). To be gay is, consequently, to feel alienated in many ways within a dominant hetero-patriarchal system that dictates the thoughts and practices of the prevailing socio-political and economical order. In a context of alienation, the way gay people see the world is often entirely different from the way those who are insiders see it.[3] Gayness does, therefore, bring a new perspective, one that is more critical on issues around lack of inclusiveness, and the way the power structure is built favouring and maintaining an androcentric system that places other important elements of our humanity in the lower sphere.

In this context of alienation, it should be said that there are many gay people who seem to conform themselves to the established order, but still do not necessarily feel part of or integrated with it. They are the ones who, at least in the public sphere, seem to have 'heterosexualised' themselves due to the restrictions imposed on them by the system and their struggle to cope with feelings of inadequacy.[4] A gay man has to act like a heterosexual person when he does not want to be reminded of his gayness by the (straight) other. In the presence of a straight man, he is made aware of his gayness and unsuitability to perform his manly duties, as prescribed by and expected from society.[5] So, there are many gay people who adopt the heterosexual camouflage in order to prove their value and capability as human beings.

In many parts of Brazil, external 'heterosexualisation' is required to avoid life threats, and not to be counted amongst the large number of unemployed. Those who have chosen not to conform themselves to the system and have decided to 'come out', have had to face the reality of being 'outsiders' or aliens within the heterosexual structures. Having 'come out', they work to subvert these structures into more inclusive and accepting ones, fighting for gay people's rights, and fighting against all the violence and stigma that gay people attract.[6]

Loving the sinner, hating the sin

The Anglican Communion's recent approaches to the issue of gayness within the church are no different from those of the Roman Catholics and many Calvinists. The 'love the sinner, hate the sin' approach has been adopted partly in order to avoid the disciplinary measure of sexual abstinence being categorised as 'homophobic'.[7] However, this approach still denies full humanity for those who are of gay or lesbian orientation. As stated above, the starting point is the sexual expression, narrowing gayness into same-sex genital contacts. This wrong starting point leads those who are the subjects of this disciplinary requirement into a whole process of disenfranchisement. Consciously or unconsciously, it imposes upon gay people Augustine's views in *City of God*, that sexual acts, as 'the greatest of all bodily pleasures ... take over the whole body and, in their intermingling of emotion and bodily desire', sinfully annihilate the capacity for self-control. Augustine argues that it would be preferable even for procreation to take place without sexual desire.[8] Here begins the process of annihilation, denying the human need for sexual intimacy.

The 'love the sinner, hate the sin' approach within the Anglican context reinforces the demand on gays and lesbians to avoid sexual contact with anyone of their own sex. However, we should always remember, as Marcella Althaus-Reid points out, that when the church speaks about morality or sinfulness, it always has its eyes turned into people's bedrooms and bathrooms.[9] The 'love the sinner, hate the sin' approach already carries with it the difficulty the church has had in dealing with sexual matters for centuries. It is acceptable to be gay, in the current institutions, or whatever inclination or fetish one might have, but the sin lies in penis erection. In other words, it applies a theology that denies pleasure – a 'shrinking penis theology'.[10] Often the church applies the argument that gay sex is unnatural biologically, since the biological construction of males and females makes them sexually compatible and complementary to each other. In other words, the penis was made for the vagina, and *vice versa*. Any other way of expressing sexuality is abomination. However, it should be pointed out that sex in *any* form (except that with procreative intent, with no regard to sexual pleasure, and sometimes even that is rejected) has very often been treated as unnatural or an abomination.

With the establishment of this obstacle, in which sexual pleasure is denied, the church gets itself into tremendous difficulties when addressing human sexuality generally. For example, a few years ago the Brazilian newspapers widely reported the story of a couple who wanted to marry in one of the parish churches in the state of Minas Gerais. However, the diocesan bishop blocked the wedding because the man was handicapped and unable to procreate. Therefore, the view that sexual intimacy is for procreation only leads not just the lives of gays and lesbians into fragmentation, but also those of handicapped or elderly people, who either for physical reasons or ageing cannot fulfil the procreation expectations in their sexual encounters. Full humanity, in this case, is denied not on grounds of sexual orientation, but on body capacity, as well as by an age limit, over which sexual intimacy would not, by this standard, be acceptable.

During the advent of HIV/AIDS, as one would expect, the church was speedy to state that it was God's punishment for homosexual acts. This position remained unchanged until HIV/AIDS proved to be something that could affect people from every sexual orientation. In Latin America, it is possible still to find some church leaders who see and treat HIV/AIDS as the Dark Plague, or even the result of demoniac possession, and who would deal with it with prayers and exorcisms only. (Another very significant problem is the large number of the Latin American population who hear again and again from their priests and bishops statements condemning the use of condoms.) The church's difficulty in dealing with sexual matters (or sometimes its silence on the subject) can have catastrophic consequences. In the case of HIV/AIDS, the issues are illness and death, and the countless economic and social implications due to the devastation of millions of lives throughout the world. Grace Jantzen writes of the church's common attitude towards those with HIV/AIDS:

> People with HIV/AIDS are the lepers of modern society. They are looked upon with horror, revulsion and fear. There is fear about any form of contact, from eating together to sharing a communion cup to offering an embrace or a kiss of peace and welcome. Like the lepers in medieval times, people with AIDS and HIV face not only physical revulsion but also moral disapproval, the attitude that their condition is a punishment for sin or that they have brought it upon themselves through sexual activity or drug use that is feared and condemned by the majority. Their human dignity is undervalued and undermined, not least by the church.[11]

The application of the 'hate the sin, love the sinner' discourse in the context of sexual orientation also becomes inapplicable, because the characterisation of gays and lesbians as sinners already implies a previous judgement, in which the ones who judge create a hierarchy of sins, in which homoerotic attraction is placed above all other sins.[12] Such judgement also implies the righteousness of those who place themselves as the judges. Again, as mentioned above, this phenomenon resembles the attitude of the coloniser towards colonised people. The colonisers stated that they 'loved' the colonised while rejecting their culture and way of life.

Interestingly, however, the New England Puritans did not accept this heterosexist hierarchy and placed everyone on the same level:

> ... in early New England, sodomitical sinners were not thought of as differing in their essential natures from Puritan saints. All persons' 'cursed Natures' inclined them to every variety of wickedness – the 'holiest man hath as vile and filthy a Nature, as the Sodomites', said Reverend Danforth in 1674. Even the most outwardly respectable Puritan might be inwardly guilty of 'heart sodomy', of 'heart buggery' – as well as 'heart whoredom', 'heart blasphemy' and 'heart drunkenness' – warned Reverend Shepard in 1641. No Puritan was perfectly pure. Only a deep faith in God distinguished the saved from the damned; both were equally corrupted by 'original sin', both were potential committers of sodomy – and other sins.[13]

Although the terms 'Puritan' and 'Puritanism' are often understood as aversion to sex or having strong moralistic beliefs about sex, at least it cannot be said that the Puritans established or reinforced a hierarchy of sin in which homoerotic expressions became the most serious sins, leading to the 'love the sinner, hate the sin' approach. At least among the Pilgrim Fathers, the concept of sin was broadened so that its focus was not only on one's sexual orientation (or sexuality in general), but on all kinds of sinfulness, both externalised and internalised. Thus, all can commit sodomitical sins, either in thought or practice, leaving no space for anyone to place themselves as judges.

The danger of the 'love the sinner, hate the sin' approach is that it renders a certain group of people permanently the subject of stigmatisation. A similar situation is the way that those who are born out of wedlock, 'illegitimate' children, are treated. Although they are not responsible for their biological parents' acts, they have to carry throughout their lives the stigma and prejudices attached to the way they came into existence. I often point out that in my experience as a parish priest in Brazil, most of the baptisms I performed were of children of single mothers, who could not take them to be baptised in the Roman Catholic Church. Or there are the remarried couples who can go to church but are for ever denied approaching the altar to take Communion. This concept of 'love the sinner, hate the sin', then, mixes sin and sinners, based on a hierarchical structure of sin. Thus, it maintains a class system, where those who do not fit into the ideal of family and marriage are for ever marked and classified as lesser in the class structure and in the eyes of the church.

The annihilation of gay people through their genital organs

The way the church talks about sex is in itself very immoral. It can be very masochist, and reflect all the western hypocrisy in which sex is seen as something impersonal. In this area, Marcella Althaus-Reid challenges the way some theologians do their theology, failing to recognise their own fetishisms.[14] What Althaus-Reid points out can be developed further, especially if we consider the moral theologians who seem to have orgasms when they write about the sins of sex, and take pleasure in thinking of millions of people who would panic in fear of God's wrath whenever they fail to follow each of the prescribed rules.

The problem with many moral theologians is that they love to spend most of their time and work on sex-related subjects, giving the impression that there is no sin present in other parts of our humanity and world. If we look at the way the Anglican Communion has spent millions of dollars to organise meeting after meeting to address sex-related issues, and the way these issues consume international gatherings such as the 1998 Lambeth Conference or Anglican Consultative Council meetings, we might easily conclude that our ecclesiastical leaders do not care if the world is devastated, as long as they 'get it right' sexually.

The current debate clearly shows that gays and lesbians in the church are regarded as a different class of people who do not fit into the heterosexual institutions. Their position is in the lower class. Thus, in order for their humanity and talents to be recognised, they must annihilate their gayness, avoiding sexual contacts or intimacy. But even suppressing the need for companionship and intimacy (in which part of our humanity is annihilated) does not always help the process of finding acceptance and overcoming the feeling of inadequacy. For example, in the Church of England when Canon Jeffrey John was appointed Bishop of Reading, those opposed to the consecration of gays and lesbians to the episcopate forced him to step down from his appointment because he was gay, even though it was made clear that he was not a 'practising' gay.

The annihilation process in this case did not produce any effect. The stigma was still there; the sinner and the sin were still held up together as the focus of hate and rejection. The issue was not that Jeffrey John was practising or non-practising, but the honesty with which he faced his own orientation and was not ashamed of it. So, in this case, gayness was not reduced merely to practising sexual acts with another person of the same gender, but something broader that still does not fit into the dogmatic heterosexual paradigm. There might have been the realisation of Jeffrey John's lack of those elements that are part of the predominant assumptions regarding masculinity, which surfaced when the public was made aware of his orientation. Therefore, his choice represented a threat to the established hetero-patriarchal system. Even accomplishing the demanded discipline required for the moulding of the institution did not work to break the barriers between the class institutions imposed by the hetero-system.[15]

Stripping sex from sin and sin from sex

So, we might ask, why is the church (and other institutions, and institutionalised thoughts and doctrines) threatened by gay consciousness? This question leads us to think again about how we have 'made sex a sin', something to be ashamed of, and how it is monopolised by heterosexual married couples, with a procreative function.[16] It leads us to reflect on the feeling of guilt that leads masses of people into desperation for ejaculating, for flirting or simply because they have had an erection. It leads us to question the way sexual power is structured, with its virtual class system that will always include few and exclude many. The question implies a deconstruction of the system and its paradigms, in order to envision and create new ones.

I recently came across some graffiti on a toilet wall. (It seems that public toilets are the only place people feel free to express themselves without embarrassment.) It read:

> Caution! Not for Gays
> But before you proceed, ask yourself:
> (1) When was the last time you f**ked?
> (2) Why do they say f*****g is a sin?
> (3) Why is doing sin so enjoyable?
> Or don't you enjoy it when you f**k?

Our western hypocrisy about sex does not allow me to write down openly the 'F' word. Always we have to write it using asterisks, so as not to shock the bourgeois, an example of 'sanitised speech about sex', distancing ourselves from the mass of people that prefer to use 'indecent' ways to symbolise it.[17]

One point of this 'bathroom wisdom' is that it does not ask the question of gays but of straight lads only, presumably assuming that gay people do not feel so guilty or ashamed about sex. Another point is that for the writer, sex and sin are intrinsically linked, reflecting a popular-culture view that sex, because it is a sin and forbidden, is even more pleasant. With these two points taken together, the graffiti may be read to suggest that if gay people have been able to overcome the demonisation of sex and pleasure, then gays and lesbians would be able to offer to the rest of 'society alternative institutions that are more sensual, inclusive, more alive and quickening than the ones we have inherited'.[18]

Looking at our Brazilian mentality and culture, it is possible to say that we are still struggling to find and declare the independence of our bodies and minds, in order to build a national sensuousness. Nevertheless, it seems we are far away from this point, since we are still struggling with the institutionalised guilt we inherited in the colonisation process, which disciplined the country and colonised its bodies.

When addressing our bodies and sexuality, the normal attitude we experience in Brazil (as in many parts of the world) is embarrassment. Although the Brazilian population is often stereotyped as sensual, the normal attitude towards sex and sexuality is really shame and guilt. These are the remains of Iberian and Roman Catholic colonisation, in many ways no different from many of its Protestant counterparts, and, therefore, synonymous with a Victorian mentality. In spite of the apparent sexual liberty of the semi-naked bodies on the beaches and the *mulatas* that dance naked in the street carnivals, the rules prescribed by the hetero-patriarchal paradigms about the body and sensuality prevail.

In spite of the beaches and carnivals, guilt is endemic within Brazilian society. Richard Parker, a North American anthropologist, argues that sin lies 'beneath the Equator', and pleasure lies in breaking the rules; for him it is only possible to understand the eroticism of Brazilian society through the view of transgression, that pleasure is the result of transgression.[19] I agree that no transgression is free of a feeling of guilt; therefore what causes pleasure at first also causes regret, if not immediately, later.

Hermelino Neder, a columnist in a major Brazilian newspaper, describes the Roman Catholic Church in our country as a specialist in making people feel guilty – thus, an institution that is irrelevant for depressed people and those estranged by society.[20] Religion of this sort fails to bring wholeness for the disenfranchised, or even ordinary men and women who struggle to integrate their faith with their humanity and sexuality.

During the debate on the return of religious education in the Brazilian state schools, Arnaldo Jabour wrote about his own experience as a boy studying in a Roman Catholic school. According to him, all the boys at that school had to go for confession every week, and among the questions asked by the priest was, 'How many times have you committed the *vício solitário* this week?' – a reference to masturbation. And he remembered the explanation given by one of the priests on why masturbation is a very serious mortal sin – because when it is practised, many human beings that could be born die in the toilet paper thrown and flushed into the toilet basin. Consequently he, and most likely the other boys, used to feel desperately guilty; they were worse kinds of persons than Hitler, feeling that they too had committed genocide, exterminating millions of babies through the practices of *vício solitário*.[21]

This example might be hilarious, but it is a matter of concern when one considers its effect upon children's upbringing, ultimately creating neurotic masses of people. Indeed, this kind of negativism is responsible for many people's going to the extreme of abandoning *all* social and religious values imposed upon them about sex. The main focus of this social and theological negativism is to reject 'the sensibility supporting the people's legitimate search for pleasure [with the] guarantee that they have the liberty to enjoy the blessings given to them by the Creator'.[22]

When we address the issue of pleasure and guilt, we find the demonisation of pleasure linked not only with the Roman Catholics but also with many Protestants. Surprisingly, however, the Puritans were an exception. Just as the New England Puritans maintained a broad concept of sin without an extreme focus on sex, so they maintained a more open view of sex and pleasure:

> It appeared to them that God's fundamental purpose in creating us as sexual beings was not that we might make babies, but that we might make love. It was love, intimacy, mutuality, not procreation, that was central to the divine intention of sexuality. Some puritans, for example, declared that if children were born to a marriage, that was 'an added blessing', but not the central purpose of the marriage.[23]

Even though most Protestant churches have overcome the idea that marriage is for procreation only, Protestantism has, generally speaking, been unable to rethink its broader human sexuality paradigms, maintaining many of the negative attitudes inherited from Rome.[24]

The church has had a real problem with the pleasures experienced through our humanity. It would prefer to adopt a masochist theology in which suffering and body denial are requirements for holiness and salvation. Therefore, it tends to reinforce a moral doctrine that is based on fear, rather than the joy of God's grace. Mathew Fox points out:

> The ultimate hang-up (read: concupiscence) for those threatened by gay persons is ... that gay love is non-productive love. There is no baby-making when a man or a woman makes love with one of their own sex. There can be only the pleasure, the fun, the sensuousness and the expression of love as a goal. It makes love-making now oriented; sensually oriented; non-justifying ...[25]

In Anglican formularies and statements there is no denial of pleasure when experienced within heterosexual relationships since marriage is not seen as a means of procreation only. However, the way other relationships are treated shows elements of uncertainty regarding sexual pleasure that are a residue of the medieval church; these were further developed and spread throughout the world during the colonisation period. It is no surprise, then, that most reactions against gays and lesbians in the Anglican Communion today come from those countries colonised by the British during the nineteenth century, when strong elements of a Victorian morality spread especially throughout Africa and

Asia. Foucault, in his introduction to *History of Sexuality*, writes, 'We supported a Victorian regime and we continue to be dominated by it even today. Thus the image of the imperial prude is emblazoned on our restrained, mute, and hypocritical sexuality.'[26]

People in the colonised countries held different approaches to sexuality, from polygamy or polyandry to different sorts of same-sex expressions. But on issues that favoured male dominance, such as polygamy, colonised peoples might be allowed to hold a more liberal vision.[27] On other issues, they reproduced the same model of repression and oppression that they experienced at the advent of colonisation, when their own structures and institutions were wiped out, to make way for the western heterosexual structure. Consequently, their way of thinking was disturbed and contaminated by the western view of their bodies and sexuality; this in its own time was sacralised and reproduced to fight anything that represented a threat to the new models.

Foucault is right that we are still victims of a Victorian attitude of hypocrisy towards sexuality. Indeed, the reactions we get nowadays from the former colonies are attempts to maintain a mentality that its original perpetrators themselves are trying hard to break with.

Towards an incarnating theology through gay consciousness

For Elias Mayer Vergara, a Brazilian Anglican priest and psychoanalyst, those who react strongly against gay people do so because they experience gays as a threat to their masculinity or femininity. Men fear their own feminine side. This fear, according to Vergara, develops because the categories of masculinity and femininity have never been crystallised. This situation is the reason why there is such social or individual convulsion when someone comes out as gay or lesbian.[28]

The acceptance and tolerance of gay people in institutional hierarchies challenges the way we perceive our masculinity. It leads to a revaluation of what masculinity means, especially as feminine aspects of maleness surface. This new situation challenges the power structure, since it will no longer be believed that men are always supposed to be strong, emotionless, always the ones who lead, provide and control.

James Nelson points out that to 'seek validation, love and affection from other men, however, is a fearful thing, for we have been taught to relate to other men on a different basis – competition. The gay male who symbolises affection, openness, and vulnerability of man to man symbolises what seems to be denied to the heterosexual male.'[29]

But the main consequence of this acceptance of gay people is a re-evaluation of the way we perceive God, whereby God as 'feminine' can be reintegrated into our system of beliefs and worship.[30] The acceptance of gay men entails facing the vices of the hetero-patriarchal paradigms, which, according to Andre Musskopf, are heterosexist and exclusive, while the gay consciousness is based on self-giving, mutual care, awareness of our corporeity and on liberty and inclusiveness.[31]

Awareness of corporeity is an important element to be discussed, since it is linked with weakness and pleasure. These are elements that often do not fit into the concept of masculinity. On the other hand, Christianity is a religion of the body. The core of its doctrine is the resurrection of the body, and the core of its sacramental liturgy is sharing the sacrificed and resurrected body. In this way there is no way to disassociate the body from Christianity's structure of beliefs and doctrines, which also state that the Word was made flesh. However, when it comes to moral theology, the church always has difficulty incorporating the body into its life. The body becomes the subject of denial, an expression of the same fear of the feminine elements that are attached to pleasure.

Jean Delumeau describes this fragmentation as caused by Augustinian thinking that until today reflects the western fear of the body and the feminine aspect of our humanity. Dulumeau points out that Augustine makes a surprising distinction between men and women:

> All human beings, he says, have an asexual spiritual soul and a sexual body. In the male, the body reflects the soul; this is not the case for woman. The man is, therefore, fully the image of God, but not the woman, who only is partially so – through her soul – but her body constitutes a permanent blockage to the exercise of their reason. Inferior to the man, the woman must therefore be submissive.[32]

Gays' awareness of their bodies challenges established concepts of masculinity, making the concept of masculinity more integrated and inclusive. This new concept of masculinity embraces sensitivity and sees pleasure and emotion as realities to be celebrated and not denied. This new consciousness offers an integration of the female and male elements, since gay persons are conscious of this integration in their own lives.

It is necessary to recover an integrative approach to our bodies and sexuality that does not deny pleasure and intimacy, which are fundamental for human sanity. Rubem Alves affirms that 'all religion that, in the name of a spiritual order, forces on the body a regime of systematic repression, tends to produce neurotic personalities.'[33]

The lack of the phallus, the physical symbolic element of power absent in the female genitals, seems to be the main reason for women's exclusion from the hetero-patriarchal system. However, in the case of gay men, the phallic element, the symbol of power and control, is there, but gay men are still blocked from the institutions if they are practising their gayness. This situation makes it clear that inclusion or exclusion is based not just on biology but also on sexual performance and orientation.

Here we end up having to look at the sexual hierarchy that determines who penetrates and who is the receptor in sexual relationships. In some cultures, there is no problem with a man having sex with someone of his own sex, as long as he is the one who penetrates rather than the receptor. This was the case in ancient Greece.[34] The receptive role is classified as a lower class, inferior to the one that holds the phallic power to penetrate. The dynamic is not strictly one that is imposed based on sexual performance, but follows gender hierarchy.

For gay people's sexual dynamics or expression, there is no crystallised rule regarding who is passive and who is active. (I am not referring here to sexual fetishes and their variants such as sado-masochism, which are present among people of all orientations.) Many gay and lesbian people adopt a versatile approach, in which they feel comfortable with both passive and active roles. There are others who prefer a specific role, either the receptive or penetrative roles. But gender, class or social hierarchy does not determine this decision; rather, one exercises the role that is mutually chosen. This is a dynamic of power sharing, not an approach of dominance. It is an approach of self-giving, not an approach in which one has to subjugate himself to the other's pleasure and control. But the most important issue here is the ability to overcome the gender dualism, or barrier, that is imposed by men to subjugate women.

Marcella Althaus-Reid states, 'all theology is sexual theology'.[35] This statement is correct when we see the way the dynamics of sexual encounters reflect our way of seeing the world. I have explored above the power issue in sexual encounters. A gay theology, therefore, brings the contribution of gay consciousness, in which a versatile approach is becoming more and more common in the establishment of relationships. This is an approach in which power is shared, avoiding subjugation. It is a model of generosity and self-giving, in which masculinity is not attributed to the size or even the presence of the symbolic element of power and dominance, or how many women one has managed to have sexual intercourse with, or which car one drives. Nor is the heavy social pressure of the role of family-provider dominant.[36]

Our belief in the incarnation of Jesus Christ and our belief in the fullness of humanity face real challenges when our own body is denied in the current dogmatic heterosexual paradigms. The experience of gays and lesbians has the capacity to rescue and revive the incarnation of Jesus in our lives, through a Christology that reveals Jesus as the one who allows mutual dependence, both emotional and physical, and places himself on the side of those who are excluded – women, single mothers, physically disabled, and all those whose sexual performance and consciousness differ from the heterosexual model. The bodily experience of gay men and lesbians, as well as their consciousness, denounces the sins of the hetero-patriarchal structure, and proposes new models of relation-ships, based on self-giving, care for each other, living a healthy bodily expression, based on liberty, inclusion and justice – all of these the main intention of the incarnation.[37]

NOTES

1. See 1998 Lambeth Resolution 1:10. Although the word 'gay', and sometimes the binary code ' and lesbian', will often be used in this chapter, that does not mean this essay is limited to the reality of either/both gays and lesbians, but rather involves all sexual minorities. I could use the word 'queer', which is a broader and more inclusive concept; however, this term is more often used in North America and some other English-speaking countries, with no real translation or similar word available in other languages. I avoid using the word 'homosexual', since there has been a strong debate in the GLBT community regarding the suitability of this term, which was first used in the medical field, where this orientation was seen as a medical/psychological disorder.

2. Michel Foucault, *Discipline and Punishment: The Birth of the Prison*, trans. Alan Sheridan (New York: Vintage Books, 1979), p.218.

3. John Boswell points out that in the medieval church, those of homoerotic orien-tation were considered to be 'inferior insiders'. He argues that there was even a certain level of respect and tolerance towards this type of non-procreative orien-tation. The same attitude may still be present in many levels of the church, but the characteristic of inferiority already implies that gay people do not belong entirely in the ecclesiastical institution. See Boswell, 'Homosexuality and Religious life: A Historical Approach', in James B. Nelson and Sandra Longfellow (eds), *Sexuality and the Sacred: Sources for Theological Reflection* (London: Mowbray, 1994), p.362.

4. There are a variety of behaviours or mannerisms in different cultural settings that constitute the popular belief of what characterises a gay or straight man. According to Delcio Lima, the stereotypes incorporated in the Brazilian popular mentality are the way one walks, speaks, dresses, etc, namely, rather feminine, similar to other Latino countries, especially Italy. However, when I mention those who have 'heterosexualised' themselves, I do not necessarily mean the ones who avoid the mannerisms that are part of the gay stereotype. Rather, I am referring to those who deny their homoerotic orientation in public, at work, to their fami-ly and friends, or in any public space. See Delcio Monteiro de Lima, *Os Homoeroticos* (Rio de Janeiro: Livaria Francisco Alves Editora, 1983), pp.13–14.

5. Franz Fanon explores the issue of black people and their feelings of inadequacy in a white world. He explores the way a black man is made aware of his blackness. He uses the example of the Malagasy people, and here I apply it to the reality of the gay man who is made aware of his orientation through the straight man. Fanon explains that if a Malagasy questions his humanity, it is because he has been once challenged by the arrival of the white man, and made to suffer for not being white, having all his dignity taken away and regarded as a parasite. However, there are the moments in which a black man is made positively aware of his blackness 'through others', which Fanon explains, is when the black man is among his own. This insight can be applied to those gays and lesbians who hide their orientation in the moments they express their being 'for others' (the

straight men), but have the chance to express their being 'for others' (other gay men). In the latter, they can choose either to be 'in' or 'out' of the closet. See Frantz Fanon, *Black Skin, White Masks* (London: Pluto Press, 1986), pp. 98, 109.

6. See Mario Ribas, 'The Church in the Closet', *Journal of Theology and Sexuality* 10:2 (March 2004), 83–9.

7. The bishops at the 1998 Lambeth Conference preferred to use 'irrational fear of homosexuals' instead of the word 'homophobia' in resolution 1:10.

8. See *City of God*, XIV:16.

9. Marcella Althaus-Reid, *Indecent Theology: Theological Perversions in Sex, Gender and Politics* (London and New York: Routledge, 2000), p.88.

10. Althaus-Reid reflects on penis shrinkage in Ghana, where the popular belief is often that it is caused by witchcraft. She goes further, developing the concepts of shrinking penises and shrinking bodies in political and economic settings. On capitalism and heterosexualism, for example, she comments: 'Capitalism shrinks bodies and memories in a thousand different ways, and so does heterosexualism. If the streets at night have no women walking for fear of rape, there is shrinkage of humanity at night. If people do not get jobs or lose those they have because of a different sexual orientation, there is shrinkage in the labor forces' (see Althaus-Reid, op. cit., pp.182–94).

11. Grace Jantzen, 'AIDS, Shame, and Suffering', in Nelson and Longfellow (eds), op. cit., p.305.

12. See Earl E. Shelp, 'AIDS, High Risk Behaviours, and Moral Judgments', in Nelson and Longfellow (eds), op. cit., p.315.

13. Jonathan Ned Katz, 'The Age of Sodomitical Sin, 1607–1740', in Jonathan Goldberg (ed.), *Reclaiming Sodom* (New York: Routledge, 1994), p.51. Katz also explains: 'In the early colonies, the term and concept "sodomy" had connotations that they do not generally have for present-day Americans. For the colonists, struggling to survive in the wilderness, the word "sodomy", no doubt, evoked the destruction of Sodom and Gomorrah, as much or more than illicit sex. For those early settlers perched precariously on the edge of a hostile continent, the term "sodomy" provoked thoughts of Sodom, that archetypal settlement destroyed for sin. Living from day to day with the threat of social dissolution, the early colonists no doubt felt a special kinship with that particular ancient city.'

14. Althaus-Reid, op. cit., p.88.

15. See Foucault, op. cit., p.218.

16. Michel Foucault asks, 'What led us to show, ostentatiously, that sex is something we hide, to say it is something we silence? And what we do in all this formula-ting the matter in the most explicit terms, by trying to reveal it in its most naked reality, by affirming it in the positivity of its power and its effects. It is certainly legitimate to ask why sex was associated with sin for such a long time – although it would remain to be discovered how this association was formed, and one would have to be careful not to state in a summary and hasty fashion that sex was "condemned" – but we must also ask why we burden ourselves today with so much guilt, for having once made sex a sin.' See Michel Foucault, *The History of Sexuality* (New York: Vintage Books, 1990), v.1, p.9.

17. Foucault, *The History of Sexuality*, Vo.1, p.3.

18. Matthew Fox, *Whee, We, Wee All the Way Home: A Guide to a Sensual, Prophetic Spirituality* (Santa Fe: Bear and Company, 1981), pp.236–7.

19. Império dos sentidos – Entrevista Richard Parker', *Revista Veja*, 9 October 1991. See also, Richard Parker, *Beneath the Equator: Cultures of Desire, Male Homosexuality and Emerging Gay Communities in Brazil* (New York: Routledge, 1999).

20. Hermelino Neder, 'Uma piada e uma oração', in *Folha de Sao Paulo*, on line edition of 6 June 1995 at http://www1.folha.uol.com.br/folha/colunas/diariodepressaoefama/ult2855u12.shtml.

21. Arnaldo Jabour, 'Nossas maos assassinas matavam milhoes', in *Folha de Sao Paulo*, 3 October 1995.

22. Calvani, op. cit., p.109.

23. Boswell, op. cit., p.364.

24. Lynda Roper maintains that Protestant moral discipline was 'more all-embracing and less well defined than it had been before the Reformation. Now any sexual relationship outside marriage was counted sinful and any occasion on which the sexes mingled, such as dances, might lead to sin.' See Lynda Roper, *The Holy Household: Women and Morals in Reformation Augsburg* (Oxford: Clarendon Press, 1989), p.112.

25. Fox, op. cit., p.236.

26. Foucault, *History of Sexuality*, Vo.1, p.3.

27. See, for example, 1998 Lambeth Conference resolution 26 on polygamy.

28. Elias Mayer Vergara, 'Que Gay sou EU?', text originally distributed through Integrity-Brasil, later published on the gay online magazine, http://mixbrasil.uol.com.br/troctroc/arena/quegaysoueu.asp#.

29. James Nelson, *The Intimate Connection: Male Sexuality, Masculine Spirituality* (Philadelphia: Westminster, 1988), p.62.

30. Rosemary Ruether argues that masculine monotheism reinforces a social hierarchy of patriarchal dominion through its religious system in a way that did not occur before with the paired images of god and goddess. God is modelled according to the dominant patriarchal class; and this (male) class presumes that God addresses them through his Son, that is, the male rather than the female assumes the position of mediator. See Rosemary Ruether, *Sexismo e Religiao: rumo a uma teologia feminista* (Sao Leopoldo: Sinodal, 1993), p.51.

31. Andre Sidnei Musskopf, *Uma brecha no Armario* (Sao Leopoldo: scola Superior de Teologia, 2002), p.61.

32. Jean Delumeau, *História do medo no Ocidente: 1300–1800* (São Paulo: Companhia das Letras, 1989), pp.316–17.

33. Rubem Alves, *Protestantismo e Repressao* (São Paulo: Atica, 1982), p.184.

34. David Halperin argues that in Athens during the classical period, sex between two or more people had to maintain the hierarchical structure that related to the class system. So the receptive agent must be someone of an inferior class, the 'statutory minors' who are the 'inferiors not in age but social and political status'. See David M. Halperin, *One Hundred Years of Homosexuality and Other Essays on Greek Love* (New York: Routledge, 1990), pp.29–32.

35. Althaus-Reid, op. cit., Foreword.

36. Musskopf, op. cit., p.5.

37. ibid., p.61.

Chapter 18

HOMOSEXUALITY AND THE BIBLE IN THE ANGLICAN CHURCH OF THE SOUTHERN CONE OF AMERICA

Humberto Maiztegui

Introduction: the hermeneutical point of view

I cannot go into a detailed study of the internal politics of the issue of homosexuality in the letters of the House of Bishops of the Province of the Southern Cone of America to the churches of the Anglican Communion and to the Presiding Bishop of the Episcopal Church (USA) for the simple reason I have been living in Brazil since 1991.[1] I am a Uruguayan living 800 kilometres from my country. Nevertheless, I have a permanent relationship with the Uruguayan church and I follow at a distance the developments and troubles of the Anglican Province of the Southern Cone. This distance permits a more peaceful analysis of the theological implications of this particular ecclesiological moment in the life of my original church. It is for this reason that I chose these letters of the House of Bishops of the Anglican Church of the Southern Cone of America on which to do a theological analysis (not only local but also global) of the implications of the present attitude of this province towards the inclusion or exclusion of homosexual persons by the church. At the end of this analysis I will try to provide some small suggestions for the reasons for the distinction between this province and the rest of the Latin American Anglican provinces and the way forward.

I have two reasons for taking on a biblical analysis of this argument about the inclusion or exclusion of homosexual persons by the church. First, this argument is the central focus of the position of the Anglican Church of the Southern Cone of America. Second, it is my area of theological interest and specialisation. The biblical and hermeneutical approach to the issue of homosexuality is no different from any other question. The problem is in understanding the different contexts of many centuries ago, the context of our experience today and the connection between the revelation yesterday and today. Is it possible to refer to any matter in the Bible with the supposition that the words fixed in the texts can be extended and understood immediately, without socio-historical and theological mediation, to other situations separated by historical, cultural and even religious changes? What kind of mediation is theologically coherent with the Christian revelation of God?

Such hermeneutical arguments are similar to those in other parts of the Anglican Communion and in others churches on this issue. Such arguments about the inclusion of homosexual persons in the church, with their full dignity and full human rights are, at the same time, significant to a particular local church and to the overall viewpoint of the whole Anglican Communion and all of contemporary Christianity.

The argument

The Anglican Church of the Southern Cone's 'biblical' argument against the consecration of Gene Robinson as a bishop, against any sexual activity except within marriage and against the recognition of same-sex blessings, is presented in the letter which the presiding bishop of the province addressed to the Episcopal Church following Robinson's consecration.[2] It can be summarised as follows:

(a) These developments are against the Christian witness of God's Word: these events have 'devastated our Christian witness [and reveal] a misinterpretation of the clear witness of God's Word' (§1).

(b) Jesus' example is to be open to all people but homosexual behaviour must be rejected as a sin that separates us from God: 'Following the example of Jesus, we are open to all people, but we reject as sin those acts which separate us from God and from each other' (§2).

(c) The consecration of an active homosexual man as a bishop of the church and the direct or indirect blessing of homosexual unions can cause a schism in the Anglican Communion: 'ECUSA's action has forced painful division in the Communion and is a schism of their own making. Because by its precipitous action it has formed needless division and denied the Tradition of the Church catholic . . .' And 'as a Province we believe institutional unity is meaningless unless it is based in the truth of the Holy Scriptures' (§2 and §5).

(d) The episcopal consecration of Gene Robinson as Bishop of New Hampshire is unfaithful to the Word of God: 'in faithfulness to the Word of God, we cannot accept this consecration as a valid one' (§3).

(e) The full inclusion of homosexual persons is against the Scriptures and the historic faith and it is necessary to affirm the traditional scriptural norms: 'hold fast the Scriptures and the historic faith . . . [We] must reject the erroneous decisions of ECUSA and must affirm traditional scriptural norms' (§4).

This kind of argument is present, more generally, in other documents of this province. Concerning the debate on the blessing of same-sex unions in the Anglican Church of Canada, the Primate Bishop of Southern Cone affirms, 'there is nothing in the Bible about the sanctity of homosexual

relationships'.[3] Paradoxically, when the matter is divorce, another document of the Anglican Diocese of Chile reads, 'it is not possible for us to
find a solution for the problem of divorce through the use of the Bible
like a code of legislation in which there is a section for the regulation of
matrimony.'[4] If this argument is true of divorce, why this difference for
homosexuality? This contradiction reveals that hermeneutical questions
are debatable within the biblical arguments used in this province.

The witness of God's word

The definition of the word of God as a witness has much support in the
tradition. Years ago, Charles Gore in his introduction to *A New
Commentary on Holy Scripture* (1928) affirmed:

> Anglicans may well regard themselves as the trustees of the
> ancient liberty ... We have no cause to fear that science or histori-
> cal criticism can dissolve its foundations but we have grave cause
> to fear that ecclesiastical authority may forget its limitations and
> become burdensome upon sensitive consciences, and intolerable to
> the open-minded scholar.[5]

In the same book, E. J. Bicknell advised of the consequences of an
uncritical reading of the Scripture in the development of Christian
thought: 'the nemesis that awaits the stifling of criticism is mental and
moral stagnation.'[6] Being witnesses of God's word is to give a testimony
of the acts and revelations of God in one time and one place. All the
testimony in the Scripture has historical contradictions and paradoxes,
which are the fruit of the diversity of human history, culture and life. For
this reason, the Scripture is not 'a code of legislation' but, more
accurately, a register of historical experience.

What does it mean to be a 'witness' in the Holy Scripture? In the
Biblical Encyclopedia (1903), the biblical term 'witness' is defined in the
Old Testament as 'to be present'. If the Scriptures are the foundational
word, then in the Bible this is the first word of God, but not the final word.

Contemporary Anglican biblical scholars follow the first Anglican
critical scholars such as Gore and Bicknell in this approach. For
example, Reginald H. Fuller in a recent article on Scripture writes: 'God
was the ultimate, not the immediate, cause behind the writing of
Scripture.' The problem for hermeneutical work is when the concept of
inspiration through the Holy Spirit is mixed with the concept of
inerrancy: 'The primary work of the Holy Spirit is not to guarantee
inerrancy, but to produce an authentic witness to the salvation event in
Jesus Christ.'[7]

Albert Nolan gave an important inspiration to Latin American theology. For Nolan, Jesus had the freedom, as the live representation of God

come into humanity, to question the principles, laws, rites, hierarchies, costumes and sacred institutions of his time and to radicalise the self-giving of God to the outcasts. That was the reason why Jesus was seen as a *scandal* in the most conservative sectors of Judaism. Nolan comments: 'The scandal Jesus caused in that society by mixing socially with sinners can hardly be imagined by most people in the modern world today. It meant that he accepted them and approved of them ... The effect upon the poor and the oppressed themselves was miraculous.'[8]

Jesus, 'the incarnate Word' (John 1:1), is the divine presence in the life of humanity. The witness (presence) of Jesus took the practice of faith-as-exclusion, dominant in his time, as a point of departure. Jesus went beyond this faith to an encounter with the part of society that the religious hierarchy in their intolerance denied had a place with God. The question is what kind of witness are we to be – a witness to exclusion or a witness to inclusion? What is the testimony of Scripture about Jesus, the paradigmatic Witness of God? What is the scope of inclusion or exclusion of persons with a homosexual orientation living in families and called to assume all the ministries in the church?

These questions lead to another issue: the openness of Jesus and the question of the rejection of homosexuality. Is homosexuality a 'sin' promoting the separation between God and humanity and acting to divide the church, especially the Anglican Church? Or can Christ's love be conveyed through it?

Jesus' openness to all people and the rejection of sin

Jesus in his ministry had a remarkable approach to the people who were the most rejected of his time. As today, some forms of rejection were based on the religious understanding of sin. The dominant *hamartology* (understanding of sin) promoted by the scribes and Pharisees was very limited and put a great number of people out of the line of dignity or salvation. The most rejected of sinners were the harlots and corrupt tax collectors: 'Verily I say unto you, that the publicans and the harlots go into the kingdom of God before you' (Matthew 21:31b).

The use of the term 'go before' (Greek, *proagousen*, 'preceding, prior in time, previous') is addressed to the Pharisees. This conservative religious group believed that they were without doubt the heralds of the kingdom of God. The same theology gave them sure security that prostitutes and publicans would never have any chance to reach the kingdom of God if they continued to be prostitutes and publicans.

Jesus' declaration of the precedence of the outcasts condemned the legalism and moral hypocrisy that had in the first place caused the social and religious exclusion of these groups from society. The excluded sinners were elevated to the new status of witnesses against the self-proclaimed pure and saintly. Jesus brought a new *hamartology*, lifting to the most serious sin the sin against human dignity. The worst sin is the rejection of the rejected.

In the Gospel the only insurmountable separation from God is the sin against the Holy Spirit. Why not a sin against the law or against Jesus himself or against God the Father? The Holy Spirit is the most anarchic person of the Trinity. The incarnation of Jesus through Mary was an illegal conception without marriage! The community of Matthew (formed largely by Jewish Christians with a special preoccupation with the law) described Joseph's situation as an internal Jewish problem about the legal situation of Mary. Must Joseph ('a righteous man', Greek *dikaios*) send away (*apolusai*) Mary? (See Matthew 1:19.)

Another significant biblical passage is the dialogue between Jesus and Nicodemus, a Pharisee 'master of law' (John 3). In this conversation about being 'reborn', it is remarkable that Nicodemus is an authorised representative of the official religious law. The conversation is a reflection, like the incarnation of Jesus, on the woman's womb (an eternal problem for religious law throughout history). In the middle of the discussion Jesus presents this description of the nature of the Holy Spirit: 'The wind blows where it wishes, and you hear the sound of it, but cannot tell where it comes from and where it goes. So is everyone who is born of the Spirit' (John 3:8).

Even though the interlocutor in the dialogue is a master of the law, he does not realise that the Spirit of God is not translatable into legalistic norms. The action of the Spirit does not always fall under the law but neither is it always against it. Sometimes the action of Spirit moves forward in new areas or in new forms not reached by the law.

A final example of the non-legalistic action of the Holy Spirit is in Acts where Luke shows Peter, Paul and Barnabas breaking the legal obstacles for the inclusion of new Christians from outside the determinations of the Torah. Acts 10:11–16, the vision of Peter on the way to Joppa, presents a divine initiative that includes that which is 'common' (*koinon*) and 'unclean' (*akatarton*). The law was clear about what was clean and unclean in many places (see Leviticus 7:20–21 and 10:10). God asked Peter to break the law! The explanation of that illegal proposition is the action of the Holy Spirit upon the people that the official religion classified as 'common' and 'unclean' (Acts 10:44–48).

The Jerusalem Council narrated in Act 15 used the argument of the action of the Spirit for the inclusion of non-Jewish converts.[9] The judgement of James, brother of the Lord and head of the church in Jerusalem, made a limited inclusion (see Acts 15:19–20). This judgement opened with the words, 'I judge that we should not trouble' (Acts 15:19a). The decision of James, in the first place, is not to act as an obstacle for the action of the Spirit and, only after that, to find an acceptable form for the conservative Jewish-Christian church of Jerusalem. When Paul relates this meeting, he omits the 'recommendations' of James and adds his own recommendation: 'to take care of the poor' (Galatians 2:1–10).

Willis Jenkins in a recent article writes that the argument for the inclusion of the Gentiles is a 'compelling' one as a 'scriptural pattern by which to witness the presence of the Holy Spirit in lesbian leadership and gay unions' and the 'appealing to the rights of others, calling for respect of cultural values and church unity'.[10] This position accepts the theological force of Luke's narration but can also be interpreted as a refusal to venture deeper into the action of the Holy Spirit. Speaking about the Spirit is easy when the action of God confirms our theological, ecclesiastical or missionary convictions; but it is extremely difficult to admit the action of Spirit when it is blowing through the back door of the church.

Are the conservative parts of the Anglican Communion and other theologically excluding parts of the global church insurmountably separated from God by the sin against the Spirit? The Anglican Church of the Southern Cone declares itself against the full inclusion of homosexual persons and the blessing of same-sex unions but also against homophobic attitudes. This paradox is similar in that of the Church of Jerusalem (Acts 15 and Galatians 2) in refusing to see the end of the law of Moses as a normative code, but also feeling love for the Gentiles who were full of the power of the same Holy Spirit. The question here is the conviction of these churches as to whether or not it is possible to restrain the action of the Spirit. It is perhaps not such a problem if these churches want to put in a kind of rule for the local church, as they have done in the matter of women's ordination; but it is very wrong for them to be against the deep commitment to inclusion in other churches. This carries us to the next point about church unity and communion.

Unity, diversity and schism

Since the beginning of the church of Christ, there has been the temptation of schism. Conflict and diversity walk together in history. The conflict between the two disciples who want to occupy the principal place in the kingdom (Mark 10:35–45 and synoptic parallels) and the conflict between Paul and Barnabas about the mission among the Gentiles (Acts 15:36–40) are early examples of this temptation.

The first attempts to repair the divisions of the church are documented in the gospel of John. Raymond Brown in his analysis of the fourth gospel sees the signs of an 'intra-Johannine schism'; in this conflict, 'both parties knew the proclamation of Christianity ... but they interpreted it differently.'[11] Hermeneutical matters tend towards division; inevitably, these divisions cannot be overcome by a doctrine like infallibility. The 'areas of dispute' were diverse: 'Christology, ethics, eschatology, and pneumatology'.[12] It is common that a conflict that starts with a particular question about ethics, for example, soon leads to other theological areas like Christology or ecclesiology. Today the discussion in the Anglican Communion is not only about homosexual inclusion but also about the nature of the church itself.

The fourth gospel proclaims words for all the people involved in the conflict. In this context, the unity is presented as the living desire of Jesus:

> I do not pray for these alone, but also for those who will believe in Me through their word; that they all may be one, as You, Father, are in Me, and I in You; that they also may be one in Us, that the world may believe that You sent Me. And the glory which You gave Me I have given them, that they may be one just as We are one. (John 17:20–22, NKJV)

The unity here is not based on the 'orthodoxy' of interpretation but in the vivid example of God. The great truth that the disciples are led to believe is that Jesus was sent by God, God is in Jesus and, through Jesus, God is in us, even with great differences of interpretation.

The debates about the ordination or consecration of homosexual persons and same-sex unions can result in many different interpretations, but they cannot extinguish our communion with God. If we understand, believe and feel that God is in us, no matter how different our opinions and practices, we remain one in God.

Will there be problems in the relationship? Yes. As in the early church, today we have similar problems of unity at the sacred table of the Eucharist with our Roman Catholic brothers and sisters. The dialogue and the action of the Holy Spirit will indicate the way to reconciliation. A community must expel its own members and not allow such expulsion to be done by outsiders. Here the Anglican Church of the Southern Cone is wrong in interfering in the life of the Episcopal Church (see Matthew 18:15–17; 1 Corinthians 5:1–13; etc).

The question is, basically, how all the Anglicans in the world can be part of one church despite contradictions in theologies and moral principles and very different visions of pastoral work, mission and ecclesiology. While the church is catholic and universal, it is primarily a local or regional church. For that reason the place of definition of issues is the local, diocesan, or, if it is possible, the provincial (regional) level. At the level of universal communion of different churches, it will be impossible to have a clear idea about any local matter, but it is possible and, indeed, necessary always to reaffirm the Catholic bases of faith at this level. For example, many local or regional churches have never implemented decisions of the Lambeth Conferences on social matters such as poverty, human rights, ecology and external debit. In Latin America the Consejo Latinoamericano de Iglesias (CLAI) (Latin American Council of Churches) cannot group together all the Latin American Anglicans. In CLAI are Pentecostals, Methodists, Lutherans and Congregationalists – but not the Anglican Church of the Southern Cone. Why not? Because the Province of the Southern Cone does not like the social and political engagement of this ecumenical organisation. The issue is not a problem of sexuality or worship but a broader question of hermeneutics and a fundamental disagreement about the role of Scripture and the church of Christ in Latin America in transforming society and politics.

The Anglican Communion was never a unity as a confessional church. Forty-six years ago, Stephen Neil wrote:

> There have been in recent times bishops and deans who have caused affliction to the Church by the eccentricity of their theological and political views, and by the manner in which these have been expressed ... A choice of evils is before the Church. A man of unsound doctrine certainly does harm, limited harm, where he is. But is that harm likely to be greater than the venom, the injustice, the spirit of persecution that so often accompanied heresy trials in the past?
>
> It is *confidence in the truth* that makes the Anglican Churches demand so much of the faithful.[13]

Paraphrasing Ecclesiastes, in the Anglican Communion, there is nothing new under the sun. But the problem of unity, reoccurring in history, brings to the church an accumulation of wisdom. Like biblical wisdom it must be tested time after time: 'My days are past, my purposes are broken off, even the thoughts of my heart' (Job 17:11). The challenge of times of testing is to keep faithfulness in the word of God.

Faithfulness in the Word of God

It is difficult to define what 'faithfulness' exactly means. The word has a large semantic field including, 'steady in allegiance or affection', 'loyalty', 'reliable or believable', 'true to fact', 'standard or original', 'thorough in the performance of duty'. In the biblical Hebrew, faithfulness is affirmed in the 'amen' that we repeat in every prayer.

What does it mean to say 'amen' to God? The parable of Jesus about the two sons in Matthew 21:28–32 points to an answer. The first son was faithful in words, in his belief or proposed action, 'saying: "I go, sir," but he did not go' (21:30). The second was the opposite, saying 'no' but doing the work asked by the father. The 'amen' is not 'orthodoxy'[14] ('right in belief') but a preceding 'orthopraxis' (*doing* the right thing).

This distinction very clearly emerged in Latin American liberation theology.[15] This is the same biblical text where Jesus declared the precedence of the harlots and publicans!

The tension between 'orthodoxy' and 'orthopraxy' is presented well in Jesus' introductory criticism of the scribes and Pharisees:

> Therefore whatever they tell you to observe, that observe and do, but do not do according to their works; for they say, and do not do. For they bind heavy burdens, hard to bear, and lay them on men's shoulders; but they themselves will not move them with one of their fingers. (Matthew 23:3–4, NKJV)

It seems that for the common people it was difficult to have a clear idea about what was right or wrong in the Pharisees' orthodoxy. The word 'Pharisee' is a derivation of the Aramaic *perishayya*, 'separation' (or perhaps in a more contemporary term, 'apartheid') but in later Judaism had the signification of 'sanctity' or *qodesh* (holy).[16]

Sometimes the religious life takes recourse to isolation to show a kind of superiority or purity. In Jesus' time the most radical experience of this was the Essene community in Qumran. But the monastic isolation of the Essenes had very little influence among the common people where Jesus developed his ministry. The Pharisees, more than being isolated, had the practice of distinguishing themselves from the rest of the population. Their clothes, their social behaviour, their forms of prayer and their permanent attitude of 'teaching' were the marks of this religious and political group.

Jesus' criticisms attempted to show, in popular terms, what the problem was in the Pharisees' theology. In the first place Jesus leads his interlocutors to see their 'work' (*ta erga*) and what they 'don't do' (*ou poiusin*) (Matthew 23:3). Jesus changes the centre of the discussion from discourse to religious practice. The general criticism is 'they bind heavy burdens, hard to bear, and lay them on men's shoulders; but they themselves will not move them with one of their fingers' (23:4). The question is not the determination of the law but the human situation. For the Pharisees, the correct application of law is not necessarily the practice of justice; for them, 'faithfulness' is the right application of law even when it causes suffering for many people. In Jesus' way, faithfulness is putting oneself in the place of a different person, the other.

In the new ethic of Jesus, God says 'amen' first, God loves first, God saves first the people who were excluded by the legalists. For Inácio Neutzling, Jesus, in 'choosing the poor ... put in action a new order of values'. The coming of Jesus brings a new human–divine relationship, putting the poor and excluded people first. Jesus says 'yes' to the people to whom the dominant religious and political groups of society say 'no'.[17]

Thus, we can understand 'faithfulness' as true affection for unloved people. Faithfulness is an 'amen' to the example of love present in the identification of Jesus with the loveless people of his time. Faithfulness can never be, in the way of orthopraxy, the exclusion of love, the promotion of proscription or the persecution of anybody (see Matthew 5:11–12 and parallels texts).

In Paul's words, 'but now we have been delivered from the law, having died to what we were held by, so that we should serve in the newness of the Spirit and not in the oldness of the letter' (Romans 7:6). Obviously Paul's times and ours are different but the assertion of the apostle has the same challenge for us: love beyond the law. Following the example of Jesus, Paul and many sisters and brothers in Christ, those faithful to the word of God must not be prisoners to an ethic of the law, but live an ethic of love.

Is the inclusion of Christian homosexuals against the Scriptures and the historic faith? Must we affirm the traditional scriptural norms?

When one's approach to the Bible is in a living way, the first question is answered on its own. It all depends on how we understand the 'historic faith'. The Anglican Church, like many other Christian denominations, has its original matrix in the (English) Reformation of the sixteenth century; but its historical reference is to the primitive undivided Christian church. This matrix is fixed for us in the Lambeth Quadrilateral. This matrix is not an immutable moral code. The ordination of women, the inclusion of divorced persons and even the development of democratic political and social life show this openness.

Is it not possible to understand that the inclusion of homosexual persons in God, with equal dignity, like all the other sisters and brothers of the Spirit of the revelation in Christ, is not 'against the Scripture'? 'Affirm the scriptural norms' is, essentially, to affirm the eternal values of Christ's revelation, with love at the top, as we read in the gospel, 'Beloved, let us love one another, for love is of God; and everyone who loves is born of God and knows God. He who does not love does not know God, for God is love' (1 John 4:7–8). That is the norm beyond any norm and the tradition beyond any tradition.

What could be the possible reason within the Latin American Anglican context for the very conservative reaction of the Anglican Church of the Southern Cone?

In Latin America there are five Anglican provinces, from south to north (using their English names): (1) the Anglican Church of the Southern

Cone of America; (2) the Episcopal Anglican Church of Brazil; (3) the
Ninth Province of the Episcopal Church (Honduras, Ecuador, Venezuela,
Colombia, the Dominican Republic, Puerto Rico and Venezuela); (4) the
Anglican Church of the Central Region of America; and (5) the Anglican
Church of Mexico. The only province to call itself 'orthodox' in the
exclusionary sense that I have been discussing is the Province of the
Southern Cone. The other provinces have in most cases national episcopal leadership and direction. The Anglican Church of the Southern Cone
Province had and has (in almost all cases) foreign episcopal leadership
and direction. The problem is that the hierarchy of the Anglican Church
in the Southern Cone has had a theological formation without an understanding of and sharing in the sensibilities about the culture, the reality
and the priorities of the Latin American people.

Latin America has its own theological identity built by the theology
of liberation, both as religious inculturation and political engagement. It
was not the same process as in Africa or Asia. The Anglicans in Latin
America participated remarkably well in this regional theological
process of liberation. Anglican participation in this ecumenical process
happened through the Latin American Council of Churches (CLAI).[18]
But the Anglicans of Northern Argentina, Chile, Paraguay, Bolivia and
Peru did not participate in this ecumenical theological activity and,
indeed, often opposed it.

It is ironic that the Anglican Church of the Southern Cone accuses the
Episcopal Church in the USA of neo-colonial economic superiority,[19]
and yet did not participate in any way in the ecumenical movement
against more than 500 years of colonialist power and imperialist
domination in Latin America. What is the Southern Cone's attitude to the
sin of external debit and the International Monetary Fund? For them,
what is the theological and practical connection between political action
and the kingdom of God? In the past there was a clear difference
between the Dioceses of Argentina and Uruguay and the rest of the
Province of the Southern Cone, but recently those dioceses have joined
the theological thought of the other dioceses. The theologians who have
a different opinion, especially in Argentina and Uruguay, are under
official proscription.

There seems to be a direct relationship within Latin American
Anglicanism between whether theology, leadership formation and the
episcopate are foreign or national and whether the church is more exclusive or inclusive in its ecclesiastical perspective. In one of the first
papers about Anglicanism in Latin America presented in São Paulo in
1966, there was a strong emphasis on the 'development of Latin
American churches, expressive of the genius of their own countries and
of the unity of the Anglican Communion, and ministering alike to the

needs of their societies and the wider brotherhood of the world community'. This, rather than the narrow English theology of the Southern Cone, is the main stream of Anglicanism in Latin America.[20]

More recently, another paper was presented in Panama before the first Latin American Anglican Congress (CALA). This document, published in 1987, speaks of Latin American Anglicanism as a way of participating in history, reflecting local tradition and looking for an ecclesial indigenisation incarnate in each country.[21]

Other global churches like the Methodists, Lutherans and Roman Catholics are already well advanced in the process of theological dialogue with Latin America. I hope that in this moment of crisis it will be possible, through a global transformation, for the whole Anglican Communion to be open to hear *all* the voices of all Anglican peoples in Latin America, not just the foreign leaders of the Anglican Church of the Southern Cone.

We all know that theological or biblical argument alone does not have the power to change the reactionary attitudes of the Southern Cone or any other Anglican church in the world. But the development of locally rooted theologies in Latin America, Africa and Asia shows that within a few years these theologies had the power to produce an inner transformation of the church. Therefore, the way of change is the encouragement of theological reflection, writing and praxis born in the real context of Latin America and not in some artificial colonial reflection of England. This process is very significant and requires patience, continuity and strong support and encouragement from the rest of the Anglican Communion.

NOTES

1. The Anglican Church of the Southern Cone of America consists of the Dioceses of Argentina, Northern Argentina, Paraguay, Uruguay, Chile, Bolivia and Peru.
2. Gregory Venables, 'To ECUSA and the churches of the Anglican Communion from the House of Bishops of the Province of the Southern Cone of America', 8 January 2004. The full text can be found at http://www.anglicanmainstream.net/news87.asp.
3. http://www.iglesiaanglicana.cl/sitio/matr_y_divor.php.
4. ibid.
5. Charles Gore, 'The Bible in the Church', in Charles Gore, Henry Leighton Goudge and Alfred Guillaume (eds), *A New Commentary on Holy Scripture Including the Apocrypha* (London: SPCK, 1928), Vol. 1, p.17.
6. E. J. Bicknell, 'The Function of Literary and Historical Criticism', in *A New Commentary on Holy Scripture Including the Apocrypha*, op. cit., Vol. 1, p.18.
7. Reginald H. Fuller, 'Scripture', in Stephen Sykes and John Booty (eds), *The Study of Anglicanism* (London: SPCK/Fortress Press, 1988), pp.80, 81.
8. Albert Nolan, *Jesus before Christianity*, rev. edn (Maryknoll, NY: Orbis, 1992), p.45. The Presiding Bishop of the Province of the Southern Cone, Bishop Gregory Venables, regards the consecration of Gene Robinson as a *scandal*: 'You must know that … the people in this province view that as absolutely

scandalous.' See his letter to the Presiding Bishop of the Episcopal Church, Bishop Frank Griswold, dated 8 January 2004, §2.

9. Humberto Maiztegui, 'Teologia da Inclusão a partir de Atos 15, 1–35, superando as barreiras da discriminação contra homossexuals', *Estudos Bíblicos* 66 (Petrópolis: Vozes, 2000), pp.62–9.

10. Willis Jenkins, 'Episcopalians, Homosexuality and World Mission', *Anglican Theological Review* 86 (Spring 2004), pp.301–2.

11. Raymond Brown, *The Community of the Beloved Disciple* (New York: Paulist Press, 1979), p.106.

12. ibid, p.109.

13. Stephen Neill, *Anglicanism* (Harmondsworth: Penguin, 1960), pp.422–3. The emphasis is Neill's.

14. Bishop Gregory Venables writes, 'Candidates will have to demonstrate their commitment to orthodoxy in order to be acceptable for ministry here.' See his letter to the Presiding Bishop of the Episcopal Church, Bishop Frank Griswold, dated 8 January 2004, §4.

15. Enrique Dussel, *Ética Comunitária* (Petrópolis: Vozes, 1986), pp.246–7. This author was probably the precursor of the dialectic relation between 'orthodoxy' and 'orthopraxy' in liberation theology. See also Clodovis Boff, *Teologia do Político e suas mediações* (Petrópolis: Vozes, 1978), p.92, and Phillip Berryman, *Liberation Theology: Essential Facts about the Revolutionary Movement in Latin America – and Beyond* (New York: Pantheon Books, 1987), p.85.

16. Joachim Jeremias, *Teologia do Novo Testamento: a pregação de Jesus* (São Paulo: Paulinas, 1988), p.223.

17. Inácio Neutzling, *O Reino de Deus e os pobres* (São Paulo: Loyola, 1986), p.102.

18. Dafne Sabines Plou, *Caminos de Unidad: itinerario del Díalogo Ecumênico en América Latina (1916–1991)* (Quito: CLAI, 1994), p.119. In this historical synthesis one definition of Julio Santana (a Uruguayan Methodist pastor resident in Brazil) is very clear about the spirit of the ecumenical Latin American liberation theology: 'the cause of Christian unity [is] like an anti-imperialist movement, inclusive ... at the service of the people and, therefore, in solidarity with the fight for justice and liberation.'

19. 'When the economically powerful church in America acts . . . ECUSA's leaders have shown selfish indifference to the difficulties and confusion their actions have now brought this and other provinces', Gregory Venables, 'To ECUSA and the churches of the Anglican Communion from the House of Bishops of the Province of the Southern Cone of America', §1.

20. *The Anglican Communion and Latin America: The Report of Consultation at São Paulo, Brazil, 24–8 January, 1966* (London: SPCK, 1966), p.iv.

21. José E. Vilar. 'What is Latin American Anglicanism?' in John L. Kater (ed.), *We Are Anglicans: Essays on Latin American Anglicanism* (Panama City: Episcopal Church Diocese of Panama, 1989), pp.9–20 (Spanish edition, *Somos Anglicanos [ensayos sobre el Anglicanismo Latinoamericano]*). The production and publication of Latin American Anglican theology has many problems. We do not have many books in Spanish or Portuguese written by Latin American Anglicans. If we want Latin American Anglicans to contribute towards a more inclusive church it is necessary to find a way to integrate Latin American theology into the process of developing Anglican resources and publications. In this matter it is important to recognise the work of the Theological Education Commission for Latin America and the Caribbean (CETALC) created in 1976 for the Episcopal Church province but recently having spread to most of Latin America. See 'Anglicanos', *Boletin Internacional Misionero*, 51 (July–October 2002), 3–7.

Chapter 19

GLOBAL INTIMACY: MONEY, SEX AND COMMUNION

Peter Selby

The conflict in the Anglican Communion about the lifestyle appropriate to lesbian and gay people takes place in a world of conflicts, many of which are life-threatening. That a disagreement about this topic should provoke such serious turmoil raises some hard questions. Put most sharply, by a lesbian friend to a colleague, the question as it appears to many outside the Anglican family of churches quite simply is, 'Don't you mind that people are starving?' The natural response, 'Of course we do', doesn't make the question go away. No collection of essays designed to show, from all corners of the Anglican Communion, that there are doubts among many of us whether the traditional response to homosexuality can simply go on being our only response, can avoid the question, recalled by a gay priest from the hymn 'My song is love unknown': 'What makes this rage and spite?'

For, quite apart from the outrageous conjunction of war and famine with this particular controversy, there are curious ironies too. The Archbishop of Nigeria congratulates on his re-election a President of the USA who has not hesitated to make war without the consent of the nations of the world, not least the poorest of them, and has sought to undermine the Kyoto accords on climate change, with all the terrible effects which that action will have on the most vulnerable of the world's populations. His congratulations are on the grounds of the President's clear stand on 'family values', reflected in the efforts made by his electoral supporters to secure that a resolution against 'gay marriage' should appear on the ballot paper particularly in those states on which his re-election depended.

Then there is the reverse irony also: members of the Episcopal Church in the USA and of the Diocese of New Westminster in Canada appear to express, in the tone of their utterances certainly, but often also in substance, the same exasperation with the expectation that they should take account of the views of the Anglican Communion as their political leaders did at the requirement to seek a UN mandate for the invasion of Iraq. That is, of course, made doubly ironic by the fact that without doubt most of those supporting the actions taken by those parts

of the Anglican household would have shown strong opposition to the
actions of the American government.

Yet the search for 'communion' is unlikely to be successful without
some engagement with the matters of *with whom* and *for whom* we are
in communion. The argument powerfully made in the Windsor Report,
largely the result of Archbishop Eames' gift for the discovery of common ground, that our communion with God enables and requires our
communion with each other is only half the story. What of the communion with the unloved and the poor, as the biblical touchstone of our
communion with God? If our communion with one another is embraced
at the expense of those thereby excluded from the conversation – and
such conversation is not much in evidence in the Windsor Report, nor
did the Commission consider it part of its mandate – have we really dealt
adequately with the question of communion at all?

This essay is concerned to ask whether the outrageous conjunctions
and the strange ironies already mentioned are just that, or whether there
are after all connections between them which might assist our progress
to mutual understanding.

One connection between the ecclesiastical conflict over sexuality and
the conflicts of the world is quite simply that our communion has to be
just; it cannot be purchased at the expense of some who are thereby
marginalised and ignored. There is another connection too: the conflicts
of the world arise in large measure from the relationships created by the
process of *globalisation*, a process driven principally by money and
power, with a huge influence on the morality and cultural identity of us
all. Can all that is implied in 'communion' be sustained in the face of all
that is implied in globalisation? Put another way, the claim of
Christianity in general and Anglicanism in particular to be *catholic*
raises the issue of the model of global unity that we have in mind. In part
that has to do with the church's structures and expectations, something
with which the Windsor Report is greatly concerned. But it is also
concerned with how it is possible to be pan-global – catholic – without
dependence upon the mechanisms of globalisation, by the means and the
grace of a God who rules by love.

It looked at one moment as though these issues would be the ones at
the heart of the Anglican agenda. There is no doubt about what was top
of the agenda at the 1998 Lambeth Conference: province after province
had made its wishes clear about that. The Conference had to address the
issue of international debt in general, and in particular the un-repayable
debt of nations in the South of the world.

And as the requests had come in, so it was arranged. A plenary ses-
sion on the subject took place,[1] and the Section 1 of the Conference,
'Called to Full Humanity', had the subject of International Debt and

Economic Justice as one of its key themes.[2] Section 1 presented a resolution to the Conference, Resolution 1.15, which was passed unanimously without debate.[3] And if that were not enough, the Prime Minister of the United Kingdom, Tony Blair, made economic justice and international debt the central thrust of his speech to the Conference, a speech that followed a meeting convened by the Archbishop of Canterbury, involving bishops from around the world and Gordon Brown, Chancellor of the Exchequer in the UK.[4]

That was to be the theme of top priority, and the signs were that it was so. The mind of the Conference, so far as one could know that from what it declared, was clear: an economic system which resulted in the impoverishment of millions in the two-thirds world by debts they could never hope to repay was unjust, violated the divine intention in creation, and contradicted the biblical understanding of what it was to be fully human.

This issue was painfully debated in a subsection which contained bishops from creditor nations and debtor nations, and in particular bishops whose dioceses included people seriously impoverished by debt.

As Chair of that subsection and one of the speakers in the Conference plenary devoted to the topic, I have my own strong memories of the way this matter was handled and how the outcome was reached.[5] There were the complaints made about the President of the World Bank, James Wolfensohn, who flew in and out on Concorde, delivered a speech which showed passion and defensiveness in equal degrees, and left without listening to any responses. Nor shall I forget the painful encounters within the subsection between the bishops from the indebted countries and the bishops from wealthy countries who felt themselves consistently put in the dock, and unfairly so. Yet for all that, I was clear that we had engaged in the kind of honest conversation that being part of a worldwide communion involves.

In terms of an outcome, furthermore, there could be no doubt about either the roots or the practical implications of where our subgroup invited the Conference to stand. As to the roots of our understanding, we appealed to the biblical witness to the value of persons as our inspiration:

> We see the issues of international debt and economic justice in the light of our belief in creation: God has created a world in which we are bound together in a common humanity in which each person has equal dignity and value. God has generously given to the nations immense resources which are to be held in trust and used for the wellbeing of all and also offered us in Christ Jesus liberation from all that destroys healthy human life – a pattern of giving which God desires all to follow. The healthy pattern for

relationships is of mutual giving and receiving of God's gifts. Borrowing has its place only in as much as it releases growth for human wellbeing. When we ignore this pattern, money becomes a force that destroys human community and God's creation.[6]

There could be no doubt where we were coming from. And as to the practical demands, they were addressed to 'political, corporate and church leaders and people of creditor nations', to 'political leaders, finance ministers, corporate executives, traditional rulers, religious leaders and the people of debtor nations', with a range of remedies and programmes that were intentionally even-handed. However, these demands were not simply addressed to those outside the Conference: the resolution ended with a commitment, both as Anglicans and working with those of other faith traditions, to pursue the objective of debt relief and economic justice, and with a quite specific commitment: 'Finally, we call on all Primates to challenge their dioceses to fund international development programmes, recognised by provinces, at a level of at least 0.7% of annual total diocesan income.'[7]

So the first priority item of the Lambeth Conference of 1998 had been addressed in plenary, worked at in a theme group and accepted by its section, and had issued in a resolution of the Conference rooted in Christian doctrine, addressed to the wider society and making quite specific commitments as a Communion to respond to what the Conference clearly saw as a requirement on us all. Yet if debt relief and economic justice were the Communion's top priority before the 1998 conference it has lost that status completely. It is resolution 1.10 on Human Sexuality that has been the occasion of threats of division in the Communion; it is this resolution to which some bishops (myself included) have been required to signify their assent as a condition for episcopal ministry in certain congregations; it is this resolution, the product neither of the group within the Conference charged with addressing the issue nor of the Section within which it was included, but of a heated afternoon debate with amendments introduced at the last minute, and opposed to the end by a significant minority of the Conference – it is this resolution over which the Communion is now engaged in a dispute which threatens, it is said, its survival as a Communion.

How has this shift of priorities happened? I write as one of the minority who opposed the resolution on human sexuality. I do not believe that the emergence of a theologically articulate and spiritually authentic community of gay and lesbian people within the church can be met simply by repeating a demand for celibacy: since the Council of Jerusalem as recorded in Acts 15 the church has had to respond to the fact that its evangelistic activity has attracted those whose presence raises questions about existing understandings. Not to find some way of engaging creatively with such new experiences when they are clearly spiritually fruitful in so many cases is far from being 'traditional' – let alone humane. I shall not argue that case at length here,[8] because in this essay I am concerned rather to introduce into the discussion some reflections on this shift of priorities and its meaning, in the belief that they in themselves give pause for thought about how we as Anglicans should respond to the globalised economy on the one hand and human sexuality on the other.

The global economy and the possibilities of resistance

In a different section of the Lambeth Conference the power of the global economy was seen as one of the most significant features of contemporary life affecting the understanding and practice of mission. Section 2 of the Conference, under the title 'Called to Live and Proclaim the Good News', introduced its report by remarking on the globalisation of the world economy as the single most important development since the 1988 Lambeth Conference, attributing to that phenomenon the arrival of a world in which young people, in particular, 'live in a world where nothing is certain. They are offered only opinions, not truth.'[9] The section report adds that, 'the globalisation of the market economy is threatening the identity and life of nations and communities. They often respond with the aggressive assertion of national and religious identity. In many countries this brings increased pressure on and persecution to Christian and other religious minorities.'[10]

These observations about the globalisation of the market economy have an even greater relevance to our context as a Communion now than they did at the time of the Conference. On the one hand, the consecration of a bishop who lives with a partner of the same sex and the decision of a diocese to authorise a form of blessing of same-sex unions are seen as a capitulation by the Episcopal Church in the USA and the Diocese of New Westminster to precisely that culture of relativism that the global market has brought about. On the other, we observe the countries of the 'North', in particular the United States and the United Kingdom, taking it upon themselves to use force in order to dictate to particular countries the government and political system under which they are to live.

Against the globalisation process itself nobody considers that there can be resistance. It yields the transmission of a commercially dominant culture across vast tracts of the world; and it also brings about the financial – not to mention military – dominance of the United States in particular over the whole world. About this apparently irresistible process there are huge ambiguities: the same movements of labour and capital that have made possible a vast expansion of world trade make possible also the spread of HIV/AIDS in sub-Saharan Africa;[11] the same information technology that enables capital to be transferred swiftly across the globe also enables a situation where the vast bulk of movements on the international money markets relate to currency speculation rather than trade in goods or services.[12] What makes possible immediate knowledge of the different cultures of the world – and of course therefore the imparting of the Christian Gospel by new, quicker and cheaper methods of dissemination – necessarily also enables cultures with more financial power behind them to acquire dominance at the expense of more vulnerable ones.

Part of the difficulty of grappling with such ambiguities lies in the need to admit that the globalisation process is, as Nicholas Boyle points out, a product of our desires:

> McDonald's is everywhere because everywhere there are people who want to eat Big Macs, and everywhere there are people (such as myself when I invest the proceeds of my work in my pension fund) who want shares in the business of providing them.[13]

As he rightly says, it is difficult to be honest about our wants, and the way we spend our money is a better gauge of them than what we say we think. But the problem lies in Boyle's assertion that this phenomenon is 'everywhere'. Pension funds – everywhere? Is not the most difficult aspect of the globalisation process that it provides brilliant mechanisms whereby the wants of some – individuals, classes, nations – are reflected in outcomes far more readily than the wants of others? More seriously still, if we are to be honest about wants, globalisation has produced a battery of techniques whereby people's wants can be manipulated to the advantage of producers and investors thousands of miles away.

Boyle makes a particular point of what he sees as a characteristically British neurosis in the face of globalisation, 'whether it is the advance of Golden Delicious at the expense of native varieties of apples, or the craze for fast food instead of roast dinners',[14] but the fear of a loss of cultural identity is, of course, a much more widespread phenomenon. The British fear, however, arises, as he points out, from the fact that the arch-globalisers in the three centuries before 'globalisation' became a phenomenon were the British themselves as an imperial power. The British fear of this process is more to do with their loss of their historic control of it.

That control has passed, at least for the next few decades, to the USA, with the consequence that any fear of loss of identity elsewhere is effectively a fear of Americanisation. That process, irresistible as it is, is also ambiguous: some of its products are wanted by those who find themselves receiving them, some are not. All of us would like to have the

benefits of globalisation without the sense of a loss of independence and
identity. There is bound therefore to be a search for points where western culture can be resisted, and that resistance will carry all the passion
that, we all instinctively know, cannot be successfully deployed against
an economic dominance that is effectively irresistible.

The ambiguity of the dominance of the 'North', and the USA in particular, is not merely the result of the fact that there are outcomes the rest
of the world wants and others which it does not. It arises also because of
the intensity of cultural disagreements in the nations of the 'North'.
Within the USA, and within Britain too, are intense controversies over
religious, cultural and ethical questions of all kinds, and American
dominance, therefore, is bound to result in certain controversies becoming globalised, as each side seeks to use the resistance to globalisation
for the purposes of advancing its own side of the argument. What neither
side can escape from, however, is the dominance wealthier and more
powerful nations and their cultures have in the international marketplace. For the purposes of determining the future of Anglicanism, the
Lambeth Conference of 1998 and the other institutions of the Anglican
Communion since then became that marketplace; and the result has been
the projection on to a worldwide stage of a fierce disagreement within
American society itself. The provinces of the less economically strong
South, hoping to resist the domination of the liberal tendencies they
detected in the provinces of the North, were simply drawn into taking
sides in the North's internal conflict; there was no problem about allowing a resolution on international debt to be passed since all the energy of
the conference had been diverted into this other conflict.

In seeking to comment in this way on the processes that have led to
the current impasse in the Anglican Communion, I do not intend to suggest that the controversies themselves, particularly those around sexual
ethics, do not have theological content and importance. Plainly they do.
But the reason for their arrival on the scene as the principal battleground
on which the identity and future of Anglicanism is fought out has also to
be noticed if those theological issues are to be entered into with honesty,
and that applies equally to both sides of the argument.

The globalisation of the argument about sexuality and the use of that
argument to avoid facing the reality of globalisation are two sides of the
same coin. For the argument about sexuality is not being conducted in
the calm tranquillity of an ethics seminar or even with the passionate
engagement of those who are personally affected as gay people seeking
an appropriate lifestyle. The context of the present argument is matters
such as the invasion of Iraq, the massive loss of life from lack of food
and clean water, the HIV/AIDS pandemic, especially in sub-Saharan
Africa – all dramatic symptoms of the unequal distribution of power and

resources in the globalisation process. These are all issues of major
theological importance, which nonetheless have not been cited as reasons
for the break-up of the Anglican Communion, or the disciplining of
provinces who adopt the wrong stance on these crucial topics.

The pervasive dynamic of power

Reading the many statements made in defence of Gene Robinson's
ordination as a bishop has nonetheless been a salutary if chastening
experience, especially for one broadly sympathetic with the substance of
ECUSA's decision.[15]

For much of the language used to doubt the wisdom of 'waiting for
the Anglican Communion' to assent to a different and more open view
on the subject of homosexuality sounds not that different from that used
to justify proceeding to invade Iraq without waiting for the UN Security
Council to authorise it. The searing irony in that, of course, is that many
if not most of those most in favour of the election of Gene Robinson
would also have been among those most strongly opposed to the line
taken by the Bush administration over Iraq; and equally among those
wearing the 'traditionalist' label many who belong to the 'religious
right'. Such are the ambiguities and ironies of the current debate.

The international aspect of the dispute about sexuality has also to be
understood in its complexity. It is not too hard to understand that
churches which for two centuries have been given one set of clear teachings by missionaries from the 'North' – notably Britain – and have
gained a sense of independence, and indeed have discovered patterns of
growth that elude the churches from which the missionaries came, find
it unacceptable to be told quite suddenly that a new teaching on sexuality
must be accepted.

The globalisation dimension adds a further sharpness to the international reaction. The successors of the missionaries are in countries
possessed of such global dominance in economic and military terms it
is only to be expected that the churches of Africa and South-East Asia
demand the right to be heard in defence of what they have been taught
in the past, and what, they learn, 'traditionalist' minorities are in any
case seeking to defend in the life of ECUSA, the Anglican Church of
Canada and the Church of England. Neither is the international scene
clear and tidy: the Province of Southern Africa represents a different
viewpoint on the African continent, not least because it has emerged
from the apartheid era with its own suspicions of conservative
Christianity and its own relatively strong economic role.

All this makes it virtually certain that members of ECUSA and the
other provinces of the 'North' who defend liberal views about homosexuality will be heard as quite simply asserting a dominance which,

while having to be accepted in the realms of economics, politics and military power, is at another level deeply resented. Put bluntly, a bishop of the Episcopal Church in the USA defending the consecration of the Bishop of New Hampshire will sound like Condoleezza Rice defending the coalition's policies in Iraq. In some cases, where the language is militant in its defence of a 'liberal' theological position, that will perhaps merit the charge of being a new imperialism.

Even those, however, who express the strongest professions of concern for the vulnerable (gay) members of their church, and who spend time and money inviting members of provinces in the 'South' of the world to come and exchange views, and who are deeply opposed to the military interventions of the USA in the Middle East and Iraq, will nonetheless be heard through the ears of those on the receiving end of the globalisation process. The knowledge that there are those in the provinces of the 'North' who oppose the 'liberal' views of their provinces and have been outvoted will simply confirm the impression that the liberal views of the majority are being imposed in an oppressive manner on their own people as well as on the Communion as a whole.

It seems that the power dynamics of globalisation have us all trapped. Views and actions that to one part of the Communion appeared to be acts of liberation, defending vulnerable gay and lesbian people against the harassment to which they are constantly exposed and the undervaluing of their dignity and their affection, can only appear to others as yet another piece of cultural domination imposed by those with the money, the communications techniques and ultimately the military power to do so. Meanwhile those in the 'South', having found allies among the traditionalists in the 'North', return in kind the techniques of threat, exclusion and even (by bishops going to other dioceses to care for traditionalist minorities) invasion that they learned from their colonial and post-colonial masters before.

Globalisation and sexuality

> 'Global economy' is a modern Orwellian term. On the surface, it is instant financial trading, mobile phones, McDonald's, Starbucks, holidays booked on the net. Beneath this gloss, it is the globalisation of poverty, a world where most human beings never make a phone call and live on less than two dollars a day, where 6,000 children die every day from diarrhoea because most have no access to clean water.[16]

John Pilger's title, *The New Rulers of the World*, strikes an immediate theological note, whatever may have been his intention. The quotation is typical of the directness of his book, drawing attention to the way in which the globalisation process is working itself out in contemporary events. However, his title also represents a secular version of the title of Walter Wink's *The Powers that Be*.[17] Both draw attention to the 'powers' or 'rulers' in a globalised world, the domination of money and the level of violence connected with it. This language recalls the language of the Epistle to the Ephesians (1:17–23):

> I pray that the God of our Lord Jesus Christ, the Father of glory, may give you a spirit of wisdom and revelation as you come to know him, so that, with the eyes of your heart enlightened, you may know what is the hope to which he has called you, what are the riches of his glorious inheritance among the saints, and what is the immeasurable greatness of his power for us who believe, according to the working of his great power. God put this power to work in Christ when he raised him from the dead and seated him at his right hand in the heavenly places, far above all rule and authority and power and dominion, and above every name that is named, not only in this age but also in the age to come. And he has put all things under his feet and has made him the head over all things for the church, which is his body, the fullness of him who fills all in all.

It is my contention in this essay that the events surrounding the debate on homosexuality demonstrate a serious diversion from the issues the Anglican Communion needs to be facing, issues to do with globalisation, with the power of money and the resort to violence. The selection of homosexuality as *the* issue on which the future of the Communion depends avoids coming to grips with matters over which we feel ourselves powerless but which in reality threaten us far more seriously.

Globalisation does, of course, also affect human sexual behaviour profoundly, again in ways that we may feel powerless to address. Western societies demonstrate what happens when technological advance in medicine in general and contraception in particular outstrip our corporate wisdom as societies about what belongs to our wellbeing. When sexual lifestyles are assimilated to the multiplicity of choices which developed societies come to expect in all areas of life, marriage becomes a 'lifestyle option', a contract for two people to construct as they think fit, an idea far removed from any biblical notion of marriage as a means by which human beings enter into and represent, with their bodies and their shared resources, the covenant that God has made with humankind. With the assistance of mass media of communication across the globe, sexuality does indeed become a matter of profound importance to an international communion.[18] But just as the HIV/AIDS crisis was profoundly misunderstood by being regarded as belonging to the gay community, so the effect of globalisation on our sexual attitudes and behaviour is one that affects all human beings and not just the minority over whom the battle is currently being fought out.[19] It is characteristic of the powers that acquire such dominance through globalisation that a minority (be it the terrorism of a minority or the sexual behaviour of a minority) is selected for examination or condemnation while the majority, and especially those with power, do not choose to examine their own manner of life and its effects.

Totalitarianism or catholicity?

Globalisation presents humankind with unprecedented choices and opportunities, but one choice above all. That choice is to which power we submit ourselves. The injustices of un-repayable debt and unequal trade, the foreseeable consequences of failure to engage with climate change and sustainable development are clear signs of what happens when globalisation excludes communion, when the powers of money and violence distort the human community. The question with which this essay began, 'Don't you mind that people are starving?' represents the starkest challenge to the powers to which humankind appears to have submitted itself. It is a question that calls a global communion of churches to give the highest priority to the sharing in the work of justice in the world, a priority that would itself, as the wider ecumenical movement has shown, yield fruit also in the closer communion which is threatened by the current dispute. Even in the specific area of sexuality, there is a huge potential for shared work on priority issues: the domestic violence which results from unresolved issues between the sexes, the growth of the abuse of children and the commercialisation of sex generally and the damage that does to the possibilities of commitment. These are issues as serious for the heterosexual majority as for the lesbian and gay minority and demand our shared engagement.

Instead there is every sign that the homosexuality debate within Anglicanism has been invaded by precisely the powers of money and violence that we see as the by-products of globalisation within the world at large. That should not surprise us but it should challenge us. On both sides of the argument the language of exclusion and sanctions threatens to drown out the large number who, notwithstanding deep disagreement, are working together and exploring the issues with openness and care for one another. Even attempts like the Windsor Report end up unable to avoid the possibility of sanctions and breaking of communion. It is surely more than time to ask whether those real theological and ethical issues that are the presenting ones in debate have been overwhelmed by some of the dynamics – the powers – that come not from the much-proclaimed need to stand for truth and justice but from the pervasive forces that globalisation has let loose. And if that is indeed the case, it will be important to rediscover the means to communion. The Ephesians passage above, a biblical statement of a constant biblical theme, makes the point that there is a *choice* of powers, and that communion has to be established, if not necessarily over against globalisation, at all costs by drawing on that power which is uniquely the means the church has to employ – Jesus Christ in his justice, his search for those at the margins of the world's life, and by his means of grace.

At the end of his majestic survey of the effect of the global market on our sense of identity, Nicholas Boyle holds out a vision of 'the only goal compatible with the rational self-respect of human beings who understand their dependence on each other and on the world that has been given to them: a permanently peaceful global order, freely chosen by all its citizens'.[20]

For a church that knows its communion as no more than the first fruits of such a glorious harvest, its choices about the kind of communion it is able to have in the meanwhile are crucial. Boyle's comment is a call to a genuine *catholicity*, one that does not replicate histories of oppression and exclusion but is prepared to choose paths of patience and engagement in the search for a common mind and a shared justice across the diverse challenges that globalisation presents to us. And if patience is to be commended it can only be by its genuine acceptance by both sides in a dispute. There is no catholic church without communion, no communion that is not engaged in the patient and committed search for God's just and gentle rule.

NOTES

1. For the three presentations given at the plenary on International Debt and Economic Justice, see *The Official Report of the Lambeth Conference 1998* (Harrisburg: Morehouse Publishing, 1999) [*ORLC*], pp.345–61.
2. For the Section report on this theme, see *ORLC*, pp.107–18.
3. For the full text of the resolution, see *ORLC*, pp.384–7.
4. See *ORLC*, pp.441–6.
5. See *ORLC*, pp.360f.
6. *ORLC*, p.384.
7. *ORLC*, p.387.
8. This was the argument I developed in *BeLonging: Challenge to a Tribal Church* (London: SPCK 1991), especially pp.47–55.
9. *ORLC*, p.98.
10. ibid.
11. In January 2000 the number of children and adults living with HIV/AIDS in sub-Saharan Africa was some 24.5 million; in the rest of the world put together the total was some 9.5 million. See Gillian Paterson, 'HIV/AIDS: A Window on Development', in Charles Reed (ed.), *Development Matters* (London: Church House Publishing, 2001), p.45.
12. Peter Malcolm ('The Role of Business in Development', *Development Matters*,

pp.61–70) paints a glowing picture of the possibilities enabled by globalisation, while Rob van Drimmelen draws attention to the need for major reform in the international financial institutions. See his *Faith in a Global Economy: A Primer for Christians* (Geneva: WCC Publications, 1998). While world trade in goods and services had risen to $6,800 billion, the *daily* turnover on the foreign exchanges had reached more than $1.2 trillion. See David Held, 'Becoming Cosmopolitan: The Dimensions and Challenges of Globalization' in Peter Heslam (ed.), *Globalization and the Good* (London: SPCK, 2004), pp.4f.

13. Nicholas Boyle, 'We're All Global Players Now', *The Tablet*, 4 September 2004, p.6.

14. ibid., p.7.

15. I am particularly indebted to Louie Crew for his assiduous circulating of many press statements, articles and speeches on this topic which have appeared, mostly from sources within ECUSA, since the election and consecration of Gene Robinson, and to Ethan Flad, who edits an online website which is the successor of the former magazine, *The Witness*, which has contained numerous short articles from those supportive of Gene Robinson's election and of the recognition of same-sex unions.

16. John Pilger, *The New Rulers of the World* (London: Verso, 2002), p.2. The statistics come from a UN Development Report, cited *Guardian*, 22 October 2001.

17. Walter Wink, *The Powers that Be: Theology for a New Millennium* (New York: Doubleday, 1998), a digest of the third volume of his series on 'The Powers'.

18. I am indebted to Mark McDonald, Bishop of Alaska, for the account of his conversations with the First Nations members of his diocese about these matters. They reveal how a discussion of homosexuality can be transformed once these wider issues are allowed to be part of the agenda.

19. This is not of course to say that homosexual people are not also profoundly affected by globalisation, becoming part of the commercial scene: see Nicholas Boyle, *Who Are We Now? Christian Humanism and the Global Market from Hegel to Heaney* (Edinburgh: T & T Clark, 1998), pp.59f.

20. ibid., p.321.

Chapter 20

HOMOSEXUALITY AND THE CLARITY OF SCRIPTURE: REFLECTING WITH THE ARCHBISHOP OF SYDNEY

Scott Cowdell

The Anglican Communion is presently engaged in a highly charged dispute about the acceptability of homosexual acts. Does involvement in gay and lesbian sex preclude ordination, even in the context of monoga- mous 'marriage-like' relationships, and should such relationships be blessed by the church? The conservatives who oppose any relaxation of traditional discipline do so for a variety of reasons, but chief among them is the alleged incompatibility of gay and lesbian lifestyles with the plain teaching of Scripture. What follows is an essay about the authori- ty and clarity of the Scripture involved in this style of argument, and the case as put by one of its main protagonists.

The battle for the Bible

The Bible passages that appear on the face of it to condemn homosexu- ality are read in context and more inclusively by many non-evangelical Christians. For example, the Old Testament prohibitions are contextua- lised in terms of Israel's need to protect its divinely covenanted identity against dilution by syncretistic currents in ancient Near Eastern culture. These teachings are thus seen to warn against sexual violence or assimi- lation to pagan norms, rather than against anything resembling the monogamous same-sex relationships between equals that are wide- spread in today's West. As for New Testament prohibitions, it is widely held that they refer to culturally licensed Greek pederasty, and that the way of Christ calls for an altogether more vocational sexuality. It can be argued that 'marriage-like' gay and lesbian unions avoid this prohibition, in the direction of a recognisably Christlike pattern of relationship that we can identify with Christian marriage. Arguments like these are well represented in the literature of this debate. Yet they do not satisfy those who insist on the clarity of Scripture, because the plain and direct meaning of biblical texts is allegedly affronted. Indeed, those like me who hold such views are liable to be written off as 'trendy liberals', 'modernists', prisoners to contemporary culture, betrayers of the Gospel, enemies of God's word, and worse.

I dispute such an assessment of my own motives and those of many like me. Of course, there *is* an 'anything goes' theological liberalism abroad in western Christianity, sacrificing Christ to culture at every turn, subsuming the Gospel to whichever therapeutically minded spirituality is in favour, and as such warranting the charge of disobedience to God. But I write here as a Christian loyal to the Bible and committed to the challenges of discipleship, engaging in conversation with contemporary culture yet not in thrall to it. And I suspect I am a common type in our church, neither hard-line conservative nor out-and-out liberal. 'Post-liberal' and 'Radical Orthodox' are new names that attempt to chart this middle ground, this third way, in contemporary theology, which is anything but a limp or faithless compromise. 'The radical centre' better indicates the claim that I and many like me would make for ourselves in this debate. And we are in danger of not being heard. Many conservatives deny that we exist, because for them a liberal is a liberal is a liberal, and because there is only one form of biblical authority. Thoroughgoing liberals, on the other hand, tend to lump us together with the conservatives, because we hold out for biblical authority, and the gospel imperative that every thought be made captive to Christ.

One significant contributor to the Anglican Communion's homosexuality debate internationally is Dr Peter Jensen, Archbishop of Sydney. His case against homosexual practice based on its incompatibility with a plain reading of Scripture reflects a wider programme of fostering faith and obedience toward the God of Jesus Christ, as made known for our salvation in the words, sentences and paragraphs of a 'heavenly book', the Bible. My respect for Peter Jensen and his role in this debate has led me to study his recent book *The Revelation of God*[1] and its predecessor by a decade, *At the Heart of the Universe: What Christians Believe.*[2] I believe it is important that Dr Jensen is properly heard and, in particular, that he is not dismissed by liberals as theologically naïve or as a typical biblical fundamentalist. Plainly he is neither, in the carefully nuanced case he makes for our ability to know the mind of God through Scripture without error, while recognising the weight of scientific claims and the opaque and contradictory nature of much in the biblical material.

Yet I do not agree with Dr Jensen on a central plank of his case, namely the clarity of Scripture. I think he imports the category into the debate, both from the religious tradition he represents and the culture of modernity he condemns, imposing it on the Bible. Further, I deny that it brings the promised assurance and provides adequate guidance to the people of God. And, for argument's sake, I challenge the claim that clarity of Scripture ensures sufficiently clear guidance for the church on homosexual practice, because the Bible's only clear condemnation

seems to be of sodomy, and not the other sexual practices engaged in
widely, and often exclusively, by gay men – not to mention a similar lack
of clarity in the Bible about lesbian relationships.

Archbishop Jensen on the clarity of Scripture

While the preference in much modern theology is to seek God's revelation in still-evolving patterns of human experience and trends in history,
with the 'event' of Jesus Christ as its high point, Dr Jensen is convinced
that the Bible offers us more certainty than this, arguing his own preference for 'propositional revelation'. The person of Jesus is not the
content of faith, except as mediated by the confession of Jesus as Lord,
with reference to the scriptural text carrying that mediation – 'Christ
clothed in his Gospel', in other words.[3] God's salvation comes to us as
we submit to the covenantal grace of God mediated in the inerrant and
totally trustworthy words of Scripture. In a multi-vocal culture God has
given us a voice we can trust. And in a world where many Christians
prefer an infallible church and others an authentic personal experience,
Dr Jensen offers us something he believes to be less problematic. His is
an uncompromising religion, yet evangelistic and pastoral in its stated
motivation, offering reassurance for troubled, rootless and hopeless
modern people. Note, however, that Dr Jensen prefers the biblical notion
of 'knowledge of God' to the technical theological category of 'revelation' – the latter suggesting that information is being conveyed, while
'knowledge of God' in the Bible means that a covenant relationship
requiring obedience is established.[4]

Dr Jensen admits that a general, universal knowledge of God and
God's purposes is available to all of humanity according to the Bible, but
it is not a saving knowledge.[5] Such saving knowledge comes only in and
through Jesus Christ, and it is important for Dr Jensen (as it was for John
Calvin) to know 'the real Jesus'. Only the real Jesus saves, while any
other purported relationship with God – based on personal spiritual
experience, perhaps, or even on participation in worship and sacrament –
has to be authenticated by reference to what we know of 'the real Jesus'.[6]

The only sure reference is provided in the New Testament, supported
by what the Old Testament tells us about the purposes of God and the
coming Messiah. 'The real Jesus' is reliably present, according to Dr
Jensen, when the biblical categories of human sinfulness, covenanted
grace and the claim of Jesus' uniqueness are all in place.[7] And the
carrier of this reassurance is the biblical text itself. It is not enough for
Dr Jensen to seek Jesus in the Spirit through the contemporary
experiences either of individuals or the church, in conversation with
Scripture.[8] Rather, the Holy Spirit of God, acting chiefly as 'librarian
and reading lamp',[9] as Kathleen Boone describes it (referring to the

work of leading evangelical J. I. Packer), brings us to the sure word of
God in the Bible, which the same Spirit inerrantly inspired.

This clarity of Scripture is absolutely essential, according to Dr
Jensen, because it is what God seeks to provide for us. Clarity of
Scripture means that the God who is honest, reliable and faithful to the
covenant will neither lie to us nor leave us in the dark. And the Bible
gives this surety of faith that God wishes for God's children, promising
to guide their steps and guard their paths.[10] This clarity is understood to
be located in the text itself, not in the inspired reading of it. That would
be too unreliable, and is deemed an unnecessary risk to court, given
God's clearer provision for our guidance in Scripture.[11]

And here it is important to note that Dr Jensen distances himself
convincingly from a number of fundamentalist currents. While a self-
confessed biblical inerrantist,[12] he is not given to fantastic interpretations, preferring a simple, sober and direct approach to Scripture.[13] He
does not condemn doubt on the part of Christians, though he does insist
that the faith of Christians must be faith in the right object, even if that
faith may waver.[14] He does not impose intellectual constructs to account
for discrepancies in the Bible, as do American fundamentalists with their
dispensationalist theories, inventing different aeons in the Bible to
account for how God appears to work differently in different parts of the
Scriptures.

Nor does Dr Jensen insist that everything in the Bible has to be read
literally at the expense of our wider rationality – Dr Jensen is no
advocate of creationism, for instance, and he does not appear to have a
problem with evolutionary theory.[15] His preferred course is to welcome
apparent discrepancies in the Bible, finding in them both grist for the
mill of biblical scholarship, and reassurance that the Bible really takes
the complexity and regular unresolvedness of human life seriously,
reflecting it in its own nature.[16] Dr Jensen's doctrine of Scripture's
clarity, then, is not necessarily an assertion of its too-easy transparency.
Rather, he insists that the text needs to be struggled with within the
wider embrace of a confident biblical faith, believing that it will guide
us if we give it time – a 'doctrine of the Bible' can be compiled on any
topic, supporting the clarity of particular passages.[17] So Dr Jensen is
confident that the Bible provides sufficient resources for the church to
resolve difficult issues in the present, if we are open to its whole coun-
sel (not forgetting the wisdom literature, for instance[18]). However, there
is a biblically based freedom that Dr Jensen also claims for Christians,
emphasising their scope for independent action in a whole range of
human activities where the Bible expresses no opinion or preference.[19]
This biblical opening-up of a 'secular realm of independent human
activity', as we might call it, albeit 'under God', is an interesting

concomitant of Dr Jensen's theology, to which I will return.

In all of this, Dr Jensen has the various theological and cultural alternatives of modernity in view. In particular, the Enlightenment is a significant category in his thought. He is in sympathy with it to the extent that the Enlightenment involves a critique of human religiousness and the claims of religious tradition.[20] Chiefly, however, Dr Jensen rejects the Enlightenment for its assertion of human autonomy from God.[21] This is the core disobedience he identifies at the heart of modern woes, finding it to be fully reflected in modern theology and church life wherever the Bible is not at the centre. Whether it be church renewal taking the form of liturgical revival,[22] or the mystical, non-verbal strain in contemporary theology, through to Christian cultural capitulation in the name of personal autonomy, Dr Jensen discerns essentially the same flawed response to what God wishes for us, and has given us through the Bible. In his Epilogue to the earlier book, Dr Jensen reservedly commends the non-propositional, 'mystical, non-verbal strain' of modern theology, for reminding us 'that our God is far beyond our comprehension', while still concluding that 'It condemns us to doubt where we can have a joyful assurance instead'.[23] Yet in the more recent book there is no remaining hint of that commendation. Both the demands of a Christian's assurance of faith, and the biblical logic discerned by Dr Jensen, militate toward tight propositional control of the knowledge of God. This is God's revealed choice and it is what we need.

Tradition, modernity and assurance in Dr Jensen

It is Dr Jensen's intent to replace the authority of Church tradition and modern culture (albeit in conversation with the Bible) with the Bible's own authority. Yet it is plainly obvious to me and to others considering such evangelical arguments for the clarity of Scripture that tradition and modernity have not been excised from Dr Jensen's presentation. Rather, they have crept in by other routes. Further, it seems distinctly odd to me, not least from the energetic vigilance with which Dr Jensen presents his case, that the assurance which clarity of Scripture ought to bring needs to be so vigorously argued and defended if it is to be believed, where one might have expected it to be more obvious, less problematic and less apparently fragile. Obviously, this clarity of Scripture is a position tenaciously defended, not just a fact of life gratefully accepted.

Concerning tradition, it is a certain sort of evangelical Protestant case that Dr Jensen presents. The history of scriptural interpretation does not show that plain, literal meanings have been demanded by Christian orthodoxy. Allegorical readings flourished in antiquity, and a distinction between the literal and the spiritual sense of Scripture emerged in the Middle Ages. Protestant biblical interpretation produced a variety of emphases, with a major distinction evident in matters of church order between the Lutheran tradition and Dr Jensen's own Reformed tradition in their treatment of Scripture, with further differences between evangelicals and fundamentalists, and among the various types of fundamentalist. Is it not entirely obvious that while Scripture is allowed to challenge tradition (for non-evangelical Anglicans and Roman Catholics as well as for evangelical Protestants), nevertheless the power of tradition remains a constant feature of everyone's relationship with the Bible?

The evidence for this dependence is in the way in which the clarity of Scripture is defended by Dr Jensen. As we have seen, he infers it from the reliability and honesty of God, from the need for assurance on the part of God's people, from the assumption that God is ultimately the author of the Bible, and the further assumption that everything about Christ we read there is meant to provide an accurate record, both in words and deeds. But these elements whereby Dr Jensen defends the clarity of Scripture are then confirmed and guaranteed by assuming the same literal authority and clarity of Scripture – this is what the Bible says, so we can and must believe it. Here we have what appears to be a circular argument. That is, on the one hand we are told that God wills and provides for our reassurance in certain ways, from which we infer the clarity of Scripture; but then, on the other hand, we can be sure that God offers such reassurance because of the clarity of Scripture. In addition to this sort of cumulative case, however – a case built upon a range of convictions about God's purposes, and the role of Scripture – Dr Jensen also points to particular passages in the Bible about the trustworthiness of Scripture and its efficacy. But many non-evangelicals trust the Bible, and trust that God will lead us using the church's perennial conversation with the Bible, without inferring biblical inerrancy from these passages. The allegorical and spiritual reading of Scripture remains the Christian norm outside evangelical Protestant circles.

The clarity of Scripture, then, is at least as much a conviction brought to the Bible as an article of faith drawn from the Bible.[24] We cannot miss a creating, covenanting God in the Bible, the crying need of humanity, the grace of God in Jesus Christ, his world-transforming mission, his saving death and liberating resurrection, Jesus' presence with a missionary church in the Spirit, and his coming again to make all things new. But the clarity of Scripture as a support for the sole authority of the Bible's plain meaning is not there to be read off, and made the guarantee of Christian faith. Rather, the clarity of Scripture is a necessary assumption if you are to prosecute biblical authority as Dr Jensen does, as spokesman for one type of evangelical tradition in theology, and that sector of Protestantism persuaded by it. In other words, it is a piece of Protestant religious tradition, deployed to support the Bible's authority, with the Bible's authority in turn underpinning the authority of that tradition.

As for the modernity of Dr Jensen's case, it is plain in his emphasis on clarity. This prime Enlightenment virtue, setting aside obfuscation, the weight of existing tradition and unscientific mystification, in favour of cool and dispassionate rationality, dominates Dr Jensen's own presentation. The Bible as he reads it brings the true Enlightenment, liberating humanity from religious superstition, creating equality by establishing the parity before God of every reader, and creating an authority free of spiritual double meanings. The plain facts of science and human nature became the charter of the Enlightenment, and it is not too much a stretch of the imagination to see the same Enlightenment sun shining on the page of Dr Jensen's Scriptures to reveal a plain message. So while his later book begins with a response to the Enlightenment challenge, and everywhere he critiques the autonomous spirit of disobedient humanity identified with modernity, nevertheless *The Revelation of God* is (in this sense) a recognisably modern-minded book.

Another modern feature of Dr Jensen's case is its univocist trend, with a totalising interpretation brooking no dissent. This is fully in keeping with the ideological overconfidence of 'enlightened' modernity. But this overconfidence has broken down in recent times, with postmodern or late-modern trends pointing to the feet of clay shared by every purportedly all-embracing view of reality. My identification of tradition and the spirit of modernity in Dr Jensen's case is an example of this deconstructive spirit in contemporary criticism, bringing its other loyalties to light. Yet this is also a spirit that can claim warrant and precedent in the prophetic tradition of Scripture.

The role of power in the production of truth is one feature of this new consciousness. One would have thought that a vague and malleable Scripture would best suit the needs of a power elite in the church, allowing them to exercise a determinative role in biblical interpretation. But a clear Scripture can also boost the power of interpretive elites, whose authority in the church is enhanced by their uncompromising stance. Clear language and a clear message thus serve a clear line of authority. Part of the clear message in Dr Jensen's theology is the threat of hell for all who do not have a saving knowledge of God, which means having the wrong Jesus if they are Christian, which in turn means having the wrong view of the Bible. This is a powerful inducement for agreeing with the preferred interpretation. Surely, however, such an approach risks co-opting Scripture in the cause of an authority that is really located elsewhere – in evangelical tradition and church leadership. Indeed, the authority of Scripture, its force redoubled by claims for the clarity of Scripture in support of a plain reading, is a necessary part of evangelical tradition. To wield the Bible, to carry and display it on one's person, to deny the biblical faith of opponents, and their obedience to God, because they disagree with the emphasis of one's own evangelical tradition, is to show how the authority of the Bible, the authority of tradition and the personal authority of church leaders are woven fine in this approach.

One other concern I have about the Enlightenment tone of Dr Jensen's position is the way it separates God from the felt realities of human experience, with knowledge of God conveyed by the Bible independent of our lived life in the world. Such an approach has consequences. It resembles another strategy of Enlightenment theology, which sought God in the continuities of nature, the underpinning of ethics or in the philosophical requirements of human selfhood (Newton, the Deists, Descartes, Kant). Thus God came to serve as a theoretical explanation or metaphysical necessity rather than a reliable reality of personal conviction. The idea was to give God a firmer foundation. But the strategy failed, when better science and a rising awareness of cultural relativism in philosophical anthropology brought to an end the metaphysical necessity and explanatory power of God. With the mathematician Laplace and his (alleged) assertion to Napoleon that God had become an unnecessary hypothesis, the God who had been co-opted for scientific and metaphysical duty suddenly became surplus to requirements. The characteristic God of Enlightenment theology thus became an outsider to the world, whose action was limited to intervention and who too readily slipped from belief before a confident secularism. And this was a secularism theologically created.[25]

As for Dr Jensen's case, of course biblical inerrantism was not one of the Enlightenment's options, with its denial of revelation in favour of reason. But by turning exclusively to the Bible and denying other means of coming into significant relation with God, the effect is the same. God's action and our knowledge of God is moved out of the realm of regular human knowing and experiencing, into a special realm only accessible to the right sort of evangelical faith. And while such recourse to the authority of the Bible is meant to bring clarity and assurance, its effect is actually to reduce living faith to will-driven fideism, which compels few today because it connects as a deep personal reality with few today. Even among evangelicals, the real reasons for Christian faith are far more complicated than this, and are tied as ever to the whole range of human experience with God, shaped in conversation with the Bible to be sure but not confined to it. This is a subtle point, for Dr Jensen is no Enlightenment rationalist. But he is like an Enlightenment rationalist in his distrust of religious tradition and priestcraft, along with mysticism and other 'soft' ways of knowing. Yet, *de facto*, most if not all believers find such means indispensable – and, moreover, to exclude them is to court atheism, as reflection on related theological strategies of Enlightenment times has demonstrated. God has not put all the eggs in one basket, even if that basket is the Bible.

The last point I want to make in response to Dr Jensen on the clarity and authority of Scripture has to do with the priority of assurance in the case as he presents it. We need assurance of salvation to have a genuine faith, and God wants to provide it, according to Dr Jensen's tradition, and thus the clarity of Scripture is mandated. Yet I am concerned that evangelicals are so worried about being deceived, and so protective of their claims. It seems that the ground of their assurance in the Bible is constantly under threat by almost everyone in the church – even by less correctly aligned evangelicals, not to mention theological liberals and the non-Christian world. The mood of such a faith is fearful, aggressive and defensive, rather than mellow, poised and open. There is a mystical stillness that mocks the claim of a nervous, strident evangelicalism to offer assurance of faith. Such a faith does not rely on propositional revelation, yet it knows Christ and is anything but doctrinally dissolute. Here I think of Rowan Williams and his mystically tinged christological orthodoxy.

For argument's sake ...

I now want to shift gear, offering a *reductio ad absurdum* argument showing how the clarity of Scripture may be less helpful on the homosexuality issue than evangelicals commonly believe. Let there be no misunderstanding, however: I am not proposing that this argument be deployed 'positively' as a major plank in the debate. It is simply to show that Scripture is not clear enough to entirely resolve the homosexuality issue for us, as claimed in evangelical circles.

It could be argued that for all its apparent clarity on the matter, Scripture provides no clear condemnation of homosexual acts apart from sodomy. Similarly, we are unable to find unequivocal scriptural condemnation of lesbian sex. And, while Dr Jensen believes a 'biblical doctrine' can be compiled on any matter, bringing a lot of texts together in the act of discernment and interpretation, it remains at the heart of evangelical condemnation of homosexual acts that they are unequivocally forbidden in specific Bible texts, with no such wider case needing to be made. But it has dawned on me that this 'plain reading of scripture' argument is not entirely convincing, as only sodomy is clearly condemned.

It is important to realise, however, that not all gay men are sodomites. Many gay men find anal intercourse to be personally repellent, as do many (but not all) heterosexual women. Oral sex and mutual masturbation are the sole sexual activities of many gay men, just as they are the regular recourse of many heterosexual couples. My question is, does the plain teaching of Scripture forbid this range of intimate activities? If Bill (the Baptist) Clinton was confident that he 'did not have sexual relations with that woman – Miss Lewinsky', might a similar Bible believer be in need of greater clarity on the matter of homosexual fellatio? Biblical teaching on fornication will not help us here, except by extension beyond the plain meaning of texts, as fornication is a heterosexual phenomenon according to the Bible.

The most challenging passage on these matters is Romans 1:26–27:

> For this reason God gave them up to degrading passions. Their women exchanged natural intercourse for unnatural, and in the same way also the men, giving up natural intercourse with women were consumed with passion for one another. Men committed shameless acts with men and received in their own persons the due penalty for their error. (NRSV)

Is this a blanket condemnation of all sexual activity that is not straight-forwardly heterosexual? Or on this important matter is Scripture simply less than clear?

First, is there a lesbian allusion in this passage? Is its reference to 'exchanging natural intercourse for unnatural' on the part of women referring to lesbian physical intimacy, or might it target women offering themselves to men to be sodomised? Some have even claimed that it condemns the 'woman on top' position in heterosexual intercourse as unnatural! So it is not obvious that lesbian sex is being plainly referred to here. And if not here, then where in the Bible is there a clear condemnation of lesbian sex to match that of sodomy?

Second, what really is being said about male same-sex desires and acts in this passage? Must we say that men 'consumed with passion for one another' are condemned out of court, meaning that a state of homo-sexual passion as well as any particular physical outcome with another man is forbidden – the desire as well as the act? However, we note that in Sydney Diocese it is not same-sex desire that is reckoned as sinful, but the physical act expressing that desire – penitent, celibate homo-sexuals are nowhere condemned. So, it would seem that this text, about being 'consumed by passion', must refer to physical acts rather than desires. But, then, can we claim that the shameful acts on the part of men referred to in the passage, 'in the same way also', extend beyond sodomy – which is, after all, the only homosexual act condemned elsewhere in the Bible (and sodomy is characteristic of the pagan practices Paul is criticising in the wider context of this passage)? Further, a plain reading of the passage might well see its censure restricted to heterosexual men who have turned to same-sex relations, for whatever reason. On such a view, the passage need not be read as saying anything at all about men of consistent same-sex orientation who have never desired or practised intercourse with women. In other words, it may only condemn men who go against their natural desires in matters of sexuality.

Dr Glenn Davies, Bishop of North Sydney, who has championed a case for the plain and incontrovertible meaning of such texts in the Doctrine Commission, reads this passage as a blanket condemnation of homosexual activity.[26] But I would like to see him demonstrate from the text that Romans 1:26–27 refers to every form of that activity. Because, to my mind, this passage is just not sufficiently clear. So how are we to deploy it?

As Protestants read the Bible, those of the Lutheran tradition tend to allow what Scripture has not forbidden, while Dr Jensen's Reformed tradition has tended to seek scriptural warrant before allowing something. Yet Dr Jensen does advocate something like a realm of secular freedom for the Christian, within the bounds of explicit biblical teaching. Rather than risk the dilution and distortion of the knowledge of God in the Bible by countenancing contemporary revelations and vocational leadings, Dr Jensen prefers to leave Christians in a religiously evacuated world, with no sacred intrusions. We have the Bible, and the rest does not matter. This is a robust faith that does not need experiential confirmation – indeed, unsustainably so, as I have argued – but it is one that leaves a lot to the individual Christian's personal choice. So I wonder if Bible-believing homosexuals, following Dr Jensen's hermeneutical lead, might justify their favourite intimate acts in the same way that Bill Clinton justified his with Monica Lewinsky. If the answer is 'No!', then this must be a matter of asserting the authority of tradition, or arguing on the basis of a reasonable reading of the intention of Scripture. Well and good, and I for one would certainly agree that all genital activity with another person is sex, but it must be recognised that the clarity of Scripture is not the sole or even the most important reason for the prohibition.

Beyond this *reductio ad absurdum* discussion of the clarity of Scripture, 'for argument's sake', how would I assess homosexual acts from a Christian ethical perspective? What I have sought is a scripturally informed, theological and ethical position on human relationships and sexuality as a whole. I conclude in favour of a 'vocational sexuality' that would not split hairs over the means of its physical expression. My case is for seeing the blessing in church of monogamous gay and lesbian unions as a development in the doctrine of Christian marriage,[27] and I take my stand in fidelity to the mind of Christ as I discern it in the Bible as a whole, and not in a few decontextualised scriptural snippets.

Surely we need to reflect more broadly on the nature of humanising relationships between people, of which I believe Christian marriage provides the norm and critical standard, seeing physical acts of whatever (non-abusive and consensual) sort in terms of their contribution to such a humanising bond, rather than separating them out from their relational context into the realm of moral infringement or taboo. This does not mean that anything goes, however. What it does mean is that human sexuality, with all the typical physical practices expressing it, is fulfilled and blessed in committed relationships after the pattern of Christian marriage.

Conclusion: a third way on biblical authority

I have tried to argue for a biblical hermeneutic that takes the Bible seriously. The approach I commend is one that trusts God, not fearing that the church is always poised on the brink of devastating fundamental error. It is a biblical approach, seeking the mind of God in a conversation with Scripture where church tradition and the modern world are our partners. I have argued that Dr Jensen's case has not excluded these conversation partners and, moreover, that his presentation is not as full of assurance as claimed, nor indeed as clear, failing to provide sufficient clarity in an area where Dr Jensen might well deem the clarity of that word to be crucial – the range of allowable homosexual practice.

The alternative, to which I and many in our church are committed, is not that of unfettered liberalism in thrall to theological delusion at best and active disobedience to God at worst. Rather, it is my claim that one can read the Bible as seriously as Dr Jensen but not as unequivocally. The knowledge of God in Jesus Christ remains pivotal, yet an evolving understanding of God's mind within the unchanging consistency of God's purposes is welcomed, rather than dismissed out of hand. Such an approach may risk the loosening of control, but it may also put me, and others like me, on the right side of obedience to God after all.

Appearing in Scott Cowdell and Muriel Porter (eds), *Lost in Translation? Anglicans, Controversy and the Bible* (Papers of the Doctrine Commission of the Anglican Church of Australia) (Melbourne: DesBooks, 2004), pp. 114–30. Dr Jensen's critical response to Scott Cowdell's article appears subsequently in *Lost in Translation?*, pp. 131–8.

NOTES
1. Peter Jensen, *The Revelation of God* (Leicester: InterVarsity Press, 2002).
2. Peter Jensen, *At the Heart of the Universe: What Christians Believe* (Leicester: InterVarsity Press, 1991/1994/2002).
3. Jensen, *The Revelation of God*, e.g. pp.47ff, 67, 83, 87ff.
4. ibid., e.g. pp.32, 37.
5. ibid., e.g. pp.105ff.
6. ibid., e.g. pp.62, 120ff, 131–44.
7. ibid., p.131.
8. ibid., pp.131–44.
9. Kathleen C. Boone, *The Bible Tells Them So: The Discourse of Protestant*

Fundamentalism (Albany, NY: State University of New York Press, 1989), p.36. This is a very helpful study of how the clarity and authority of Scripture functions as part of a total discourse or worldview, in the hands of evangelicals and fundamentalists.

10. Jensen, *The Revelation of God*, e.g. pp.183, 195, 197ff.
11. ibid., e.g. pp. 235f, 252f, 264.
12. ibid., p.199.
13. ibid., pp.201ff.
14. ibid., p.62.
15. ibid., p.201.
16. ibid., pp.193f, 203.
17. ibid., p.226.
18. ibid., p.277.
19. Jensen, *At the Heart of the Universe*, p.70.
20. Jensen, *The Revelation of God*, e.g. p.196.
21. ibid., pp.153, 159.
22. ibid., p.269.
23. Jensen, *At the Heart of the Universe*, p.173.
24. This is persuasively argued by Kathleen Boone, op.cit, and by American evangelical James Callahan as the conclusion of his exhaustive study, *The Clarity of Scripture: History, Theology and Contemporary Literary Studies* (Downers Grove, IL: InterVarsity Press, 2001).
25. See my book, *A God for this World* (London and New York: Continuum, 2000), Ch. 2. There, I was indebted to the analyses of Michael J. Buckley SJ, *At the Origins of Modern Atheism* (New Haven, CT: Yale University Press, 1987) and William C. Placher, *The Domestication of Transcendence: How Modern Thinking about God Went Wrong* (Minneapolis, MN: Westminster John Knox Press, 1996).
26. Glenn Davies, 'Homosexuality in the New Testament', in *Faithfulness in Fellowship: Reflections on Homosexuality and the Church* (Melbourne: John Garratt Publishing, 2001), pp.63–74; see especially p.65.
27. See my article, 'Anglican Moral Theology and the Challenge of Same-Sex Unions' in *Faithfulness in Fellowship*, pp.141–60. For a fuller discussion of Christianity, sex and relationships, see my book, *God's Next Big Thing: Discovering the Future Church* (Melbourne: John Garratt Publishing, 2004), pp.169–87.

Chapter 21

THE ONLY THING THAT COUNTS: FAITH ACTIVE IN LOVE[1]

Gertrude Lebans

'Context is everything', some ethicists would say. Others would contend that there are standards for human behaviour that have been ordained by the God who stands outside of time and context. I am writing this essay in the summer of 2004 following the General Synod of the Anglican Church of Canada and I think that the debate on the participation of gay and lesbian people in Canada is very much contingent on context. And in addition, I would say that a god who stands outside of time and context has little relevance to the concerns of mortal, struggling humans. I am interested in a God who is self-revealing through history, through the world, and through human relationships. I think that this is the tradition and model of Jesus who seemingly had less interest in philosophy and more involvement with the struggles of people for justice and for meaning. This model calls us to be open to learning and change. In my opinion, to be an adherent of Jesus is to be willing to confront my own prejudices and limitations with courage and faith that in God all is being revealed, even if very slowly and contingent upon human readiness.

For months before the 2004 General Synod the community discussed endlessly how to frame a motion on same-sex unions and how it would be received. Some camps of the church began an early propaganda campaign; others attempted to encourage their own followers to have courage. An active electronic and 'snail' mail campaign was launched at bishops and at delegates of General Synod. Perhaps because the outcome of the debate at General Synod was unexpected, the church then responded with a diversity of opinion on the significance of the decisions. In one sense nothing happened; in another sense, the gathered community reflected the general problems that dominate the church in Canada and that paralyse our leadership. One of these issues is obviously the question of human sexuality. The acknowledged participation of gay and lesbian Christians is the focus, but not the limit, of these discussions. Tied to this focus are questions about authority within the Communion (power, in other words), the authority and limits of Scripture, the very nature of God in relationship with all creation and the influence of knowledge on theology.

It seems to me that the weight of the debate on gay and lesbian membership in the church has less to do with moral theology than with a growing strain in what Christians think we are doing, who we think God is and why the church exists at all. Eric Beresford, former ethics consultant for the Anglican Church of Canada, has commented that one can only solve a problem, not an opinion or a conviction.[2] The issue of the participation of gay and lesbian Anglicans in the church is not in fact a problem but a matter of conviction and a deep-seated and seemingly irreconcilable difference of opinion. I cannot deal adequately with all these issues within this chapter but they cannot be ignored because they form parts of the context and background for all discussions in our church in this time. No single issue can be discussed without an awareness of how deeply divided we are on these matters and how wide the gap is between the far points of the discussion.

At the General Synod of 2004 a motion was presented from the Faith, Worship and Ministry Committee. The motion consisted of five sections. Synod agreed to separate section 2 from the other clauses. After some amendments, the resolution ('A134 Blessing of same-sex unions: Part A') passed as follows (being made up of sections 1, 3, 4 and 5):

> Be it resolved that this General Synod:
>
> 1. Affirm that, even in the face of deeply held convictions about whether the blessing of committed same-sex unions is contrary to the doctrine and teaching of the Anglican Church of Canada, we recognise that through our baptism we are members one of another in Christ Jesus, and we commit ourselves to strive for that communion into which Christ continually calls us;
>
> 3. Affirm the crucial value of continued respectful dialogue and study of biblical, theological, liturgical, pastoral, scientific, psychological, and social aspects of human sexuality; and call upon all bishops, clergy and lay leaders to be instrumental in seeing that dialogue and study continue, intentionally involving gay and lesbian persons;
>
> 4. Affirm the principle of respect for the way in which the dialogue and study may be taking place, or might take place, in Indigenous and various other communities within our church in a manner consistent with their cultures and traditions; and
>
> 5. Affirm that the Anglican Church is a church for all the baptized and is committed to taking such actions as are necessary to maintain and serve our fellowship and unity in Christ, requesting the House of Bishops to continue its work on the provision of adequate episcopal oversight and pastoral care for all, regardless of

the perspective from which they view the blessing of committed same-sex relationships.

The original clause 2 ('A134 Blessing of same-sex unions: Part B') read as follows:

> Be it resolved that this General Synod:
> 2. Affirm the authority and jurisdiction of any diocesan synod, with the concurrence of its bishop, to authorize the blessing of committed same-sex unions.

It was debated only after the others had been discussed and voted on. The response to this clause was to defer its consideration until the meeting of General Synod in 2007, to request the Primate to ask the Primate's Theological Commission to review whether the blessing of same-sex unions is a matter of doctrine and to make a report to the Council of General Synod by its Spring 2006 meeting. That report would then be distributed to each province, each diocese and the House of Bishops for consideration.

Following this vote to defer consideration of clause 2, the Rev. Garth Bulmer from the Diocese of Ottawa implored the Synod to consider the gay and lesbian members of the Communion who were looking for reassurance from this gathering. He then submitted what was first considered an amendment to A134 and was eventually recognised as its own motion, renumbered and passed by a clear majority. It read, 'Be it resolved that this General Synod: Affirm the integrity and sanctity of committed adult same-sex relationships.'

Later that evening, nine bishops who had gathered independently of the rest of the House of Bishops read a statement that deplored the resolution:

> In recent days the Synod has made a number of contradictory decisions which may be causing confusion in the church. On the one hand, the Synod has deferred a decision concerning the blessing of same-sex unions for three years. On the other hand the Synod appears to have pre-empted this work by summarily expressing the opinion that it affirms the 'sanctity' of committed same-sex relationships. We regret that it also ignores the work of the Lambeth Commission. We must point out that General Synod's opinion is in error and contrary to the teaching of Scripture and the tradition of the undivided Church.[3]

The response to the letter accentuated the divisions within the Synod but was certainly a more moderate reaction than many were anticipating.

The debate on the blessing of same-gender unions had its origin in

1976 in a discussion in the House of Bishops on the ordination of gay and lesbian persons as priests. In 1979 the House stated that, 'We believe that as Christians, homosexual persons, as children of God, have a full and equal claim with all other persons, upon the love, acceptance, concern, and pastoral care of the church.' The statement, however, repudiated the idea of 'homosexual unions'. By 1995, after ongoing discussion, the statement had been updated to read, 'The Anglican Church affirms the presence and contribution of gay men and lesbians in the life of the church and condemns bigotry, violence and hatred directed toward any due to their sexual orientation.' The Doctrine and Worship Committee was then directed by that Synod 'to initiate broad based consultations within the Anglican Church of Canada concerning the liturgical recognition of committed same-gender unions'. The churches were encouraged to undertake study and discussion. At the time, the overt decision was that gay and lesbian persons must undertake to live a life of chastity because the bonds of marriage were not available to them. Covertly, some bishops cast a blind eye to the living arrangements of clergy and others undertook a 'purging' of suspect clergy.

The Episcopal Church in the USA began to talk about same-gender unions in 1973 and elected its first openly gay bishop amid great furore in 2003. At the Canadian General Synod in June 1998 a motion that contained six human rights 'principles' – 'the right to be treated with courtesy, compassion and integrity; the right to fair treatment; the right to vote; the right to be considered for election; the right to be considered for service; and the rights of employees in positions not requiring ordination' – was approved by lay and clergy delegates and voted down by the House of Bishops. The key complaint was that the human rights principles called for 'protection from discrimination on the basis of age, sex, sexual orientation, family or marital status, race, colour, ethnic origin, ancestry, disability, creed and socioeconomic status'. There was a great deal of discussion, mostly concerned with the inclusion of gay and lesbian people. In 2003 the Bishop of the Diocese of New Westminster, after increasingly successful motions at three synods, gave his assent to the blessing of same-gender unions. Again a great deal of anger and division resulted.[4] In 2004 the provincial legislatures of Quebec, Ontario, British Columbia, the Yukon and Nova Scotia recognised 'gay' marriages. In late 2004 the Supreme Court of Canada upheld this recognition. In July 2005 the national Parliament legalised same-sex marriage, making Canada the fourth nation to do so. These events have forced the church to become conscious again of the changing world around us.

On one side of the question, the Anglican Church stands accused of being wilfully insensitive to the convictions of churches on other continents. At the General Synod of 2004 Canon Gregory Cameron, Director of Ecumenical Affairs for the Anglican Communion and Secretary of the Lambeth Commission, addressed the Synod thus:

> If you say, 'no' to the motions before you, you will be in danger of letting down the thousands of gay people in your midst, who are part of your Canadian family, as well as all those who are looking towards the Anglican Church of Canada to set a new standard of dealing with this issue. But if you say, 'yes', the work of the Lambeth Commission becomes horribly complicated, because we will be told that the Anglican Church of Canada refuses to hear the voice, and to heed the concerns, of your fellow Anglicans in the growing provinces of the Global South, who are your international family ... You must do what you believe God is calling you to but the implications of your decision for the unity of the Anglican Communion, perhaps even its survival in its current form, are just about as serious as it could get.

We are also accused of not listening to our own aboriginal people and forging ahead despite their protests. The picture that is presented is of an urban church determined to sanction the secular (and therefore sinful) morals of its own context despite the 'correction' and concern of others. Of course, this is an overly simplistic picture. There are gay and lesbian people in every context, every religious group, every place, whether urban or rural areas. Gay and lesbian people who live in places of oppression look to the church to affirm their lives, their context, and to rescue them from prejudice and intolerance. Indeed, many heterosexual Anglicans cannot understand the level of prejudice and rage the conversation has incurred. For many of these people the church's reluctance to act affirmatively speaks of a deep hypocrisy about who we are and the love we claim to share. The question of acceptance troubles not just gay and lesbian Anglicans, but all Anglicans who claim a church where faithfulness means inclusivity and change.

Our bishops are caught in this quandary. Bishops who speak openly and approvingly about the full inclusion of gay and lesbian people find themselves vilified and written about contemptuously. Their dioceses are threatened financially and in terms of membership. They personally receive volumes of hate mail.[5] As well, some bishops say they need to be bishops to the whole church and so believe that they must attempt to affirm gay and lesbian people while stalling any decision-making that would unleash the forces of hate and rage. Other bishops have come to see that prejudice cannot be tolerated in the church as they understand it and so endure incredible personal persecution for their courage. The nine bishops who confronted the General Synod of 2004 have made it clear that they do not feel bound to honour the House of Bishops, nor to contain their dissension. We are not in danger of schism; our ecclesial structure is broken now, whether our bishops choose to acknowledge this reality or not. Many people at the grassroots are asking what the price of unity is and if it is not already too late to pretend to a solidarity that clearly does not exist.

The discussion of human sexuality has been a continuing debate. Our current understanding of how to behave and what is 'natural' has been formed by a quasi-historical picture of the post-biblical era. In these eras, 'noble' children often were betrothed at birth and married in their early teens.[6] Marriage was clearly for the purpose of transmission of property to legitimate sons or for trade or political advantage. For the poor and the peasantry of feudal times, marriage was casual because issues of property and progeny were insignificant.

In order not to be distracted by questions of polygamy in the time of the patriarchs, I will begin the 'biblical' discussion in what we understand to be the context in Jesus' time. Then, marriage was also largely a matter of significance only amongst the affluent and powerful. Women and children were understood to be property.[7] Jesus' insistence on treating women as persons had to be one of the most shocking and scandalous of his behaviours.[8] Marriage was for reproduction, for economic benefit and only accidentally for friendship or pleasure.[9] Romantic love as we think of it did not enter the equation. Among Gentiles, the love between men was thought to be the highest form of relationship. Among Jews, friendships based on discussion and shared values occurred among men also. In none of these times would anyone have understood the concept of sexual orientation. The role of wives was to care for men and raise their legitimate sons to inherit their father's property. The society of men provided the world of ideas and friendship.[10]

Paul suggested two things about marriage. In 1 Corinthians 7:25–28 he says:

> Now concerning virgins, I have no command of the Lord, but I give my opinion as one who by the Lord's mercy is trustworthy. I think that, in view of the impending crisis, it is well for you to remain as you are. Are you bound to a wife? Do not seek to be free. Are you free from a wife? Do not seek a wife. But if you marry, you do not sin, and if a virgin marries, she does not sin. Yet those who marry will experience distress in this life, and I would spare you that.

In other words, there really are no 'rules', but the emphasis is on remaining committed to the mission of Christ. And in Ephesians 5:28ff, the apostle compares marital love to the relationship between Christ and the church. Better not to marry, but if you must, then make it a sign of the love of Christ and a shared witness to the Gospel. In other words, as far as Paul was concerned, marriage was not for property or progeny, or even primarily to satisfy desire, but to further the Way as companions on the journey.[11] That would seem to make the discussion about the genders and sexual orientation of the partners less significant than the quality of purpose and mission of the union. Indeed, at most churches in urban areas, it is quite common for gay couples to be active members of the congregation and for people to speak openly about their gay relatives. In metropolitan areas, clergy attend the Gay Pride parades in their clericals and with their bishops' consent and, sometimes, even encouragement.

Whenever I officiate at a wedding, I am reminded how soap operas have created a 'tradition' for ordinary people. Most people think the norm that has existed for the last century has in fact existed since the time of Jesus. Not surprisingly, they argue against changing a tradition that has 'lasted millennia'. Some of us accept education about the more accurate history of gender politics and customs and some of us ignore it. For those who understand that marriage is a social custom and has relatively little to do with theology, the transition to the blessing of same-gender unions is fairly easy. For those who continue to believe that at one moment in human history, marriage was both invented and organised by God for the primary purpose of reproduction, the whole discussion, not only of same-gender unions, but of divorce, sexual activity outside of marriage (and other similar subjects) is a minefield of potential damnations.

A troubling but interesting aspect of the debate about same-gender unions is the fixation of many on the actual behaviours and body parts involved in a gay union. At first I dismissed this as prurient curiosity, but now I think it has to do with the church finally coming to terms with what it means to have bodies that are not merely reproduction machines.[12] Most of the opponents of same-gender unions speak about what it is 'natural' to do sexually and by that they mean activities that either are or mimic reproductive behaviour, as long as everyone has the appropriate corresponding parts. Pleasure that is mutually acceptable between consenting adults is not considered a good reason for sexual activity. The contradiction to this anti-erotic stance is found in the Canadian *Book of Alternative Services*: 'marriage is so that a couple may know each other with delight and tenderness in acts of love.' Clearly, procreation is a secondary aim of the modern marriage canon.

The debate around the ordination of women is frequently compared to these discussions on the inclusion of gay and lesbian people. People who are opposed say that there is no comparison and people in support say that the rhetoric is similar, as are the threats. I think both are

somewhat true but the ordination of women caused us to enflesh
the priesthood for the first time. I remember a bishop commenting that
the presence of a woman priest would make us think about sex during
church, especially if she were pregnant at the time. What I think did
happen is that the presence of women allowed us to see the faith as truly
incarnate, despite albs and other vestments. Men could no longer
pretend to be the image of the divine, since women would be included
and women could now be conceived of as being a living icon for Jesus.
Men had to come to terms with the reality of being creatures for whom
the priestly clothing could no longer hide the body, its desires and
its mortality. The loss of this shield against reality also meant that
bodies were a topic for discussion about boundaries, behaviour and
individuality in a way that had been more covert in other eras.

In several forums on the blessing of same-gender unions, people in
opposition have made two consistent points. The first is that since the
ordination of women, the church has been led by the world into dangerous
and damning decisions, including inclusive language, the move away from
the Book of Common Prayer, the changes in understanding about
Confirmation and Baptism, the growing practice of open table (welcoming unbaptised persons to the Eucharist) and an ethical laxity in matters of
sexual behaviour. Moreover, even how we understand obedience has
changed. It is common to hear clergy say that they are obedient to the
Gospel of Jesus Christ as it is written in Scripture, but they really mean the
teachings of Paul. Yet their oath of obedience is to their bishop, not to the
Bible. When I was ordained, despite my great discomfort with the promise, I agreed to obey my bishop. For a radical like me, it was a frightening
moment of submission. My method for maintaining my own integrity has
been to be as forthcoming as possible about what I really think, regardless
of what is required of me. And so, I have some problems with the priests
and lay people who use the smokescreens of anger and hate both to resist
their ecclesiastical obligations and make intelligent debate impossible. I
think that refusing to participate in the life of a diocese, refusing to submit to one's bishop, refusing to allow for the diversity that is part of
Anglican culture is, at least for priests, a violation of the oaths we swore
at ordination and a betrayal of what each church has received as the
member of a diocese. This self-righteous power-mongering must be
named for what it is. Our bishops have attempted to appease dissenters and
to woo them. I think some honest confrontation is now in order. I think that
each of us assumes that we are doing the right thing and that our
perspective is the most accurate reading of how to be the church.

I am troubled by the idea that some discussions have reached their
terminus and there is no more to be learned. If we believe that creation
is still unfolding and humans are still developing, then there will contin-

ue to be changes to everything we think about God, the church and how we live in the world. If, however, we believe that everything that we need to know has already been revealed, at least insofar as human biology, morality and reproduction are concerned, then there can be some final rules based on whatever moment in history we want to freeze as definitive. At that point, we could ask our bishops to stop thinking and learning and changing their minds because we would have the final version. How would we choose that moment and who would set the norms? Would we reverse our decision on the ordination of women and on divorce, based on the biblical injunctions ascribed to Jesus, for example?

If we believe that we have received the mind of God unadulterated by language, translation or interpretation, then I think debate has ceased. If, on the other hand, we believe that we have received a version of events, teachings and liturgy that is a product of a time, a perspective and a particular knowledge base, then we are free to adjust this material to contemporary reality. Jews say that Torah is alive in every era. For that to be true for contemporary Christians, we need a continuing *midrash* that helps us understand what ideas might mean in our own context. It is also a fact that we have no idea what Jesus really said or did because we have no eyewitness accounts. Even if we did, we think and know differently now. We cannot undo, nor should we want to undo, our knowledge about both the microscopic and macroscopic universes, about our tiny, wonderful presence in a grand cosmos, about the mysteries that form us and that continue to intrigue us. The knowledge we have at the moment is 'partial' as it was for Paul; it is all still unfolding.

Letters, narratives, poetry have become Scripture so that we might feel drawn to the faith. To ask Scripture to respond to how we make decisions about sexuality would be disrespectful of the culture and conditions of the biblical era. It would also dispute the evidence and experience of faithful gay Christians who have a language and a self-definition that has never before existed in the world.[13] We can ask Scripture what the norms are for Christian relationships. That is fairly easy to ascertain. Be generous and hospitable. Forgive one another. Gather to pray and to plan how you will serve the poor, the sick and the oppressed of the world. That is the mission for which Jesus called us to be responsible. I think the vitriolic and acrimonious debate around whether or not we approve of Christians joining in covenantal love to serve Christ is at the least unfaithful and at the best, blasphemous and disobedient to the spirit of the Gospel.

How we understand our relationship with God has weight in the debate also. For the ancients, the idea of covenantal love had less to do with a warm feeling and more to do with the response of a slave to its rightful and benevolent owner. God, like a landowner (Isaiah 5:1–7), had the power to create and to sustain but also the power to punish for an insincere or half-hearted obedience. In the 'school' of Jesus, the emphasis shifted from absolute dependency to willing service, a radical restating of Isaiah that required the Jews of the time to look beyond their own boundaries and assumptions about how they thought God wanted them to act. Today, some of us think of God as benign but powerless or as a fantasy for those afraid to confront the grim reality of mortality. Some of us retain our picture of the sovereign God who will one day reward or punish, who arbitrarily delivers some and ignores other prayers, who has an absolute set of rules to be obeyed and interpreted very narrowly. For many, though, God is a power source, a living connection for those who seek ways of acting for justice and compassion. This God wants us to grow up, to learn how to be peaceful and healthy communities. The God we choose affects how we respond to that God in terms of our ethics, our faith and our witness.

Faith is always a risk. Jesus did not ask us to be safe but to follow the road of doubt, of difficulty, of misunderstanding. The parable of the Good Samaritan is about taking the initiative to act compassionately without assessing the politics of a situation. When Jesus calls Zacchaeus the tax collector out of the tree, he shows that even the most despised members of society can become the hosts of justice and love. And when Nicodemus decides to learn from Jesus, we are reminded that power cannot justify wearing blinkers. So let's get on with helping each other out of ditches with other Samaritans, and out of trees with tax collectors who think they are unworthy, and out of power-brokering that embarrasses the mission to free, to heal and to love.

NOTES

1. The title of this essay is taken from a discussion of the law and freedom found in Galatians 5:1–6.
2. For a useful history of how the motion to General Synod developed and the thinking behind that motion, it is helpful to read Eric Beresford's 'Background Paper on the Same-Sex Blessings Motion before General Synod, 2004'.
3. The statement in its entirety was available from the *Anglican Journal* website.
4. In November 2004 three motions were presented to the Diocese of Niagara Synod. The first to be debated was a vote to defer all actions with regard to same-gender unions until after the General Synod in 2007. It was narrowly defeated. The second motion was to express support for the Windsor Report. This was also defeated, as much because of the ecclesiological changes the report recommended as because of any opinion it expressed on same-gender unions. The third motion suggested that when a same-gender couple who had been legally married by the state came to have their union blessed by the church, the priest might be permitted to affirm the sanctity and integrity of their union, according to the action of the 2004 General Synod. This motion passed by 67 per cent but the diocesan bishop denied his assent at that time, while expressing his personal

agreement with the motion. Shortly afterwards in the Diocese of Toronto, the Synod agreed to defer any action on same-gender unions until after the General Synod of 2007.

5. 'Virtuosity, The Voice for Global Orthodox Anglicanism', self-named, in a web article by David W. Virtue, said, 'It makes little difference whether one wears a purple shirt with a pectoral cross or a black shirt with a Swastika, the mentality behind both is the same.' This is typical of the anonymous invective that our bishops receive on a regular basis.

6. See John Boswell, *Same-Sex Unions in Premodern Europe* (New York and Toronto: Vintage Books, 1995), p.35, and Peter Coleman, *Christian Attitudes to Marriage, From Ancient Times to the Third Millennium* (London: SCM Press, 2004), p.7.

7. In *Dirt, Greed & Sex: Sexual Ethics in the New Testament and their Implications for Today* (Philadelphia: Fortress Press, 1990), William Countryman notes, 'Property denotes something which is understood as an extension of oneself, so that a violation of my property is a violation of my personhood' (pp.147ff).

8. On Jesus' relationships with women, see Coleman, *Christian Attitudes to Marriage*, p. 91.

9. ibid., pp.51 and 55.

10. See Boswell, *Same-Sex Unions in Premodern Europe*, pp.76, 135 and 159.

11. See Countryman's discussion of Paul and sexual relationships in the early church, *Dirt, Greed & Sex*, pp.190–213.

12. See Countryman, op. cit., p.266, for a further discussion of contemporary but biblical sexual ethics.

13. Probably the closest we have to an understanding of sexual orientation in the ancient world is from Plato's *Symposium* on the myth of androgyny. As Coleman notes, 'There were originally three forms, male, female, and hermaphrodite, and their abilities were such that they became a threat to the gods. So Zeus decided to split them in half, with the result that they spent their time searching for their other halves. Half males searched for male lovers, female halves found each other and became lesbian couples, the hermaphrodites, who combine some of the characteristics of the other two species, found halves of the other gender and did the breeding' (p.57). See also Boswell's comments on Jewish perspectives on androgyny, op. cit., p.366.

Chapter 22

GOOD AND GAY?

Duncan B. Forrester

'Lord, make my spirit good and gay' – George MacDonald, the Scottish
Congregationalist writer who deeply influenced C. S. Lewis, could not
have anticipated how these words from his wonderful morning hymn, 'O
Lord of life, thy quickening voice awakes my morning song', would be
heard and understood today. It is the contention of this essay from
Scotland that gay can be good and that gay people may have a specific
vocation or calling, a special service they may render to the church and
to the broader community. We can all learn from gay people about the
importance of friendship, about how to keep on loving even when one is
subjected to contempt, prejudice and derision, about keeping one's
integrity when one is abused and feared.

In Scotland as elsewhere, the whole discussion of sexuality in the
churches is highly charged emotionally. And nothing arouses so much
irrational feeling and intense prejudice as the question of homosexuality,
or rather the place, if any, for gay people and gay ministers in the church
of Jesus Christ. In the Church of Scotland, as elsewhere, when the issue
arises the usual strategy of church managers is to kick the issue into
touch by enjoining the whole church to study the matter for some years
before a formal position is taken. And then for a time things go quiet.

My purpose in this essay is not to investigate the sources of the
passions aroused by the mere mention of the topic or to challenge and
dissect the irrational prejudice that dominates so many Christians' thinking on the matter. I want simply, by way of introduction, to note how
easily the Christian tradition has been distorted and misunderstood in
order to buttress a basically unchristian homophobia. Only when we
have brought into the open the subtle ways in which theology may be
used, or rather abused, to legitimate conventional prejudices, are we in a
position to venture statements which may be more authentically
Christian, and firmly rooted in the Gospel rather than our own society's
nervous values and prejudices.

Christians' understanding of the nature of human sexuality is, and has
for decades been, in a state of flux, as traditional formulations are
increasingly questioned and account is taken of modern developments in
theology and biblical studies, and of new knowledge coming from the
human sciences. This is *not* to say that the tradition is being, or ought to

be, jettisoned. Indeed my own view is almost the opposite of this: that despite distortion and abuse, the Christian tradition preserves an understanding of human sexuality of unequalled profundity and perennial relevance. But the tradition has to be re-examined, reviewed, tested, reformulated; accretions and misunderstandings have to be removed, if it is to commend itself as a relevant and challenging contribution to modern people's self-understanding.

I would like to mention three sources of distortion which have deeply, and harmfully, influenced the Christian understanding of sexuality.

'The mastery of sex'

First, from certain strands in Greek philosophy there came a deep suspicion of the emotional life, of the Dionysian element in life. Sexuality, so necessarily united with the emotions, was seen as something dangerous, threatening, requiring to be controlled, curbed, channelled, if it is not to be demonic. Sexuality involves, according to the preamble to the Book of Common Prayer Marriage Service, people having 'carnal lusts and appetites like brute beasts that have no understanding'. These are to be controlled and restrained, usually in marriage, which is to be entered into (again, according to the Book of Common Prayer) 'as a remedy against sin and to avoid fornication, that such persons as have not the gift of continency may marry and keep themselves undefiled members of Christ's body'.[1] A not dissimilar attitude was shown by the title – and much of the contents – of a book on sexuality by Leslie Weatherhead which was still popular in my student days, *The Mastery of Sex*.

This sense of sex as a dangerous enemy that is to be feared and mastered is not, I believe, authentically Christian, but it has penetrated deeply into the Christian tradition, making it hard to affirm the goodness of sexuality and giving much sexual ethics an extraordinarily repressive skew. According to this view, sexuality is not something to be celebrated and enjoyed, a vital dimension of all worthwhile and lasting relationships. It has become rather a frightening force that must be restrained within as narrow a compass as possible because it cannot be eliminated. When such attitudes become influential, it is hardly surprising if minority forms of sexuality attract particularly vigorous condemnation. Such condemnation highlights the negative and sub-Christian attitude towards sexuality as a whole which has been so influential, and so harmful, within the Christian tradition.

What is natural?

The second distortion is most clearly evidenced in natural law thinking, but it is by no means confined there. If we ask what is the nature of sexuality, what it is there for, what good it is intended to achieve, we clearly do not have a simple question capable of a simple answer. But unfortunately rather glib and superficial answers have only too often been given to this question. For instance, it has repeatedly been affirmed that sexuality is for procreation, or primarily for procreation; it is that part or aspect of human nature which is devoted to the propagation of the species. It follows that any use of sex which does not have procreation primarily in view is illegitimate and unnatural. This may make some kind of biological sense, but it wholly neglects the fact that human beings are more than biological entities. Humans are complex creatures, and human sexuality performs a range of functions. I think it was Berdyaev who long ago lamented that so many Christian books on sex read like treatises on cattle breeding; they leave out the personal dimension, the integration of sexuality into the understanding of love and of relationships, the central core of what it means to be human. Sexuality is, of course, necessarily involved in procreation, even in an age of in-vitro fertilisation (IVF) and the possibility of reproductive cloning, but that is not all that sexuality is about, and to suggest that it is involves a drastic impoverishment of the whole understanding of sexuality, and indeed a dehumanising of human sexuality. Sexuality is concerned with love and relationships primarily, and only if this is recognised very clearly is the procreative and nurturing role of sexuality put in its proper context.

There is another trap into which natural law thinking about sex can very easily fall. It is this: to allow, consciously or unconsciously, the conventional view of the time to define what is, and what is not, 'natural' behaviour. The danger here is of what purports to be an objective approach to ethics becoming simply an expression of the prejudices of the age. Not uncommonly, the claim that homosexuality is 'unnatural', boils down to a belief that behaviour that differs from that of the majority, or the opinions of an influential minority, must be wrong. But in either case all that is happening is that the prejudices of many are being passed on and reinforced without serious critical examination. If we choose to speak in terms of natural law, it is good to be aware how easily it may be manipulated and misused for the buttressing of unthinking prejudice.

The Bible and sexuality

Similar dangers lurk in the use of the Bible, 'the supreme rule of life and doctrine'. It is easy to fall into the trap of reading the Bible in such a way that what it implies reflects back to us our own prejudices and assumptions, confirming opinions that were not in any real sense derived from Scripture. The danger of the spirit of the age controlling the interpretation is particularly liable to occur when the Bible is used as a quarry of proof-texts deployed in an argument without regard to their context or original meaning. I would go along with Henry Morton's rejoinder to the extreme Covenanters in Walter Scott's novel, *Old Mortality*:

> I revere the Scriptures as deeply as you or any Christian can do. I look into them with humble hope of extracting a rule of conduct and a law of salvation. But I expect to find this by their general tenor, and of the spirit which they uniformly breathe, and not by wresting particular passages from their context, or by the application of scriptural phrases to circumstances and events with which they have often very slender relations.

Yet, again and again Christian opinions on homosexuality have been based on proof-texts, which turn out on examination to have little if any bearing on the issue. It is, for example, blatantly absurd to base a blanket condemnation of homosexuality on passages in the Old Testament which condemn sexual assault or cultic prostitution. Such a way of proceeding is to take neither the Bible nor people with adequate seriousness.

A second danger is that of regarding the Bible as primarily a rule-book. There *are* rules in the Bible, it is true, some of them time-bound but others of apparently universal validity. The exegete has to attempt to distinguish between the two sorts of rules, and to see even in antique structures of law what cannot and must not be applied today as matters of perennial significance. But always the Christian must remember that the Bible is primarily Gospel, good news and promise, and only second-arily and derivatively, law. The Gospel is prior to the law. It is about love, forgiveness, new beginnings, grace, fulfilment, abundant life, rather than about condemnation, rejection, repression and the meticulous observance of a battery of rules.

We should never forget that in the New Testament sexual sins are quite systematically treated as of themselves of much less importance than other sorts of sins: pride, callousness, oppressing the poor, and so on. There is very little in the Bible about homosexuality; and any Christian and biblical understanding of homosexuality must pay attention not only to these passages, peripheral as they are, but also to the far more significant and central: the plentiful things that the Bible has to say about love and relationships and the place of sexuality in loving relation-ships. A Christian understanding of homosexuality must be rooted in 'the general tenor' of Scripture; it must arise out of real dialogue, a mutual questioning between Scripture and our modern understandings and assumptions. The Christian Gospel questions not only our assumptions, but also *us*, particularly if we feel ourselves to be righteous, good, 'all right'.

Persons in love

In attempting to outline a Christian understanding of humanity, the necessary starting point is that there is no such being as the isolated individual; persons are to be understood in relation. The triune God is united in the loving dance of *perichoresis*.[2] Our relationships – to God, mother, father, siblings, peers, spouse, children – not only show what kind of people we are, but they make, shape and form us. Sin, the theological term to indicate the human predicament, the problematic side of human existence, the flaw in the human condition, is primarily a matter of broken relationships, of fear of relationships at depth, and, consequently, of incapacity for relationships. Augustine and Luther aptly described sin as the condition of being *incurvatus in se*, turned in on oneself and, consequently, turned away from one's neighbour. C. S. Lewis, in his autobiography, *Surprised by Joy*, tells how before his conversion he was obsessed with himself and with his own inner working. His experience of becoming a Christian involved liberation from being obsessed with himself and a new free and spontaneous openness to others. Thus free and confident relatedness to the neighbour is a central component in the Christian understanding of humanity. It is not good for a human being to be alone, for destiny, maturity and completeness involve fellowship.

Human beings' capacity for relationship is founded upon the fact that we are beings loved by God, loved so much that God sent his Son to show God's love, ultimately in dying for those who loved him not. God's love is mediated to us in all sorts of ways, some normal, even mundane, others extraordinary or even miraculous – through the love of parents, brothers, sisters, friends, spouses, partners. The experience of being loved is absolutely necessary for growth, maturity, confidence, indeed for sanity. The Christian tradition has all along known well the teaching of modern psychology, that in being loved we learn to love: 'We love because he first loved us' (1 John 4:19). And the Christian faith goes further and affirms that in loving we come to know God – there is no other way to knowledge of him – and to enter into the mystery of God's own being, for God is love: 'Beloved, let us love one another, because love is from God; everyone who loves is born of God and knows God. Whoever does not love does not know God, for God is love'(1 John 4:7–8).

Let me take the discussion a bit further by looking at three New Testament passages.

1 Corinthians 13

This is as familiar as it is profound and challenging. It tells us that love is patient, love is kind; love is not envious or boastful or arrogant or rude.

Love doesn't take offence. It is not conditional, something that we earn. It is the greatest of the three things that last for ever – faith, hope and love. Love and fidelity, love and faithfulness are inseparable. Love is constancy – utterly reliable. It cannot be predatory, or exploitative or episodic.

1 John 4:7–21
This passage is full of amazing statements. God is love; love flows from God. In Jesus we see the full reality of God's love. God loves us first, and this sets us free to love, to obey the strange and wonderful command: 'Beloved, let us love one another, because love is from God.' And then the amazing words: '*everyone* who loves is born of God and knows God.' Yes, *everyone*. People who love know God, even if they don't recognise it. People who love are in touch with the very mystery of God's own being. And people who don't love, however disciplined, however hardworking, however good at keeping the rules, however much they may be pillars of the Kirk, don't know God.

Luke 7:36–50
In this passage we find the familiar story of the woman with the alabaster box of ointment, who gate-crashed a dinner given for Jesus, and washed and anointed his feet. Embarrassing! Everyone knew she was a prostitute, a woman who made her living from sex, not a respectable person, someone who was universally despised and shunned, in public at least. She bursts into the party and in an impulsive act of love and generosity she pours the expensive ointment over Jesus' feet, and washes them with her tears, drying them with her hair. Embarrassing! We don't like, any more than the Pharisees of long ago, public displays of emotion, of love, especially from such a woman. Jesus should have known what kind of a woman she was. He should have been very cautious and judgemental in all his dealings with her.

There is a problem in the text, over which the translators have fretted. Towards the end of the passage Jesus says, 'her sins, which are many, are forgiven (*hoti* = *because*), for she loved much.' *For she loved much.* That's pretty strong. It suggests that in all the uncertainties and the degradations of the life of a whore, this woman had tried to love, and had learned to love. Her great love had often been distorted, and oftener, no doubt, exploited. But Jesus recognised it as love, a love more real than the love of the Pharisee and his kind. And so her sins are forgiven, and she can go in peace.

All this is rather much for some of the translators. Some of them add some words to the text and say that her love *to Jesus* shows that her sins are forgiven (Phillips), or that 'her great love *proves* that her many sins have been forgiven' (NEB), or 'her sins, which are many, have been forgiven, *hence* she has shown great love' (NRSV). Anything to avoid the suggestion that her loving has brought her close to God in Jesus, sitting at the table. Anything to avoid the suggestion that Jesus accepted this whore without qualification, and proclaimed that her sins were forgiven because she loved so much. Anything to avoid what John says so clearly in this passage: 'Everyone who loves is born of God and knows God.'

Love, then, is completely central and definitive for the Christian understanding of human beings. Indeed I think it could be quite appropriate to define human beings as creatures who are loved and are accordingly capable of loving. This would at least be better than the common obsession with sin and human incapacity and, consequently, with the need for restraint and coercion. Love, of course, exists in various modes, as C. S. Lewis reminds us in his book, *The Four Loves*. And so, I make three affirmations about love:

- Love in any of its modes excludes using the other as a means to one's own ends. Loving relationships are non-exploitative, non-manipulative and equal. They involve self-giving, *kenosis* (Philippians 2:5–9) and are quite incompatible with using the other for one's own gratification or as a tool for one's own purposes.
- Fundamental relationships (for example, to God, parent, child, spouse or partner) have a necessary quality of exclusiveness, so that when they are threatened, jealousy is naturally engendered.
- Fidelity is the condition for growth in love. God's fidelity is absolute; so should be the fidelity of those who truly love.

People are sexual beings, with varying sexual drives, orientations and appetites. Sexuality is an integral dimension of what it means to be a person. These sexual drives and orientations are in themselves morally neutral; their goodness or badness depends on how they are mobilised and used and how effectively they are integrated into the personality.

Christian confusions
We have already seen how the Christian tradition has been deeply infected with a pagan fear of sexuality, which joined hands with a more genuinely Christian rejection of the idolatry of sex. In combination, these two elements made it hard for Christians to give sexuality its proper place in their understanding of human life. Only too often sex was seen as something to be repressed, controlled or ashamed of. Virginity and celibacy were given a quite exaggeratedly high status in comparison with all forms of active sexuality. Sex was regarded as allowable because necessary for procreation, but not as something to be

enjoyed or celebrated, let alone as a channel or strengthening of love. Prudery, guilt and embarrassed silence have only too often been substitutes for a serious attempt at a Christian consideration of the place of sexuality in human life.

And the failure of the church has been to a large extent responsible for what I call the modern sexual heresy. This involves the reduction of love to sexual intercourse, the identification of sexual fulfilment and human fulfilment, understood in rather crude terms as the widest possible variety and intensity of sexual experience. There is here as total a separation between sex and procreation as the two were closely allied in the older Christian tradition. Sexual expression is artificially separated from loving, reliable relationships, and these become strangely idealistically considered.

At this point something must be said about the Christian placing of sexuality. Where does it belong in the understanding of personality? How are we to regard it? St Francis used to refer to his body as 'Brother Ass' – a useful reminder, perhaps, that we should not be over solemn or pretentious in matters affecting our bodies or our sexuality. Sex is often funny. But people are far more than simply sexual beings, and labelling people in terms of their sexual orientation can be a dangerous thing – reducing, freezing, limiting, dehumanising. One of the oldest games a society plays is to label a feared or subtly attractive minority in such a way as to degrade and humiliate it, and to draw clear and tight frontiers around the minority, insulating it from the rest of society. I understand why oppressed and threatened minorities feel they must affirm their group identity by strengthening solidarity among themselves. But this should not be more than a stage to the acceptance of the one true label – a person, or child of God – and the comprehensive solidarity of humankind.

Before addressing directly the question of homosexuality, let me recount two true stories about homosexual people, who like everyone else are made to love and to be loved. These two events deeply affected my thinking on these matters and questioned some of my prejudices.

Some years ago I was involved in a group of Christians discussing sexuality. One middle-aged woman called Pat said – and it was heartfelt – 'The very idea of homosexuality disgusts me.' She wasn't the only one who thought that. Then someone else asked her: 'Pat, if your son or your daughter came to you and said, "Mum, I'm gay and I have a partner whom I love dearly," would you reply, "Johnny (or Helen), you disgust me"?' Pat thought for a moment, and then she said, 'Of course not. You see, I love them, and as a mother and as a Christian I couldn't say that. I need to love them as they are, to love them in their difference, and to trust that their love is faithful and generous and lasting.' She really believed, you see, that 'Everyone who loves is born of God and knows God.'

My second story is an experience which profoundly challenged and changed some of my prejudices. It is this. Years ago I was chaplain at a university in England. One day I was called in and told that a middle-aged woman from the School of Education had died. I went immediately, of course, to call at the home. When I got there I found a woman who had been in a lesbian relationship with the dead woman for many years. The dead woman's friend and partner was in deep grief. As I spoke with her, I learned of their constant, reliable and loving relationship over some fifteen years. I heard of the rich gifts and experiences they had shared over many years, of the problems they had faced together, of the way their love had grown through times of difficulty and times of joy, of how they had supported and encouraged one another.

And, of course, she spoke of her grief, of how she had tended her partner through her long and painful illness. Like almost everyone else who has been bereaved, she wanted to tell the stories of her loved one, and their relationship. She wanted to share her grief. But to her partner's family she was an embarrassment. They wanted her to be forgotten, excluded, her very existence denied. Neither in the law nor in her partner's family circle did she, or her grief, or her love, have a place.

As I listened to this woman, almost despite myself I had to recognise that the love that she and her partner had shared was not different from the love that unites my wife, Margaret, and me. The words of 1 John came into my mind: 'Everyone who loves is born of God and knows God.' And I was heart sore that, whereas the love that Margaret and I have for one another and for our children is recognised, supported and encouraged by church and society, the love of these two women is still to many an embarrassment and an offence. It gets neither recognition nor support. It is still for many people dismissed as disgusting and wrong.

Ethics for gay people?

Years ago I accepted an invitation to speak at a conference about 'ethics for gay people'. But the more I reflected on the subject I had been given, the more I became convinced that there wasn't such a thing as an ethics for heterosexual people and another ethics for gay people, any more than there is an ethics for English people and a different ethics for Scots! Even the ethics that Jesus taught his disciples claimed to have a universal bearing, to be, potentially at least, an ethics for everyone.

I feel it makes no sense whatever for a Christian to condemn, or for that matter, to commend, a homosexual orientation. It is not that sort of thing. For most people their sexual orientation is part of the *givenness* of their personal situation and a Christian should regard this as a vocation or talent to be used to God's glory and for the good of God's children.

Some who would accept what I have just said about orientation would nevertheless draw a sharp distinction between orientation and behaviour, and affirm that homosexual genital behaviour is inherently wrong. Accordingly, the homosexual should be a lifelong celibate. Now, it is fashionable to speak a good deal of nonsense about celibacy today. Many people seem to believe that celibacy is impossible as well as undesirable. The celibate, they feel, cannot be a full, satisfied and mature person. This is, not to spin things out, complete nonsense. Some people of all types of sexual orientation have a vocation to celibacy and find it a high, wonderful and fulfilling vocation. Some of the celibates I know are the most vital, complete and loving of people.

But celibacy is a *special* calling; it must be something freely chosen, not imposed from outside. It is a destructive state of life unless it is chosen, embraced and lived in firm conviction. While I accept that some people find that the eschewing of any particular sexual attachment is for them the way to a wider and richer loving directed towards God and their neighbours, I also believe that for most people their ability to love is rooted in the basic primary relationships. If these relationships are reliable, consistent, honest and accepting, a confident openness towards others results. I do not believe that all homosexual people are called to celibacy, although some undoubtedly are.

But perhaps, as many like the former Moderator of the General Assembly of the Church of Scotland, my friend Professor Ian Torrance, suggest, gay people and gay ministers are fine as long as they are celibate. And certainly some people are called by God to be celibates. For others, imposed celibacy is an impossible burden and a well of loneliness. Most of us continue to learn how to love and grow in love in the context of faithful, exclusive and loving relationships.

And I do not believe that what happens, or doesn't happen, in the bedroom is nearly as important as some people suggest. Love is communicated in many ways – physical, emotional, material, spiritual. Gay people, like the rest of us, are made to love and to be loved. We can often learn from them about friendship, love and fidelity. What matters for gay and straight, single and married, parents and children is love. For those who love much are, like the woman with the alabaster box of ointment, forgiven and accepted and loved by God, and 'Everyone who loves is born of God and knows God.'

In what I have said about celibacy, I have not suggested that continence and sexual restraint are either impossible or undesirable. I happen to believe that continence before marriage is a good thing, and

even within a heterosexual marriage there are times when sexual intercourse is inappropriate or undesirable. In a good and growing relationship, sexual expression and its place should be sensitively explored, and
sensitivity sometimes involves continence and restraint. Christian
marriage is not a licence to rape one's partner – would that all talk of
'conjugal rights' were forgotten, and people realised that there is a
wrong use of sex within marriage as well as without.

What are the conditions within which homosexual acts may be
regarded as legitimate and good? Very simply, I would suggest that these
are precisely the same as for heterosexual acts. In other words, they
should be expressions of love rather than exploitation, and they should
be concerned for the deepening of a relationship of care and self-giving.
They should confirm and strengthen a relationship that is reliable – and
this means as far as I can see permanent, honest and exclusive, i.e. non-
promiscuous. Such a relationship is, to my mind, chaste and faithful.

I am, of course, commending the pattern of monogamous heterosexual marriage. But in doing so, some difficulties need to be faced.
First, while for heterosexual people there are still strong, sometimes too
strong, confirmations of monogamy, precisely the opposite is true for
homosexual people. Homosexual unions have in most places neither
social nor religious nor legal recognition; and such social pressures as
there are still encourage furtiveness, promiscuity and instability in
relationships. Indeed, society goes a long way in encouraging the kind of
behaviour among homosexual people which it then denounces as 'vices
characteristic of the gay condition'. Putting the same point another way:
the lack of social support for homosexual partnerships from church and
society makes it even easier for them to come unstuck.

I believe that the church should help by affirming the Christian worth
of homosexual unions and by providing support, recognition, counselling and blessing to help gay and lesbian couples to grow in love
through difficulties as well as joys. There is also a pressing need on the
part of the churches to provide more sensitive and honest pastoral help
when a union is broken through death or otherwise.

One final point: because homosexual unions are not procreative and
because for homosexual people sex is a vehicle of love, relationship,
tenderness and caring, but is not usually capable of producing children,
we all have, I believe, things to learn from the gay experience in an age
when heterosexual sex is more commonly a way of communicating love
than a way of producing children. We have things to learn about sexuality apart from procreative intent – about tenderness, care, self-giving,
reciprocity. And gay people often have much to teach us all about the
importance, and the value, and the nature of friendship, and of networks
of friends.

We all need to learn from one another, and ultimately from God, about love. But this is only possible if we recognise that Christ on his cross has broken down the walls of suspicion, hostility and distrust among people and only if we have the courage to live and to love in the freedom Christ has given us.[3]

NOTES

1. The early Scottish marriage orders, 'Knox's Liturgy' (1562) and the *Westminster Directory* (1645), are markedly more positive in their assessment of sexuality and indeed of marriage as a primordial form of fellowship than is the Book of Common Prayer.
2. On *perichoresis*, see Colin E. Gunton, *The One, the Three and the Many: God, Creation and the Culture of Modernity* (Cambridge: Cambridge University Press, 1993), pp.163–79.
3. A version of this chapter has also been published in *Theological Fragments: Essays in Unsystematic Theology* (London: Continuum, 2005).

Chapter 23

THE CHURCH OF ENGLAND AND
HOMOSEXUALITY: HOW DID WE GET HERE?
WHERE DO WE GO NOW?

David Atkinson

How we got here

In 1914 E. M. Forster finished his novel *Maurice*, eventually published in 1971. He wrote it, he says, to argue that homosexual love can be ennobling and that any perversity in the matter lies with the society which persecutes those who love in this way. 'The man in my book is, roughly speaking, good, but Society nearly destroys him; he nearly slinks through his life furtive and afraid and burdened with a sense of sin.'[1] Forster died in 1970. Ten years earlier he had said that unless the recommendations of the Wolfenden Report of 1957 became law, *Maurice* would have to remain in manuscript.[2] In fact, the Wolfenden Report became the basis for the English 1967 Sexual Offences Act, which said that homosexual behaviour between consenting adults in private should no longer be a criminal offence.[3] This unlocked the door to the closet, enabled homosexual people to be more visible, homosexuality to be more talked about and created a movement of change in public and political attitudes that in England has swung more liberal and then more conservative over subsequent years. The changes in the Church of England's attitudes to homosexual people, particularly since 1957, need to be seen in the light of such social changes.

The 1960s and 1970s: from crime and neurosis to tolerance

Until 1967 gay sex in England was a crime. Psychiatric textbooks were including homosexuality as a 'neurosis', 'deviation' or 'disorder'.[4] The 1960s saw a major shift in the West in the social significance of sex.

There was also rising political and social pressure for attitude change in relation to homosexual people. In 1969 the Stonewall riot in New York saw the birth of a new gay cultural movement that quickly affected England: the Gay Rights lobbies, the GaySoc in the universities, the flood of pro-gay literature.

D. S. Bailey's 1955 ground-breaking study *Homosexuality and the Western Christian Tradition* sought to interpret the Bible in the light of contemporary understandings of homosexual experience.[5] One of the few major evangelical ethicists to address the topic in the 1960s was Helmut Thielicke who struggled with a way to understand Scripture that does not 'diminish the humanity' of homosexual people.[6] He effectively argued for an optimum morality for a less than ideal world.

There was a flood of popular Christian writing.[7] One symbolic milestone was theologian Norman Pittenger's *Time for Consent?*, first published in 1967, arguing for social acceptance of gay relationships.[8] That book was notable for its description of the wide range of tender and affectionate aspects of physical relationships practised by gay people.[9]

In some of our Anglo-Catholic theological colleges in the 1970s a significant proportion of ordinands were gay, and there was a well-established gay sub-culture.[10] As far as I am aware, this was not adequately addressed theologically or morally. Evangelical colleges had their gay ordinands too, but this was hardly acknowledged. Is this history part of the background to some of the major divisions in today's Church of England?

In the mid-1970s the theological college principals privately asked the House of Bishops for some guidance. One response came in 1979 with the church's first major report, *Homosexual Relationships*. This argued that there were 'circumstances in which individuals may justifiably choose to enter into a homosexual relationship with the hope of enjoying a companionship and physical expression of sexual love similar to that found in marriage'.[11] The Report was not accepted by the church.

The 1980s: a conservative reaction

The 'Thatcher decade' of the 1980s saw a swing back in public discourse from the liberalising 1960s and 1970s. Jeffrey Weeks suggests that the symbol of the 1980s in relation to homosexuality was 'Section 28'[12] a clause in the Local Government Act 1988 designed to prevent the 'promotion' of homosexuality by local authorities. Perhaps there was a widening gap between official sanctions and popular culture? There were certainly three significant social changes in that decade. First, the rise of the political New Right; second, the effects of the new municipal radicalism seen, for example, in some local authorities aggressively pushing equal opportunities policies and promoting a positive image of homosexuality; third, the impact of AIDS – on the one hand, sometimes described as the 'gay plague', on the other, providing many examples of loving pastoral care within gay communities.

The 1980s were also the 'Runcie Decade' in the Church of England and some conservative trends in society were countered by some liberalising trends in the church. However, there was a highly publicised debate in General Synod in 1987, which affirmed (among other things) 'the biblical and traditional teaching on chastity and fidelity in personal relationships ... and that homosexual genital acts fall short of God's ideal and are to be met by a call to repentance and the exercise of compassion'. (An amendment requiring that 'appropriate discipline among the clergy should be exercised in cases of sexual immorality' was defeated.) Many observers believed that the Synod felt caught between wanting to be faithful to Christian sexual morality as traditionally understood and sympathetic to the testimonies of Christian gay people.

One instructive feature of that debate was that one speaker spoke about sin and the judgement of God. Another spoke about falling short of God's ideals, and the picture was of a God of forgiving grace. Yet a third spoke of God as love and of the splendid variety of God's creation. These three approaches never engaged with each other. It became clear to me that our guiding metaphors for God are most likely to dictate the way we shape the moral and pastoral questions. It is probable that part of the lack of fruitful dialogue today derives from the fact that protagonists in the 'debate' are working from different fundamental metaphors for God and therefore defining the theological issue in different terms.

In 1986 a Board for Social Responsibility working party was set up to advise the bishops on questions concerning homosexuality and lesbianism. Their largely descriptive (unpublished) report sought to be faithful to Scripture, tradition and reasoned reflection on what Christian homosexual people had to say about their lives. It helpfully distinguished between the theological task, the pastoral task and the quest for justice in the public realm. It took the view that homosexuality is an issue on which conscientious differences of opinion may be held.

The 1990s: an uneasy truce, holding unity despite diversity

The beginning of the 1990s was marked on the one hand by more sexually explicit TV and videos, and on the other by Prime Minister John Major's 'Back to Basics' call for a return to family values. This decade also saw the substantial growth of the Lesbian and Gay Christian Movement and other Christian gay groups such as Changing Attitude. The work of Christian 'ex-gay' organisations such as True Freedom Trust and Courage were also more widely promoted. Whereas both the latter evangelical organisations sought to help homosexual people either change their orientation through healing, or (much more usually) to live celibate lives, by 2001 Courage had changed its approach. They had come to the view that 'change' is very elusive and that in the New Testament, singleness is a gift and celibacy could not be insisted upon, that developing a close committed same-sex relationship is valid and valuable, and that many sincere lesbian and gay Christians have need for intimate relationships.[13] This decade also saw the emergence of Reform: a conservative evangelical network, whose understanding of God's way of life for his people includes 'the rightness of sexual intercourse in heterosexual marriage and the wrongness of such activity both outside it and in all its homosexual forms'.[14]

In 1991 the House of Bishops published *Issues in Human Sexuality*, in order 'to promote an educational process' within the church, calling for prayerful study and reflection.[15] It argues that there is in Scripture 'an evolving convergence on the ideal of lifelong, monogamous, heterosexual union as the setting intended by God for the proper development of men and women as sexual beings'.[16] Although the bishops could not commend a loving, faithful and intentional lifelong homophile partnership they 'do not reject those who sincerely believe it is God's call to them. We stand alongside them in the fellowship of the Church, all alike dependent upon the undeserved grace of God.'

In the case of homophile *clergy*, however, their exemplary, pastoral and teaching function means that clergy cannot claim the liberty to enter into sexually active homophile relationships.[17] *Issues*, though intended to educate and promote discussion, became in effect a sort of policy statement. General Synod commended the Report for study in 1997. *Issues* enabled bishops to 'hold the line' but it was widely criticised, notably by Jeffrey John, as effectively removing needed pastoral support for gay clergy and seeming to promote inconsistency between bishops' private pastoral responses and their public statements.[18] Another prominent critic was Michael Vasey whose *Strangers and Friends* made out a case for affirming gay relationships.[19] He argued that even if the 'double standard' approach in *Issues* could be defended theologically, it was less clear – given the current situation of the church and of gay clergy within it – that it was workable.

The flow of literature has continued from biblical scholars, pastors and pressure groups.[20] The 'St Andrew's Day Statement' from evangelicals argued against the danger of constructing any ground for Christian identity other than our redeemed humanity in Jesus Christ.[21] There has been growing awareness of the significance for biblical interpretation of the social construction theories of homosexuality, arguing that the concept of homosexuality as we now use it is comparatively modern and that there is considerable variety in the meaning of sexual acts in different contexts.[22] In 1998, the working group on human sexuality at the Lambeth Conference confessed – in a magnificent understatement – that they were 'not of one mind' about homosexuality.[23] They say that 'the challenge to our Church is to maintain its unity while we seek, under the guidance of the Holy Spirit, to discern the way of Christ for the world today with respect to human sexuality.' The Resolution 1.10 of the full Conference endorses the most conservative emphasis.

Attitudes harden

Since Lambeth 1998, attitudes in the Church of England have hardened and positions have polarised, whereas for a significant number of non-church English people there is puzzlement why this has become such an issue. In 2003 the House of Bishops produced a further report, *Some Issues in Human Sexuality: A Guide to the Debate*.[24] This substantial report, outlines the debate and seeks to model and inform discussion for the future. Some other significant publications in the United Kingdom include Gareth Moore OP, *A Question of Truth*; D. Petersen (ed.), *Holiness and Sexuality*; and *True Union in the Body*.[25] At the time of writing, the first Civil Partnerships are being registered in the UK, and the bishops have provided guidelines which recognise clergy's right to enter such partnerships while holding them to the standard of behaviour expressed in *Issues*, and ruling out public blessing of such partnerships as if they were gay marriages.

Where now?

Personal reflections

In 1979 I wrote *Homosexuals in the Christian Fellowship* focusing on the standard biblical texts that refer to homosexual behaviour. The story of homosexual rape in Sodom seemed to have little to contribute to contemporary debates. The Levitical purity laws in the Holiness Code need to be handled carefully in the light of the Christian Gospel, but seem, I argued, to form the basis for the New Testament understanding of homosexual behaviour as out of line with the Creator's purposes for human sexuality and a by-product of idolatry (Romans 1), as inappropriate for citizens of the kingdom of heaven (1 Corinthians 6) and as falling short of the demands of the Decalogue (1 Timothy).

Since then I have come to question what it is that the New Testament texts are referring to, and to see that a concentration only on these texts does not engage with many of the questions which the contemporary expression of homosexual identity is posing for the church. Since 1979 I have become more aware of the way the Levitical purity laws also reflect a view of gender – of male ownership and female subordination – which has been overturned by the example and teaching of Jesus concerning the full reciprocity of the sexes. I have also learned more of the shamefulness in Roman society, with its views of masterful masculinity, of a man allowing himself to be used 'as a woman'.[26] St Paul's use of homosexuality to illustrate his argument in Romans 1, therefore, depends in part at least on his negative view of the domination and subordination throughout Roman society. It needs to be read alongside his revolutionary approach to sexual equality in 1 Corinthians

√ 7, that sex is not about ownership but about mutual self-giving.

The concern of 1 Corinthians 6 is to call the Corinthian church to act together as a community of faith to condemn the use of secular litigation, which can only lead to further injustice, and to affirm the new identity in Christ of those who are baptised. The disputes within Corinth are met by Paul's plea that the Corinthians remember they are the baptised people of God. The passage often quoted as confirming Christian opposition to gay relationships (6:9–11) is part of a section specifically addressing the problems of taking fellow Christians to court – and is on the side of the oppressed and marginalised and opposed to those who are 'greedy'.[27] The primary import of 1 Corinthians 6:1–11, therefore, is to urge Christians to reflect primarily on our life together as the people of Christ. The vice list of verses 9–11 itemises aspects of behaviour which are not compatible with belonging to the baptised community. Since every other item on the list refers to actions that diminish, hurt, oppress or harm others, it is at least arguable that the reference to homosexual behaviour should be read in the same way. St Paul's most obvious reference to homosexuality is likely to be related to the culture of slavery, idolatry and the domination of the strong over the weak within the world of Corinth, and it is that to which he is referring and objecting. It is, therefore, at least arguable that loving, faithful, stable, same-sex friendships which reflect something of the character of God are not within his sights.

My membership of the Osborne working party (1986), and growing pastoral ministry to homosexual people, created in me a considerable quandary about the mismatch between the tone of these texts and the testimonies of many Christian gay people. When gay persons can thank God for the gift of a partner to love and who loves them, when their life shows signs of healing and blessing in place of anguished loneliness and when their partnership bears the marks of faithfulness, stability and the fruits of the Holy Spirit, what is a biblically informed response?

The question presses: to what extent are the 'standard' texts addressing at all the contemporary experience of gay Christian people in loving, stable and committed relationships? If Romans 1 *is* talking about such Christians, are they deluded in their claimed experience of God? Or was St Paul wrong? – not a view that I as an evangelical will readily admit. Or are there new realities which the New Testament texts simply do not directly address – the awareness of homosexuality as an unchosen orientation and the freedom (since Wolfenden) for gay Christian people to be more open about their loves and relationships, of which earlier generations were largely unaware? While it is clear that there could be no biblical endorsement for the promiscuity which characterises much of our contemporary secular gay subculture, it is much less clear to me that

the testimony of stable, faithful and loving gay relationships can so
quickly be dismissed. We need a biblical gospel hermeneutic from which
to evaluate the mismatch between the standard interpretation of the relevant texts and the contemporary testimony of gay Christian experience.

A way forward for evangelical theology

As the 'St Andrew's Day Statement' makes clear, orthodox theology is
trinitarian. In Jesus Christ we know God and human nature as they truly
are; the Spirit of Jesus Christ bears witness to the Gospel in Holy
Scripture, directs us in the task of understanding human life and experience through the Scriptures, declares Christ's power and forgiveness in
mutual encouragement and exhortation to holiness; and the Father of
Jesus Christ restores broken creation in him. These are 'first order'
principles. In light of our earlier reference to 'guiding metaphors', we
need to hold all this together, and not be betrayed into a legalism of
moral rules on the one hand, or an antinomian individualism which
focuses only on individual autonomy, on the other. The 'Statement' then
argues that there is no such thing as 'a' homosexual or 'a' heterosexual:
there are human beings, male and female, called to redeemed humanity
in Christ and on the journey of discipleship towards the fulfilment of all
things in God.

Lambeth Resolution 1.10 properly recognises that there are persons
within the church who experience themselves as having a homosexual
orientation and the bishops rightly commit themselves to listening to
these experiences, assuring such people that they are loved by God and
that all baptised believing and faithful persons are full members of the
Body of Christ. Our identity is found in being made and loved by God
and strengthened by his grace. Gay and lesbian people are not defined
by their sexuality. But the interpretation of homosexual emotion and
behaviour is a Christian 'task' still inadequately addressed and the
church must be open to empirical observation as well as governed by the
authority of apostolic testimony.

In that task, what place is to be given to freedom of conscience before
God? There are many matters on which evangelical Christians, while
firmly holding to the 'fundamentals' of the Gospel, give each other freedom of conscience to disagree: abortion, remarriage after divorce, the
permissibility of war, contraception. The question is whether the debate
about faithful stable gay relationships comes in this category. I shall try
to argue that it does.

Covenant

One of the basic biblical models for human relationships which reflect
something of the divine Trinity is covenant: an exclusive relationship

between two parties based on promise and marked by faithfulness, patience and forgiveness. As Barth put it, creation is the external basis for covenant, and covenant is the internal meaning of creation.[28] In other words, our human covenants one with another are intended to reflect something of the nature of God who is Creator and covenant Lord. The Holiness Code of Leviticus is a good example of the way human covenants among the people of God are intended to reflect God's character: 'You shall be holy for I the Lord your God am holy'; 'I am the Lord' (Leviticus 19:2 etc.). This theme is reinforced in the Sermon on the Mount and elsewhere in the New Testament (Matthew 5:48; 2 Peter 1:5). As a recent symposium from the Oak Hill School of Theology rightly argues (though I disagree with some of their pastoral conclusions), 'Holiness is an expression of the covenant relationship in which God has placed us. We are to bear witness to a fallen world of God's character and intentions for humanity by our distinctive, God-determined life-style.'[29] One particular form of human covenant is friendship.

Friendship

Two of the central characters of Old Testament covenants, Abraham and Moses, are also described as God's 'friends'.[30] This intimacy of relationship with God comes into clearer light in the Upper Room when in the synoptic gospels Jesus, breaking bread with his disciples, speaks of 'my blood of the covenant', whereas in the fourth gospel he says to them 'You are my friends.'

There has been a welcome recovery of the importance of Christian friendship in some recent writing, with the reminder of a long Christian tradition of deep and covenanted friendships between people of the same sex and of the opposite sex.[31] One of the primary features of many Christian homosexual relationships is the quality of friendship. Alan Bray's book traces the development of friendship from the deeply intimate and public friendships of the late medieval time to the privatised friendships of today. He explores examples of the tradition of two men swearing lifelong 'brotherhood' to each other – often blessed by the church. He quotes examples of prayers from liturgical forms of 'making brothers' that are remarkably similar to the wording of the marriage service. There are examples of sworn friendships between women also. In particular Bray examines the tomb monuments of friends buried together in ecclesiastical settings but draws a sharp contrast between the intimacy of public same-sex friendships which such monuments display and 'sodomy'. The latter is wild, sinful and subversive; the former wholesome, orderly, publicly accepted and socially cohesive. Today we have lost much of the deep intimacy of same-sex friendships, though many relationships which today would be called lesbian or gay are essentially recovering the intimacy of friendship, some at the 'ordinary' level of a desire to share life with someone, to have someone to go shopping with, to go on holiday with, to be there when you are ill, to look after you when you are dying; and some at the much deeper level of committed love and shared embrace. Many within the church are again finding ways to celebrate friendship, including the possibility – largely lost in contemporary western culture – of the passionate intimacy expressed by David for Jonathan (2 Samuel 1:26), and of the depth of loyal affection from 'the disciple whom Jesus loved' and who was lying close to his breast at the table (John 13:23).

What is sex for?

If within such a context we ask what our sexuality is for, the Christian tradition has usually replied, pleasure (for example, the erotic poetry in the Song of Songs), companionship (reflecting the loving friendship of God) and creativity (including, importantly, procreativity). According to Christian moral tradition all these three ideally belong together.

The church has not always been very good at talking about pleasure, the 'joy of sex'. It has made much more of relationships and of creativity – at least procreativity and the importance of family. The Bible does not hide the fact that sex can also be painful, alienating and destructive. When human sin and selfishness spoil something as powerful as sex, it is extremely damaging. This is why nearly every society has laws and taboos to regulate sexual behaviour, to prevent sex becoming abusive and to offer guidelines for its pleasure, companionship and creativity.

Upholding marriage

Human sexual relationships are meant to be expressed – the Christian tradition has always said – in a relationship of a man and a woman that is loving, faithful, reliable and permanent. That is what Christians mean by the covenant of marriage, a primary category of friendship.[32]

In the Matthean discussion on divorce, Jesus refuses to engage in disputes between Pharisaic schools and points first to the work of the Creator: 'He who made them from the beginning made them male and female.' The implication is that human beings exist in the image of God as males or females. Then follows the quotation from Genesis 2 about heterosexual marriage. This is the basis for the bishops' statement in *Issues* that in Scripture there is 'an evolving convergence on the ideal of lifelong, monogamous, heterosexual union as the setting intended by God for the proper development of men and women as sexual beings'; and for Lambeth 1.10 properly to uphold faithfulness in marriage between a man and woman in lifelong union. The Book of Common Prayer illustrates how marriage is understood as an ordering of desire:

the desire for children, the desire for sexual expression and the desire for intimacy.[33] At its best marriage can be a relationship of mutual healing, sustenance and growth,[34] reflecting Christ's love for the church (Ephesians 5:31–32). St Paul argues that to express sexual commitment with your body but not be committed as a whole person is to divide up what belong together (1 Corinthians 6:15–20). That rules out sex in transient relationships – or sex without relationship. Those who are not married, the tradition has said, express their sexuality in other ways – as Jesus did – in the celibate life, with a range of loving friendships and other ways of being creative apart from having children. There is a special gift of marriage and a special gift of celibacy.[35] But how are we to be faithful to Scripture as we seek to respond to the whole range of human experience, in particular to those whose unchosen orientation towards the same sex means that marriage is not an option, but who have received no calling to celibacy?

Holiness in a fallen world

There are times when human beings – heterosexual and homosexual – do not or cannot fit into the biblical 'ideal'. The Matthean divorce material recognises the reality of a fallen world and, alongside the Creator's purpose, also indicates the need to find an optimum morality in a less than ideal situation (Matthew 19:8). Jesus does not hold everyone to 'the command of creation' but refers to a divine 'concession' to human need. The central question for Christian disciples is how we are to live holy lives as sinners in a less than perfect world, a world in which compromises are inevitable. All of us in different ways fall short of God's ideals (Romans 3:23). Some people have bad early experiences, which mean that sex is not a pleasure. Some people have psychological needs, which make it hard for them to be good companions. Some people cannot have children. And what of those who because of genetic predisposition, or early learning experiences or other reasons which no one knows, find that their sexual feelings are towards the same sex and not the other sex? Their experiences offer us certain evidences, which we need to evaluate today, that question the adequacy of the way we have traditionally expressed the biblical ideal. What, for such people, is a biblically informed response?

The Bible and 'homosexual practice'

One of the most substantial and influential conservative contributions to current debate comes from Robert Gagnon. *The Bible and Homosexual Practice* is an exhaustive exegetical study, but unfortunately proclaims a certainty which I do not believe his argument supports. In his defence of traditional exegesis, Gagnon argues from

Genesis 1:26–27 that 'the fullness of God's image comes together in the union of male and female in marriage.'[36] But this claims too much: it does not give much space for single people – or for our unmarried Lord himself. Gagnon further wishes to link being made in the divine image with 'procreative purpose' (Genesis 1:28), but Jesus does not make any reference to Genesis 1:28 in his quotation from Genesis 1:26–27 recorded in Matthew 19. There is something about the importance of being in the divine image that cannot be reduced to procreative capacity. Compared with the Old Testament, in which procreation was an essential feature of the self-understanding of the people of God, the gospels show little interest in procreation. And there are important sexual dimensions to the celibate life to which Gagnon does not refer at all. Gagnon further argues that anatomical complementarity of male penis and female vagina itself demonstrates the normativeness of heterosexuality, that same-sex intercourse therefore violates nature, and that this must underlie St Paul's argument. But nowhere does St Paul talk about anatomy and Gagnon's argument at this point is derived not from exegesis but from his own assumption of what is 'natural'. In his concentration on anatomy and on the morality of sexual actions without reference to their context in a relationship, Gagnon gives no acknowledgement of the fact that, to some extent at least, context determines the moral value of actions.[37] This is universally accepted in the heterosexual world, where married sexual love is recognised as wholly different in meaning from rape. One of my primary difficulties with Gagnon's lengthy thesis is that the entire focus is on the morality of actions separated from any consideration of the contexts that give them meaning. To abstract behaviour from the whole context of a person's motivation, relationships and moral vision fails to do justice to the biblical emphasis on 'the heart'. It concentrates only on discrete acts, not the way those actions are woven into a person's character and quest for moral values. It leads to a morality of rules, rather than to a personal morality of allegiance to the covenant Lord.

Lambeth Resolution 1.10

In the context of the above discussion, when we turn back to the Lambeth resolution we find that it fails to recognise homosexual friendships or to point to any way forward for homosexual people to 'order their desires'. Furthermore, when Lambeth 1.10 rejects 'homosexual practice' as being 'incompatible with Scripture', I have difficulties. To my mind the resolution at this point is not being 'biblical' enough. It assumes several things that need to be disentangled.

First, it assumes that the Bible is unambiguously clear when it refers to homosexuality. As I have argued, however, many faithful homosexual

THE CHURCH OF ENGLAND AND HOMOSEXUALITY

Christians do not recognise themselves within the standard texts in Romans and 1 Corinthians.[38]

Secondly, Lambeth resolution 1.10 assumes that 'homosexual practice' is unambiguously clear. But this phrase is used without any adequate context. The 'standard' biblical texts are presumably about anal penetration, which carried a particular meaning of male dominance in Canaanite and Greco-Roman cultures.[39] But what is a biblical response to two loving Christian men living together with varying degrees of physical intimacy short of intercourse? Is homoerotic love allowed or not? To read St Anselm, one is almost embarrassed by the rich homoerotic tone of his letters to friends, but he would be opposed to what we would call 'homosexual intercourse (anal)'.[40] As I understand it, anal intercourse is by no means normative for gay sexuality and there are many meaningful possibilities for physical expressions of tenderness and affection for gay persons in a loving relationship with each other. Lambeth 1.10 does not show any awareness of the debate about the social construction of homosexualities, nor that different cultures have very different understandings of same-sex intercourse, nor that cultural and relational context is essentially part of the meaning of the actions.

Thirdly, the Lambeth Resolution 1.10, like Gagnon, supposes that it is a straightforward matter to move from the texts of Scripture to questions of contemporary homosexual practice without acknowledgement of the complexities and compromises of living in the world as it is. When Romans 1 refers to homosexual practice as being contrary to 'nature', it does so as an *illustration* taken from contemporary understanding, in an argument about something else. I accept that 'nature' is referring back to the doctrine of creation. The question is how to live holy lives before the Creator in this world. In this context, Thielicke (as long ago as 1964) argued that, while 'homosexuality cannot be put on the same level with the normal created order of the sexes' (though, to be clear, this is to understand it as only *one* form of the disordered sexuality which we *all* share in this fallen world), the pastoral task is to enable homosexual people to achieve the 'optimum ethical potential'. To deny this, he argues, would mean a degree of harshness and rigour not required of anyone else.[41] To be sure, to discover oneself to have a homosexual orientation may be a calling from God to a life of celibacy, and such a life may itself be the road of healing and personal growth. There are many testimonies, very many not without struggle, of the grace of God enabling such a life to be lived joyously to the full. But just as St Paul recognises that for heterosexual people 'it is better to marry than to be aflame with passion' (1 Corinthians 7:9), is it not better for homosexual people, for whom the option of marriage is not available, to order their desires within a covenanted stable and faithful friendship of love than to be tempted into a life of promiscuity?

Fourthly, the Lambeth Resolution offers no space for biblical evalua-
tion of what vocation a homosexual person fulfils within the church. It
gives little incentive for Christian mission to gay communities. It gives
little place for grace. One of the characteristic features of the ministry of
Jesus was the fellowship he had with people whom others regarded as
outsiders. His example suggests that a church that is as inclusive as the
Gospel will require our acceptance of different Christian lifestyles and
of those with whom we disagree.

In a gay subculture that is dominantly promiscuous, a covenanted
faithful relationship which reflects something of the covenant of God's
grace could be a demonstration of the Gospel calling gay Christians to be
counter-cultural. If, instead of asking first about God's law, we ask 'How
am I going to move nearer to a life of holiness?' or 'How am I going to
find more integrity in my life?', the human reality is that some Christian
gay people answer that in terms of a covenanted friendship of love, with
the gospel marks of healing, sustenance and growth. That answer, it
seems to me, needs to be affirmed. The first word some gay people hear
from the church is a call to repentance, which is not the first word of the
Gospel. Law belongs within grace. It is only after we first hear and
receive the word of God's grace that the question of change arises. Many
in the church now believe that a homosexual relationship that bears the
marks of love, joy, peace, faithfulness, goodness, meekness and self-
control is one which can be seen as bearing the marks of God's Spirit.

To argue as I have done is to risk alienating Christian brothers and
sisters who see things differently, though I hope we can give one another
freedom of conscience to disagree. It also risks alienating English
Muslims whose traditional understanding of these matters is very conservative. And in our English context I am well aware of the need to be
fully sensitive to the very different cultural questions that affect
Christian brothers and sisters in other parts of the Anglican
Communion.[42] But I would argue that cultural sensitivity is a mutual
task and wish to follow Rowan Williams in requesting some recognition
of the fact that 'those who want to argue for ... a revisionist position on
the possible legitimacy of "sexual expression" for the person of homosexual inclination may, like their opponents, be trying to find a way of
being faithful and obedient to the givens of revelation.'[43]

Conclusion

In conclusion, I believe Lambeth 1.10 proves too blunt an instrument for
an appropriate pastoral response to those for whom this is a pressing personal question, too unclear an instrument for forming any constructive
Christian mission to gay communities, and too insensitive an instrument

for affirming and accepting what is of God in the lives of many Christian gay people. While we all seek further the mind of God for us as a church, can there be a willingness (as with many other moral and pastoral questions) to give each other the freedom of conscience to disagree in love, while we all continue prayerfully to seek God's will and purpose for us and for God's church?

NOTES

1. E. M. Forster, *Maurice* (Harmondsworth: Penguin Books, 1977 edn), p.9.
2. ibid., p.221.
3. *Report of the Committee on Homosexual Offences and Prostitution* (London: HMSO, 1957).
4. As recently as 1973 homosexuality featured in the list of recognised mental disorders agreed by the American Psychiatric Association.
5. Longmans, 1955.
6. H. Thielicke, *The Ethics of Sex* (London: James Clarke, British edn 1964).
7. Some of this is documented in David Atkinson, *Homosexuals in the Christian Fellowship* (Oxford: Latimer House, 1979).
8. SCM Press, reissued as a third and revised edition without the question mark in the title eleven years later.
9. It served as a counter to the prevalent (and wrong) assumption that gay men are only interested in anal penetration. It is worth noting that in 1978 Jeffrey Weeks made the comment that 'anal intercourse is still the exception, even among homosexuals' (Jeffrey Weeks' introduction to Guy Hocquengham, *Homosexual Desire* [London: Allison and Bushby, 1978], p.24).
10. See the novel by A. N. Wilson, *Unguarded Hours* (London: Secker & Warburg. 1978), which may be somewhere near the truth.
11. *Homosexual Relationships: A Contribution to Discussion* (The 'Gloucester Report') (London: CIO Publishing, 1979), §168.
12. Jeffrey Weeks, *Coming Out* (London: Quartet Books, 1977, revised edition 1990).
13. See www.courage.org.uk.
14. A recent Reform discussion paper affirmed that 'Sexual intercourse within same-sex relationships is not a matter for debate,' believing that 1 Corinthians 6:9–11 settles the matter by arguing that such behaviour excludes homosexually active people from the kingdom of God.
15. A Statement by the House of Bishops of the General Synod of the Church of England (London: Church House Publishing, 1991).
16. ibid., p.18, §2.29.
17. 'The world will assume that all ways of living which an ordained person is allowed to adopt are in Christian eyes equally valid', *Issues*, 5.13.
18. Jeffrey John, *Permanent, Faithful and Stable* (London: Darton, Longman & Todd, 1993 and 2000), a powerful argument for the acceptance and blessing of permanent, faithful and stable homosexual relationships as sacramental ways of holiness, justified by orthodox theology and biblical understanding.
19. Michael Vasey, *Strangers and Friends* (London: Hodder & Stoughton, 1995).
20. Jeffrey Heskins, *Unheard Voices* (London: Darton, Longman & Todd, 2003), is the moving story of how St Luke's Church, Charlton, South London, has for the past twenty years been offering pastoral services of blessing for gay and lesbian couples.
21. Timothy Bradshaw (ed.), *The Way Forward?* (London: Hodder & Stoughton,

1997; 2nd edn, London: SCM Press, 2003).

22. For example, David Greenberg, *The Construction of Homosexuality* (Chicago: University of Chicago Press, 1988).

23. Their report serves as an outline of the various viewpoints currently held within the Church of England (and Anglican Communion). The working group wrote: 'Our variety of understanding encompasses:

- those who believe that homosexual orientation is a disorder, but that through the grace of Christ people can be changed, although not without pain and struggle;

- those who believe that relationships between people of the same gender should not include genital expression, that this is the clear teaching of the Bible and of the Church universal, and that such activity (if unrepented of) is a barrier to the Kingdom of God;

- those who believe that committed homosexual relationships fall short of the biblical norm, but are to be preferred to relationships that are anonymous and transient;

- those who believe that the Church should accept and support or bless monogamous covenant relationships between homosexual people and that they may be ordained.'

The Official Report of the Lambeth Conference 1998 (Harrisburg, Pennsylvania: Morehouse Publishing, 1999), p.93ff.

24. Archbishops' Council (London: Church House Publishing, 2003).

25. Moore (London: Continuum, 2003); Petersen, *Papers from the Seventh Oak Hill College Annual School of Theology* (Milton Keynes: Paternoster Press, 2004); *True Union in the Body*, a paper commissioned by the Archbishop of the West Indies, undated (published in Oxford, 2003).

26. See Peter Brown, *The Body and Society* (London: Faber and Faber, 1989), ch. 2.

27. See R. B. Hays, *First Corinthians*, Interpretation Bible Commentary (Louisville: John Knox Press, 1992).

28. K. Barth, *Church Dogmatics* III/1 (Edinburgh: T & T Clark, 1958).

29. David Petersen (ed.), *Holiness and Sexuality* (Milton Keynes: Paternoster, 2004), p.34.

30. Isaiah 41:8; 2 Chronicles 20:7; see James 2:23 and Exodus 33:11.

31. For example, Peter Atkinson, *Friendship and the Body of Christ* (London: SPCK, 2005).

32. Thomas Aquinas regards friendship as a more fundamental category than marriage. See Atkinson, *Friendship and the Body of Christ*.

33. Angela Tilby address to Southwark Cathedral Seminar, January 2004.

34. These are Jack Dominian's helpful categories in *Marriage, Faith and Love* (London: Darton, Longman & Todd, 1981).

35. 1 Corinthians 7:7. See C. K. Barrett, *A Commentary on the First Epistle to the Corinthians*, 2nd edn (London: A & C Black, 1971).

36. Robert Gagnon, *The Bible and Homosexual Practice* (Nashville: Abingdon Press, 2001), p.58.

37. See, for example, the many Protestant critiques of *Humanae Vitae* for its concentration on sexual actions rather than on the context of a relationship.

38. A recent letter from a Christian man in his seventies says, 'the prohibitions in Leviticus and St Paul (let alone Sodom) do not even come near to what I know and experience in my relationship with P – thirty-six totally happy years. They are simply condemning something else that I have known and experienced once upon a time but not now ... I am quite certain that the writers do not know

∠   anything of a same-sex life together of "mutual society, help and comfort".'

39. See Brown, op. cit..

40. See Richard Southern, ch. 7, 'The Nature and Importance of Friendship', *Saint Anselm: A Portrait in a Landscape* (Cambridge: Cambridge University Press, 1990).

41. Thielicke, op. cit., p.285.

42. However, when on a recent visit to southern Africa I asked a pastor who was also a medical doctor about homosexuality, the reply was revealing: 'If you are asking the pastor, it does not exist; if you are asking the doctor, it is as significant a feature of life as anywhere else, but we do not talk about it.'

43. Rowan Williams, 'Knowing Myself in Christ' in Timothy Bradshaw (ed.), *The Way Forward?* 2nd edition (London: SCM Press, 1997), p.19.

Chapter 24

HOW SHALL WE KNOW?

Charles Hefling

> And no one after drinking old wine desires new; for he says, 'The
> old is good.' *Luke 5:39*

Beneath all the overheated rhetoric, the political posturing and the
apocalyptic journalism, there are issues at stake in the current turmoil
over sexuality that are solidly theological. They are not new. They are
coeval with Anglicanism, and they have erupted, again and again, at
various points on the theological map. Since theology is speech about
God and about all things in relation to God, different things raise different theological questions. Just now, the disputed question is how sexual
desire, sexual 'orientation' and sexual activity are or ought to be related
to God. Behind that, however, is the more fundamental question that
Daniel Hardy, with his usual clear-sightedness, has identified. The
present quarrel, he writes, revolves around 'the form in which the truth
of God is known'.[1] On what basis do we speak *truly* about all things in
relation to God, sex among them?

It is that fundamental question which lies behind the notorious
Mtetemela clause in Lambeth Resolution 1.10(d). A certain sort of
behaviour, we are told, is to be rejected. Why? Because it is 'incompatible with Scripture'. But even if this incompatibility is a fact, we may
legitimately ask what makes it a *relevant* fact, a fact that Christian
people are obliged to take account of in deciding how to act. It will not
do simply to answer that Scripture is authoritative. So it is – but not
directly. Authority is a personal or, better, an interpersonal reality. Books
do not exercise it, in and of themselves, even if they are books of the
Bible. As the Windsor Report rightly observes, 'the authority of
Scripture' is a potentially misleading shorthand, used for referring to the
authority of *God* mediated by a certain collection of meaningful words.[2]
Everything hangs, then, on what the mediating consists in. How, in
short, is Scripture itself related to God?

Anglicanism had its birth in the throes of controversy over that question, and the answer I am going to argue for takes its bearings from the
'classical' Anglican theology that was born. My argument is not primarily historical. On the other hand, neither does it attempt to ally itself
with postmodern eclecticism, radical orthodoxy, or any of the other

recent trends that can be discerned in Anglican theology. Not only do I think that those who find Lambeth 1.10(d) unacceptable ought to have reasons for opposing it; I also think the reasons will be all the better for being recognisably continuous with the tradition that has nourished those who give them. At the same time, however, theological reasoning always goes on within some context in the present. This essay is no exception. As I was beginning to write it, I was put in mind of its context by attending a diocesan meeting – a routine and unremarkable event, and thus a good one to offer by way of illustration.

Present at this meeting were the newly accepted postulants for holy orders, whom the bishop had invited to supper along with a few of the other people who take part in the process of discernment and formation for ordained ministry. It began, as meetings like this always do, with a round of self-introductions. As they described themselves, the fifteen postulants mentioned all the things you would expect – their families and parishes, their work and schooling. Several spoke about their children, one about her forthcoming marriage, and so on. The speeches were interesting, personal, lively, but hardly unusual. There was nothing dramatic in the way they were spoken or listened to. When they were finished, that was that, and the bishop went on to the business of the evening. All very ordinary.

By saying there was nothing unusual about these get-acquainted speeches, I have characterised a context. From two or three of them, you might have gathered that the speakers were raising their children with partners of the same gender. You might have noticed that the woman about to be married would be marrying another woman.[3] But you would have heard nothing unheard-of, nothing that called particular attention to these speakers. They did not label themselves. There was no need. Sexuality, as such, had not been significant for the commissions, interviewers, committees and psychologists who advise the bishop on potential ordinands. Nor is it a contentious issue for the diocese as a whole. Of some three hundred active clergy, a dozen or so are gay, spokenly if not outspokenly.[4] Many of these are rectors, vicars and priests-in-charge. The parishes in the diocese vary, as parishes do, but for the most part you are likely to find it true that 'The Episcopal Church Welcomes You', as the denominational street-sign says, if you happen to be gay. The day-to-day work of ministry goes on without taking special notice of gay people, one way or the other, much as it went on at the meeting I have mentioned.

None of this makes the diocese unique. It is not typical either. But what a typical diocese might be is difficult to say. On matters of sexuality the Episcopal Church is a house of many mansions, as it has generally been on every other divisive issue. The saying that America is not so much a nation as a world applies to American Christianity as well, and not least to our branch of Anglicanism. Besides the standard ecclesiastical parties, imported from England, there are home-grown movements and traditions, often regional, rooted in histories that have been complex and sometimes conflictual. Broadly speaking, Episcopal churches in the Great Plains, say, are apt to have a different character from those in the Deep South, or in New England, or on the West Coast. Some of the differences are a result, others a source, of different opinions on issues of sexuality. But generalisations are dangerous. A social history of the Episcopal Church and its gay members would have to take account of many local variations as well as wide diversity.

Such a survey might be difficult to write, however, for another reason. There is a lack of data. Much has happened that will never be known, because until recently the whole subject was taboo. In the church as elsewhere, gay people lived their lives under an old policy that has lately taken a new name: 'Don't ask, don't tell.' So long as there was no 'grave scandal', no public acknowledgement, no formal approval, the institutional church did not often concern itself very closely with anomalous domestic arrangements on the part of its members, lay or ordained. Some people are 'not the marrying kind'. That was understood. They did not call attention to the fact, however, and neither did anyone else. That would have been unseemly. Such a tacit gentlemen's agreement suited the Episcopal Church quite well in the days when it was even more a church for gentlemen and ladies than it is today. Even now there are those who think discreet reticence is the best way to deal with these matters. As recently as 1997 an attempt was made at General Convention to turn the old, unstated rules into an official policy, explicitly applicable to 'non-celibate gays'.

The attempt failed. It failed, partly and perhaps mainly, because of what has been a fact of American life for twenty or thirty years: more and more of those affected most directly by the ethos of 'Don't ask, don't tell' have become less and less willing to accept their side of the bargain. To put it in the gay vernacular, they have chosen to be out of the closet – to be unashamedly and publicly honest, to speak, even in church. Despite the obvious social advantages of 'passing' as straight, gay hypocrisy has been weighed against 'gay pride' and found wanting. Among those who find it so, and who now decline to play by the old rules, are gay Christians, for whom 'coming out' has often been an experience of grace and conversion. It is their visible and audible presence in the church, as the persons they find themselves to be, that has probably done more than anything else to change their fellow Christians' minds and hearts.

That is not to say that being 'out' meets with the same unperturbed acceptance in all Episcopal circles as in the diocese I belong to. On the contrary. But neither is there the slightest reason to think it is a trend that is going to turn around or go away. That is why the church finds itself in its present difficulties. Under the policy of discreet reticence, it was usually possible to avoid overt dissonance between formal precept and actual if unacknowledged irregularities. No one *had* to notice. By now, dissonance has become crashingly obvious, especially though not only at the two flashpoints, ordination and marriage. Neither of these is an action that constitutes the church – the Eucharist does that – but they do embody and display particular aspects of how the church understands its own constitution and what it stands for. And whether they are or are not sacraments, marriage and ordination are surely outward and visible signs of inward and spiritual commitment. The question, then, in the Episcopal Church as in the Anglican Communion at large, is whether the commitments these rites signify and effect can exist together with a certain way of being sexual which those who accept and enact it are no longer keeping secret.[5]

With that, we arrive at theology. For centuries it was above all the church that told gay people they had something to hide, and it was the church's moral teaching that shaped the laws and customs which penalised them if they failed to hide it. Their coming out of hiding has now begun to be endorsed and affirmed in various practical ways. If these new practices imply new teaching – and they do – the implication ought to be made explicit. It is one thing to disregard or tolerate private deviations from the public norm. To reconfigure the norm is something else, and to reconfigure it out of sentiment or under pressure, instead of for good and sufficient reasons, is irresponsible at best. A reasonable case needs to be made for such a corporate change of mind, and the reasoning needs to be theological.

If that is what the Windsor Report has called for, it cannot be said there is an answer ready to hand. So far, in America anyhow, theological argumentation has been left to catch up as best it may with innovations in practice. As happened with the ordination of women, the broadly liberationist view that the church should 'act its way into thinking' has taken the lead, while the arguments that do get advanced tend to revolve, again as with women's ordination, around the theme of justice. Advocates for the 'full inclusion' of gay people in the church's life are apt to stress that what they are advocating is only fair, only right, only just, and – therefore – theologically warranted.

This is an argument that appeals to American sensibilities. As there ought not to be second-class citizens in a nation 'with liberty and justice for all,' so there ought not to be second-class church members. If baptism confers full church membership and qualifies the baptised to receive the greatest blessing the church has to mediate, the Eucharist, then baptism likewise bestows entitlement to receive the special blessings of ordination and marriage, other things being equal. The only question is whether other things are made *un*equal by the active sexuality of baptised persons who are gay. If not, excluding such persons from holy orders on that ground alone is unjust. Similarly, even if marriage must by definition be limited to mixed-gender couples, at least same-gender couples have the right to claim a blessing.

So runs a fairly common line of reasoning. It is not wrong, as far as it goes, but neither is it altogether satisfactory. The difficulty is not that it appeals to justice. Justice, in the classical sense of rendering to each and everyone what is his or her due, is one of the cardinal virtues, indeed the chief and sum of them all. The difficulty is that justice in this sense is not one of the *theological* virtues, not what the Gospel is primarily concerned with. There is no right or entitlement to the glorious liberty of the children of God: there is only the undeserved gift of being drawn to the Father by the Son. To the extent that such a further, specifically Christian dimension is missing from arguments that take their stand on justice, they are open to objections such as this: 'It may well be that everyone, gay or straight, deserves the same freedoms and protections in civil society, and that sodomy laws, for instance, should therefore be repealed. All the same, there are many things which are not criminal, but *are* sinful, and gay sex is one of them. So, even if members of the church are committed by their baptismal promises to strive for justice and respect the dignity of every human being,[6] it remains that the church itself exists to call sinners to repentance, and that church members *as* church members are held to a standard that may be higher than the standards that happen to be imposed by civil law or social sanction.'

I have just outlined two arguments. The first is an egalitarian argument against discrimination. I take it to be representative of the way many, perhaps most, Episcopalians who approve of their church's innovations with regard to gay people would justify their approval. The second argument, which invokes the theological category of sin, I take to be the gist of the most estimable case for *not* conferring holy orders or liturgical blessings on Christians who are gay. As stated, the two arguments have no common ground. If the basic premise of the second is true – if gay sex is always and by definition sinful – then the first argument is irrelevant, theologically speaking, though it may still have a bearing on civil legislation. A lot therefore turns on whether that premise *is* true. Is it? The church has no doubt adhered to it, officially anyhow, for centuries. But consensus by itself is no guarantee of truth. 'The church hath erred', even in great matters, as the nineteenth Article of Religion avers. The circumstances in which Anglicans now find themselves make it imperative to ask what *grounds* there are for adhering, officially or otherwise, to the moral judgement that sexual congress between two women or two men is evil, or that only husband and wife may have sex without sin. What makes that judgement true, if true it is?

Ultimately, the one explanation that matters to Christian believers is God. Why is any true moral judgement true? Because it is God's; because it coincides with what divine wisdom approves or disapproves. Insofar as there is reason to believe that the received judgements about sexual conduct do so coincide, they ought to be upheld and acted on. Anyone who would take issue with them, and do it on Christianly relevant grounds, has to show that these judgements do *not* coincide with God's intention. That is why the next question is crucial, as I said at the outset. For the next question is: How do we *know* the purposes of God, what God would have us be and do?

The simplest, most straightforward answer is the one in the Sunday-school song. How do I know? 'The Bible tells me so.' That is the answer a great many Christians in America would give, in one form or another. It is also the answer to which Lambeth Resolution 1.10(d) appeals. There are two things to be said about it, and saying them will occupy most of the rest of this essay. The first is that it is not an answer that stands on its own. It never did, even under the more impressive name of the *sola scriptura* principle. It rests on a whole theology, a view of the world in relation to God and, especially, of the kind of God the world is related to. The second is that the theology on which such an answer rests is foreign to what I take to be the classically Anglican position on judging matters of conduct. In fact, the Anglican position was in part hammered out precisely in opposition to the theology of which 'the Bible tells me so' is a lineal descendant. If this is the theology meant, as it certainly seems to be, by those who take 'biblical orthodoxy' for their watchword, the Anglicanism of their position can be questioned.

Let me return, then, to where this essay began, and lay out in very abbreviated terms an argument that I believe to be more in keeping with an Anglican approach to moral theology. To repeat the point at issue: Is gay sex 'incompatible with Scripture'? Yes, of course it is, if by that you mean the Bible contains passages which condemn it. There can be more than one opinion on just what the Sodom and Gomorrah story is driving at, but not on what St Paul would say in an epistle to the Diocese of New Hampshire, or on what the redactors of Leviticus would do at the blessing of a same-gender union – they would rend their clothing aghast. So far, all sides ought to be able to agree. But notice what we ought to agree on. We should agree that certain persons, a known Christian apostle and some unknown Jewish scribes, committed to writing, at certain times, certain evaluations of certain behaviours. We may be reasonably sure of what these persons thought about gay sex. Theirs, in the first instance, are the judgements conveyed in the two relevant biblical passages that are flat, unambiguous condemnations. But that is not the end of the matter, and never has been. Why should *we* think as these persons thought, and conform our moral judgements to theirs?

That is a question to which (with honourable exceptions) not enough attention has been paid. It is not an exegetical question. The exegetical question has been answered, over and over. It is, rather, a *theological* question about 'the form in which the truth of God is known'. I propose to consider it, briefly and theologically.

That holy Scripture is 'the Word of God' is a doctrine to which every deacon, priest and bishop in the Episcopal Church is committed by solemn oath. So far, so good. What does that doctrine mean? Not that the eternal Word, who was in the beginning with God and *is* God, became a text and dwelt among us. The Bible is not the incarnation of one of the persons of the Trinity. Only Christ himself is that. Scripture is truly named the word of God inasmuch as it means what Christ meant, so that the marks on the pages are instruments by which other men and women can share in the mind of Christ. How the marks got there should not be made to vanish by dialectical sleight of hand or by rhetoric that erases the distinctions between different meanings of the word 'word'. For the marks got onto the pages through a thoroughly historical, vastly complicated process of writing, revising, compiling, selecting and gathering, which did not bypass the human minds of the writers, compilers, editors, and the like. So and not otherwise has God 'caused all holy Scriptures to be written', as the Bible Sunday collect puts it.[7] These books were not delivered by an angel, all complete, like the Book of Mormon. Still less are they divine in themselves. To say, nevertheless, that the great, sprawling miscellany that is the Bible means what Christ meant is to say that it came to be written, in the providence of God, for the same reason that the Word was made flesh – written, the collect goes on to say, 'for our learning', written so that we might 'embrace and ever hold fast the blessed hope of everlasting life ... given us in our Saviour Jesus Christ'.

That is what Scripture is *for*. Its purpose or point or end or design is to make us 'wise for salvation through faith in Christ Jesus' (2 Timothy 3:15, New International Version). We have reason to 'read, mark, learn, and inwardly digest' these words inasmuch as doing so directs us towards what *we* are for, towards the 'last end' or ultimate destiny of humankind. That end, for which we are made, is one that surpasses anything we can be or do in this present life. In theological parlance it is 'supernatural'. We could not know about it, not even as a possibility, had it not been 'revealed'. To such an extravagant, supernatural end, the means is likewise supernatural. That means is faith. The ordinary, natural means by which we reach ordinary, natural ends – our native intelligence, the light of reason – does not suffice. Informed, conscientious deliberation does tell us the difference between right and wrong, good and evil. What it does not tell us, and what could only be revealed, is that our doing those things which we know we ought to do is pleasing and acceptable to God just insofar as our motivation in doing them is the love of God and our aim or intention in doing them is God's glory. So while it is faith, not fulfilment of moral obligation, that brings us to our last end, there is no discontinuity, for in revealing that end, 'the blessed hope of everlasting life', God has revealed as well that to fulfil our moral obligations is to do his will on earth as it is done in heaven.

What does all this imply about Scripture? Two things. The first is that on matters of *faith*, on what Christians are to believe for their souls' health, Scripture is the sole authority. The second, however, is that Scripture is not and cannot be the complete, all-sufficient criterion by which to discern our moral duty. It makes no such claim for itself. In fact it says just the opposite, and says it in the same passage that includes the verses most frequently quoted in the current debate about sexuality – the end of the first chapter of Romans and the beginning of the second. For if that passage means anything, it means that people who did *not* have the light of supernatural revelation were nevertheless quite capable of knowing, by the light of their own natural reason, what was morally good. Otherwise – if they had not been able to know their duty – they could not be held responsible for failing to do it. By holding the Gentiles responsible, as he so clearly does, St Paul lays down the principle that moral obligation does not, in and of itself, have to be revealed.

It *was* revealed – to a particular people in particular circumstances. Consequently, the character of the writings which, for St Paul, mediate this revelation is such as to call for something more. The biblical law, with its mélange of precepts, statutes, commands, proscriptions, recommendations and permissions, demands that distinctions be drawn. Even if the Bible were entirely a manual of instructions, which it is not, there are no instructions for how the instructions are to be applied. No written code does that, or ever could. Unless all the Old Testament rules are equally obligatory for Christians – an idea abandoned by the church at the outset – they have to be sorted and assessed. That is what the church has always done, and it has done so in the light of 'natural reason', that is, judgement based on the most serious and intelligent moral deliberation Christians could bring to bear. To take the example that stands for all the rest, the Ten Commandments have long been regarded as a compendium of duty to God and neighbour. They have this status, however, not simply because of their source as revealed in Scripture, but because they sum up precepts that are universally acknowledged to be fundamental. And even so, they do not provide a Christian rule of life, and never have done, without being extended, interpreted and applied, as they are in catechisms like Luther's or the one in the Prayer Book. Such a catechism is, in fact, a hermeneutical exercise. Before the Commandments can be acted on, they have to be *understood* in a context different from the one in which they were given.

In sum: the Bible discloses 'what God has prepared for those who love him'. It tells us that our acts and attitudes are fitting responses to divine love insofar as they are motivated by that love. It tells us which acts and attitudes such a response consists in, that is, what God would have those who love him be and do. Between those acts and attitudes, and the obligations set by sound moral judgement, there is no disparity, much less conflict, because revelation focuses and strengthens the innate human ability to know what humans ought to make of themselves and their world. Duty as revealed in Scripture coincides with obligation as illuminated by the light of natural reason. True, that light falters and fails. True, we deceive ourselves as to our own ends. True, the devices and desires of our own hearts are all too often at odds with our best moral judgement. It remains – and this is the point everything hinges on – that *God* is not at odds with our best moral judgement. The human capacity to know the good is not only a capacity he has created but also, what is more, a likeness and a taking part in his eternal Word, the true light that enlightens every man and woman.

Lest anyone should suppose that in holding the position I have just set out I am bowing to the Baals of Enlightenment rationalism, autonomous individualism, humanist modernism, or what have you, I would empha- sise that every substantive point in the preceding four paragraphs comes directly and sometimes verbatim from one of the revisers of the 1662 Book of Common Prayer – Robert Sanderson, who also wrote the preface.[8] Sanderson's lectures on conscience, one of which I have been following to the point of plagiarism, were given at Oxford just before he was expelled from his post by the same party he had been lecturing against – the Puritans, with their legalistic insistence on the 'plain sense' of Scripture. That party has not disappeared. Among its present-day successors are those who issue the most dogmatic diatribes against gay sex (among other things) on Bible-says-so grounds. In America, their characteristic way of appealing to Scripture is more likely to be found outside the Episcopal Church than in it. Puritanism was brought here by colonists who left England precisely in order to leave behind them the church that Sanderson was defending, and Anglicanism has been seen ever since as an alternative to the Puritan outlook. But that outlook has been a potent force in American culture and politics at large, and one that has had its effect on Episcopalians as well as others.

Nor has the question disappeared that was at issue between Sanderson and the Puritans of his day. It was, and is, a question that turns not only on the sense in which Scripture is the word of God, but even more fundamentally on the kind of God that Scripture reveals. Sanderson was a traditionalist, taking one side of the same dispute that had given rise to a distinctively Anglican theology. The principle he was maintaining and elaborating was one that Richard Hooker had insisted on, half a century earlier, already in opposition to the Puritans: 'They err who think that of the will of God to do this or that, there is no reason besides his will.'[9] God is a God of order, and what he orders (in the sense of commanding it) is identical with what he orders (in the sense of giving it purpose and direction). What God sets in order is intelligible, not chaotic. What God wills is reasonable, not arbitrary. The two statements are equivalent.

There you have the real issue: the enormous difference between holding, in the tradition of Hooker and Sanderson, that there are understandable reasons for what God wills, and holding that what God wills, he simply *wills* – full stop. It will be worthwhile to spell out the difference, not least because unfamiliarity with this admittedly difficult region of theology contributes to the thinness of much present discussion. I shall call the first position Anglican, for so I judge it to be, and the second Puritan.

On the Anglican position, the first divine attribute is wisdom. It belongs to wisdom to set things in order, and God orders all creation 'sweetly and mightily'. On the Puritan position, the first divine attribute is freedom. Nothing precedes God's deciding, much less restricts it. What God chooses is good simply and solely because God chooses it. On the Anglican position, divine law means the orderly movement of all things to their divinely appointed ends, and this movement is intrinsic to their being the kinds of things they are as components of the universe God has in fact created. On the Puritan position, divine law is extrinsic, something over and above what things *are* by nature, something imposed on them by fiat.

On the Anglican position, there is ultimately harmony between the moral duties that follow from natural tendencies, and the imperatives God has revealed. Biblical commandments and 'natural law' coincide. Hence, to quote Sanderson, by revelation 'we are informed to more advantage of what was naturally known to us'. On the Puritan position, there is nothing morally relevant to be learned from the nature of things, because there is nothing morally relevant outside of what God has decided to command. Ethics has no empirical element.

On the Anglican position, willingly to violate any moral law is self-destructive. It frustrates the finality of some created order, obstructing the outcome God intends, which is the wellbeing of the violator. Vice, therefore, is its own punishment, virtue its own reward. Supernatural rewards and punishments continue the same trajectory beyond what we experience in this life. That is what '*super*natural' means. On the Puritan position, violating a revealed commandment opposes its commander. That is all it does. That is also all that matters. Rewards and punishments are arbitrarily assigned to certain types of action or, in the extreme predestinarian version, assigned to certain individuals irrespective of their actions, for no other reason than that God so chooses.

From the Anglican position, two consequences follow that bear on the subject at hand. In the first place, it follows that to ask *why* is legitimate. God has reasons for ordering what he does, as he does. We may ask what those reasons are. We *ought* to ask what they are, because to ask for explanation, to ask *why,* is in itself to obey a 'natural law'. Raising such questions is one of the inherent inclinations of beings who are created in the image of God. On the Puritan position, asking *why* can only be insubordination, prideful daring, and incipient disobedience. In the second place, and most importantly, it follows from the Anglican position that there can be development in morals, just as there is development in Christian doctrine, and for the same reason. Growth in human understanding is itself a finality that belongs to the order of the universe, which is not static but dynamic and historical. It changes, as do we. What we learn about pork should alter our assessment of the kosher laws. What we learn about the circulation of money should alter our assessment of the prohibition of usury.[10] And so on.

In light of the distinction I have been drawing, let us return to St Paul and to that most notorious pronouncement he makes – in the course of a far larger argument – at the end of the first chapter of his Letter to the Romans.

It is not at all a Puritan argument. It is an Anglican argument, and that in two ways. The first I have mentioned: St Paul holds that those who did not have the blessing of being 'informed to more advantage of what was naturally known' to them nevertheless did know it, naturally, and, if they did not, they ought to have done. The second point concerns the sort of behaviour, sexual behaviour in particular, that to St Paul's mind is a consequence of ignorantly following base passions. He does not say that God inflicts an extrinsic punishment on those who so behave. On the contrary, he says the penalty is contained in the behaviour itself. That is what the 'wrath of God' comes down to, always: the working-out of the inevitably destructive results of irrational and irresponsible conduct. That is precisely the evidence of its irrationality and irresponsibility.

Take both these points together, and a question arises: Exactly what *is* the self-inflicting penalty intrinsic to the sexual behaviour of which St Paul disapproves? That, whatever it is, will be what clinches the argument that such behaviour is behaviour that offends God. In other words, we are dealing with a question of truth, as Gareth Moore has insisted at length[11] – not one of the truths of faith that concern 'what eye hath not seen nor ear heard', but the empirical, verifiable, naturally knowable truth of how life in the existing universe is wisely ordered, by a wisely provident God, for the good of his human creatures.

Let me repeat the point. 'God is not offended by us, except by what we do against our own good.'[12] If what gay people do, inasmuch as they are gay, does offend God, as St Paul no doubt thought it does, probably with Leviticus in mind, then *on his own argument* there must be evidence for the offence. Somehow or other, it must be the case that gay people who are not celibate inevitably obstruct the orderly unfolding of the human good in which, as human creatures made in God's image, they are embedded. If, on the other hand, there is no such evidence, then what St Paul undoubtedly thought is not what he should have thought or what any other Christian should think. The question, then, is what this obstruction consists in, this penalty that gay people bring on themselves or their society or both.

St Paul does not tell us. He says, notoriously, that the behaviour he disapproves is 'against nature', but that is just another way of naming the question, not an answer that explains his disapproval. To say something is against nature is to say that natural human intelligence can grasp what makes it so – that its being 'unnatural' is something we can, by nature, know. Unless we know it, therefore, unless there is an explanation, unless it can be shown that gay sex does, here and now, in this world, always and as it were automatically corrupt human wellbeing, there is no more *reason* for Christians to agree with St Paul on this point than there is to agree with him about women's silence or men's haircuts.[13]

There are, of course, a great many arguments that attempt to fill this gaping hole in St Paul's reasoning and supply what he takes for granted – arguments to the effect that gay people who act on their sexual desires in any way at all do so to their own ruin. Not all these arguments address the question of truth by an appeal to facts, to intelligible structures and tendencies of human life in the actually existing universe. Those that do make such an appeal must, on the position I have been outlining, be taken seriously.[14] The end of a short essay is not the place to do that.[15] And even if it were done, even if all the arguments for the intrinsic viciousness of gay sex had been defeated once and for all, the result would be no more than a double negative. 'Not vicious' is not equivalent to 'virtuous' or 'wholesome' or 'godly'. Stamp-collecting is not intrinsically vicious, but neither does the philatelic behaviour of stamp-collectors commonly have the momentous meaning, the moral and spiritual significance, that their sexual behaviour may have. A positive assessment of what sexual intimacy between women or between men *can* mean is a more urgent and important theological project, in the long run, than negating the Levitical and Pauline negations of bodily acts that are potentially meaningful. But it is on these negations that the Puritan way of thinking takes its stand, and since it can now claim Lambeth Conference support, I have devoted most of this essay to the necessary but merely preliminary project of marking out the ground on which I would maintain that Anglicans (including bishops) ought to be standing instead. What is really needed, however, and would have to be built on that ground, is a case for holding that faithful Christians who are gay have something to choose besides the two options set before them by the bishops at Lambeth: sin and celibacy. In other words, what is needed is an argument to the effect that gay sex can be – not that it is, but that it can be – holy.

Such an argument, presumably, will play an important part in any response the Episcopal Church makes to the Windsor Report's specific request for a reasoned contribution to ongoing discussion.[16] If it is to be an Anglican argument, standing in the tradition of moral theology that Sanderson stood for in his day, it will do two things. I have suggested both already. It will ask a certain kind of question, and it will apply the answer by appealing to a certain kind of evidence. The question will be a question about *ends*, and the appeal an appeal to concrete realities – to *facts*. In the first place, sex has a for-the-sake-of. What is it? That is the basic question. A sexual act or practice or relationship, of any kind whatever, is virtuous or vicious, wholesome or unwholesome, insofar as it does or does not fulfil an intrinsically intelligible function. Then, in the second place, if the ends which make sex what it is *are* being fulfilled, the fulfilment is a matter of fact. Likewise, if an act or practice or relationship fails, as judged in relation to those intrinsic ends, that too is a matter of fact. The judgement, one way or the other, is empirical, and the evidence for making it, one way or the other, is the concrete evidence of what sexual behaviour really does, to and for real human beings.

The way this reasoning would apply to the issue at hand should be clear. No one doubts that gay sex can be, and sometimes is, stultifying, predatory, trivial, obsessive, immature, manipulative, hedonistic and self-indulgent: an abomination, if you like. The same is true of non-gay sex. Perhaps, then, the problem is not that gay sex is gay but that it is sex. And perhaps the good which it can and sometimes does fall short of is not all that different from the good that belongs to what has always been, statistically speaking, the more common sort of sexual activity, namely the sort that involves one male and one female. Hence the question that I have stated comes first: What *is* that good? What is sex *for*?

It is by no means a simple question. Human sexuality, inasmuch as it is human, is extremely complex. It has not only chemical, hormonal and biological but also psychic, affective, emotional, spiritual, social, political and historical dimensions. Actualising it, 'having sex', is neither the instinctive copulation of animals nor the ethereal coalescence of disembodied souls. It is the activity of psychosomatic unities, whole persons, who touch, feel, desire, think, play, intend, hope, judge, choose, love and pray. Consequently, just as sex is not simple, neither is its finality or directedness or end. It has more than one for-the-sake-of. The obvious end of (some) sexual activity is reproduction. That is not, however, and never has been, the only thing sex is good for. Sex unites. It communicates one incarnate self to another, reciprocally, and so founds the community that is two-in-one-flesh. None of this happens automatically, much less in a single act. The relational good of sex is personal. Like persons, it comes into being over time, as a story constituted by a more or less coherent series of intentional choices.

Quite clearly this interpersonal good, as enacted by husband and wife, is what manifests and takes part in the relation between Christ and church, according to Ephesians 5. Clearly too, it is a good distinct from the good of procreation. That very important distinction was recognised and affirmed half a century ago, at the ninth Lambeth Conference. The bishops began, in the traditional manner of Anglican moral theology, by raising just the sort of question I have raised: What good is sex? It goes without saying that they did not raise it in order to address the issue of how gay people should behave. They had other problems to deal with. Their conclusion, however, is very relevant and very clear: 'Sexual intercourse is not by any means the only language of earthly love, but it is, in its full and right use, the most revealing ... it is a giving and receiving in the unity of two free spirits which is in itself good.'[17] Not only does this mean, as the statement goes on to say, that it is 'utterly wrong' to maintain that there must never be sexual intercourse without the deliberate intention of having children. It means as well – and this was recognised at the time – that to affirm the integrity of the relational, unitive good of sexual activity has implications beyond those which the Conference explicitly drew. For there are other sexual acts besides the one that sometimes, in certain circumstances, results in the initiation of a new biological life. That being so, the possibility of actualising the distinct, distinctively human goodness of sexual activity does not depend on the biological difference between a male and a female organism. It depends on the personhood of persons.

I have said that an argument rooted in genuinely Anglican ground would have two components, and I have pointed the direction I think the first should take.[18] If there is to be reasoned discussion of gay sex, it will have to take place in the context of an account of the role that sexual activity plays in the unfolding of the human good, social and individual. Equally important, however, if not more so, will be the second component. Suppose that sexual intercourse is, as the Lambeth Conference put it in 1958, the most revealing language of earthly love. Suppose that what it is *for* is communication and community. Can gay people 'speak' this language, perhaps in a dialect of their own? If they can, then the Anglican poet-theologian-novelist Charles Williams was right: 'Men can be in love with men, and women with women, and still be in Love.'[19] Dante scholar that he was, Williams meant 'the Love that moves the sun and the other stars', the Love that God is, sweetly and mightily ordering all things to their proper ends, so as to draw them home to himself. Whether women in love with women, men in love with men, *do* take part in this universal homecoming, whether 'gay' is a somewhat uncommon but quite meaningful way to speak the earthly language that best speaks of God – that, once again, is a question of fact. By that I mean it is to be answered, not on the *a priori* ground that what it asks about cannot be so, or on the legalistic ground that this must not be so, but on evidential grounds. *Is* it so?

Seventy years ago, when Williams wrote, those who could give first-hand evidence to confirm his statement would not have been inclined to give it publicly. Closet doors were firmly shut. Now the situation has changed, in America if not everywhere. In that regard, it is quite appropriate that the Windsor Report singles out the Episcopal Church to provide the reasoned reflection the report requests. We have, in our corner of the Anglican world, evidence to reflect on that has yet to come to light in most other provinces. And should it ever happen, in the providence of God, that the one hopeful sliver of Resolution 1.10 – the bit about listening to gay people – comes to be taken seriously, those who do listen may find themselves recognising that Williams knew something St Paul did not. There would still be a need for theological reasoning, and I have drawn some of the lines I think Anglican reasoning might most authentically follow.[20] But willingness to entertain an argument, mine or any other, is not produced by arguing. That prior condition of willingness is met, humanly speaking, in the irreducibly personal encounter that meets another, face to face and heart to heart.

NOTES

1. 'The Situation Today: March 2001', pp.198–206 in Daniel W. Hardy, *Finding the Church* (London: SCM Press, 2001), p.202.
2. The Lambeth Commission on Communion, *The Windsor Report 2004* (London: The Anglican Communion Office, 2004), §54.
3. In a civil ceremony. The marriage of two men or two women has been lawful in the Commonwealth of Massachusetts since May 2004. All members of the clergy are empowered by the Commonwealth to act as its officers in conducting (lawful,

civil) marriages. In our diocese, which is one of two in Massachusetts, Episcopal presbyters may exercise this delegated power only if the marriage they are to solemnise also meets the definition of the Prayer Book and the canons of the church.

4. A note on nomenclature: there is not yet a commonly agreed language for naming the persons about whose sexual desires and practices the disputes that prompted this book have arisen. In the USA, public discourse seems (for the sake of brevity if nothing else) to be settling on 'gay' as a unisex term, applicable to men and women alike. On the one hand, there are those who think 'gay and lesbian' or 'lesbigay' or 'LGBT' (lesbian, gay, bisexual, transgendered) would be better. On the other hand, the Episcopal Church's most recent official document about gay people declines to let *any* of the terms they use of themselves appear in print, lest the Anglican Communion at large be offended. Instead, the theology committee of the House of Bishops opted for 'homosexual'. But 'homosexual' is like 'negro' – antiseptic, perhaps correct in a technical or scientific sense, yet doubtfully neutral. It is not used in this essay.

5. I have made some suggestions on this aspect of the matter in 'What Do We Bless and Why?', *Anglican Theological Review* 85 (2003), 87–96.

6. See the Episcopal Church's *Book of Common Prayer* (1979), pp.294, 305.

7. The Second Sunday of Advent in the classical *Book of Common Prayer*. Recent Anglican Prayer Books move the collect out of Advent, usually to a Sunday in November.

8. Born in 1587, Sanderson was Regius Professor of Divinity from 1642 to 1648, when he was ejected. His ten lectures on the obligation of conscience were delivered in 1647, but not published until 1660, the year in which he was reinstated and, later, made Bishop of Lincoln. He died in 1663. I have drawn mainly on the fourth lecture, which considers the 'adequate rule' of conscience, in *De Obligatione Conscientiae* (London: Cambridge University Press, 1851), pp.90–125.

9. Richard Hooker, *Of the Laws of Ecclesiastical Polity* I, 2.5. (Everyman's Library edition, London: J. M. Dent & Sons, Ltd., 1907), Vol. 1, p.153.

10. Charging interest on loaned money was long regarded as a sin, and a mortal one at that. I have sketched the parallel between the (im)morality of usury and the (im)morality of gay sex in 'By Their Fruits: A Traditionalist Argument', in Charles Hefling (ed.), *Our Selves, Our Souls and Bodies* (Boston: Cowley Publications, 1996), pp.159–61.

11. Gareth Moore, OP, *A Question of Truth: Christianity and Homosexuality* (London and New York: Continuum, 2003).

12. Thomas Aquinas, *Summa contra Gentiles*, III, para.122.

13. On natural knowledge that men ought not to wear their hair long, see 1 Corinthians 11:14.

14. This applies, for example, to the question of gay marriage. On the face of it, the argument that the institution of husband–wife marriage will be undermined by adding wife–wife and husband–husband marriages to the social fabric is very implausible, but if there is evidence to support it, the argument should not be dismissed.

15. Moore does it in *A Question of Truth*, ch. 8, pp.216–80. He writes in a Roman Catholic context, but that is where the most serious moral theology is to be found at present. His final paragraph states a position Anglicans could and should arrive at for themselves: 'The conclusion of this book is ... not that it is good to be gay, but that it is irrational for serious, reflective Christians ... to accept

church teaching on homosexuality ... This is not a matter of dissent or material-
ism; it is simply that the church at the moment produces no good arguments to
assent to. Regrettably, in this area, the church teaches badly' (p.282).

16. *The Windsor Report*, §135.

17. The Lambeth Conference's report is quoted in *Continuing the Dialogue: A
     Pastoral Study Document of the House of Bishops to the Church as the Church
     Considers Issues of Human Sexuality* (Cincinnati: Forward Movement
     Publications, 1995), p.53.

18. There is a somewhat fuller account of a parallel argument in Hefling, 'By Their
     Fruits', pp.166–73.

19. Charles Williams, *Descent into Hell* (1937; reprint, Grand Rapids, Michigan:
     William B. Eerdmans Publishing Company, 1972), ch. 9, p.174.

20. They are drawn in the knowledge that the linguistic tools I have used to draw
     them are old-fashioned. Virtues, cardinal and theological, vices, revelation, the
     natural and the supernatural, the 'light' of reason, ends, will and willing,
     conscience – these are not prominent notions in ethical discourse at present.
     Their meaning can, I think, be transposed for contemporary use. Meanwhile, it
     is not as though some *other* conceptuality was a matter of common agreement
     among moral theologians generally and Anglicans in particular. That, in fact, is
     our real problem. In relation to it, the issues that surround sexuality are sec-
     ondary at most. Towards solving it, there may still be something to learn from
     our 'classical' tradition.

BEYOND LIBERTARIANISM AND REPRESSION: THE QUEST FOR AN ANGLICAN THEOLOGICAL ASCETICS

Sarah Coakley

This essay offers a short theological 'afterword' to the varied 'voices' that have sounded in this volume, many of them – but not all – of leading Anglican representatives from the Southern hemisphere who have previously been unheard, or unheeded, in Britain and North America. It is an affecting matter to read, and listen to, these voices; and no one, surely, could attend to them without realising that a central plank of the current anti-homosexual lobby within Anglicanism has now collapsed: 'homosexual orientation' is by no means the preserve of the Northern hemisphere, or indeed of a privileged and supposedly 'corrupt' society. It is a worldwide phenomenon, with many faces of cultural difference.

It is thus an honour for me to be asked to comment here, at the close of this rich, powerful and multifaceted book. But what credentials do I have to do so?

I write as a systematic theologian who has lived for over a decade now – during the whole of the crescendo into the Anglican Communion's current crisis over homosexuality – in two cultures. My academic year is spent as a professor in North America, in the predominantly 'liberal' Episcopalian Diocese of Massachusetts. I spend much time at Harvard in my office hours talking with highly intelligent gay, lesbian and transgendered students who long to give a richly theological account of their orientation and of their place in the churches they serve. These interactions have been, and continue to be, amongst the most profound and moving of my priestly life. My summers are spent in England, in the (theologically much more divided) Diocese of Oxford, where Anglican conversations on homosexuality are seemingly more fraught and tense. I am English and canonically resident in the Oxford Diocese; but I assist during the year in two very different parishes: one American, suburban and affluent; one English, socially deprived and struggling. So I own that what I want to say on the subject addressed in this book is much affected by my peripatetic, even chameleon-like, ecclesiastical and academic life. What I see and hear in these two contexts, and what I signally do *not* hear in either (despite their contrasting theological and political presumptions), deeply informs the argument I offer below.

But for what it is worth (since it is profoundly relevant to this book's concern to 'contextualise' sexual ethics), I have also lived for nearly a year, much earlier in my life, in an extremely deprived part of Southern Africa – in Lesotho, the land-locked former British protectorate surrounded by South Africa, which remains one of the poorest countries in the world. Partly because of its extreme poverty and lack of natural resources, and the absence of large proportions of its adult male population at any one time doing manual work in South Africa, HIV/AIDS infection has now reached a staggering estimated 75 per cent of the population in some townships of the country (including that of Mohale's Hoek, in which I worked as a volunteer student teacher in 1970). Unprotected and promiscuous heterosexual contact is undeniably responsible for almost all of this spread of disease, along with social instability, poverty and malnutrition, poor or non-existent education, and desperate lack of medical resources. But this is also a culture which has traditionally not spoken openly about homosexuality, a state of affairs that – in missionary contexts, especially – could easily lay it open to secretive forms of promiscuity or abuse. Lesotho, now, is a country dying silently on its feet; it represents for me the forgotten and tragic face of the privileged world's gross mismanagement of the whole 'economy of desire'. As I shall argue below, sexual desire cannot, in this or any other context, finally be divorced from other forms of desire (for food, wealth, power, status, peace and, finally, for God) – not, that is, when 'desire' is itself properly, and *theologically*, reflected upon.

Beyond 'liberalism' and 'biblicism'

This short essay proceeds in a pincer movement. In this first, and longer, section I reflect briefly on the current Anglican debate on homosexuality as witnessed in this volume, and urge that – despite much enrichment provided by the pan-Anglican perspectives given here – the characteristic disjunction between 'liberal' and 'biblicist' opinions remains insufficiently disturbed by them, and that neither of these options (as currently purveyed) seems sufficiently rooted in reflection on 'classic Anglicanism'. I shall thus probe a little beneath these categories and suggest that they hide another, more insidious and false, *modern* disjunction, that between 'libertarianism' and 'repression'. In my latter section, then, I shall propose a move beyond this second disjunction, one that would reintroduce the category of 'asceticism' into a distinctively Anglican quest for a holy or devout life (whether heterosexual or homosexual), an asceticism that would seek to chasten and purify *all* our desires before God. This conclusion necessarily fits ill with classic 'liberalism', and hence can only sound yet one more voice in this volume, a voice not necessarily in tune with much that has preceded it. It is a paradox of the modern history of homosexuality, I shall suggest, that only 'liberalism' has fostered the courage to enable its public and political acknowledgement, but only 'asceticism' can provide a proper matrix for its theological representation in relation to desire for God.

Let me look at the 'liberalism' 'biblicism' divide briefly first. It will be clear that all the writers in this volume resist 'biblicism' in the forms of biblical *literalism* or *fundamentalism*, especially as they relate to the scattered biblical injunctions against sodomy or lesbian relations. Many of the authors reflect deeply on the complex 'hermeneutical' processes that are involved in any attempt to relate such injunctions to contemporary life in a variety of cultural contexts. But there is still a danger, in some writers in this book, of assuming that 'hermeneutics' (so-called) is somehow only the prerogative of the 'liberal': this slippage in semantic use must surely be firmly resisted, since it merely plays into the hands of the opponent. (It also does no justice to highly *sophisticated* biblical scholarship done on the conservative wing of the debate.) No, any serious spiritual engagement with the authority of Scripture is necessarily 'hermeneutical', involving a demanding process of scriptural application that in no way ensures easy resolutions with contemporary mores or 'local' practices.[1] And indeed Anglicanism historically has its own distinctive and classic views on this process of interpretation, precisely in connection with the Holy Spirit's inspiration (a prime Calvinist emphasis), and the subtle relation to 'reason', 'tradition' and 'justice' (a prime additional Anglican emphasis). A few authors in this book rightly start to probe back here to Richard Hooker's sophisticated discussion of the relation of Scripture, tradition, reason and 'natural law' in Book V of the *Laws of Ecclesiastical Polity*.[2] But much more remains to be done, frankly, than could have been attempted in this volume, to raise the current worldwide Anglican debate to the level of complexity and subtlety in Hooker's account. Scarcely, for instance, can we call the Windsor Report itself a consciously 'Hookerian' document; on the contrary, its short section on 'Scripture and Interpretation' makes no mention of Hooker and his own painful debates with more staunchly literalist opponents on the Calvinist wing (a narrative quite revealing for today's contretemps). Nor does it engage with Hooker's complex understanding of 'natural law' as itself in the process of only gradual unfolding to the church's view, and its important relation to the primary authority of Scripture.[3] Indeed, the novel ecclesiological suggestions made in the Windsor Report (regarding a proposed 'covenant' between various parts of the Communion) smack more of Presbyterian polity than they do of specifically Anglican understandings of ecclesiastical order as found in Hooker and others. In short, the pole of 'biblicism' in the current Anglican disjunction of opinion hides a multitude of deeper issues which demand careful, and historically nuanced, attention.

If the 'biblicist' option is a 'straw man' (even as represented in this volume), what of the 'liberal' wing of the debate? This is obviously given much greater voice in this book as a whole; but I would like here, again, to give brief attention to certain axioms, or presumptions, which surface in its enunciation, and which I believe require deeper theological analysis, just as in the ostensibly opposite case of 'biblicism'.

Political 'liberalism' and theological 'liberalism' are by no means the same thing, and their European and North American forms are also importantly different from one another;[4] but political and theological forms of 'liberalism' do share some common presumptions and historical roots, and are often inextricably entangled, especially – I find – in the United States. Here in the USA the Bill of Rights seems to most folk as 'natural' as mother's milk – so obvious, in fact, as to need no explanation or defence at all (let alone a probing of its own religious underpinnings). And herein lies so much of the difficulty in our current dispute in the Anglican Communion: to so many on the political 'left' among US Episcopalians, the proper approach to homosexuality is simply a matter of 'rights', 'liberty', 'justice' and the 'pursuit of happiness', and there is really no need to complicate it with discussion of arcane biblical proscriptions. Add to that a historic grudge against the original 'colonialism' of Britain and its state church, and you have the potent mix of resentments that fires the current trans-Atlantic dispute.

However, it is not only in the United States where the language of political 'liberalism' dominates the ecclesiastical dispute about homosexuality. The discerning reader will have noted the following 'liberal' lines of argument present in the writing of many of the authors in this current book (although these are of course by no means the only arguments): (a) Sex is 'private', and not a matter for prurient intervention by church or state; as long as no abuse is involved, and sex is 'consensual', it should be of no 'public' concern. (b) Everyone has a 'right' to 'happiness', including the happiness of sexual expression and pleasure (a subtext here is that celibacy is presumed impossible, except for a tiny minority of people with an unusual 'vocation' to it). (c) 'Tolerance' and 'acceptance' of various different forms of sexual practice should be promoted, even demanded, in a 'liberal' society. (d) There are many more terrible ills of 'injustice' going on in the world (economic debt, poverty, war, ecological disaster) than those to do with sexuality, and since sex is 'private' and (mostly) 'harmless' we would do better to focus our ecclesiastical energies on those more pressing topics.

Perhaps we may add to this list another two 'liberal' lines of argument which also sound in this book, but are arguably more the product of 'postmodern' mores than of classic 'modern' thinking: (e) Statistics show that divorces are increasing, and it is important that the church show compassion and understanding to those who cannot find happiness with the same person throughout a long life; if the church is 'accepting' of divorced folk, it certainly should be also of homosexuals, lesbians, bisexuals and transgendered people. (f) The infinite variability of sexual mores and gender roles found in many parts of the world suggests that no one standard of sexual uprightness can be imposed worldwide; indeed it would be imperialist to try to do so. We should support a non-coercive plurality of models for sexual expression in different cultural contexts.

Not everyone in this book shares all, or any, of these presumptions or arguments: that should be firmly stressed. A few contributors might want to distance themselves from all or most of them (especially the latter two).[5] But it has to be admitted that these arguments are present in this book, however fleetingly, in one form or another. And what I want to note, again from a theological perspective, is that none of these arguments – *as stated* – is overtly Christian, let alone explicitly 'Anglican'. Some of them do indeed have a Christian (or Jewish) ancestry of deep importance, but it is buried beneath an 'Enlightenment' form of expression, and requires excavation. Others seem to me more questionably Christian, particularly the appeal to the 'privacy' of sexuality (with its accompanying presumption that sexual expression does not affect anyone except the partners themselves). To be fair: I have isolated these 'liberal' strands of argument here in a sort of typological caricature, and many of the authors in this book do indeed attempt the work of their theological excavation with some profundity, conjoining one or more of them with rich appeals to Bible, tradition and 'experience'. But my point is merely this: to the extent that these 'liberal' arguments remain *unexamined*, *uncriticised*, and *unconnected* to the hard, Hookerian, task of conjoining obedience to scriptural authority with a consideration of the inheritance of ecclesial tradition, and a close examination of the ways that 'reason', 'natural law', 'common sense' and 'wisdom' now seem to point the way forward afresh, then the task is not finished. It is not yet an 'Anglican' argument.

So far I have been attempting to show that the polarised wings of Anglicanism that most commonly attract attention in the press and public are, at best, only residually 'Anglican' in their theological method. This is a bold claim, and cannot be further spelled out in this short essay; but it is essayed here merely to draw attention to the need for the varied voices in this current volume, which so interestingly complicate and enrich the discussion, to be heard in an authentically *theological* auditorium of reinvigorated Anglicanism. And not only that: for my further hypothesis is that, beneath the regrettable churchly divide between 'biblicists' and 'liberals' that I have briefly discussed lies a more profound, and perhaps occluded, *worldly* divide between 'repression' and 'libertarianism' that fuels the passion of the debate. For it is not for nothing that 'biblicists' are often accused of enforcing sexual 'repression', and 'liberals' of encouraging sexual 'libertarianism'. These are modern, psychoanalytic and political, categories, lurking under the veneer of ecclesiastical debate. But they also demand our brief theological attention in closing.

Beyond 'libertarianism' and 'repression'

Amid all the furore caused by churchly rows on homosexuality, not enough attention is drawn to the completely novel phenomenon of our generation – a 'new thing' in the best, Isaianic sense. That (some) gay and lesbian couples wish now to make public, and publicly accountable, life-long vows of fidelity,[6] is – I submit – the true moral achievement of this painful cultural and ecclesiastical transition. Such 'witness'[7] is indeed an ascetic one, cutting against the grain not only of remaining cultural and churchly disapproval of homosexuality itself, but, perhaps more significantly, consciously resistant to the widespread collapse of bonds of faithfulness in society at large. In this sense we might see our current ecclesiastical furores (whether Protestant or Roman Catholic) as not finally about homosexuality or failed celibacy per se (although these attract the scandal-mongering), but more deeply about a crisis in the workings and siftings of 'desire', *tout court*. Seen thus, and theologically, the crisis is about the failure, in this Web-induced culture of instantly commodified desire, to submit all our desires to the test of divine longing.[8] For the key issue in the ascetic 'training of desire' is a lifelong commitment to what we might call the 'long haul' of personal, erotic transformation, and thereby of reflection on the final significance of all our desires before God. This is a profoundly counter-cultural perspective, bringing many of the 'liberal' presumptions earlier stated into some sort of question (Is sex 'private'? Is the 'right' to various pleasures superseded by the call to fidelity? Is my desire for wealth at the cost of Africa's ravaging ultimately disconnected from my assessment and testing of other desires –- including sexual desires –- before God?). Thus to bind all one's desires 'into a tether' is to move out beyond the false secular disjunction between 'libertarianism' and 'repression', which presumes that freedom is found only by throwing off constraint. It is in contrast to re-glimpse a vision of 'freedom' obtained precisely by certain (freely chosen) ascetic *narrowings* of choice, fuelled finally by prioritising the love of God.[9]

But herein lies our final paradox, at which I hinted at the outset. For gay men and lesbian women to find even minimal acknowledgement and support in the Anglican Church has involved years of painful and courageous activism, which – arguably – only a 'liberal' politica agenda could have sustained; and that battle is certainly not over, as this book so memorably displays. The quest for 'liberation', 'acknowledgement', and 'justice' is hard enough to maintain in the current climate; the ascetic quest for holiness, *conversio morum*, fidelity, and certain forms of consciously chosen constraints of desire, may seem to sit uneasily, even oppressively, alongside such a quest. But just as the battle between 'biblicism' and 'liberalism' in the Anglican homosexuality wars is, I have here argued, forcing us back into a deeper reconsideration of our Anglican theological heritage so as to re-mint it for today, so here, too, the witness of gay and lesbian couples, choosing to make public vows (and thus cutting not once, but twice, against cultural expectation), demands of all of us a deeper reconsideration of the meaning, and costliness, of such vows in a world of rampantly promiscuous desires, oppression of the poor, and profligate destruction of natural resources. Seen thus, I suggest, one can no longer say of the 'voices' in this book (in classic 'liberal' mode), 'Can we talk about something else? The poor are dying and the oppressed are suffering, and *you are obsessing about sex?*'. No, the voices in this book themselves demand attention to the other ways, all the ways, in which our desires may be at odds with God's. In sum, the task for the Anglican Communion is, at its deepest level, theological and spiritual: not merely to reconsider its subtle and distinctive heritage on Bible and 'reason', but to re-enliven its demanding vision of the 'devout life'.

NOTES

1. This particular issue is quite sensitively discussed in *The Windsor Report* (London: The Anglican Communion Office, 2004), paras. 57–62.

2. For the relevant portions of Book V, see *The Works of That Learned and Judicious Divine, Mr. Richard Hooker*, ed. John Keble (Oxford: Oxford University Press, 3rd edn, 1865), II, 13–41. Note especially Hooker's opening premise, that 'So natural is the union of Religion with Justice, that we may boldly deem there is neither, where both are not' (Bk V, I: *ibid.*, 14).

3. Hooker puts it, famously, thus: 'what Scripture doth plainly deliver, to that the first place both of credit and obedience is due; the next whereunto is whatsoever any man can necessarily conclude by force of reason; after these, the voice of the Church succeedeth. That which the Church by her ecclesiastical authority shall probably think and define to be true or good, must in congruity of reason overrule all other inferior judgments whatsoever' (Bk V, VIII.2: *ibid.*, 34). At this point Hooker has just elaborated his principle that the 'Church being a body

OTHER VOICES, OTHER WORLDS

which dieth not hath always power, as occasion requireth, no less to ordain that which never was, than to ratify what hath been before ... *Laws touching matters of order are changeable*, by the power of the Church; articles concerning doctrine not so' (*ibid.*, 33, my emphasis).

4. It is instructive here, for instance, to compare the political and religious 'liberalism' of John Locke (as closely correlated to the church/state arrangements in England), with the religious 'liberalism' of Thomas Jefferson in America.

5. There is no space to develop my own position here more systematically; but suffice it to say that, with the possible exception of axiom (c), I subscribe to none of these views (as formulated here). Axiom (f) demands particularly close critical attention, because it slides from 'contextualisation' to actual moral relativism ('what is moral *is* moral relative to, and in virtue of, a particular context, c'). It is possible, I would argue, to be extremely sensitive to the variables of context, culture and local expectation, and still maintain a non-relativistic ethic. Once again, questions of 'hermeneutical' application become all-important here.

6. I choose not to enter here into the (to my mind, somewhat fruitless) question of whether gay alliances should be called 'marriage'. This question of terms has legal implications in the USA, of course; but since 'marriage' has in any case become so debased in its meaning in secular culture (often involving no serious commitment to fidelity), I would propose that 'lifelong vows of fidelity' is a better expression theologically, and nicely avoids the issue of whether we can – or should – call heterosexual and homosexual 'marriages' 'the same' in all particulars.

7. The Orthodox tradition of thinking of marriage as a 'martyrdom' may sound grim to western ears, but seems to me entirely theologically appropriate. Marriage is indeed both a public 'witness' (*martyr*) and also, inevitably, the commitment to some forms of loss, suffering and transformation in relation to the 'other'. Both these modes of 'witness'/martyrdom can be christologically conceived.

8. The view that 'desire' or 'longing' is found primordially in *God* (though without loss or change, in God's case), and from there implanted in humans as a clue to their ultimate source in God, is both a biblical and a Greek philosophical (Platonic and Neoplatonic) notion. The idea is developed with particular power in the late fifth-century pseudo-Dionysius the Areopagite, *Divine Names*, IV. In my forthcoming book, *God, Sexuality and the Self: An Essay 'On the Trinity'*, I build on this heritage to give new coinage to an ascetic analysis of 'desire'.

9. This approach, note, makes 'life vows' in heterosexual and homosexual partnerships curiously similar to monastic vows of celibacy, and notably different from a careless or faithless approach to 'marriage'. I have recently spelled out further the ideals of such a proposed 'theology of desire', and explicated its contrast to the Freudian notion of Eros, in 'Pleasure Principles: Toward a Theology of Desire', *Harvard Divinity Bulletin*, (Autumn 2005), 22–33.

LIST OF CONTRIBUTORS

DAVID ATKINSON is Bishop of Thetford in the Diocese of Norwich. He has been a Fellow of Corpus Christi College, Oxford, and Archdeacon of Lewisham in the Diocese of Southwark, and is the author of a number of books including *Pastoral Ethics* and some *Bible Speaks Today* volumes for InterVarsity Press.

MARTIN BROKENLEG is Director of the Native Ministries Programme and Professor of First Nations Theology at the Vancouver School of Theology. He has been a priest since 1972, is a Canon of Calvary Cathedral of the Diocese of South Dakota, a Benedictine Canon and honorary assistant at St James' Church, Vancouver.

STUART E. BROWN has been the Executive Director of the Canadian Centre for Ecumenism in Montreal since October 2004. Previously, he worked extensively in Christian–Muslim relations in several countries of Africa as well as in the Dialogue department of the World Council of Churches.

TERRY BROWN is Bishop of Malaita and Senior Bishop of the Church of the Province of Melanesia. He served as Regional Mission Coordinator, Asia/Pacific of the Anglican Church of Canada from 1985 to 1996.

SARAH COAKLEY is Edward Mallinckrodt, Jr., Professor of Divinity, Harvard Divinity School, and an Anglican priest of the Diocese of Oxford. She is the author of a number of books, including *Religion and the Body* (ed., 1997), and *Powers and Submissions: Philosophy, Spirituality and Gender* (2002). She is at work on a systematic theology that attends centrally to the category of 'desire' (the first volume is forthcoming as *God, Sexuality and the Self: An Essay 'On the Trinity'*).

SCOTT COWDELL is Rector of St Paul's Church in Canberra, Australia. He is a theological teacher and writer, and a member of the Australian Anglican Doctrine Commission.

DULEEP DE CHICKERA is the Bishop of Colombo in the Anglican Church of Ceylon (Sri Lanka). He is a member of the Anglican–Oriental Orthodox International Commission and of the World Council of Churches' Commission on Diakonia and Development.

DUNCAN B. FORRESTER was an educational missionary in South India from 1962 to 1970, and was ordained in the Church of South India. He taught for eight years in the University of Sussex, and then back in Scotland, where he was Professor of Christian Ethics and Practical Theology in Edinburgh University from 1978 to 2001.

ARUNA GNANADASON, Church of South India, coordinates the work on Justice, Peace and Creation of the World Council of Churches and is also responsible for the Women's Programme of the WCC.

WINSTON HALAPUA is Bishop for Polynesia in New Zealand/Aotearoa and Dean of The College of the Diocese of Polynesia, St John's College, Auckland, New Zealand. He is the author of two books on marginalisation and militarism and has contributed various chapters to other books and journals.

CHARLES HEFLING is a professor of systematic theology at Boston College and examining chaplain to the Bishop of Massachusetts and editor-in-chief of the *Anglican Theological Review*.

GERTRUDE LEBANS has been a priest of the Anglican Church in Canada for twenty years, formerly in the Diocese of Niagara and now in New Westminster. Her writings and workshops focus on a renewed vision of the church, a rethinking of our theological metaphors in the light of our present knowledge and how Christians engage in moral discourse in the twenty-first century.

TUCK-LEONG LEE is the Secretary for the Centre for Reflexive Theology and is currently running projects for lay theological education and spiritual formation with the Free Community Church, Singapore.

LENG LIM is a Singaporean and an Episcopal priest of the Diocese of Los Angeles. He is an executive coach who works with professionals and businesses in the field of organisational transformation and leadership development.

ROWLAND JIDE MACAULAY is a pastor with the Metropolitan Community Church, North London. He is a qualified Christian theologian, an author, poet, preacher, teacher, a dynamic and an inspirational speaker.

HUMBERTO MAIZTEGUI is Professor of Old Testament in the Egmont Machado Krischke Seminary in Porto Alegre, Brazil. A Uruguayan, since 1987 he has lived and worked in Brazil, where he was ordained a priest and recently completed his doctorate at the Ecumenical Postgraduate Institute in São Leopolodo, Brazil.

ESTHER MOMBO is Lecturer in African Church History and Women's Theologies and Academic Dean at St Paul's United Theological College, Limuru, Kenya. She is a member of the Circle of Concerned African Women Theologians and the Inter-Anglican Doctrinal and Theological Commission and served on the Lambeth Commission that produced the Windsor Report.

KAWUKI MUKASA is a consultant in congregational development for the Anglican Diocese of Toronto. He was raised and ordained in the Church of Uganda.

RENTA NISHIHARA is Associate Professor at Rikkyo University, Tokyo, specialising in Systematic Theology and Anglicanism. He is priest of the Nippon Seikōkai and Vice-Moderator of the National Christian Council of Japan.

JULIUS POWELL, JR is Chair of the Policy/External Relations Committee for the New York City Department of Health and Mental Hygiene HIV Prevention Planning Group, and former member of the Board of Education and Youth for the Diocese of Jamaica and the Cayman Islands in the Church of the Province of the West Indies. He currently serves as Secretary for the Episcopal Diocese of New York's Reparations Task Force.

MARIO RIBAS, one of a new generation of Latin American theologians, is a priest of the Episcopal Anglican Church of Brazil. He holds degrees from Trinity College, University of Bristol and the Methodist University of Sao Paulo, and is currently engaged in doctoral studies at the University of Cape Town, South Africa.

DAVID RUSSELL is retired Bishop of Grahamstown, Church of the Province of Southern Africa. He is former Dean of the Province, and Chair of the Southern African Anglican Theological Commission.

PETER SELBY, whose ministry has been in the fields of mission and laity formation, is Bishop of Worcester and Bishop to Her Majesty's Prisons in England and Wales. He was formerly Professorial Fellow in Applied Christian Theology in Durham University and is the author of *Grace and Mortgage: The Language of Faith and the Debt of the World.*

JENNY PLANE TE PAA is Ahorangi or Principal at the College of St John the Evangelist in Auckland, Aotearoa New Zealand. She is a member of several international Anglican bodies including the recent Lambeth Commission.

PEDRO TRIANA is a priest and biblical scholar. He is Professor of Old Testament and Vice-President in the Union Theological Seminary, Matanzas, Cuba. He is also Director of the Study Center of the Cuban Council of Churches.

KEVIN WARD is Senior Lecturer in African Religious Studies in the Department of Theology and Religious Studies at the University of Leeds. Ordained in the Church of Uganda, he worked for many years in theological education in Uganda as a mission partner of the CMS.

ROSE WU has been an active participant in the women's movement and other social and political movements in Hong Kong since the 1980s. She is the author of *Liberating the Church from Fear: The Story of Hong Kong's Sexual Minorities* and *A Dissenting Church.*

KIM-HAO YAP is the Pastoral Advisor for the Free Community Church, Singapore. He has previously served as the Bishop of the Methodist Church in Malaysia and Singapore and the General Secretary for the Christian Conference of Asia.

241
245

303